MW01014986

Piper Aircraft

The development and history
of Piper designs

by

Roger W. Peperell

An Air-Britain Publication

ISBN 0 85130 253 X

Published in Great Britain by

Air-Britain (Historians) Ltd.,
12 Lonsdale Gardens, Tunbridge Wells, Kent

Sales Department,
5 Bradley Road, Upper Norwood,
London SE19 3NT, England

or e-mail barrie@air-brit.demon.co.uk

Printed by Martins the Printers Ltd
SeaView Works, Spittal
Berwick-on-Tweed
TD15 1RS England

Cover photographs:

Front - PA-18-150 Super Cub s/n 1809053 registered in Switzerland as HB-PMN photographed at Prangins, near Geneva in 1990 by Roger W. Peperell.

Rear upper - PA-32R-301 Saratoga II HP s/n 3213097 registered in the U.S.A. as N495WF photographed at Vero Beach in 1995 by Roger W. Peperell.

Rear lower - PA-46-350P Malibu Mirage s/n 4622190 registered in Brazil as PT-WJP photographed at Vero Beach in 1995 by Roger W. Peperell.

Piper Aircraft is the most detailed book covering the development and history of one of the most well-known aircraft manufacturers in the world. The book begins with the forerunner aircraft, the Chummy and Taylor Cub. It describes each of the Piper aircraft designed and built, designed and not built, and those which were considered for acquisition by Piper. It gives information on prototypes, production histories, specification details and performance data of the different designations. The production data tables are based on the official company microfiche. The specification details and performance data are taken from sales brochures or engineering reports. Production data is according to Piper and is correct to the end of 1996. Also listed in the book are details of the Piper foreign assembly programmes and the many 'in the field' conversions. There are many appendices including a Piper serial number / U.S. Armed Forces serial number cross reference and details of the floods at Lock Haven.

Author Roger W. Peperell stands next to his own aircraft, PA-28-180 Cherokee F s/n 28-7105210 registered G-AZLN. The photograph was taken by his daughter Carrie at Fenland, England in 1993.

The author has been an Air Britain member for more than 25 years and lives in Oxfordshire, England. Piper Aircraft represents the culmination of 30 years of research undertaken with the fullest co-operation of the Piper Aircraft Corporation and the New Piper Aircraft Inc.

Piper Aircraft

Contents

INTRODUCTION

I am very pleased to present this book on Piper Aircraft, which is a fully revised version of 'Piper Aircraft and their Forerunners' published in 1987 and brings production up to 1996 and includes many new and previously unpublished designs.

I would like to thank The New Piper Aircraft Company and their predecessor The Piper Aircraft Corporation for opening their engineering files which has enabled me to considerably update my own extensive records to produce this book. Many thanks also to Colin Smith for all his help on registration data and checking the draft material and to my wife Hazel and Grahame Gates for checking the text. A special thanks to my family who have supported me whilst I prepared this book.

Over the past 34 years I have spent many a happy hour talking with current and past employees of Piper and many other aviation people, borrowing photographs and recording events. I would like to thank them all and hope that I have not forgotten to mention anyone in the list below:

American Avn. Hist. Soc.
Aerospace Publishing
Air-Britain
Ben Baker
Bill Barnhouse
Melvin Bartholomew
Dave Benson
Madeleine Blesh
Ann Bowers
Peter Bowers
Earle Boyter
Bill Bubb
Erwin Bulban
John Bryerton
Neal Carlson
CASA
Al Casper
Jim Cavanagh
Chris Chatfield
Chincul, S.A.
Dick Clark
Joe Caprio
Charlie Cresswell
Chuck Diefendorf
CSE Aviation
Cub Clues
Cub Flier
David Donald
Keith Donald
Phil Dunnington
Bob Edelstein
Embraer
ENAER
Paul Everly
Warren Finch Jr.
Flight International
Fran Fowler
Grahame Gates
John Geise
Guido A. Ghiretti
Wayne Giles
Jim Griswold
Jennifer Gradidge
Dan Hagedorn
Mal Halcomb
Werner Hartlieb
Tom Heitzman
Jim Hensen
Dennis Hoffman
Ted Hooton
Walter Jamouneau (deceased)
Ray Johnson
George Kasote
Peter Keating
Bill Kelly
Henry van Kesteren
Ralph Kimberlin
Jess Krall
Dave Lawrence
George Leamy
Howard Levy
Dave Lister
Lock Haven Express
Curt LoPresti
Suzie Luther-Stringfellow
Dave Marshall
Joe Maurielli
Ian McConnell
Jack McNulty
Jake Miller
Mississippi Sate Univ.
Frank Mitchell
Clarence Monks
Vince Montuoro Jr.
Bill Moreu
Alfred Munro (deceased)
Jay Myers
NASA
Elliott Nichols
The New Piper Aircraft Inc.
Gene Ohl
Pete Peck
Chet Peek
Ed Phillips
Geoff Phillips
Piper Aircraft Corp.
Piper Aviation Museum
Piper Pilot
Bill Piper Jr.
Joe Ponte
Rick Richardson
Hannu Riihela
Kenny Rooke
Rosie Rosenmehier
Dave Schwartz
Dave Scott
Sentimental Journey
Rod Simpson
Clyde Smith Sr.
Clyde Smith Jr.
Colin Smith
Doug Smith
Martin Smith
Richard Smith
Smithsonian Institution
John Stahly
Colleen Steinhoff
Daisy Strickland
Ed Swearingen
Robert Taylor
John Taylor
Norman Thelwell
Charles Trask
John Underwood
U.S. Air Force
U.S.C.A.R.
Ken Wakefield
Clark Walker
Fred Weick
Kurt Wetzel (deceased)
Jack Wetzel
Kim Wheeler
Cal Wilson
Bob Yoder

Any comments, additions or amendments will be gratefully received by the author.

Roger W. Peperell
51 Church Street
Kidlington
Oxford
OX5 2BA
England

December 1996

This book begins with the forerunner aircraft, the Chummy and Taylor Cub. It describes each of the Piper aircraft designed and built, designed and not built, and those which were considered for acquisition by Piper. It gives information on prototypes, production histories, specification details and performance data of the different designations. The production data tables are based on the official company microfiche. Where the microfiche does not show the year or model year, then company fiscal year is used (1st October to 30th September). The specification details and performance data are taken from sales brochures or engineering reports. Some of the data has been converted from metric to imperial or vice versa to keep data consistent within a type. Production data is according to Piper and is correct to the end of 1996. Also listed in the book are details of the Piper foreign assembly programmes and the many 'in the field' conversions. The book is presented in type number order, which is approximately equal to date order. There are many appendices.

In order to avoid having large columns the model details are shown in abbreviated form. Some examples of the full expanded designations are as follows:

PA-18 '95'	=	PA-18 Super Cub 95
PA-18 '135'	=	PA-18 Super Cub 135
PA-18-135	=	PA-18-135 Super Cub
PA-24-260 'B'	=	PA-24-260 Comanche B
PA-32R-301 'II HP'	=	PA-32R-301 Saratoga II HP

Throughout the book the abbreviation used for manufacturing serial number is 's/n', written off is shown as 'w/o'.

The first Cub, Taylor Cub s/n 11 registration 10547 with C.G. Taylor and pilot at Bradford in 1930. (via R. Taylor)

Piper family taken in the mid 1960s. William T. Piper Senior (bottom centre), then clockwise Mary Harford (daughter), Howard 'Pug' Piper (son), Margo Piper (Tony's wife), Thomas 'Tony' Piper (son), Helen Piper (Howard's wife), Bill Piper Junior (son), 'Pud' Piper (Bill Junior's wife) and Elizabeth Harford (daughter). (via F. Weick)

20,000th Piper Cub, PA-12 Super Cruiser s/n 12-59 registration NC20000 with E-2 Cub s/n 254 registration NC15336 at Lock Haven in May 1946. (Piper Aviation Museum)

50,000th Piper, PA-23 Apache s/n 23-1829 registration N4328P at Lock Haven in November 1959. (Piper Aircraft Corporation)

100,000th Piper, PA-31T Cheyenne s/n 31T-7620023 registration N100MP in April 1976. (Piper Aircraft Corporation)

125,000th Piper, PA-34-220T Seneca III s/n 34-8233146 registration N125PA in May 1982. (Piper Aircraft Corporation)

FOREWORD

Piper is held in high esteem throughout the world for the quality of the designs it has offered and the fine workmanship in every aircraft it delivers.

It all started with the forerunner companies the North Star Aerial Service and the Taylor brothers Aircraft Manufacturing Company led by Clarence G. Taylor. The Piper Aircraft Corporation, led by William T. Piper, produced its first aircraft in November 1937. Piper's first annual report dated September 1938 shows revenue of $768,144.83 and a net profit of $14,031.45. By November 1959 50,000 aircraft had been produced; by April 1976, 100,000; the 125,000th came off the Vero Beach production line on the 4th of May 1982 and by the end of 1996 over 128,500 aircraft covering hundreds of different types have been built. PIPER is famous for aircraft like the Cub, the Aztec, the Cherokee and the Navajo.

In 1965 the U.S. Commerce Department presented Piper with the Government 'E' award for export achievement - 877 aircraft or 19.7% of Piper's sales were exported in that year. In February 1967 Piper delivered its 10,000th export aircraft.

W. (William) T. Piper Senior and his sons had managed Piper from 1937 through to 1969, except for a brief period in the late 1940s when the company was managed by a Mr. Schriver. In January 1969, Chris-Craft, famous for building boats, started buying Piper shares in order to take control of Piper Aircraft. Piper were not happy about the prospect, so tried to set up deals with other companies. In February 1969 Piper proposed a merger with Grumman Aircraft but the deal was dropped. In March 1969 Piper negotiated a deal with the United States Concrete Pipe Co., but the deal was overruled by the Stock Exchange Board of Governors in April 1969. By May 1969 Bangor Punta acquired a considerable number of Piper shares which resulted in both Bangor Punta and Chris-Craft owning approximately half the stock each. Bangor Punta seemed to end up with more stock, but the courts ruled that they were not allowed to vote some of it for five years. This effectively moved Chris-Craft into the pilot's seat. So on the 12th of August 1969 Chris-Craft and Bangor Punta took control. Thomas (Tony) Piper who had left the company in 1960, left the board of directors but Bill Junior, who had been the president since 1960, remained as President. Howard (Pug) Piper left the board of directors but remained part of the administration. William Piper Senior worked at the factory each day until he was taken into hospital on the 19th of November 1969. On the 15th of January 1970 William Piper Senior died. Pug Piper left to join Beechcraft Aircraft and Bill Junior left, so by the early 1970s all the Piper family had left the Piper Aircraft Corporation.

Joe Mergen, who became President in 1971 resigned in early 1974 due to ill health. William Gunn took over until Lyn J. Helms arrived later in 1974. By 1977 Bangor Punta had taken overall control of the company and Max Bleck became President in October 1978.

The 1977 annual report shows sales of $268 million and net income of $13.5 million.

In 1978, when the aircraft manufacturers were producing the greatest number of aircraft, Piper had six factories. They were:-

Vero Beach, Florida covering 618,000 square feet
Lock Haven, Pennsylvania covering 754,000 square feet
Lakeland, Florida covering 623,296 square feet
Quehanna, Pennsylvania covering 257,750 square feet (prefabricated parts)
Renovo, Pennsylvania covering 65,500 square feet (glass-fibre components)
Santa Maria, California (Aerostar)

On the 1st of March 1984 Lear Siegler took over Piper's parent company, Bangor Punta. Frank Manning was appointed President of Piper in 1985 and reported to Robert Wyma, who was re-appointed a vice-president of Lear Siegler.

5,253 Piper aircraft were delivered in 1979, the last 'good' year before the light aircraft industry decline of the 1980's. In the mid 1980's the general aviation world was in a recession and the U.S. product liability laws resulted in huge insurance premiums for the aircraft manufacturers. With the excess of available second-hand aircraft, light aircraft manufacturing shutdown for months. Only 325 Piper aircraft were delivered in 1986.

Aircraft awaiting delivery at Lock Haven in 1975. (R.W. Peperell)

Cherokees at Vero Beach in 1969. (Piper Aircraft Corporation)

Navajos at Lakeland in 1976. (R.W. Peperell)

By the end of 1985 Piper had consolidated its total operation to one plant, Vero Beach, which had been expanded to more than one million square feet. Piper sold off most of its inventory of spares for models produced at Lock Haven instead of transporting them to Vero Beach. In March 1985 Univair Aircraft of Aurora, Colorado, acquired the entire inventory of spares for certain out of production Piper models. The types involved were J-3, J-4, J-5, PA-11, PA-12, PA-14, PA-15, PA-16, PA-17, PA-20 and PA-22. At the same time Duncan Aviation of Lincoln, Nebraska, acquired the spares for the PA-18, PA-23, PA-23-250, PA-24, PA-24-400, PA-30, PA-36 and PA-39.

Forstmann Little & Company acquired Piper in early 1987 and it was sold to M.S. (Stuart) Millar (Romeo Charlie Inc. of California) on the 12th of May 1987.

Clarence G. Taylor died at the age of 89 on the 29th of March 1988 in Houston, Texas.

Things looked good for Piper at the end of the 1980s with new models, rising production and a growing workforce. Romeo Charlie set up LoPresti Piper with Roy LoPresti as president to develop new models. Piper North was to be established at Lock Haven with Pennsylvania State Government funding and with John Piper as president, but this failed to materialise due to the company's cash flow crisis. Pipers troubles started in late 1989 when suppliers stopped shipping parts to Piper due to non-payment. Piper stopped production in January 1990 and started laying off staff. Restricted production restarted in March concentrating on the Cheyenne and Mirage and the 70 aircraft that were part completed. Production had to stop again whilst funding and / or a partner was found. A series of companies were then involved in trying to purchase Piper. Transisco of San Francisco, CA in June 1990 - called off in July; Aerospatiale of France in January 1991 - called off in March. Piper filed for Chapter 11 (bankruptcy) protection in the first week of July 1991. Cyrus Eaton of Canada announced its intentions to purchase Piper in January 1992 and move to British Columbia or Saskatchewan within three years. They were also going to certify a Russian twin-jet. By May of that year Saskatchewan and Manitoba provincial governments were involved and a new company, Dan-Can of B.C. After failing to find finance to keep Piper going, Millar left in May 1992, Chuck Suma took over as President to orchestrate Piper's escape from the Courts control. In November 1992 Pilatus of Stans, Switzerland wished to purchase Piper and included in the proposal was the world-wide assembly of the PC-12 aircraft. This became a very serious plan in April 1993, but by June another company was also interested in Piper, 2I, a French-Italian consortium. In September the court at Miami rejected the bids. In January 1994 Vero Holdings of Philadelphia proposed buying Piper, but this fell through. Finally a group consisting of Dimeling, Schreiber & Park (50%), Teledyne Industries (25%) and a trust of Piper's creditors & shareholders (25%) agreed to purchase the assets for $95m. This was agreed by the courts on the 10th of July and signed on the 17th of July 1995. Piper Aircraft Corporation had died, but the New Piper Aircraft Inc. was born. With the birth of New Piper, new serial number blocks were started for the seven models in production.

1st New Piper, PA-46-350P Malibu Mirage s/n 4636001 registration N954SB at Vero Beach. (The New Piper Aircraft Inc.)

1
THE BEGINNINGS

Clarence Gilbert Taylor was born in Rochester, New York State on the 25th of September 1898, son of Mr. and Mrs. Arthur Taylor. Arthur was a skilled tool and die maker and a self taught engineer and set up his own company in 1889, so C.G. grew up around machinery. At a very early age he dreamt of designing and building his own aircraft. The Taylor family moved to Newark, N.Y. just 20 miles east of Rochester in August 1922. C.G. and brother Gordon set up a small business in a machine shop (an old coal storage shed) on East Union Street, next to the Barge Canal (now the Erie Canal) and their first project was a large ice-sled, propeller driven, designed to operate on frozen lakes. Mr. Jack Loomis of Binghampton, New York advertised a World War I surplus Curtiss JN-4D Jenny s/n 5060 for sale. The buyer would be taught to fly as part of the sale. C.G. purchased the aircraft for $750 and spent the winter of 1925 / 26 restoring the aircraft. He continued to modify it during 1926. This included three cockpits rather than two, the nose radiator was removed and replaced by a vertical one, rudder pedals replaced the rudder bar, metal landing gear added, the stagger changed on the wings and the wing panels re-rigged. This aircraft carried the registration 285 from June 1927 onwards (it was not mandatory to register aircraft in the U.S. until April 1927). On the 21st of April 1926 C.G. and Gordon, with H. Mertz of Palmyra, N.Y. set up the North Star Aerial Service Corporation at Newark. C.G. Taylor learned to fly and began barnstorming activities in the Upper New York State area.

Jack Loomis was impressed by C.G. Taylor's modifications, so he asked the brothers to build another aircraft. This was carried out at Rochester, N.Y., the Taylors moving back from Newark in the Spring of 1926. The aircraft was purchased from Mr. David Basil in August 1926 who had originally completed it in 1925. This aircraft, known as the 'Loomis Special', was rebuilt as a three-seater monoplane with an open cockpit for one and an enclosed cabin for two. It was fitted with a 110 hp Anzani 10 cylinder radial engine, and carried the registration 2594 (it was not registered until May 1927), and was s/n 2. This aircraft crashed on the 30th of August 1927 and it is thought that it was partially repaired and then returned by road to Rochester in 1928. Following a complete rebuild and conversion to a 4-seat open cockpit aircraft, it was fitted with a 135 hp Hallett engine. The registration 2594 was disallowed and on the 23rd of February 1929 it took up registration 2954 with the s/n now quoted.

In 1927 the brothers formed the Taylor Brothers Aircraft Manufacturing Company with H. Brigham and W. Britton. In September construction of the Arrowing A-2 Chummy began. The Chummy name was derived from the seating arrangement of a side-by-side 'Chummy' layout. This was completed in February 1928 as s/n 3 registration X4203 and Gordon was the test pilot for its first flight. It was a high-wing strut braced side-by-side two-seater monoplane powered by a 90 hp Anzani engine. The fuselage was built with molybdenum-carbon steel tubing and the wings were of spruce and mahogany. Both fuselage and wings were fabric covered. The wings were braced to the fuselage with 3 tubes arranged to form an N-strut. The Chummy was offered for sale at $2,300.

On the 26th of March 1928 the company name was changed to Taylor Brothers Aircraft Corporation, and in April s/n 4 registration X4901 appeared. This was a refined version of s/n 3 above and was designated the Taylor A-2 Chummy, the main difference being that a 96 hp Ryan-Siemens 7 engine was fitted (the German Siemens-Halske SH-11 imported by T. Clyde Ryan). This aircraft was built for the Detroit exhibition of April 1928 and it was there that it crashed on the 24th of April killing Gordon Taylor.

Following this came two 4-seat specials, s/n 5 for Eugene Wuriman of Syracuse, N.Y. and s/n 6 for a Mr. Bishops in Pennsylvania. However s/n 6 is shown as never finished. Despite this, s/n 6 registration 7698 appeared in September 1928 as a 4-seat monoplane powered by a 180 hp Hispano-Suiza engine. It is thought that this aircraft was actually s/n 5 modified for another owner, George Kallfetz, also of Syracuse.

The experience gained with the two A-2 Chummy aircraft, enabled C.G. Taylor to offer the model B-2 Chummy aircraft as a production aircraft. Initially it was offered with a choice of engines, the 96 hp Ryan-Siemens or 90 hp Kinner K-5 (from the Kinner Aircraft and Motor Corporation of Glendale, California). The prototype was s/n 7 registration 7303 appearing in June 1928. It was fitted with a 90 hp Kinner engine. The first aircraft suffered several minor accidents, which meant that some re-design became necessary.

Taylor's machine shop at Newark. (via R. Taylor)

Ice Boat on the Barge Canal at Newark. (via R. Taylor)

Early aircraft PRODUCTION DETAILS

Year	Serial Number Range From	To	Type	Total	Comments
1926	(1)		JN-4D	1	NASC, Rochester
1926	2		North Star 'Loomis Special'	1	NASC, Rochester
1928	3		Arrowing A-2 Chummy	1	TBAMC, Rochester
1928	4		Taylor A-2 Chummy	1	TBAC, Rochester
1928	5 *	6	Taylor Special	1	TBAC, Rochester
1928	7	8 *	Taylor B-2 Chummy	1	TBAC, Rochester
1929	9		Taylor B-2 Chummy	1	TBAC, Rochester
1929	(10) *		Taylor C-2 Chummy	0	TBAC, Bradford
1930	11		Taylor B-2 Chummy	1	TBAC, Bradford
1930	12	14 *	Taylor B-2 Chummy	2	TBAC, Bradford
1930	15		Taylor B-2 Chummy	1	TBAC, Bradford
1930	15A		Taylor D-1 Glider	1	TBAC, Bradford
	16 *		Taylor B-2 Chummy	0	TBAC, Bradford

A total of 5 aircraft in the batches marked * were not delivered, instead they were updated and given new serial numbers. See table below.
Total manufactured 12

Early aircraft SERIAL NUMBER CHANGES

Model	Old Serial Number	New Serial Number	New Model (if different)
Special	5	6	
B-2	7	10	C-2
B-2	8	11	
B-2	13	15	
B-2	16	Not completed	

At this stage C.G. Taylor could see that the Rochester premises would not be large enough for the production that he envisaged, so alternative premises were sought. At the same time Bradford was seeking new businesses to boost the local economy, which was suffering from the fast disappearing local oil production. As an incentive for Taylor Aircraft to move to Bradford, a citizen's committee offered to purchase a large amount of Taylor stock and the use of a small ironworks bordering the local airport. The result was that the Taylor Bothers Aircraft Corporation moved to Emery Airport, Bradford in Pennsylvania in September 1928 (this included one completed Chummy aircraft 7303, parts / assemblies and six employees). Some of the money was spent on building a new factory at the airport. One of the oil-men was a certain Mr. W.T. Piper. Before long Mr. Piper was on the Taylor board of directors.

William Thomas Piper was born in Knapp Creek, N.Y. State on the 8th of January 1881, son of Thomas and Sarah Piper. William was a partner in an oil recovery business called the Dallas Oil Company in Bradford, Penna which was started in 1915.

The first local person hired by the Taylor Company was Warren Finch (Warren worked for the company for 45 years, retiring reluctantly in late 1974 at Lock Haven). It was still a family affair with Mrs C.G. Taylor in charge of sewing, and father Arthur in assembly and C.G. in charge.

Another Chummy, s/n 8 registration X140E appeared in November 1928, was for exhibition purposes only and was never flown.

Jenny registration 285. (via R. Taylor)

North Star 'Loomis Special' s/n 2 registration 2594. (via R. Taylor)

Another view of the North Star 'Loomis Special' s/n 2 registration 2594. (via c. Peek)

Early aircraft SPECIFICATION & PERFORMANCE			
SPECIFICATION	North Star 'Loomis Special' s/n 2	Taylor s/n 2	Arrowing A-2
Engine	110 hp Anzani	135 hp Hallett	90 hp Anzani or 96 hp Ryan-Siemens
Engine TBO (hrs)			
No of seats	3	4	2
Wing Span (ft/ins)	42/0	41/0	34/0
Length (ft/ins)	24/6	26/0	22/0
Height (ft/ins)			7/6
Useable fuel capacity (US gal)			28
Gross weight (lbs)	2300	2450	1485
Empty weight (lbs)			985
Useful load (lbs)			500
PERFORMANCE			
Max speed			110 mph
Cruise speed			100 mph
Efficiency (gph)			
Stall speed - flaps / gear down			38 mph
Climb @ sea level (fpm)			850
Range with reserves			500 sm
Service ceiling (ft)			

The first production aircraft s/n 9 was first registered as X492 in February 1929 and was fitted with a Kinner engine. While this did not qualify for a full Approved Type Certificate (ATC), it did receive the lesser Category 2 certificate 2-114 on the 27th of August 1929, it's registration changing to C492, but now without the N-strut just a double strut. Later it became NC492. Taylor offered two Chummies: the Trainer and the Sport. These were identical, offering dual control sticks, adjustable stabilizer, detachable swing-away engine mount and 'fabrickoid' leather upholstery. In addition, the Sport offered a cabin heater, wheel brakes, tail wheel, airspeed indicator and magnetic compass. The Kinner or the 90 hp Brownbach engine were the alternative powerplants offered.

Later in 1929, s/n 7 was rebuilt as s/n 10 retaining registration 7303. This rebuild was the Taylor C-2 Chummy and was a special for the Daniel Guggenheim International Safe Aircraft Competition which took place in November and December 1929 at Mitchel Field, Long Island, N.Y. It arrived for the competition by air on the 1st of November and departed after trials were completed on the 4th of December. It had failed by 1.5 mph as the maximum speed had to be a minimum of 110 mph. This aircraft had a variable incidence wing (which rotated about 7.5 degrees), but officials of the competition commented that this feature was of little value and added complication and weight to the aircraft. (Although the designation was changed in the published registers, the s/n was not amended, staying as 7).

The second, unflown, prototype s/n 8 was then rebuilt in March 1930 as s/n 11 registration NC592V. This was still designated as a model B-2 Chummy. Three further B-2's were built with s/n 12 registration 314W, s/n 13 and s/n 14 registration NC992V in 1930. It should be noted that s/n 13 was changed to s/n 15 registration NC5E prior to registry. All these models were fitted with the Kinner K-5 engine; the Brownbach Tiger engine was not used in any Chummy. The last Chummy, s/n 16 was sold incomplete and without an engine to Skyways Inc. of Cleveland, Ohio much later in December 1934.

Taylor A-2 Chummy s/n 3 registration X4203. (via T. Heitzman)

Taylor A-2 Chummy s/n 4 registration X4901. (J.W. Underwood)

Taylor B-2 Chummy s/n 7 registration 7303. (Piper Aircraft Corporation)

Early aircraft SPECIFICATION & PERFORMANCE			
SPECIFICATION	Taylor Spec s/n 6	B-2 Chummy	C-2 Chummy
Engine	180 hp Hispano Suiza	90 hp Kinner K-5	90 hp Kinner K-5
Engine TBO (hrs)			
No of seats		2	2
Wing Span (ft/ins)	43/0	34/0	34/0
Length (ft/ins)	26/0	22/6	22/6
Height (ft/ins)		7/6	8/0
Useable fuel capacity (US gal)		24	30
Gross weight (lbs)		1643	1667
Empty weight (lbs)		1082	1197
Useful load (lbs)		561	470
PERFORMANCE			
Max speed		110 mph	108.5 mph
Cruise speed		90 mph	
Efficiency (gph)			
Stall speed - flaps / gear down		38 mph	45.5 mph
Climb @ sea level (fpm)		750	
Range with reserves		400 sm	
Service ceiling (ft)			
Take off (Ground run)(ft)			
Take off (over 50ft obst)(ft)			
Landing (Ground roll)(ft)			
Landing (over 50ft obst)(ft)			

The price of the Chummy was over $4,000 and it was not selling. The company was rapidly going broke in 1930 because aircraft were not selling due to the Depression. That year saw many well established aircraft factories closing their doors. In the middle of 1930, Taylor Brothers Aircraft Corporation went into voluntary liquidation and closed its doors for three months. W.T. Piper purchased the assets of the business and from these assets formed the Taylor Aircraft Company, with C.G. Taylor as Chief Engineer. In July 1930 a single seat Taylor D-1 Glider was produced. This had a tubular steel framework, a bicycle saddle for a seat and very primitive controls, lightweight wings with wire bracing and skids rather than wheels. It's s/n was 15A but no registration was assigned. Mr. Piper and C.G. Taylor used to pull it along behind an automobile up and down the runway at the airport each week-end. This was eventually sold to Mr. Clarence Fischer of Buffalo, N.Y. in July 1936.

Taylor B-2 Chummy s/n 9 registration NC492 at Bradford. (via R. Taylor)

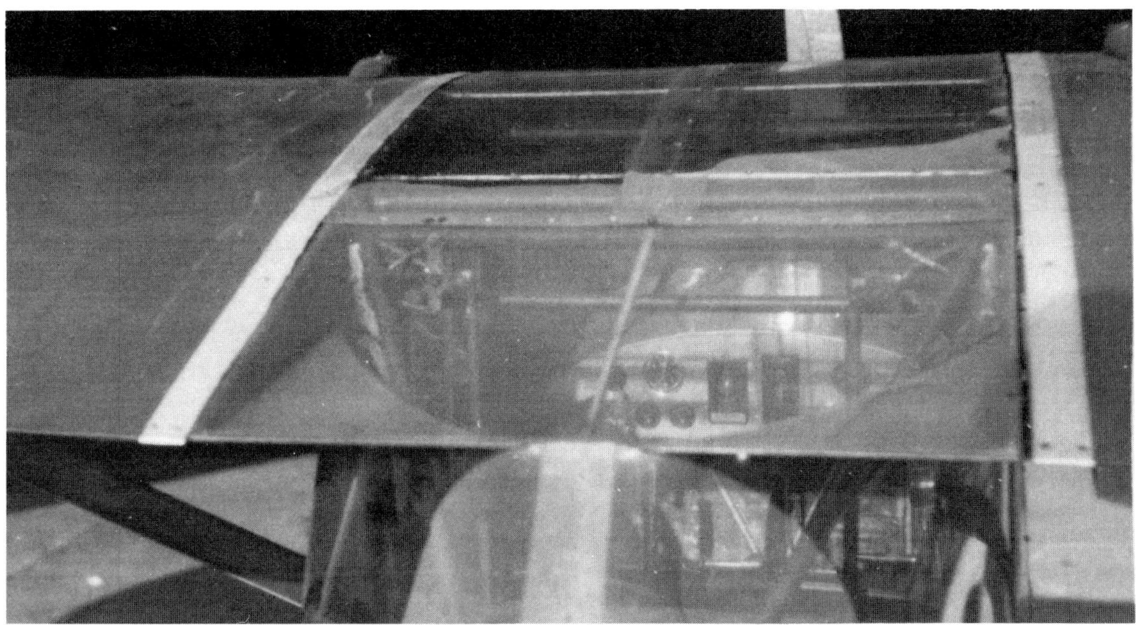

Taylor C-2 Chummy s/n 10 registration 7303 showing the variable incidence wing controls. (via R. Taylor)

Taylor B-2 Chummy s/n 14 registration 314W at Bradford. (via W. Finch Jr.)

Taylor D-1 Glider at Bradford. (Piper Aircraft Corporation)

2
CUBS

The experience with the Glider gave rise to the thought that maybe a light aircraft could be built. Mr. Piper wanted to produce a simple low-powered trainer that was economical for flight instructors to operate and therefore lessons would be inexpensive. So C.G., Arthur Taylor and Kenneth Tibbets set to work and in about four weeks put together the aircraft, called the Taylor E-2, s/n 11 registration 10547. (The Glider was the model D and the -2 indicates 2 seats). The E-2 was a two-seat tandem low powered aircraft with a high-wing and fabric covered tubular steel fuselage, fabric covered wooden wings and open cockpit. The choice of an engine was a problem though.

The aircraft sat in the factory for three weeks waiting for a French Salmson engine to arrive from New York. This was a small nine cylinder radial engine of 40 hp. In the meantime, C.G. and Mr. Piper had been searching for an engine that could be obtained in quantity. They had made a number of trips around the east side of the U.S. which ended up at the Continental Motors Company of Detroit, Michigan, but their new engine was not yet available. The Light Manufacturing and Foundry Company of Pottstown, Penna, whom they had contacted, had a small two cylinder 20 hp engine called the Brownbach Tiger Kitten. A Mr. George Kirkendall was sent to Bradford with the engine. This engine was much too small, but it was this engine that engendered the name of the aircraft, because Tiger Kitten equals Cub, and the name stuck. It was fitted to the aircraft and Mr. Kirkendall did manage to get it airborne on the 12th of September 1930 to a height of one foot for a distance of 10-15 feet. Mr. Kirkendall was thanked and sent on his way. The first successful flight of the Cub was made by Bud Havens at the end of September after the Salmson D-9 engine was installed. This engine was deemed suitable in power output, but it was considered to be too expensive and anyway it was built to metric sizes. For a time the project was shelved, whilst an alternative power plant was sought.

C.G. decided to try the unproven 37 hp A40 engine from Continental Motors. This engine was a four cylinder, air-cooled horizontally opposed engine. This was fitted to a new airframe, s/n 12 registration NC10594, which was completed on the 9th of April 1931. (Piper purchased s/n 12 registration N10594 on the 7th of November 1989 and was in the production building at Vero Beach in 1996). This motor proved to be problematic during testing and was returned to Detroit several times for repair and modification. Continental received approval for their A40 engine on the 15th of May 1931, which allowed the Taylor E-2 Cub to be first certified on the 15th of June 1931 under group 2 approval number 2-358 that covered the first 14 examples. Production Cubs had the 9 gallon fuel tank moved from above the centre of the wing to between the panel and the firewall. Production of the Taylor E-2 Cub got underway with the Continental A40-2 engine, commencing with s/n 13 registration NC10784. The basic aircraft was painted silver and red, no equipment or accessories were available. It's price was $1325. The first aircraft exported was an E-2 Cub, s/n 14 which was completed on the 18th of June 1931. This was exported to Canada in August 1931 under export number E424 and was registered CF-ARA. Final approval on Approved Type Certificate A455 was granted on the 7th of November 1931 covering s/n 26 and up. These were classified as 'new models' having a new gas tank, better seats and an updated fuselage. Serial number 26 registration NC11674 was completed at the factory on the 9th of October 1931.

Aircraft s/n 32 was completed on the 11th of December 1931 as registration X12627. This was owned by Kenneth Tibbets, but Mr. H.P. Augustine of Buffalo, N.Y. installed an Augustine R4-40 engine. This was returned to the Factory in August 1932 in order to repair some damage and replace the engine.

In 1932 an enclosed cockpit became standard by installing a wrap-around rear windshield in the gap between the wing and fuselage at the rear of the cabin. The first aircraft with this was s/n 35 registration NC12630 completed on the 9th of February 1932.

The first serious accident was to aircraft s/n 36 registration NC12664 on the 5th of September 1932.

The Continental A40 engine proved not to be entirely satisfactory, frequently stopping in flight. An Aeronca engine was mounted on a Cub, but it was hopelessly rough. They did update their engine to the A40-2 which had two thrust bearings instead of one, making it more reliable. The first Cub with the A40-2 engine was s/n 69 completed in August 1933. It was about this time that Continental announced its intentions to stop making aircraft engines. (Later they changed their minds). The search for suitable alternatives resulted in three further versions of the basic design.

Taylor E-2 Cub s/n 11 registration10547 at Bradford with pilot Bud Haven. (via W. Finch Jr.)

First Cubs PRODUCTION DETAILS

Fiscal Year	Serial Number Range From	To	Type	Total	Comments
Prototype	11		E-2	1	
1931	12	32	E-2	21	
1932	33	54 *	E-2	22	
1933	55	72	E-2	18	
1934	73		E-2	1	
Prototype	74		F-2	1	
1934	75	139 *	F-2 and F-2	64	
Prototype	140		H-2	1	
1934	141	148	E-2	8	
Prototype	149 *		G-2	0	to H-2
1935	150	358 *	E-2 and H-2	206	
1936	359	380 *	E-2	5	

A total of 22 aircraft in the batches marked * were not delivered, instead they were updated to the next model and given new serial numbers or not built. See table below.
Total manufactured 348 (All built at Bradford)

First Cubs SERIAL NUMBER CHANGES

Model	Old Serial Number	New Serial Number	New Model (if different)
E-2	48	S-557	J-2
E-2	134	949	J-2
E-2	149	522	J-2
E-2	244	614	J-2
E-2	324	719	J-2
E-2	364-380	Not built	

The first was the 3 cylinder radial Aeromarine AR3-40 of 40 hp, which was first fitted to s/n 74 registration X13272, completed on the 4th of October 1933. Production commenced with s/n 75 registration NC825M, completed on the 3rd of January 1934. Also s/n 66 registration X2735 was converted by the factory from an E-2 to have an Aeromarine engine on the 27th of January 1934. This version was designated the Taylor F-2 Cub and the Approved Type Certificate A525 was granted on the 16th of February 1934. The F-2 Cub had a removable engine mount.

Taylor then tried to use a 40 hp engine of their own design, the T-40 engine. This was fitted to s/n 149 registration X14756 as the Taylor G-2 Cub and was completed on the 2nd of February 1935. This was not a very successful fitting as this aircraft re-emerged in April 1935 as the Taylor H-2 Cub fitted now with a Szekely engine.

Earlier, Taylor had put a 35 hp Szekely SR-3-35 engine on s/n 140 registration X14733 also completed on the 2nd of February. Another H-2 aircraft was experimented with at the factory, s/n 180 registration X15001 completed on the 26th of April. The model H-2 was granted an Approved Type Certificate A528 on the 28th of May 1935. The only production model, s/n 263, was delivered without an engine but with a Szekely engine manual.

The only other variant to be built by the factory was the float equipped model F-2S s/n 115 registration X14729, completed on the 17th of October 1934. This was on Edo model 990 floats.

The Szekely engine had a magnesium alloy crankcase. In 1933 the ATC was revoked.

Only 30 F-2 aircraft were completed before Taylor dropped it as an option for the Cub. In the meantime Continental Motors updated their engine again to the model A40-3, but still of 37 hp. This then became the engine used in production E-2 Cubs from s/n 178 onwards, which was completed on the 13th of April 1935.

Taylor E-2 Cub s/n 12 registration NC10594. (via R. Taylor)

1st Cub with an enclosed cockpit, Taylor E-2 Cub s/n 35 registration NC12630 at Bradford. (via R. Taylor)

Taylor F-2 Cub s/n 75 registration NC825M. (via R. Taylor)

First Cubs SPECIFICATION & PERFORMANCE

SPECIFICATION	E-2	F-2	H-2
Engine	37 hp Continental A40-2 or 3	40 hp Aeromarine AR-3-40	35 hp Szekely SR-3-35
Engine TBO (hrs)			
No of seats	2	2	2
Wing Span (ft/ins)	35/3	35/3	35/3
Length (ft/ins)	22/3	22/0	22/1
Height (ft/ins)	6/6	6/6	6/6
Useable fuel capacity (US gal)	9	9	9
Gross weight (lbs)	925	943-988	943-988
Empty weight (lbs)	532	536-545	536-545
Useful load (lbs)	393	407-443	407-443
Propeller			
Floats available			
PERFORMANCE			
Max speed	80 mph	85 mph	82 mph
Cruise speed	68 mph	75 mph	72 mph
Efficiency (gph)	3	3.5	3
Stall speed - flaps / gear down	28 mph	30 mph	30 mph
Climb @ sea level (fpm)	450	600	550
Range with reserves	180 sm	240 sm	220 sm
Service ceiling (ft)	12,000	14,000	12,500
Take off (Ground run)(ft)	120	100	110
Take off (over 50ft obst)(ft)			
Landing (Ground roll)(ft)	95	100	100
Landing (over 50ft obst)(ft)			

One aircraft, a model F-2 s/n 112 registration PP-TAW, had an accident in Brazil prior to being officially registered. This was rebuilt and fitted with a 50 hp Walter Mickron engine and then officially registered during February 1937. This machine, after its rebuild, did not look like a standard model F-2.

The final production E-2 was s/n 363 registration NC15931 built in February 1936. The last 17 aircraft (s/n 364 - 380) were cancelled on the 9th of November 1935 when it was decided to proceed with the J-2 model.

Taylor G-2 Cub s/n 149 registration X14756 at Bradford. (via W.T. Piper Jr.)

Taylor H-2 Cub s/n 140 registration NC14733 at Bradford. (via R. Taylor)

Taylor F-2S Cub Seaplane s/n 115 registration X14729. (Piper Aircraft Corporation)

J-2 Cub

Walter Jamouneau reworked the Cub, with a new type airfoil wing with rounded wing tips and a new tail shape, a refined nose for better engine cooling and a wider track landing gear with a revised shock cord and tension strut arrangement. The rear turtledeck structure was raised to fair the fuselage into the wing and create a closed cabin with a three-piece windshield. The experimental aircraft was s/n 48 which had been returned to the factory after an accident in June 1934. Now with registration X13118 it was converted / repaired in early 1935.

It was when C.G. Taylor saw what had happened to his Cub design in 1935 that he decided to leave the company. C.G. Taylor was ill during the winter of 1934 / 35. Walter Jamouneau had been hired into the company as an engineer in January 1931. C.G. wanted to manage all design work and this was impossible as he was not at work. He also wanted to design a side-by-side aircraft which conflicted with Mr. Piper's wish to upgrade the tandem Cub using the ideas of Walter Jamouneau. Mr. Piper bought out C.G. Taylor's share of the company and C.G. went off to set up the Taylor-Young Company (later Taylorcraft). His first design was the Taylor-Young A s/n 25 registration X16393, a side-by-side high-wing mono-plane. This first flew at the Pittsburgh-Butler airport in April 1935.

The first J-2 production aircraft was completed on the 18th of December 1935 as s/n 500 registration X15951. This new version followed logically from the previous model, the H-2, so became the J-2 Cub, which was quite a coincidence as the name of the design engineer who was responsible for the redesign was Walter Jamouneau. The engine used was the 37 hp Continental A40-3 and, following the issue of the Approved Type Certificate A595 on the 14th of February 1936, production commenced with s/n 501 registration NC15956. The standard colour scheme for the J-2 was silver. Initially priced at $1,470 later it was reduced to $1,270. From s/n 510 onwards the landing gear tread was widened. In September 1936 the engine fitted was changed to the 40 hp A40-4, starting from s/n 820.

J-2 Cub s/n 600 registration X16792 was completed on the 14th of July 1936. During the rest of 1936 and 1937 the design was updated - including a re-shaping of the vertical tail surfaces, fitment of wheel brakes, tail wheel, balanced rudder, additional standard panel equipment and larger seats. This aircraft was the prototype of the next model and became the J-3 in October 1937.

The J-2 model with Edo floats was the J-2S, the prototype was s/n 700 registration X16395, completed in May 1936. The first production aircraft with seaplane fittings was s/n 658 registration NC16643 completed on the 16th of June 1936.

In late 1936 and early 1937 some J-2 aircraft were shipped to Aircraft Associates at Long Beach, California for completion. The first aircraft shipped to Aircraft Associates was s/n 899 in October 1936. These were known as the Western Cub and were approved on a separate Approved Type Certificate, A620 issued on the 23rd of December.

A few J-2 aircraft were sold with the Everel single blade propeller. An example was s/n 886 registration X17220 in early 1937.

Originally all production work was done in one building, from welding to final assembly. As demand for more production increased, additions were made to the original building in the form of long Ls, eventually giving a floor space of 36,000 square feet. Since it was a frame building inaccessible to the City water hydrants and the process of 'doping' was very hazardous, the fire insurance rates were too high for a struggling company to afford coverage of more than $10,000 per year. Disaster struck on the night of the 16th / 17th of March 1937 when the Bradford factory was destroyed by fire, which originated in the dope room. Ten J-2 aircraft (s/n 1316 registration NC17882 to s/n 1325 registration NC17891) on the production line were lost in addition to some others damaged and one lost outside the factory. Technical drawings were lost, tools and jigs were damaged.

However, many Cubs were built at Bradford following the fire. The ATC was re-issued on the 24th of March with number ATC595 for the J-2 built after the fire. As it could be seen that the Bradford facility would not be large enough, alternative premises were sought in which to restart production.

The Taylor factory at Bradford. The aircraft in the centre is the experimental J-2 Cub s/n S-557 registration NC13118. (Piper Aircraft Museum)

Taylor J-2 Cub s/n 503 registration NC15958 at Bradford. (Piper Aircraft Corporation)

J-2 PRODUCTION DETAILS

Fiscal Year	Serial Number Range From	To	Type	Total	Comments
Experimental	48		J-2	0	Taylor at Bradford
1936	500	555	J-2	56	Taylor at Bradford
1936	S-556	S-560	J-2	5	Taylor at Bradford
1936	561	599	J-2	37	Taylor at Bradford
Experimental	600 *		J-2	0	Taylor at Bradford
1936	601	699 *	J-2	99	Taylor at Bradford
Prototype	700		J-2S	1	Taylor at Bradford
1936	701	872 *	J-2	170	Taylor at Bradford
1936	C838		J-2	1	Cub Aircraft at Hamilton
1937	873	898	J-2	26	Taylor at Bradford
1937	899	902	J-2	4	Aircraft Associates at Long Beach
1937	903	969	J-2	67	Taylor at Bradford
1937	C906 & C909		J-2	2	Cub Aircraft at Hamilton
1937	970	992 *	J-2	22	Taylor at Lock Haven
1937	1000	1122 *	J-2	121	Taylor at Bradford
1937	C1005, C1006		J-2	2	Cub Aircraft at Hamilton
1937	C1080, C1082 & C1083		J-2	3	Cub Aircraft at Hamilton
1937	C1089, C1091 & C1092		J-2	3	Cub Aircraft at Hamilton
1937	1201	1244	J-2	44	Taylor at Bradford
1937	1245	1246	J-2	2	Aircraft Associates at Long Beach
1937	1247 (1)		J-2	1	Taylor at Bradford (w/o on delivery)
1937	1247 (2)		J-2	1	Taylor at Bradford
1937	1248	1262	J-2	15	Aircraft Associates at Long Beach
1937	1263	1291 (1)	J-2	29	Taylor at Bradford (1291 (1) w/o by Fire)
1937	1291 (2)	1325 *	J-2	25	Taylor at Bradford
1937	1500	1647	J-2	148	Taylor at Bradford
1937	1648	1856 *	J-2	208	Taylor at Lock Haven
1937	1858	1875	J-2	18	Taylor at Lock Haven
1937	1920 & 1922		J-2	2	Taylor at Lock Haven
1938	993	999	J-2	7	Piper at Lock Haven
1938	1123	1124	J-2	2	Piper at Lock Haven
1938	1150	1153	J-2	4	Piper at Lock Haven
1938	1155	1162	J-2	8	Piper at Lock Haven
1938	1166	1178 *	J-2	3	Piper at Lock Haven
1938	1316 (2)	1319 (2)	J-2	4	Piper at Lock Haven
1938	1876	1918	J-2	43	Taylor at Lock Haven
1938	1857, 1919, 1921, 1923		J-2	4	Piper at Lock Haven
1938	1927 & 1928		J-2	2	Piper at Lock Haven
1938	1924	1926	J-2	3	Taylor at Lock Haven
1938	1927	1928	J-2	2	Piper at Lock Haven
1938	1929	1936	J-2	8	Taylor at Lock Haven
1938	1937	1975 *	J-2	14	Piper at Lock Haven

The experimental aircraft 48 has been included as S-557 in the manufactured total. A total of 53 aircraft in the batches marked * were not delivered, instead they were updated to the next year's model and given new serial numbers or not built. See table below.

Total manufactured 1158 (Taylor & Piper)
11 (Cub Aircraft - s/n are C followed by fuselage number)

J-2 SERIAL NUMBER CHANGES			
Model	Old Serial Number	New Serial Number	New Model (if different)
J-2	600	1999	J-3
J-2	646	768	
J-2	728	1312	
J-2	833	1291 (2)	remained registered as s/n 833
J-2	975	1647	
J-2	1101-1102	Not built	
J-2	1168-1177	Not built	
J-2	1316 (1)-1325	Not built, destroyed by fire	
J-2	1800	2000	J-3
J-2	1948-1949	Not built	
J-2	1951-1960	Not built	
J-2	1962-1974	Not built	

A number of towns began wooing Taylor their way. Jacob (Jake) Miller, a Cub distributor, and Lock Haven city officials met with W.T. Piper. Thus Taylor Aircraft moved to Lock Haven, in Pennsylvania, taking over the property formally occupied by the Susquehanna Silk Mills, which was a large concrete two storey building and 16 acres of adjoining ground space located next to the airport. The Susquehanna River which flows through Lock Haven, afforded excellent facilities for seaplane flying. Production of the J-2 transferred there in July 1937 with s/n 1652 completed on the 7th. (s/n 1648 to 1651 followed a few days later at Lock Haven).

Even though the company name was not officially changed to the Piper Aircraft Corporation until the 13th of November, it was effective as of the 1st. The first aircraft to carry the Piper plate was s/n 1937 registration NC20137 completed on the 2nd of November. Piper Aircraft Corporation went public with a stock offering in March 1938.

Taylor J-2 Cub with Everel single blade propeller, s/n 886 registration X17220. (via W.T. Piper Jr.)

Taylor J-2S Cub Seaplane s/n 700 registration X16395. (Piper Aircraft Corporation)

'The New Silver Cub' at the New York show, Taylor J-2S Cub Seaplane s/n 1223 registration NC17288. (via W.T. Piper Jr.)

Taylor J-2X Cub with a Glenn D. Angle radial engine, s/n 1718 registration NX19518. (P. Bowers collection)

Record breaker Taylor J-2 Cub s/n 1701 registration NC19501 at Motor City Airport, Detroit, Michigan. (Piper Aviation Museum)

Taylor J-2 Cub aircraft being put into a rail car on delivery. (via W.T. Piper Jr.)

J-2 SPECIFICATION & PERFORMANCE

SPECIFICATION	J-2	J-2S
Engine	37 hp Continental A40-3 or 40 hp Continental A40-4	37 hp Continental A40-3 or 40 hp Continental A40-4
Engine TBO (hrs)		
No of seats	2	2
Wing Span (ft/ins)	35/3	35/3
Length (ft/ins)	22/5	
Height (ft/ins)	6/8	7/7
Useable fuel capacity (US gal)	9	9
Gross weight (lbs)	970 1000 (s/n 600+)	1058
Empty weight (lbs)	563	657
Useful load (lbs)	407	410
Propeller	Sensenich	Sensenich
Floats available		Edo 1070 / 1140
PERFORMANCE		
Max speed	87 mph	75 mph
Cruise speed	70 mph	65 mph
Efficiency (gph)	3	
Stall speed - flaps / gear down	30 mph	35 mph
Climb @ sea level (fpm)	400	360
Range with reserves	210 sm	200 sm
Service ceiling (ft)	12,000	10,000
Take off (Ground run)(ft)	125	
Take off (over 50ft obst)(ft)		
Landing (Ground roll)(ft)	100	
Landing (over 50ft obst)(ft)		

The acquisition of the new plant and the cash from going public laid the groundwork for revolutionising aircraft manufacturing. Many of the straight-line production techniques saw their first use in the Cub factory. An industrial engineering company was hired to implement efficient constant-flow methods. Among the most outstanding developments which speeded construction was the 'ferriswheel' in the dope room. This rotary device, which had a capacity of twelve wings and six fuselages, enabled the workers to spray the units with maximum efficiency; by the time each unit came round the second time, it had dried sufficiently to be painted again. Production was stepped up at least ten percent by the introduction of a suspended assembly line, which consisted of an overhead monorail system connecting with all departments by means of switches, crossovers and sidings. A fuselage or wing on leaving its jig was put on this 'railway' and passed at a steady pace for more than a mile through all stages of installation and painting direct to final assembly.

The final few J-2 aircraft, serial numbers 1975, 1945 and 1946 were completed in April and May 1938 with s/n 1947 not completed until later in that year.

Aircraft s/n 1701 registration NC19501 was used for an endurance record in 1937 staying aloft for 34 hours and 24 minutes, taking off and landing at Motor City, Detroit, Michigan.

Aircraft s/n 792 registration PP-TCX was registered as a model H-2 in Brazil. It was fitted with a Szekely SR-3 engine in place of the Continental, therefore they could not register it as a J-2.

In the field, Taylor J-2 s/n 1289 registration NC17854 was modified with increased wing dihedral and merged exhaust stacks. Aircraft s/n 1718 had a Glen D. Angle 5-60 radial engine fitted in 1938 and wore the registration NX19518. Several aircraft have been fitted with a 65 hp Continental A65-8 engine, an example being s/n 980 registration LN-FAB in 1965.

After the fire at Bradford in March 1937. (Piper Aircraft Corporation)

Aerial view of the factory at Lock Haven in 1938. (Piper Aircraft Corporation)

J-3 Cub

J-2 Cub s/n 600 registration X16792 was originally completed at Bradford on the 14th of July 1936. During the rest of 1936 and 1937 the design was improved - including a re-shaping of the vertical tail surfaces, fitment of wheel brakes, tail wheel, balanced rudder, new wings, additional standard panel equipment and larger seats. SAE X-4130 steel tubing was used for the fuselage allowing the installation of higher powered engines. The s/n was changed to 1999 and the type to J-3 as of the 8th October 1937. The J-3 was granted an Approved Type Certificate A660 on the 30th of October 1937 with the prototype now registered NC16792. A second J-3 was s/n 1800 completed at the end of October 1937 as NC20000. The s/n of this aircraft was changed to 2000 as of the 2nd December 1937 still as NC20000 (even though NC20200 was allocated). J-2 and J-3 Cub aircraft were built together at Lock Haven in early 1938. It is possible that as many as 51 J-2 aircraft were converted in early 1938 into J-3 aircraft, but unfortunately it has not been possible to confirm this. (Registrations allocated to 51 serial numbers in the range 1945 - 1998 were used by serial numbers in the range 2198 - 2280). When launched the J-3 Cub Trainer was on sale for $1,249 then $995 and later $1,270. A Cub Sport was also available at $1,395.

The initial power plant was the 40 hp Continental A40-4. Subsequently a variety of other engines in the 40 to 65 hp range was fitted. Aircooled Motors Corp. of Syracuse, N.Y. introduced the 40 hp Franklin 4AC-150-S40 motor to compete with the Continental A40. Aircooled Motors had purchased aircraft s/n 2069 registration NX20269 in January 1938. They installed their own 40 hp Franklin in it and this was the first J-3F. This was approved on ATC660. Later the horse power was increased and the J-3F-50 was approved on certificate A692 on the 14th of July 1938. Piper used aircraft s/n 1937 registration NX20137 to test out the new 50 hp Continental engine in February 1938. The J-3C-50 Approved Type Certificate A691 was granted on the 14th of July 1938. Later in the year the Lenape Papoose radial engine was tested, (this was previously the Aeromarine AR-3). The J-3P was approved on certificate A695 on the 23rd of August 1938. Lycoming Motors Corporation purchased aircraft s/n 2513 registration NX21631 on the 2nd of September 1938 with their own 50 hp engine installed. The J-3L-50 Approved Type Certificate A698 was granted on the 17th of September 1938. Piper had planned to offer the J-3 Cub with a 50 hp Menasco M-50 engine in 1938, the J-3M-50. Unfortunately only dual ignition engines were being approved by then and the Menasco was single ignition, so it was a non starter.

Aerodynamically balanced friese type ailerons were available for the J-3 in October 1938. These were tested by Piper in September on aircraft s/n 2548 registration NX21662.

In 1939 and 1940 more horse-power was available, with Type Certificates being granted as follows: J-3C-65 on the 6th of July 1939, J-3L-65 on the 27th of May 1940, J-3F-60 on the 31st of May 1940 and J-3F-65 on the 7th of August 1940.

Over the years Piper worked on increasing the gross weight and therefore the useful load of the J-3 as the engine horse power increased. They strengthened the airframe and reinforced the landing gear. Gross weight was increased to 1160 pounds in mid 1941, up to 1200 pounds in late 1941. J-3L-65 aircraft s/n 7080 registration NC38510 and J-3C-65 s/n 7776 registration NX41177 were used for development and testing between June and the end of 1941. In 1943 increases to 1260 pounds were made and finally in 1946 the gross weight was up to 1300 pounds.

Civil production lasted from December 1937 to December 1941 and from September 1945 until January 1947 at Lock Haven. The standard colour scheme for the J-3 was yellow with a horizontal black stripe and a teddy bear on the tail.

Most versions of the J-3 series have also been fitted with floats, often Edo (Edo was short for Earl D. Osborn, the builder), and can be identified by the S at the end of the designation, e.g. J-3C-50S. This version was advertised during 1944 as the Cub Sea Scout. Several float designs were offered to Piper for fitment to the J-3 in addition to the metal Edo, e.g. McKinley pneumatic in 1939 on s/n 2548 registration X21662, Wollam plywood in 1941, Heath and Capre floats. Approved Type Certificates were granted for various versions on the following dates:- J-3L-50S on the 21st May 1939, J-3C-65S and J-3L-65S on the 27th May 1940, J-3F-60S on the 31st May 1940 and J-3F-65S on the 4th January 1943.

Experimental Taylor J-2 Cub s/n 600 registration X16792 at Bradford in 1936. (Piper Aviation Museum)

J-3 Cub s/n 2009 registration NC20209. (Piper Aircraft Corporation)

J-3 Cub s/n 2060 registration NC20260 at the Chicago International Air Show in January 1938. (via W.T. Piper Jr.)

J-3P Cub s/n 2471 registration NC21621 of Russel Flying Service, Kansas. (via T. Heitzman)

J-3L Cub s/n 2946 registration NC23160 with wheel pants at Lock Haven. (Piper Aircraft Corporation)

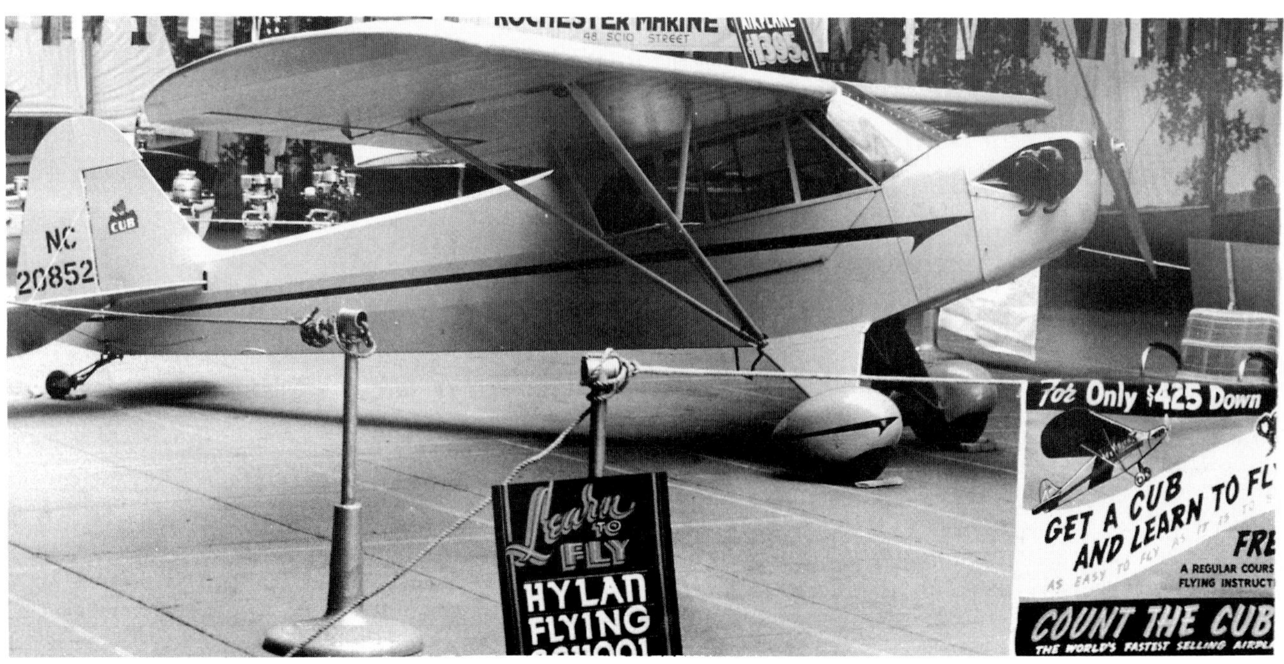

J-3 Cub Sport s/n 2151 registration NC20852 at Rochester Sportsmans Show in 1938. (via T. Heitzman)

The production variants of the J-3 are as follows:

Model	Engine	hp	Known on floats	First known examples (earliest found in production records) Land	Floats
J-3	Continental A-40-4	40		NC16792 s/n 1999	
J-3C-40	Continental A-40-4	40	Yes	NC21539 s/n 2385	NX21409 s/n 2253
J-3C-50	Continental A-50-1	50	Yes	NC21480 s/n 2327	NC21519 s/n 2350
J-3C-65	Continental A-65-1	65	Yes	NC25077 s/n 3649	NC30614 s/n 5028
J-3F	Franklin 4AC-150-S40	40		NX20269 s/n 2069	
J-3F-50	Franklin 4AC-150-S50	50	Yes	NX21491 s/n 2325	NC21589 s/n 2453
J-3F-60	Franklin 4AC-171 or 4AC-150-SA	60	Yes	NX23367 s/n 3106	NC27956 s/n 4476
J-3F-65	Franklin 4AC-176-B2	65	Yes	NC30774 s/n 5104	NX33455 s/n 5983
J-3L	Lycoming O-145-A1	50	Yes	NC21678 s/n 2490	NC22759 s/n 2706
J-3L	Lycoming O-145-A2	55	Yes	NX23118 s/n 2909	NC23265 s/n 3169
J-3L-65	Lycoming O-145-B1	65	Yes	NC24906 s/n 3530	NC30538 s/n 4968
J-3P	Lenape LM-3-50	50	Yes	NX20280 s/n 2080	NX21662 s/n 2548
J-3R	Lenape LM-3-65	65	No	NX21806 s/n 2595	
J-3X	Continental A-65-8	65	No	NX42111 s/n 9110	

Many experimental models were produced at the factory. Some of these are listed below:

Type	s/n	Registration	Date Manufactured	Comment
J-3F-60	3106	NX23367	7th June 1939	Inverted flight equipment
J-3L-55	3151	NX23395	13th June 1939	Freedman Burnham Propeller
J-3F-60	3377	NX24711	9th August 1939	60 hp Franklin
J-3C-65	4671	NX28288	28th June 1940	Special lighter wings
J-3C-75	4901	NX30588	31st July 1940	Experimental Trainer
J-3C-65	5585	NX32750	22nd October 1940	Experimental 65 hp

During the period 18th to 20th of May 1938 aircraft J-3P s/n 2080 registration NX20280 was used for record breaking flights by flying non-stop from Newark to Miami and back to Newark. It was airborne for 63 hours, 54 minutes. Refuelling en-route was carried out by picking up cans of fuel from cars speeding down airport runways. Aircraft J-3C-50 s/n 2564 registration NX21679 was used for an endurance record between the 23rd of October and the 2nd of November 1938, staying airborne for 218 hours 23 minutes. Also between the 30th of September and the 30th of October 1939 aircraft J-3C-50S s/n 3002 registration NX23233 was used to establish an endurance record of 726 hours.

The J-3R s/n 2595 registration NX21806 was originally completed on the 7th of October 1938 as a J-3P with wings which had slotted flaps.

The only clipped-wing Cub built by the factory was J-3C-75 s/n 6943 registration NX38333 completed on the 2nd of June 1941. This was built for Bevo Howard, a stunt flier based in South Carolina.

Fifty J-3 aircraft were sold in the U.S. in the spring of 1941, one being assigned to each Piper distributor in each of the 48 States and the two Territories, Alaska and Hawaii. They were used in the U.S. to promote the Royal Air Force benevolent fund. They were called 'Flitfires' and painted silver rather than yellow. The first one was a J-3F-65 s/n 6600 registration NC1776 completed on the 21st of March. The other 49 were a combination of Continental, Franklin and Lycoming powered, in the serial number range 6666 to 6720 and registration range NC35959 to NC37935 completed between the 10th and 22nd of April 1941.

J-3P-S Cub Seaplane s/n 2548 registration X21662 with McKinley pneumatic floats. (NASM Smithsonian Institution, SI Neg No 95-8803)

The only clipped-wing Cub made by the factory was for Bevo Howard, J-3C-75 s/n 6943 registration NX38333. (via J. Caprio)

J-3 PRODUCTION DETAILS

Fiscal Year	Serial Number Range From	To	Type	Total	Comments
1938	1125	1130	J-3	6	
1938	1154		J-3	1	
1938	1163	1165	J-3	3	
1938	1995	1998	J-3	4	
Prototype	1999		J-3	1	ex J-2 s/n 600
Prototype	2000		J-3	1	ex J-2 s/n 1800
1938	2001	2588	J-3	588	
1939	2589	3625 *	J-3	1036	
1940	3626	5406 *	J-3	1780	
1941	5407	7683	J-3, YO-59	2277	
1942	7684	8276	J-3, O-59, NE-1	593	
1942	8277-1	8277-40	J-3, NE-1	40	
1942	8278	8815 (1)	O-59A	538	8815 (1) w/o
1942	8815 (2)	8852 (1)	O-59A	38	8852 (1) w/o
1942	8852 (2)	9101	J-3, O-59A, L-4A	250	
1942	9352	9666	L-4B	315	
1942	10332	10335	J-3	4	
1942	G-1	G-29	TG-8	29	
1942	G-31 & G-33		TG-8	2	
1943	9667	10331	L-4A, L-4B	665	
1943	10336	10568 (1) *	J-3, L-4A, L-4H	233	10568 (1) w/o
1943	10568 (2)	10847 *	L-4H	279	
1943	2356A		J-3	1	
1943	G-30 & G-32		TG-8	2	
1943	G-34	G-253	TG-8	227	
1944	10848	11148 (1)	L-4H	301	
1944	11148 (2)	11456 (1) *	L-4H	308	Two 11148 built 11456 (1) w/o
1944	11456 (2)	11500 (1)	L-4H	45	11500 (1) w/o
1944	11500 (2)	12284 (1)	L-4H	785	12284 (1) w/o
1944	12284 (2)	12824	L-4H, L-4J	541	
1944	2357A	2362A	J-3	6	
1944	9110		J-3X	1	
1945	12825	13469 (1)	L-4J	645	13469 (1) w/o
1945	13469 (2)	13476 (1)	L-4J	8	13475 (1) & 13476 (1) w/o
1945	13475 (2) & 13476 (2)		L-4J	2	
1945	13477	14091	J-3, NE-2, L-4J	615	
1945	14092	14290 *	L-4	0	
1945	14291	14368	J-3	78	
1945	2363A	2370A *	J-3	7	
1946	14369	17967 (1)	J-3	3599	17967 (1) w/o
1946	17967 (2)	19796 (1)	J-3	1831	19796 (1) w/o
1946	19796 (2)		J-3	1	
1946	19798	20237	J-3	440	
1946	101C	230C	J-3	130	Built Canada
1946	21991	22094	J-3	104	Built Ponca city

J-3 PRODUCTION DETAILS (continued)

Fiscal Year	Serial Number Range From	To	Type	Total	Comments
1947	20238	21080	J-3	843	
1947	22095	23180	J-3	1086	Built Ponca City
1947	231C	249C	J-3	19	Built Canada
1952	C250		J-3	1	Built Canada

A total of 204 aircraft in the batches marked * were given other serial numbers or not built. See table below.

Total manufactured 19,906 J-3 in USA
150 J-3 in Canada
253 TG-8
(All built at Lock Haven unless stated otherwise)

J-3 SERIAL NUMBER CHANGES

Model	Old Serial Number	New Serial Number	New Model (if different)
J-3	2760	Not completed	
J-3	4698	Not built	
J-3	10338	2356A	
L-4	11150	Not built	skipped as two 11148 built
L-4	14092	14290	Not built
J-3	2370A	14291	

Piper along with other light aircraft manufacturers tried to get the U.S. armed forces to use their aircraft. In August 1940 a J-4 Cub Coupe was sent to Fort Beauregard, Louisiana and later a J-3 Cub to Fort Knox, Kentucky in February 1941. In June 1941 trials took place at Camp Forrest, Tennessee to ascertain whether or not the Cub, and its competitors from Taylorcraft and Aeronca, could be used for observation purposes by the U.S. Army (U.S.A.A.F.). These trials used up to 8 standard civilian production J-3C-65 aircraft loaned to the Army for the purpose. Further trials took place in July at Fort Bliss, Texas and Biggs Field, El Paso. These aircraft were nicknamed the 'grasshopper'. Four YO-59 aircraft were ordered and taken on strength in September 1941.

Following this, a batch of 40 similar aircraft was ordered under the designation O-59 and all were taken on strength on the 28th of November 1941 at Fort Sill. These had a radio antenna in the form of a reel which extended from the cabin to the top of the rudder.

Piper experimented with several J-3 aircraft for these trials. Aircraft s/n 7080 registration NC38510 was completed on the 30th of June 1941 with additional cabin glazing. Aircraft s/n 7935 was completed for the U.S. Army on the 19th of November 1941 in Olive Drab & Grey paint with a large top deck window and J-5 lift struts. Piper installed an RCA radio, transmitter and RCA reel antenna in s/n 8025 registration NC41367 in December 1941. The test aircraft for the 'greenhouse' type cabin glazing installation was s/n 8175 registration NX41555, completed on the 9th of January 1942.

In February 1942 the first big orders were placed for the O-59A, which was the first version to have the 'greenhouse'. On the 2nd of April 1942 whilst the second batch was being delivered, a big re-designation programme took place by the A.A.F. with the introduction of Liaison (L), the O-59A being changed to the L-4A, the YO-59 and O-59 being retrospectively redesignated as the L-4. Following on from the orders for the L-4A came an order for the L-4B which was similar apart from the lack of radio. A further order was then placed for L-4A aircraft. This had an improved Scott tail wheel and military instruments. This order started with aircraft s/n 10339 U.S.A.F. serial 43-29048 completed on the 17th of May 1943. Another update took place and most of this order for L-4A aircraft was delivered as L-4H. (The first L-4H was s/n 10538). A new revised U.S. Star insignia with white rectangles and red border was first used on s/n 10618.

J-3F-50 Cub s/n 4155 registration NC26756 at Lock Haven. (via J. Myers)

Record breaker J-3C-50S Cub Seaplane s/n 3002 registration NX23233. (P. Bowers collection)

Flitfire J-3F-65 Cub s/n 6600 registration NC1776 at Lock Haven. (Piper Aviation Museum)

Next was the L-4J which was to have the Beech Roby R002 controllable-pitch propeller, but problems prevented it being fitted. The first L-4J aircraft were fitted with a fixed pitch Sensenich propeller starting with s/n 12341 U.S.A.F. serial 44-80045 completed on the 15th of July 1944. From November 1944 the Beech Roby propeller was installed on L-4J aircraft, however few, if any, of these L-4J aircraft reached combat zones still fitted with these propellers. In August a one-piece plexiglas windshield and sliding window were fitted starting with s/n 13981 completed on the 12th.

During the War, civilian owned Cub aircraft in the U.S.A. were organised into a U.S. Army air forces auxiliary, called the Civil Air Patrol (CAP).

Details of U.S.A.A.F. / U.S.N. designations of J-3 variants were:

USAAF / USN	**Piper**	**Number built**	**Contract Numbers (See Appendix A for further details)**
YO-59	J-3C-65	4	AC2263
O-59	J-3C-65D	40	AC5657
O-59A / L-4A	J-3C-65D	948	AC24952 and AC36506
L-4B	J-3C-65D	980	AC30126
L-4C	J-3L-65	(11)	AC31394 (impressments)) This contract
L-4D	J-3F-65	(4)	AC31394 (impressments)) number only
L-4E *	J-4E	(15)	AC31394 (impressments)) applies to the 100
L-4F *	J-5A	(43)	AC31394 (impressments)) with serial numbers
L-4G *	J-5B	(32)	AC31394 (impressments)) 43-2909 to 43-3008
L-4H	J-3C-65D	1801	AC36506
L-4J	J-3C-65D	1680	AC36506
'L-4'	?	(6)	AF3005 (in 1951 for Iran)
L-4K		(15)	Post war conversions ex L-4A, L-4B, L-4H
UC-83 *	J-5A	(4)	impressments, to L-4F
C-83A	J-3L-65	(2)	impressments, to L-4C
C-83B *	J-4A	(1)	impressment, to L-4E
TG-8	TG-8	253	AC31898
XLNP-1	TG-8	(3)	AC31398 (ex TG-8)
NE-1	J-3C-65	224	498-A (1st 6 only) and 2873A
HE-1 *	J-5C	100	NX7053
L-14 *	J-5D	5 (850 ordered)	AC5897 / AC9133
* For details of these see the appropriate following sections, they have been included here for completeness.			

All production military Cubs were fitted with the 65 hp Continental O-170-3 which was the military designation of the A65-8.

There are many stories involving the Piper Cub that have emerged from World War II. Three L-4 aircraft were launched from the U.S.S. Ranger during the invasion of North Africa in November 1942. In 1943 Landing Ship Tank (LST) craft were used with L-4 aircraft for the invasion of Sicily. In 1944 in the Pacific arena, L-4s were recovered from the LST using the Brodie device, a system that allowed the L-4 to be retrieved by hooking onto a cable suspended between supports.

When manufacturing for the civil market had to cease in December 1941, Piper had stocks of Cubs at Lock Haven. The J-3F-65 were virtually all sold to Brazil, but a small number went to Argentina. The J-3C-65 stocks were purchased by the U.S. Navy, who used them under the designation NE-1, and these aircraft retained the standard civil cabin glazing. A total of 230 were bought. In August 1945 the U.S. Navy took delivery from the U.S.A.A.F. of 20 brand new L-4J aircraft, which were given the designation NE-2.

J-3 Cub No 3 on U.S. Army manoeuvres with W.T. Piper Sr. Note the grasshopper insignia. (NASM Smithsonian Institute SI Neg No 92-2383)

YO-59 s/n 7513 U.S. Army serial 42-460 at Lock Haven. (Piper Aircraft Corporation)

J-3 SPECIFICATION & PERFORMANCE

SPECIFICATION	J-3 / J-3C-40	J-3F
Engine	40 hp Continental A40-4 or -5	40 hp Franklin 4AC-150-S40
Engine TBO (hrs)		
No of seats	2	2
Wing Span (ft/ins)	35/3	35/3
Length (ft/ins)	22/3	22/3
Height (ft/ins)	6/8	6/8
Useable fuel capacity (US gal)	9	9
Gross weight (lbs)	1000	1000
Empty weight (lbs)	578	
Useful load (lbs)	422	
Propeller	Sensenich	Sensenich
Floats available	Edo 1070 / 1140 / 1320 / 1400	
PERFORMANCE		
Max speed	87 mph	87 mph
Cruise speed	72 mph	72 mph
Efficiency (gph)		
Stall speed - flaps / gear down	32 mph	32 mph
Climb @ sea level (fpm)	425	
Range with reserves	210 sm	
Service ceiling (ft)	10,000	10,000
Take off (Ground run)(ft)	125	
Take off (over 50ft obst)(ft)		
Landing (Ground roll)(ft)	100	
Landing (over 50ft obst)(ft)		

The TG-8 was a 3-seater (tandem) glider conversion of the J-3 with longer canopy. The first TG-8 was under construction as a J-3 s/n 9102 before being modified to a glider, s/n G-1 U.S.A.A.F. serial 43-3009 and was completed on the 17th of June 1942. The Approved Type Certificate GTC10 was granted on the 19th of August. In September 1942 the U.S.A.A.F. commenced taking delivery of a total of 253 TG-8 gliders, of which three were transferred to the US Navy for trial purposes where they were given the designation XLNP-1. Many TG-8s were sold at the end of the war and were then converted into powered Cub variants, e.g. J-3F-65 s/n G-1 registration NC46490, J-3C-65 s/n G-251 registration NC46306, J-3L-65 s/n G-83 registration NC65410.

Between 1943 and 1945 fifteen J-3C-65 Specials were completed with s/n 2356A to 2370A, the first one s/n 2356A registration NC42056 being converted from s/n 10338 in 1943 and it has been suggested that the others were rebuilt L-4J's.

Piper built an experimental J-3 aircraft during February of 1944 with s/n 11840 registration NX33522. Later it was used in an aircraft parachute test at Hicksville, Long Island, N.Y. on the 13th of December 1945. Unfortunately the test failed to prevent the aircraft being written off.

Piper used an L-4 aircraft s/n 10336 registration NX42049 for several experimental programmes. In October 1943 it was used for wing flap development for the L-4X, and a 113 hp Franklin engine was installed in April 1944 in support of the Skycoupe project. Another project was the testing of castoring gear in February 1944. NX42049 was used to evaluate this gear's advantages in assisting cross-wind landings. In July 1944 a 100 hp Lycoming engine was installed in support of the J-3X project. Aircraft s/n 2359A registration NX33525 was used for several programmes. In January 1945 it had co-ordinated controls similar to the Ercoupe. By December it was flying with a 80 hp Continental C80 engine, wing slots and flaps.

During May and June 1944 Piper tested two L-4H aircraft on floats on the Susquehanna River at Lock Haven. These were s/n 11330 US Army serial 43-30039 and s/n 11925 US Army serial 44-79629.

L-4B s/n 9914 U.S. Army serial 43-1053. (Piper Aircraft Corporation)

L-4J with the Beech Roby controllable pitch propeller at Lock Haven. (Piper Aviation Museum)

Experimental L-4 with castoring gear, s/n 10336 registration NX42049 at Lock Haven. (Piper Aviation Museum)

NE-1 s/n 8020 U.S. Navy serial 26199 coded 63. (Piper Aircraft Corporation)

NE-2 s/n 13971 registration N67635 marked as U.S. Navy serial 29685 at Lakeland, Florida. (K. Donald)

TG-8 s/n G-1 U.S. Army serial 43-3009 at Lock Haven. (via T. Heitzman)

J-3 SPECIFICATION & PERFORMANCE

SPECIFICATION	J-3C-50	J-3F-50	J-3L
Engine	50 hp Continental A50-1, -3 -5	50 hp Franklin 4AC-150-S50	50 hp Lycoming O-145-A1
Engine TBO (hrs)			
No of seats	2	2	2
Wing Span (ft/ins)	35/3	35/3	35/3
Length (ft/ins)	22/3	22/4	22/4
Height (ft/ins)	6/8	6/8	6/8
Useable fuel capacity (US gal)	12	12	12
Gross weight (lbs)	1100	1100	1100
Empty weight (lbs)	635	635	635
Useful load (lbs)	465	465	465
Propeller	Sensenich	Sensenich	Sensenich
Floats available	Edo 1140	Edo 1140	Edo 1140
PERFORMANCE			
Max speed	90 mph	90 mph	90 mph
Cruise speed	80 mph	80 mph	80 mph
Efficiency (gph)			
Stall speed - flaps / gear down	35 mph	35 mph	35 mph
Climb @ sea level (fpm)	500	500	500
Range with reserves	250 sm	250 sm	250 sm
Service ceiling (ft)	10,000	10,000	10,000
Take off (Ground run)(ft)			
Take off (over 50ft obst)(ft)			
Landing (Ground roll)(ft)			
Landing (over 50ft obst)(ft)			

The J-3X s/n 9110 registration NX42111 was known as the 'Cantilever Cub' which was a J-3C-65 Cub fitted with a cantilever wing and first flew on the 29th of November 1944. This was developed to make the J-3 go faster - it succeeded on speed (111 mph versus 87 mph standard) but failed on cost. Changes made included: shock struts streamlined, slots closed by covering with fabric, trailing edges of wing and tail faired with tape, J-5C nose cowl and airscoop, J-4 stabilizer fillet, landing gear filleted, control horns faired, various places on the wing and fuselage smoothed out, tail wheel replaced by wooden block, turtle deck rounded, wing tips faired, clipped wings. Prior to the J-3X being completed, Piper tested the new streamlined gear on aircraft s/n 2362A registration NX33528 on the 23rd of October 1944.

In 1945 Piper experimented with the 75 hp Continental A75-8 engine in two J-3 Cubs. These aircraft were s/n 4592 registration NX28082 and s/n 10337 registration NX42055.

Piper tested a duster unit and sprayer unit in 1945. They installed the duster unit in aircraft s/n 2358A registration NX33524 and first flew as such on the 25th of May and then first flew with the sprayer unit installed on the 29th June. Next they put a duster unit in aircraft s/n 20596 registration NC7369H.

J-3 SPECIFICATION & PERFORMANCE

SPECIFICATION	J-3P	J-3C-65	J-3F-65
Engine	50 hp Lenape LM-3-50	65 hp Continental A65-1, -3, -7, -8	65 hp Franklin 4AC-176-B2, -BA2
Engine TBO (hrs)			
No of seats	2	2	2
Wing Span (ft/ins)	35/3	35/3	35/3
Length (ft/ins)	22/4	22/3	22/4
Height (ft/ins)	6/8	6/8	6/8
Useable fuel capacity (US gal)	12	12	12
Gross weight (lbs)	1100	1100 (1939) 1220 (1946)	1100
Empty weight (lbs)	630	640 (1939) 680 (1946)	640
Useful load (lbs)	470	460 (1939) 540 (1946)	460
Propeller	Sensenich	Sensenich	Sensenich
Floats available		Edo 1140 / 1400	Edo 1140
PERFORMANCE			
Max speed	92 mph	92 mph (1939) 87 mph (1946)	92 mph
Cruise speed	81 mph	82 mph (1939) 75 mph (1946)	82 mph
Efficiency (gph)	3.5	4	
Stall speed - flaps / gear down	35 mph	35 mph	35 mph
Climb @ sea level (fpm)	500	575 (1939) 450 (1946)	575
Range with reserves	270 sm	250 sm (1939) 220 sm (1946)	250 sm
Service ceiling (ft)	12,000	12,000 (1939) 11,500 (1946)	10,000
Take off (Ground run)(ft)			
Take off (over 50ft obst)(ft)			
Landing (Ground roll)(ft)			
Landing (over 50ft obst)(ft)			

From March 1946 onwards the J-3 was built with metal wing spars. This was first tested on aircraft s/n 10332 registration NX42047 during 1944. The 1946 J-3C-65 had a one piece windshield and a carburettor air filter that sloped with the cowling. For 1947 the J-3C-65 was marketed as the Cub Special.

In early 1946 Piper submitted an improved L-4J for the U.S. army L-15 liaison aircraft contract. This was a written only bid, no aircraft was used. The contract was won by Boeing with their Scout.

After the war, a second production line was set up at Ponca City in Oklahoma, where production lasted from August 1946 until March 1947, when it was replaced on the line by the PA-11. Aircraft s/n 17871 registration NC70851 which had been completed at Lock Haven on the 10th of June 1946 was shown off to the press at Ponca City on the 26th July as the first built. (It may have been dismantled and re-assembled by Ponca City to prove out the production line). The first J-3 assembled at Ponca City was s/n 21991 registration NC77500 completed on the 12th of August.

Some J-2 and J-3 aircraft were built from kits by Cub Aircraft of Hamilton, Ontario, Canada between 1936 and 1937. Post war the J-3 Cub Prospector aircraft was built from late 1945 to 1947 with one additional aircraft appearing in 1952. The Cub Prospector had an enlarged baggage compartment, and an auxiliary fuel tank could be installed to increase the range to 375 miles.

J-3C-65 Cub s/n 17871 registration NC70851 shown as the 1st built at Ponca City on the 26th of July 1946. It was built at Lock Haven in June, the first J-3 to be completed at Ponca City was not until the 12th of August. (via W.T. Piper Jr.)

Aerial view of Ponca City Airport showing the Piper factory. (Piper Aviation Museum)

J-3 SPECIFICATION & PERFORMANCE		
SPECIFICATION	J-3L-65	TG-8
Engine	65 hp Lycoming O-145-B1, -B2	None
Engine TBO (hrs)		
No of seats	2	3
Wing Span (ft/ins)	35/3	35/2.5
Length (ft/ins)	22/4	23/1
Height (ft/ins)	6/8	5/2
Useable fuel capacity (US gal)	12	
Gross weight (lbs)	1100	1060
Empty weight (lbs)	640	522
Useful load (lbs)	60	538
Propeller	Sensenich	
Floats available		
PERFORMANCE		
Max speed	92 mph	122 mph
Cruise speed	82 mph	
Efficiency (gph)		
Stall speed - flaps / gear down	35 mph	
Climb @ sea level (fpm)	575	
Range with reserves	250 sm	
Service ceiling (ft)	10,000	
Take off (Ground run)(ft)		
Take off (over 50ft obst)(ft)		
Landing (Ground roll)(ft)		
Landing (over 50ft obst)(ft)		

Many other engine installations have been used over the years, some resulting in new designations and others that did not. Some of these are listed below, together with examples:

Type	Engine	Registration	s/n
J-3L-75	75 hp Lycoming O-145-C2	NX23118	2909
J-3L-75D	75 hp Lycoming O-145-C2	NX25999	3878
J-3F-50	Motor Development 50	NX21894	2675
J-3C-85	Continental C-85	N51506	10022
J-3C-90	Continental C-90-12F	D-EGZA	10086
J-3C-115	Lycoming O-235-C1B	N88038	15655
J-3F-90	Franklin 4AC-199-D	N40608	7361
J-3C-100	Continental	HB-OXR	12611
	75 hp Praga D	SP-ARF	9501
	90 hp Pobjoy Radial	N42456	14723
	Coventry Victor Flying Neptune	G-AIYX	10993
	65 hp PZL-A65	SP-AOA	11506
	60 hp Walter Mikron III	SP-ALA	12885

The light aircraft industry took off at the end of the war as hundreds of thousands of men trained to fly war aircraft returned to civilian life wanting to fly aircraft. Piper increased production levels to meet this demand. The greatest number of aircraft produced of a single type in any one calendar year was achieved by Piper in 1946 when 6,432 J-3 Cubs were completed. The manufacture of the final production J-3 aircraft s/n 23180 registration NC78439 was completed at Ponca City on the 4th of March 1947.

J-3X (P-5) Cantilever Cub s/n 9110 registration NX42111 at Lock Haven. (Piper Aircraft Corporation)

J-3C-80 Cub with wing slots, flaps and a high tail, s/n 2359A registration NX33525 at Lock Haven. (via W.T. Piper Jr.)

J-3 Cub Prospector s/n 208C registration CF-EGG. (Piper Aircraft Corporation)

A number of J-3 variants have been brought up to PA-11 standard, e.g. s/n 4852 registration LV-FCF. Several J-3C-65 Cubs are known with tri-cycle gear, one being s/n 22589 registration NC3388N converted in 1948. Many J-3 aircraft have had their wing span reduced (by 12 feet) and are referred to as a 'clipped wing' J-3. Aircraft s/n 3801 registration N25845 was flying with a 150 hp Lycoming O-320 engine in 1996 and is registered as a PA-18-150. Some of the Piper L-4 aircraft in Czechoslovakia are known as the Letouny K-68, an example being s/n 11525 registration OK-YKG.

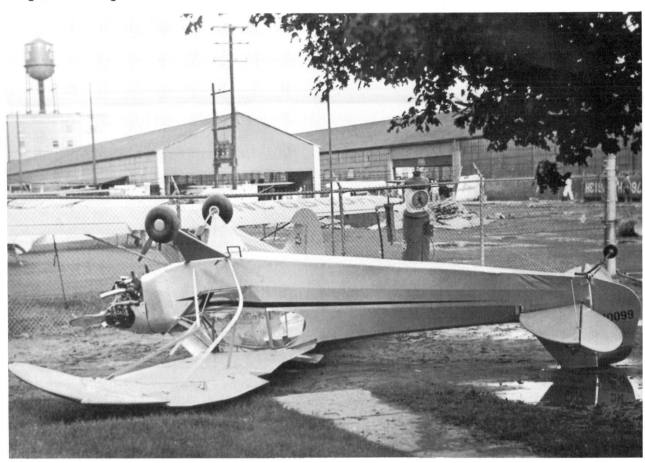

J-3C-65 Cub s/n 19796(1) registration NC6600H written off in a wind storm at Lock Haven. (Piper Aircraft Corporation)

J-3C-65 Cub duster s/n 20596 registration NC7369H at Lock Haven. (Piper Aircraft Corporation)

J-4 Cub Coupe

Piper first experimented with a side-by-side aircraft at the end of 1937. They built J-3 s/n 2014 registration NX20214 in December with a widened fuselage with space for two seats side-by-side. This configuration led to the design of the Cub Coupe. This was an improved side-by side two seat touring version of the Cub. These improvements included a 105 pound capacity baggage compartment, fabric-lined cabin, sprung landing gear and a better instrument panel. It had a forward-hinged door on the right side of the fuselage. The prototype was registration NX21599 and first flew in May 1938. Power was supplied by an unproven 60 hp Skymotors Tank motor. Skymotors was a new company based in Milwaukee, Wisconsin. The engine was replaced by a 50 hp Continental A50-1 engine in August 1938. On the 13th of August s/n 4-400 was assigned to the prototype (which implies that it was originally s/n 1 ?). The Approved Type Certificate A703 was granted on the 26th of October 1938. Production got under way with s/n 4-401 registration NC21835 completed also on the 26th of October. It was powered by the 50 hp Continental in a cowl with exposed cylinder heads. The J-4 was first shown to the public at the 1938 National Air Races and was priced at $1,995. It was available at 1200 or 1300 pounds gross weight.

This was followed by the 65 hp Continental A-65-1 powered J-4A which had a fully cowled engine and an optional 9 gallon fuel tank in the left wing root. Production of the J-4A commenced with the s/n 4-490 registration NC22824 completed at the end of February 1939. The Approved Type Certificate was granted on the 4th of March 1939. The engine in the J-4A was upgraded to the 65 hp Continental A65-3 and again later to the A-65-8, a small number had the A65-7 engine. From October 1939 a Freedman Burnham propeller was an option in place of the standard Sensenich.

The float equipped J-4A-S seaplane was also available, the first known example being s/n 4-604 registration NC23388 built in June 1939. This was Type approved on the 25th July.

Very soon the J-4B was offered with the 60 hp Franklin 4AC-171, the test aircraft being s/n 4-481 registration NX21696, completed on the 13th of February 1939. The derivative won its Approved Type Certificate A708 on the 16th of March 1939. Open and closed cowlings were available. Franklin Motors tested J-4B s/n 4-557 registration NX23223 with experimental magnetos and propeller in May 1939.

A customer tested a J-4 s/n 4-468 registration NX22781 with a Lenape engine at the end of January 1939. Lenape tested J-4 s/n 4-502 registration NX22881 with a 50 hp Lenape AR-3 Model 160 engine in March 1939. This became the J-4C, but no production was carried out.

J-4 PRODUCTION DETAILS

Fiscal Year	Serial Number Range From	To	Type	Total	Comments
Prototype	4-400		J-4	1	
1939	4-401	4-464	J-4	64	
Experimental	4-465		J-4D	1	
1939	4-466	4-480	J-4	15	
Experimental	4-481		J-4B	1	
1939	4-482	4-501	J-4, J-4A, J-4B	20	
Experimental	4-502		J-4C	1	
1939	4-503	4-800	J-4A, J-4B	298	
1940	4-801	4-866	J-4A, J-4B	66	
Experimental	4-867		J-4F	1	
1940	4-868	4-1267	J-4A, J-4B, J-4F	400	
1941	4-1268	4-1377	J-4A, J-4F	117	
Experimental	4-1378		J-4E	1	
1941	4-1379	4-1384	J-4A, J-4F	6	
1941	4-1385	4-1608	J-4E	224	
1942	4-1609	4-1649	J-4E	41	
Experimental	RX-2		J-4RX	1	Rose-slotted wing
Total manufactured 1251 (All built at Lock Haven)					

Prototype J-4 Cub Coupe s/n 4-401 registration NC21599 at Lock Haven. (Piper Aircraft Corporation)

1st J-4 Cub Coupe with an enclosed cowl, J-4B s/n 4-481 registration NX21696 at Lock Haven (via W.T. Piper Jr.)

J-4 SPECIFICATION & PERFORMANCE

SPECIFICATION	J-4	J-4A	J-4B
Engine	50 hp Continental A50-1, A50-3	65 hp Continental A65-1, -3, -7, -8, -9	60 hp Franklin 4AC-171
Engine TBO (hrs)			
No of seats	2	2	2
Wing Span (ft/ins)	36/2	36/2	36/2
Length (ft/ins)	22/6	22/6	22/6
Height (ft/ins)	6/10	6/10	6/10
Useable fuel capacity (US gal)	16	16, 25 optional	16
Gross weight (lbs)	1200	1200 or 1300	1250
Empty weight (lbs)	710	740	730
Useful load (lbs)	490	560	520
Propeller	Sensenich	Sensenich	Sensenich
Floats available	Edo 1140 / 1320		
PERFORMANCE			
Max speed	93 mph	100 mph	96 mph
Cruise speed	83 mph @ 85%	92 mph @ 85%	85 mph @ 80%
Efficiency (gph)	3.6 @ 85%	4.2 @ 85%	4.0 @ 80%
Stall speed - flaps / gear down	35 mph	37 mph	36 mph
Climb @ sea level (fpm)	480	600	550
Range with reserves	325 sm @ 85%	360-460 sm	340 sm @ 80%
Service ceiling (ft)	10,500	12,000	11,000
Take off (Ground run)(ft)			
Take off (over 50ft obst)(ft)			
Landing (Ground roll)(ft)			
Landing (over 50ft obst)(ft)			

Naturally a Lycoming engined version was to appear, the J-4D, the test aircraft was s/n 4-465 registration NX22777 completed on the 20th of January 1939 with a 55 hp Lycoming engine. This aircraft was owned by Lycoming. It flew with a 75 hp Lycoming O-145-C3 engine in July 1939. No production of the J-4D was undertaken. This aircraft also flew with a 65 hp Lycoming O-145-B engine with the designation J-4F.

The J-4E was next. It is not known which aircraft was used but one was tested with a 75 hp Continental A75-3 engine in early June 1939. This was not put into production until 1941.

The improved 1940 version of the J-4A was called the J-4-40. The experimental aircraft was s/n 4-828 registration NX25892 completed on the 28th of November 1939 with the 65 hp Continental A65-8 engine. A Detroit industrial designer worked on this model with improvements including a muffler reducing engine noise and an increase in speed and range.

The J-4F finally appeared with a 65 hp Lycoming O-145-B2 engine, the first Piper example was s/n 4-867 registration NX26726 completed on the 31st of January 1940 as a J-4A with a 65 hp Lycoming. The Approved Type Certificate A721 was granted on the 22nd of March 1940. The first production J-4F aircraft was s/n 4-970 registration NC26955 completed on the 1st of April 1940.

The J-4E appeared later in 1940 and the test aircraft s/n 4-1378 registration NX33499 was completed on the 17th December 1940. This was powered by a 75 hp Continental A75-9 and the gross weight was increased to 1400 pounds. Production commenced with s/n 4-1385 registration NC35230 completed on the 1st of February 1941 even though the Approved Type Certificate A740 for the J-4E was not granted until the 28th of April.

Designed in late 1938, the J-4RX first flew on the 11th of May 1939 using an experimental J-4 airframe fitted with the William Rose wing with slats, slotted ailerons and flaps. This was powered by a 75 hp Continental A75-8, with s/n RX-2 and registration NX22941. This variant was not found to be a success, but was kept at Lock Haven for a couple of years.

The J-4 model saw military service since the C-83B was a J-4A impressed, this was re-designation as an L-4E to join a further 14 J-4E aircraft which were impressed directly as L-4E's.

J-4A Cub Coupe Seaplane s/n 4-670 registration NC24657 on the Susquehanna River at Lock Haven. (via W.T. Piper Jr.)

J-4 Cub Coupe for 1940, s/n 4-828 registration NX25892. (Piper Aircraft Corporation)

J-4RX Cub Coupe with the William Rose wing, s/n RX-2 registration NX22941. (via W.T. Piper Jr.)

J-4F Cub Coupe s/n 4-972 registration NC27000 at Lock Haven. (Piper Aircraft Corporation)

J-4 SPECIFICATION & PERFORMANCE

SPECIFICATION	J-4E	J-4F
Engine	75 hp Continental A75-9	65 hp Lycoming O-145-B2
Engine TBO (hrs)		
No of seats	2	2
Wing Span (ft/ins)	36/2	36/2
Length (ft/ins)	22/6	22/6
Height (ft/ins)	6/10	6/10
Useable fuel capacity (US gal)	25	16, 25 optional
Gross weight (lbs)	1400	1300
Empty weight (lbs)	865	740
Useful load (lbs)	535	560
Propeller	Sensenich	Sensenich
Floats available	Edo	Edo
PERFORMANCE		
Max speed	105 mph	100 mph
Cruise speed	96 mph @ 80%	92 mph @ 85%
Efficiency (gph)	4.9 @ 80%	4.2 @ 85%
Stall speed - flaps / gear down	40 mph	39 mph
Climb @ sea level (fpm)	600	600
Range with reserves	460 sm @ 80%	360-460 sm
Service ceiling (ft)	12,000	12,000
Take off (Ground run)(ft)		
Take off (over 50ft obst)(ft)		
Landing (Ground roll)(ft)		
Landing (over 50ft obst)(ft)		

The last J-4 s/n 4-1649, which was completed on the 11th of December 1941, was exported to Brazil where it was registered as PP-TTW.

Some J-4 aircraft were converted in the field. Three of these were: J-4 s/n 4-757 registration NX24902 which had a 60 hp Skymotors 70A tank engine installed, J-4F s/n 4-867 registration NX26726 which had a 75 hp Franklin 4AC-176 engine installed, and J-4 s/n 4-462 registration NX22780 was fitted with a Monocycle Model 1 engine, horse power unknown. These conversions were carried out in the 1940's.

J-4E Cub Coupe s/n 4-1387 registration NC35429. (Piper Aviation Museum)

J-5 Cub Cruiser

The J-5 Cub Cruiser was the three-seat version of the J-4, with the pilot in front and two passengers behind. The prototype s/n 5-1 registration NX24573 first flew in July 1939 and was followed by s/n 5-2 registration NX26071 completed on 6th of December 1939. Both were powered by 75 hp Continental A75-8 engines.

Production commenced in 1940 with the 75 hp Continental A75-8 powered J-5A, the first aircraft being s/n 5-3 registration NC26876, completed on the 16th of March. The J-5A was granted an Approved Type Certificate A725 on the 13th of April, priced at $1,798.

At the end of October 1940 Piper tested the A75-9 engine in J-5A s/n 5-407 registration NX32898. Production J-5A were powered by Continental A75-9 engines from s/n 5-570 onwards.

In the middle of 1940 a 75 hp Lycoming GO-145-C2 powered version appeared, the J-5B. Two test aircraft were used, Prototype NX26071 and s/n 5-106 registration NX28071, which was owned by Lycoming. The Approved Type Certificate was granted on the 17th of June. Production of the J-5B commenced in June.

In May 1940 McKinley rubber floats were installed on J-5 aircraft s/n 5-54 registration NC27918 for Airways Inc. Aircraft J-5A s/n 5-64 registration NC27949 was built at the factory with special fuel tanks in the wings and was used for a flight endurance record.

J-5 PRODUCTION DETAILS

Fiscal Year	Serial Number Range From	To	Type	Total	Comments
Prototypes	5-1	5-2	J-5	2	5-2 later to J-5B
1940	5-3	5-105	J-5A	103	
1940	5-106	5-333	J-5A, J-5B	228	
1941	5-334	5-1227	J-5A, J-5B	894	
1942	5-1228	5-1308	J-5A, J-5B	81	
Experimental	5-1309		J-5C	1	
1942	5-1310	5-1384 *	J-5A, J-5B	73	
Experimental	5-1385		J-5C	1	
Experimental	5-1386		J-5CA	0	
Experimental	5-1387 *		J-5CO	0	
Experimental	5-1388 (1) *		HE-1	0	
1942	5-1388 (2)	5-1389	J-5C	2	
Experimental	5-1396 *		J-5C	1	
1942	5-1400		HE-1	1	
1943	5-1401	5-1499	HE-1	99	
Experimental	5-3001		L-4X	1	
1945	5-1390	5-1395	J-5C	6	
1945	5-3002	5-3005	YL-14	4	
Experimental	5-1601 *		J-5C	0	to PA-12
1946	5-1602	5-1615 *	J-5C	0	to PA-12
1946	5-3006	5-3014 *	L-14	8	
1946	5-3015	5-3850 *	L-14	0	
Prototype	01		J-5D	1	

A total of 857 aircraft in the batches marked * were not delivered, instead they were converted to the other models and given new serial numbers or not built. See table below.
Total manufactured 1506 (All built at Lock Haven)

The second prototype J-5 Cub Cruiser s/n 5-2 registration NX26071 at Lock Haven. (Piper Aircraft Corporation)

J-5A Cub Cruiser s/n 5-553 registration CB-BIM-1 ready for delivery at Lock Haven. (Piper Aviation Museum)

J-5B Cub Cruiser with W.T. Piper Jr. at Lock Haven. (Piper Aviation Museum)

Experimental 100 hp J-5C Cub Cruiser s/n 5-1309 registration NX41333 at Lock Haven. (Piper Aircraft Corporation)

J-5 SERIAL NUMBER CHANGES

Model	Old Serial Number	New Serial Number	New Model (if different)
J-5	5-1323	Not completed	
J-5	5-1325	Not completed	
J-5CO	5-1387	01	J-5D
HE-1	5-1388 (1)	5-1400	HE-1
J-5C	5-1396	5-1601	J-5C
J-5C	5-1601	12-1	PA-12
J-5C	5-1602	12-2	PA-12
J-5C	5-1603	12-3	PA-12
J-5C	5-1604	12-4	PA-12
J-5C	5-1605	12-5	PA-12
J-5C	5-1606	12-6	PA-12
J-5C	5-1607	12-7	PA-12
J-5C	5-1608	12-8	PA-12
J-5C	5-1609	12-9	PA-12
J-5C	5-1610	12-10	PA-12
J-5C	5-1611	12-11	PA-12
J-5C	5-1612	12-12	PA-12
J-5C	5-1613	12-13	PA-12
J-5C	5-1614	12-14	PA-12
J-5C	5-1615	12-15	PA-12
L-14	5-3013	Not completed	
L-14	5-3015 to 5-3850	Not built	

Piper increased the fuel capacity on both the J-5A and J-5B in 1941. Aircraft J-5A s/n 5-690 registration NX35593 had a 7 gallon header tank installed on the 24th of February 1941. This option was available from s/n 5-784 onwards.

Piper installed an 80 hp Continental A80-8 engine in s/n 5-1283 registration NX41185 in late June 1942. This derivative received an Approved Type Certificate on the 31st of July 1942. There was no Franklin powered version of J-5.

In November 1941, the J-5C was developed with a 100 hp Lycoming O-235-C engine. The experimental aircraft was s/n 5-1309 registration NX41333. A second experimental aircraft s/n 5-1385 registration NX41599 was completed on the 4th of February 1942. Production commenced with aircraft s/n 5-1388 (the second) registration NX42000 completed on the 10th of September 1942. The Approved Type Certificate was granted on the 21st December. The J-5C was tested on floats. The first one was aircraft s/n 5-1389 registration NC42001 which first flew as such on the 7th of October 1943. This version was known as the Cub Super Sea Scout. In May 1942 two experimental J-5C aircraft were completed. These were the J-5CA, a two litter ambulance (with one litter above the other) with s/n 5-1386 registration NX41551 on the 8th, and the J-5CO, an observation aircraft with s/n 5-1387 registration NX41552 on the 25th.

After tests with NX41551, the US Navy chose the single litter J-5C ambulance, the top decking of the rear fuselage being removable to enable a single patient on a stretcher to be carried. The prototype was s/n 5-1388 U.S. Navy serial 30197 completed on the 28th of July 1942. This was later converted to s/n 5-1400 on the 31st August so that all production could be in one serial number block. A total of 100 of these was delivered between November 1942 and June 1943 under the designation HE-1, later amended to AE-1 when the letter H became useable only in helicopter designations. Power for the HE-1 was the same 100 hp Lycoming as in the J-5C and flew on the same Approved Type Certificate.

The two-litter experimental J-5CA ambulance s/n 5-1386 registration NX41551 at Lock Haven. (via W.T. Piper Jr.)

The J-5CA s/n 5-1386 registration NX41551 showing the two litters. (via W.T. Piper Jr.)

HE-1 s/n 5-1400 U.S. Navy serial 30197 at Lock Haven. (Piper Aircraft Corporation)

J-5 SPECIFICATION & PERFORMANCE

SPECIFICATION	J-5A / J-5A-80	J-5B	J-5C / HE-1
Engine	75 hp Continental A75-8, -9, or 80 hp Continental A80-8, -9	75 hp Lycoming GO-145-C2, -C3	100 hp Lycoming O-235-C
Engine TBO (hrs)			
No of seats	3	3	3
Wing Span (ft/ins)	35/6	35/6	35/6
Length (ft/ins)	22/6	22/6	22/6
Height (ft/ins)	6/10	6/10	6/8
Useable fuel capacity (US gal)	18 later 25	25	25
Gross weight (lbs)	1450	1450	1550 (J-5C) 1426 (HE-1)
Empty weight (lbs)	760	830	855 (J-5C) 906 (HE-1)
Useful load (lbs)	690	620	695 (J-5C) 644 (HE-1)
Propeller	Sensenich	Sensenich	Sensenich
Floats available			
PERFORMANCE			
Max speed	95 mph	96 mph	110 mph
Cruise speed	85 mph @ 80%	86 mph @ 80%	90 mph @ 80%
Efficiency (gph)	4.9 @ 80%	4.7 @ 80%	6.3 @ 80%
Stall speed - flaps / gear down	42 mph	42 mph	45 mph
Climb @ sea level (fpm)	450	460	600
Range with reserves	300 sm @ 80%	430 sm @ 80%	385 sm @ 80%
Service ceiling (ft)	10,000	10,200	15,000
Take off (Ground run)(ft)		640	
Take off (over 50ft obst)(ft)			
Landing (Ground roll)(ft)		410	
Landing (over 50ft obst)(ft)			

The J-5CO was further developed during 1943. A 125 hp Lycoming O-290-A engine was installed and first flew on the 16th of June, thus it was re-designated a J-5D. Rear glazing was added in October. Long stroke landing gear with shock struts and wing flaps were added during 1944. (This was the first Piper aircraft with wing flaps). Development continued and the L-4X s/n 5-3001 registration NX33529 appeared in 1944 with a 125 hp Lycoming engine, a bulged fuselage with glazing, wing flaps and balanced elevators. It first flew on the 9th of September. Then the definitive L-14 was completed with a flat sided fuselage (with extra glazing on top of the rear fuselage and glazed doors), a new high-lift wing with slots and faired undercarriage shock struts. This was s/n 5-3002 registration NX33534 and first flew on the 29th of February 1945. Meanwhile Piper tried a 125 hp Continental C125 engine in NX33529 in March. The U.S. Army ordered 850 of the 125 hp Lycoming O-290-C powered flat-sided version. NX33529 and NX33534 were delivered to the U.S.A.A.F. during May and a further three in June 1945. All five aircraft were designated YL-14. The (Y)L-14 won an Approved Type Certificate A760 on the 31st of July 1945. Production of this Army Cruiser was just starting in August 1945 when the balance of the order was cancelled. Eight of the nine aircraft under construction at that time were completed in 1946 to civilian standards under designation L-14, starting with s/n 5-3006 registration NC41399.

The post war version of the J-5C Super Cruiser was a development of the 1942 model J-5C Super Cruiser. The differences being that two wing tanks were fitted (with metal wing spars), the interior was updated and a few aerodynamic changes were made to clean up the appearance. The prototype was J-5C s/n 5-1601 with registration NX41561, which first flew on the 29th of October 1945. Power unit was the Lycoming O-235-C of 100 hp. The s/n on this aircraft was originally 5-1396, being changed to 5-1601 before its first flight. Production commenced in early 1946, and the first aircraft was s/n 5-1602 registration NC87800 completed 22nd of February at Lock Haven. In March it was decided to change the type designation to the PA-12, the first fifteen aircraft had their serial numbers converted from 5-16xx to 12-x (e.g. 5-1601 became 12-1). Aircraft NX41561 was tested on floats by Edo Corporation in early 1946.

Experimental observation J-5CO s/n 5-1387 registration NX41552 at Lock Haven. (Piper Aviation Museum)

Experimental observation J-5CO with long stroke landing gear with shock struts at Lock Haven. (via W.K. Giles)

L-4X s/n 5-3001 registration NX33529 at Lock Haven. (via W.K. Giles)

J-5 SPECIFICATION & PERFORMANCE

SPECIFICATION	L-14
Engine	125 hp Lycoming O-290-C
Engine TBO (hrs)	
No of seats	3
Wing Span (ft/ins)	35/10
Length (ft/ins)	23/5
Height (ft/ins)	7/0
Useable fuel capacity (US gal)	30
Gross weight (lbs)	1800
Empty weight (lbs)	1000
Useful load (lbs)	800
Propeller	
Floats available	
PERFORMANCE	
Max speed	115 mph
Cruise speed	100 mph @ 80%
Efficiency (gph)	8.0 @ 80%
Stall speed - flaps / gear down	40 mph
Climb @ sea level (fpm)	600
Range with reserves	300 sm @ 80%
Service ceiling (ft)	12,000
Take off (Ground run)(ft)	
Take off (over 50ft obst)(ft)	
Landing (Ground roll)(ft)	
Landing (over 50ft obst)(ft)	

Piper continued to develop the J-5D for the civilian market. A 125 hp Lycoming O-290-A engine had been installed in aircraft NX41333 and first flew on the 26th August 1944. Another was s/n 01 registration NX91902 converted from aircraft J-5CO s/n 5-1387 registration NX41552. This first flew on the 26th of March 1946. Unfortunately it crashed in September after catching fire in flight.

As shown under the J-3 Cub heading, 4 J-5A aircraft were impressed as C-83's, later becoming L-4F joining an additional 43 aircraft, and a further 32 J-5B's were impressed under the L-4G designation (see appendix A).

One J-5 aircraft, s/n 5-82, was converted in late 1956 by installing two 65 hp Lycoming engines on the wings. This was registered as a Miller M-6, s/n 106 and registration N9074C.

The definitive L-14 s/n 5-3002 registration NX33534. (via W.K. Giles)

3
MISCELLANEOUS AIRCRAFT 1940 TO 1946

Ray Applegate designed and built his Duck Amphibian in early 1937. This was a high wing 2-seater with an aluminium hull powered by an Essex radial motor fitted in pusher style rather than tractor. It was s/n 1 and registration NX17866. He wanted Piper to manufacture it, so in 1940 Piper tested it, the Essex motor being replaced by a 60 hp Lenape Papoose engine. Piper reworked the aircraft with J-5 wing panels, lift struts, control surfaces and systems and other parts from the J-3 and J-4. The landing gear was relocated ahead of the lift struts. The Lenape engine was replaced by a 75 hp Continental A75-9. The aircraft was re-registered NX27960 and carried the Piper designation P-1 with s/n P1. During testing it was fitted with 75 hp Lycoming GO-145 engine and later a 90 hp Franklin 4AC-199-E2 engine. Piper planned to market it as the Piper Amphibian (PA) or Cub Clipper with a 125 hp engine. This was not a successful venture made more difficult by the shortage of aluminium due to the start of World War II. In the middle of 1941 the project was dropped.

Next, in September 1941, came the model P-2 Cub s/n 0 with registration NX33281. This was a high wing 2 seater powered by a single Franklin 4AC-171 of 60 hp. Later a Continental A75-8 of 75 hp was fitted. This was similar to the J-3 but with a cowled engine and a one-piece hinged door. This would have replaced the J-3 on the production line in 1942 had WW II not started. In 1946 a Continental A80-9 was fitted.

It has been suggested that the P-3 designation was used for the J-4RX 'Rose Slotted Wing' Cub Coupe s/n RX-2 registration NX22941 produced in 1939 and was still around in 1941. (See J-4 section).

In 1941 the Piper P-4 Cub appeared, which was a 4 seater, with the usual high wing and a single fully cowled 120 hp Lycoming O-290 engine, s/n 1 registration NX38300. It was first built with a cambered tail surface which was later changed to a flat adjustable elevator. A 130 hp Franklin engine was tried during development. This also would have entered production in 1942 had WW II not started.

Miscellaneous aircraft PRODUCTION DETAILS

Year	Serial Number Range	Type	Total	Comments
1940	1 *	Applegate Duck	0	
1940	P1	P-1 Cub Clipper	1	
1941	0	P-2 Cub	1	
1941		P-3	0	J-4RX ?
1941	1	P-4 Cub	1	
1943	1	PT-1 Trainer	1	
1944	1	PWA-1 Skycoupe	1	
1944	9110	P-5	1	J-3X
1944	1	LBP-1 Glomb	1	built by R. Barber
1945	2 & 3	LBP-1 Glomb	2	
1946	6-01	PA-6 Sky Sedan	1	
1947	6-1	PA-6 Sky Sedan	1	
1945	-	PA-7	0	Not flown
1944	1	Cub Cycle	1	
1945	2 *	Skycycle	0	
1945	8-01	PA-8 Skycycle	1	
1945	-	PA-9	0	Not built
1946	-	PA-10	0	Not built

The J-3X has been included in the J-3 manufactured total.
A total of 2 aircraft in the batches marked * were not delivered, instead they were updated to other models and given new serial numbers. See table below.
Total manufactured 12 (All built at Lock Haven unless stated otherwise)

Ray Applegate with his Duck s/n 1 registration NX17866 with Essex engine at Lock Haven. (P. Bowers collection)

Applegate Duck s/n 1 registration NX17866 with Lenape Papoose engine at Lock Haven. (Piper Aviation Museum)

Piper P-1 s/n P1 registration NX27960. (Piper Aviation Museum)

Piper P-2 Cub s/n 1 registration NX33281 at Lock Haven. (Piper Aviation Museum)

Piper P-4 Cub s/n 1 registration NX38300 at Lock Haven. (Piper Aviation Museum)

Piper PT-1 Primary Trainer s/n 1 registration NX4300 at Lock Haven. (Piper Aircraft Corporation)

Miscellaneous aircraft SERIAL NUMBER CHANGES

Model	Old Serial Number	New Serial Number	New Model (if different)
Applegate Duck	1	P1	P-1 Cub Clipper
Skycycle	2	8-01	PA-8 Skycycle

Miscellaneous aircraft SPECIFICATION & PERFORMANCE

SPECIFICATION	P-1	PT-1	PA (PWA-1)
Engine	125 hp	130 hp Franklin 6AC-298-D	113 hp Franklin 4ACG-199-H3
Engine TBO (hrs)			
No of seats	2	2	2
Wing Span (ft/ins)	34/5.25	35/2.5	30/0
Length (ft/ins)	24/4	22/10	
Height (ft/ins)		6/6	
Useable fuel capacity (US gal)	27	34	
Gross weight (lbs)	1500	2000	1597
Empty weight (lbs)	945	1325	
Useful load (lbs)	555	675	
Propeller			
Floats available			
PERFORMANCE			
Max speed	100 mph	190 mph	120 mph
Cruise speed		135 mph	108 mph @ 85%
Efficiency (gph)			
Stall speed - flaps / gear down	45 mph	47 mph	48 mph
Climb @ sea level (fpm)		750	design 580 actual much less
Range with reserves		700 sm	352 sm
Service ceiling (ft)		12,400	11,000
Take off (Ground run)(ft)			
Take off (over 50ft obst)(ft)			640
Landing (Ground roll)(ft)			
Landing (over 50ft obst)(ft)			

Piper initiated the design of the MX-108 in March 1942. This was a design for a pilot-less glide bomb, which had no landing gear, carried a 2000 pound bomb and was made of wood. It was not proceeded with.

In 1943, the first low wing product from the Piper stable appeared, the PT-1 Primary Trainer s/n 1 registration NX4300. This was also known as the Cub PT and first flew on the 14th of March. It was a fabric covered tandem 2 seater with metal tube fuselage and wooden spar wings with flaps. It also had a retractable main gear undercarriage. Power was supplied by a 130 hp Franklin 6AC-298-D3 engine. This was developed for the advanced low-cost trainer contract with the U.S. Army Air Corps. The contract was not awarded due to the War ending. This aircraft was still registered in 1996 and is the only known survivor of the miscellaneous war-time prototypes.

Piper LBP-1 Glomb s/n 1 U.S. Navy serial 85165 at Cleveland, Ohio. (via W.T. Piper Jr.)

The portable radar. (Piper Aircraft Corporation)

In November 1943, the US Navy placed orders for the pilot-less gliding bomb, nicknamed the 'Glomb'. Piper was one of the three manufacturers to receive orders. These were 100 LBE-1 from Pratt-Read (3 XLBE-1 plus 97 LBE-1), 60 LBT-1 from Taylorcraft and 100 LBP-1 from Piper. In the event only the three XLBE-1, 25 of the LBE-1 and 3 LBP-1 were built, the remainder being cancelled. The LBP-1 Glomb was designed by 'Designers for Industry' and built by Dick Barber and crew at Cleveland, Ohio in 1944. It was made from plywood and was fabric covered. It had a span of 33 feet and radio and TV controls were installed. It carried the U.S. Navy Serial 85165 and s/n 1. It was trucked to Fort Dix, New Jersey and first test flown with a test pilot in January 1945 behind a Grumman F4F Wildcat. When the programme was cancelled, it was trucked to Lock Haven and scrapped with s/ns 2 and 3 which had been completed at Lock Haven, plus a load of production parts.

Production facilities were only fifty per cent operative between 1942 and 1945, since Army requirements for the L-4 aircraft were not sufficient to keep the plant working at full capacity. Having extensive, well-equipped welding facilities and spacious assembly halls, the U.S. Army Signal Corps awarded Piper a contract for the manufacture of sorely needed secret radar equipment. This project, known as the E.S.D. or 'bedsprings', because of its resemblance, consisted of a large welded steel tube structure, which with its component electrical control parts, was the reflector screen of radar units used to detect aircraft. Contracts worked on included:- a total of 1040 Antenna between May and October 1942, 239 Antenna on a sub-contract for the Western Electric Company between December 1942 and December 1943 and 475 Antenna between May 1943 and January 1944. Toward the end of the war, Piper was awarded another contract for a quantity of 1085 of an improved radar device, the TPX between February and October 1945. This was a portable radar set consisting of a seventeen foot sectional mast with reflector mounted so that it could be turned through a 360 degree arc. With all electrical equipment installed, this improved unit was receptive in a 1,000 square mile area. For the Navy, Piper sub-contracted for the General Electric Company and manufactured 1650 parabolic radar reflector assemblies between February 1944 and May 1945. This was a steel reinforced aluminium reflecting antenna which when connected with its electrical chassis, was used for radar protection aboard Navy ships. Effective range of this type of radar unit is 22,000 yards. In addition, a quantity of 1,382 of a Navy TDZ chassis and test harness were produced between February and August 1944. Both items involved aluminium fabrications and welding as well as a large amount of basic electrical work. These items were integral parts of a new Navy radio development.

During the war Piper sub-contracted on many U.S. armed forces contracts. One of these was 500 wing and tail surfaces for the Waco CG-4A glider in April and May 1942. The order was cancelled after one wing was completed. Another was 1650 cockpit enclosures for the Boeing N2S aircraft for Navy Aviation between December 1943 and August 1944. Yet another was 720 installation cradle assembly oil tanks for Fairchild AT-21-BL Gunner aircraft for Bellanca Aircraft Corporation in December 1943. This contract was cancelled in April 1944 after 39 were completed.

Piper purchased an Ercoupe 415C s/n 31 registration NC28936 which had a 65 hp Continental engine on the 31st of December 1943 and used it as a test-bed. Bigger tails were tried in February 1944 and later in 1944 the co-ordinated controls were removed and the wings reworked, flying as NX28936.

The next Piper was the model PA (the second) which became the PWA-1 (PWA = Post War Aircraft), named the Skycoupe. This was a side-by side, 2 seat, low wing twin-boom fuselage with one engine in pusher configuration. It was fitted with a tricycle undercarriage and a 113 hp Franklin 4ACG-199-H3 engine. The prototype was s/n 1 registration NX4500 and first flew on the 18th of March 1944 at Black Mashannon, Pennsylvania. The PWA-1 did not fly too well (the climb rate was poor), as the fuselage design was too smooth. It was not flown after the end of 1944. The 4 seat version of the PA was the PB, designed in late 1943 with the PA and updated in early 1944, but this did not leave the drawing board. The design had retractable gear, room for four, modified tail and booms and a 160 hp Franklin 6ACG-298-P3/8 engine. The PA-7 was a new design similar to the Skycoupe with twin booms but with a high tail and a 113 hp Franklin pusher engine. Assembly was started in mid 1944 with fabric covered wings and fuselage. It was developed to see if it was more efficient with a high wing as compared to the Skycoupe low wing. The project was cancelled before it was flown.

Piper purchased a General Aircraft G1-80 Skyfarer s/n 19 registration NC29032 on the 5th of August 1944. It had a 75 hp Lycoming engine, differential ailerons and fixed rudder and flaps. Piper used this and the Skycoupe for testing ideas, e.g. twin tails, controls, etc.

Piper borrowed a Dart G s/n GK21 registration NX20912 in 1944. Unfortunately it was damaged in a forced landing. Perhaps Piper was considering buying the design. At the end of 1945 Applegate & Weyant purchased the Dart design and built ten aircraft. The design then became the Culver Cadet.

Piper manufactured canopy on the Boeing N-2S-3 Kaydet, this aircraft is s/n 7807 U.S. Navy serial 75-7411 at Lock Haven. (Piper Aviation Museum)

Ercoupe 415C being reworked at Lock Haven, s/n 31 registration NX28936. (Piper Aircraft Corporation)

General G1-80 Skyfarer s/n 19 registration NC29032 at Lock Haven. (via W.T. Piper Jr.)

Dart model G s/n GK21 registration NX20912 at Lock Haven. (via W.T. Piper Jr.)

Piper PWA-1 Skycoupe s/n 1 registration NX4500 at Lock Haven. (Piper Aircraft Corporation)

Unknown Piper PWA-1 Skycoupe at Lock Haven, note modified fuselage. (Piper Aviation Museum)

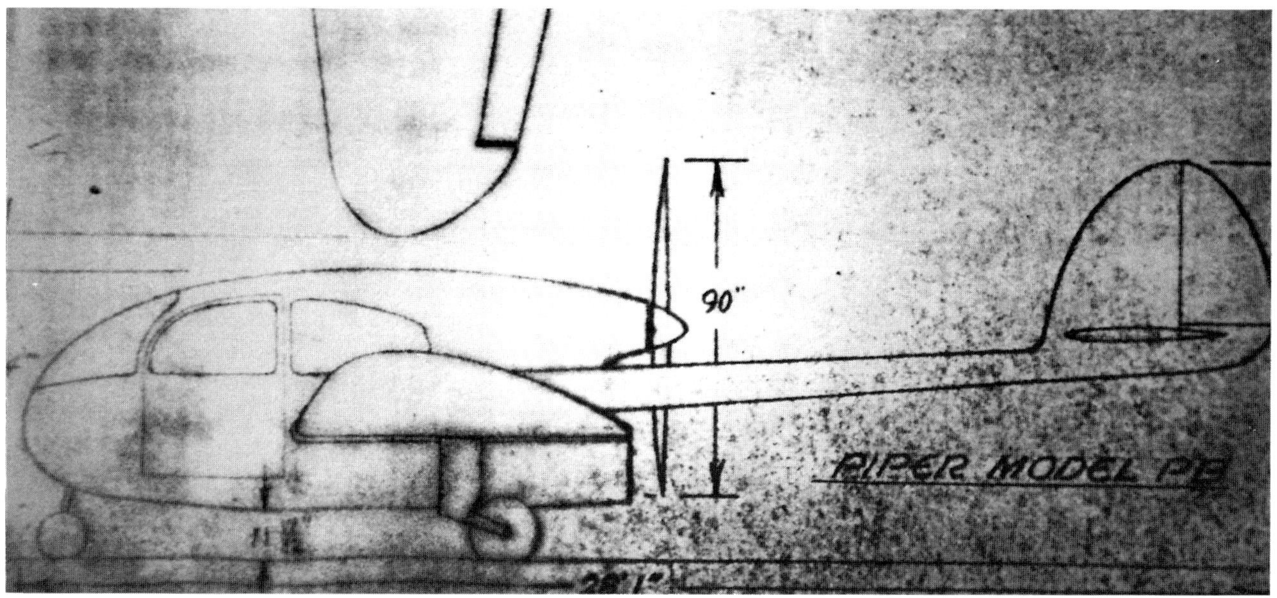

Drawing of the four seat Piper model PB. (Piper Aircraft Corporation)

Piper PA-6 Sky Sedan s/n 6-01 registration NX580 at Lock Haven. (Air Britain Historians)

Piper PA-6 Sky Sedan s/n 6-1 registration N4000M at Lock Haven. (E. Bulban)

Miscellaneous aircraft SPECIFICATION & PERFORMANCE			
SPECIFICATION	PB (proposed)	PA-6 (proposed)	PA-6
Engine	160 hp Franklin 6ACG-298-P3/8	140 hp Franklin	165 hp / 185 hp Continental E-165 / E-185
Engine TBO (hrs)			
No of seats	4	4	4
Wing Span (ft/ins)	34/0	34/8	34/8
Length (ft/ins)	28/1	26/0	26/0
Height (ft/ins)	8/9	7/0	7/0
Useable fuel capacity (US gal)			
Gross weight (lbs)			2400
Empty weight (lbs)			1360
Useful load (lbs)		1050	1040
Propeller			
Floats available			
PERFORMANCE			
Max speed		140 mph	160 mph
Cruise speed		125 mph	120 mph
Efficiency (gph)			
Stall speed - flaps / gear down		50 mph	
Climb @ sea level (fpm)			
Range with reserves			620 sm @ 140 mph
Service ceiling (ft)			
Take off (Ground run)(ft)			
Take off (over 50ft obst)(ft)			
Landing (Ground roll)(ft)			
Landing (over 50ft obst)(ft)			

The P-5 designation was used for the J-3X 'Cantilever Club' s/n 9110 registration NX42111 produced in late 1944. (See J-3 section).

In the Autumn of 1944 Piper put out a list of aircraft that it proposed to have on sale after the end of the war. One of these was the Sky Sedan, a fabric covered aircraft with metal framed fuselage and wings, a 4-seat development of the 1942 model PT-1 Trainer powered by a 140 hp Franklin engine. When the first Sky Sedan appeared in March 1946, it was designated PA-6, and a 165 hp Continental E-165 was fitted. This aircraft was s/n 6-01 and registration NX580 and first flew on the 29th. A second aircraft appeared in 1947, which was all metal, fitted with a 185 hp Continental E-185 engine (205 hp available for take-off), hydraulic main gear with a fixed tail-wheel and a one piece windshield, which had s/n 6-1 and registration NC4000M. This aircraft was scrapped after the undercarriage failed and subsequently the tail was put on the PA-23 experimental aircraft. No more were built, but the first six production fuselages were built by Schweizer and delivered to Lock Haven. The project was cancelled due to the collapse of the aircraft market.

The Skycycle was another of the proposals announced in the Autumn of 1944. An aerodynamic test airframe was built to which a small two cylinder Franklin 2-AC-99 engine was fitted, it had s/n 1 and the registration NX47Y. This aircraft was completed on the 8th of July and was initially known as the Cub Cycle and attempted to get airborne on the 27th of August 1944, but failed The Franklin engine was replaced by a 37 hp Continental A40-3 and still failed to get airborne with this engine on the 12th of September 1944. It was this Continental powered version that was proposed for the Skycycle at the end of hostilities. It had a fabric covered mid wing, single engine, single seat with tail-wheel undercarriage. The fuselage was made from the droppable belly fuel tank as fitted to the U.S. Navy Vought F4U Corsair fighter aircraft.

Piper Cub Cycle s/n 1 registration NX47Y at Lock Haven. (C. Smith Sr.)

Piper Skycycle s/n 2 registration NX47Y with N. Carlson, C. Cupp, H. Eclsmar and A. Butler.(Piper Aircraft Corporation)

Piper PA-8 Skycyle s/n 8-01 registration NX47Y with improved canopy at Lock Haven. (Piper Aircraft Corporation)

Miscellaneous aircraft SPECIFICATION & PERFORMANCE		
SPECIFICATION	MX-108 (proposed)	PA-8
Engine	None	37 hp Continental A40-3 or 55 hp Lycoming O-145-A2
Engine TBO (hrs)		
No of seats	0	1
Wing Span (ft/ins)	12/0	20/0
Length (ft/ins)		15/8
Height (ft/ins)		5/0
Useable fuel capacity (US gal)		14
Gross weight (lbs)	2460	630
Empty weight (lbs)		
Useful load (lbs)	2000 lb bomb	
Propeller		
Floats available		
PERFORMANCE		
Max speed	565 mph (dive)	120 mph
Cruise speed		95 mph
Efficiency (gph)		
Stall speed - flaps / gear down	146 mph	55 mph
Climb @ sea level (fpm)		875 (55 hp)
Range with reserves		400 sm
Service ceiling (ft)		
Take off (Ground run)(ft)		
Take off (over 50ft obst)(ft)		
Landing (Ground roll)(ft)		
Landing (over 50ft obst)(ft)		

The first Skycycle was scrapped and a definitive Skycycle was built with s/n 2 and the same registration NX47Y, this first flew on the 30th of January 1945 powered by the same 37 hp Continental A40-3 engine. It was subsequently upgraded later in 1945 to be the PA-8 and given the new s/n 8-01 and a new canopy. Then a new 55 hp Lycoming 0-145-A2 engine was installed. It first flew with this engine on the 30th of April. A 65 hp Continental A-65 engine was fitted in 1946 and first flew with this engine on the 20th of March. The aircraft was eventually destroyed by fire. No production was undertaken due to cost; Mr. Piper wanted this aircraft to sell for under $1000 but the engine alone was nearly $1000.

During 1994 / 1995 Carlson Aircraft of East Palestine, Ohio produced a reproduction Skycycle made of more modern materials including some fibreglass. It used the same registration NX47Y.

The PA-9 was a Piper proposal in answer to an RFP for a field artillery observation aircraft dated the 4th of February 1946. Piper flew an Army Stinson L-5 in May 1946 in preparation for the potential Army requirement to replace them. The PA-9 design was an observation and liaison aircraft that looked very much like a Stinson L-5 Sentinel. It was to be powered by a 190 hp Lycoming O-435 or alternately a 165 hp Continental engine. Piper didn't get the contract and the design never left the drawing board.

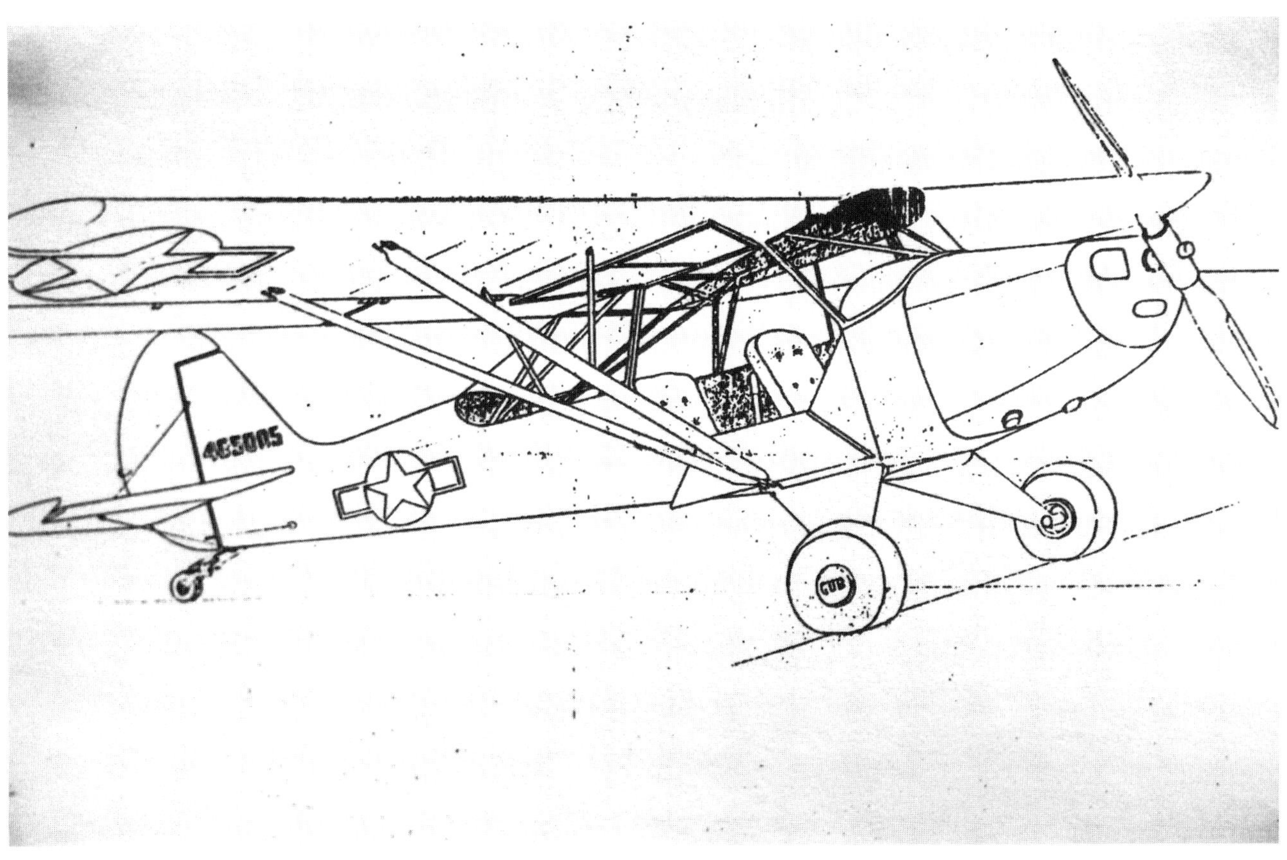

Drawing of the Piper PA-9 field observation aircraft. (Piper Aircraft Corporation)

The second prototype Thorp Sky Skooter s/n 3 registration NX91312 which was tested at Lock Haven. (P. Bowers collection)

Miscellaneous aircraft SPECIFICATION & PERFORMANCE

SPECIFICATION	PA-9 (proposed)	PA-9 (proposed)	T-11 Sky Skooter
Engine	165-185 hp Continental O-470	190 hp Lycoming O-435-11	75 hp Lycoming O-145-C2
Engine TBO (hrs)			
No of seats	2	2	2
Wing Span (ft/ins)	35/0	35/0	25/0
Length (ft/ins)	22/10.75	22/10.75	17/6
Height (ft/ins)	6/11	6/11	
Useable fuel capacity (US gal)	38 + 20	38 + 20	
Gross weight (lbs)	2000	2030	1050
Empty weight (lbs)	1353	1383	557
Useful load (lbs)	647	647	493
Propeller			
Floats available			
PERFORMANCE			
Max speed	130 mph	136 mph	112 mph
Cruise speed	104 mph @ 57%	104 mph @ 50%	100 mph
Efficiency (gph)			
Stall speed - flaps / gear down	42 mph	43 mph	45 mph
Climb @ sea level (fpm)	1130	1170	550
Range with reserves	740 sm (with extra tank)	710 sm (with extra tank)	
Service ceiling (ft)	19,300	20,000	
Take off (Ground run)(ft)			
Take off (over 50ft obst)(ft)	550	525	
Landing (Ground roll)(ft)			
Landing (over 50ft obst)(ft)	550	550	

John Thorp had developed the Little Dipper whilst he worked for Lockheed in California in the early 1940s. It was flown by Piper whilst on a trip east to Washington, DC. and Syracuse, NY. in the middle of 1945. Walter Jamouneau and John Thorp were good friends and often contacted each other on various engineering matters. John Thorp left Lockheed and established J. Thorp & Company and developed the T-11 Sky Skooter by the end of 1945. The Sky Skooter was originally designed in the early 1940s, but Lockheed wanted to produce the Little Dipper first. At the end of 1945 Piper were contemplating whether to produce the single seat Skycycle or begin design of a new two seat aircraft. Early in 1946 Piper began designing a new side-by-side low wing all-metal aircraft with a 65 hp Lycoming engine designated the PA-10. (By coincidence Piper unofficially named this design the Sky Skooter). Piper was busy with the J-3, Super Cruiser and the PA-6, so not much work was done on the design. Jamouneau kept in close contact with Thorp on his Sky Skooter project. The prototype s/n 1 registration NX91301 first flew at Burbank, California on the 15th of August 1946. By January 1947 Piper were very interested in purchasing the Sky Skooter project from Thorp so they could manufacture it, saving Piper the development time and costs. No work had been carried out on the PA-10 since early 1946. In March terms for selling the manufacturing and sales rights to Piper were drawn up. At this time Piper was busy with the Cub Special and Super Cruiser production at Lock Haven. It was suggested that Schweizer at Elmira, NY. be asked to bid to produce the 'Piper Sky Skooter', Schweizer was helping Piper on the PA-6 project. In April Thorp brought the second Sky Skooter prototype s/n 3 registration NX91312 to Lock Haven. This aircraft had the 75 hp Lycoming O-145-C2 engine. It was test flown by Piper on the 10th of April. Unfortunately the aircraft business crashed in the Spring and the resulting financial problems at Piper precluded the purchase of the Sky Skooter; the cost and tooling required for an all metal aircraft was unaffordable. Thorp left Lock Haven for California on the 14th of April and went on to further develop the T-11 Sky Skooter.

A special was designed and built by Dave Long, Piper's chief engineer in his spare time during 1947 for the Goodyear Trophy Races in Cleveland, Ohio in 1948. The aircraft was s/n 1 registration NX5111 and had an 85 hp Continental engine, single seat and fixed gear. In 1949 Schweizer were contracted to build 5 slightly modified Long Specials called the Midget Mustang. Unfortunately Dave Long died when the aircraft crashed. The design lived on, becoming the Bushbee Midget Mustang.

4
POST WAR

PA-11 Cub Special

The Cub Special was the first post war model to get beyond the prototype stage. It was a development of the J-3. The prototype was s/n 11-1 registration NX91913 and first flew on the 26th of March 1946. The aircraft was experimented with over the next six months, resulting in an improved design. The engine was fully cowled, the interior modernised and the fuel tank raised and put in the port wing (metal wing spars supporting the extra weight). The shock strut assemblies were faired in and the wing lift struts were more streamlined. The engine was still the 65 hp Continental A65-8. Two further test aircraft were built in 1946, these were s/n 11-2 registration NX2000M completed on 26th of September and s/n 11-3 registration NX2001M completed on 29th of October. These three aircraft were built using a modified J-3 fuselage and wings. The Piper board authorised the production of serial numbers 11-4 through 11-5003 in November. This was later increased to s/n 11-10000. Production got underway with the 65 hp version in March 1947, starting with s/n 11-4 registration NC4500M completed on the 10th of March. The PA-11 was approved on the 30th April using the same Approved Type Certificate as the J-3C-65.

PA-11 PRODUCTION DETAILS

Fiscal Year	Serial Number Range From	To	Type	Total	Comments
Prototype	11-1		PA-11 '65'	1	Lock Haven
Pre-production	11-2	11-3	PA-11 '65'	2	Lock Haven
1947	11-4	11-432	PA-11 '65' & '90'	429	Lock Haven
1947	11-1354	11-1486	PA-11 '65' & '90'	133	Ponca City
1948	11-433	11-879	PA-11 '65' & '90'	447	Lock Haven
1948	11-1487	11-1678	PA-11 '65' & '90'	192	Ponca City
1949	11-880	11-1111	PA-11 '90'	232	Lock Haven
1949	11-1249	11-1353	L-18B	105	Lock Haven
Total manufactured 1541					

In May 1947 Piper bid for the L-16A contract (number 33-038-47-782) for an observation aircraft for the US Army and National Guard. They used PA-11X s/n 11-5 registration NX4501M with a 85 hp Continental C85-8FJ engine and a McCauley metal propeller. This was fitted with the Continental C85 engine in February and the McCauley propeller in May. This aircraft had the L-4 type army glazing and was painted in silver. There was a fly-off with Aeronca at Fort Bragg. The contract was won by Aeronca with the Champ.

On the 22nd of January 1947 Piper tested aircraft NX2000M with a 65 hp Franklin 4AC-176-BA2 engine. Piper decided to stay with the Continental version.

In July 1947 Piper obtained approval for the Cub Special (and the J-3C-65) to be operated as an open landplane (without doors and side windows). Aircraft s/n 11-321 registration NX4810M was used for this approval.

NX4501M was also used as the development aircraft for installation of the 90 hp Continental C90-8 engine. All production stopped for four months between December 1947 and April 1948. Many unsold 65 hp Cub Specials were converted to 90 hp prior to being sold. Either the 65 hp or the 90 hp engine was available from s/n 11-434 onwards in April 1948.

The float equipped PA-11S seaplane was also available, the test aircraft was NX2000M which first flew with floats on the 16th of April 1947.

PA-11 Cub Special s/n 11-2 registration NX2000M at Lock Haven. (via W.T. Piper Jr.)

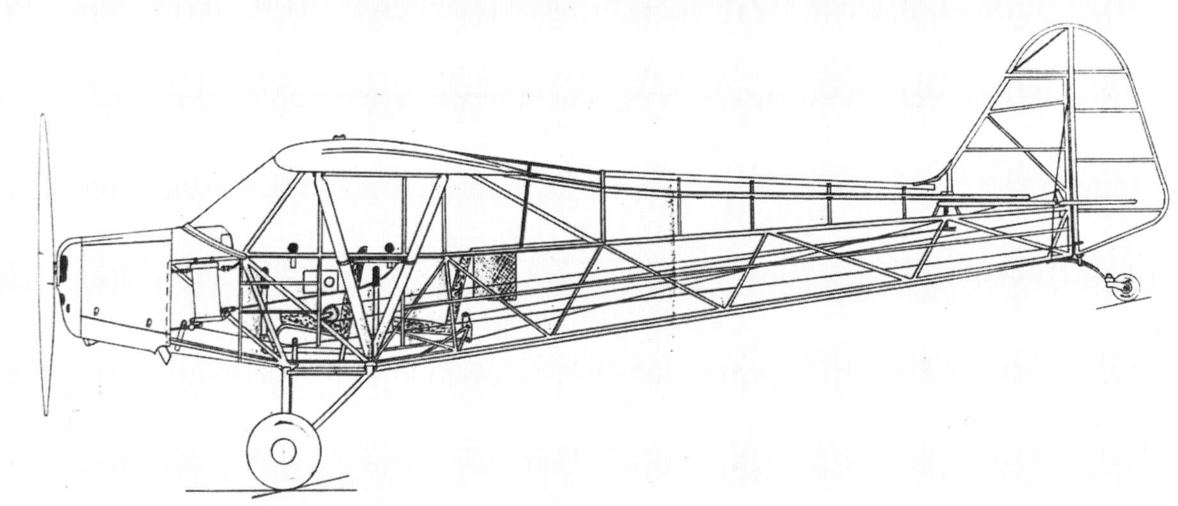

Inboard profile of the proposed PA-11 Army (L-16). (Piper Aircraft Corporation)

PA-11S Cub Special Seaplane s/n 11-2 registration NX2000M over Lock Haven. (via W.T. Piper Jr.)

PA-11 sprayer s/n 11-951 registration N5052H. (via C. Smith Jr.)

L-18B s/n 11-1249 U.S. Army serial 49-2774 for Turkey awaiting delivery at Lock Haven. (Piper Aircraft Corporation)

PA-11 Cub Special '90' s/n 11-956 registration N5057H at Lock Haven. (Piper Aircraft Corporation)

SPECIFICATION & PERFORMANCE

SPECIFICATION	11	11	11X / L-16A
Engine	65 hp Continental A65-8	90 hp Continental C90-8	85 hp Continental C85-8FJ
Engine TBO (hrs)			
No of seats	2	2	2
Wing Span (ft/ins)	35/2.5	35/2.5	35/2.5
Length (ft/ins)	22/4.5	22/4.5	22/4.5
Height (ft/ins)	6/8	6/8	6/8
Useable fuel capacity (US gal)	18	18	17
Gross weight (lbs)	1220	1220	1220
Empty weight (lbs)	730	750	771
Useful load (lbs)	490	470	449
Propeller	Sensenich or Hartzell	Sensenich	McCauley
Floats available	Edo 1400	Edo 1400	
PERFORMANCE			
Max speed	100 mph	112 mph	107 mph
Cruise speed	87 mph	100 mph	70 mph @ 76%
Efficiency (gph)			
Stall speed - flaps / gear down	38 mph	40 mph	38 mph
Climb @ sea level (fpm)	514	900	
Range with reserves	300 sm	350 sm	
Service ceiling (ft)	14,000	16,000	10,000
Take off (Ground run)(ft)	350	250	400
Take off (over 50ft obst)(ft)		475	800
Landing (Ground roll)(ft)	290	290	300
Landing (over 50ft obst)(ft)		550	600

During 1948 Piper developed the PA-11 into an agricultural aircraft, making available Whitaker dusting and spraying equipment (from Art Whitaker of Portland, Oregon). Aircraft s/n 11-892 registration N4999H which was completed on the 29th of December 1948, was painted in a new colour scheme identical to the 1948 PA-14 scheme. This was later converted into the first PA-11 duster. Aircraft s/n 11-951 registration N5052H tested the sprayer equipment. The first production duster was s/n 11-947 for export and the first production sprayer was s/n 11-956 registration N5057H both completed in March 1949.

In June 1949 the US Army ordered 105 L-18B aircraft with the 65 hp Continental engine, which were supplied to Turkey. The L-18B type approval was granted on the 29th of June. The first production L-18B was s/n 11-1249 US Army serial 49-2774 completed on the 15th of August.

For the 1949 model year the PA-11 was marketed as the PA-11 Trainer.

Production continued at Lock Haven until s/n 11-1111 was completed on the 26th of September 1949 for export to a French overseas colony. In the meantime a second line had been set up at Ponca City where production commenced in September 1947 with s/n 11-1354 registration NC78536 and continued there until the 26th of January 1948. Twenty five of the final twenty six aircraft were exported to Argentina in June 1948 (along with vast numbers of the PA-12). Production of the PA-11 never reached the 10,000 units they had planned.

A small number of PA-11 aircraft have been fitted with tri-cycle undercarriage. One such is s/n 11-1039 registration N5536H. Another interesting conversion was carried out by Harold Wagner of Portland, Oregon, by joining a J-3 and PA-11 fuselage together into a twin engined aircraft each with a 85 hp Continental engine. This was registered N1334N.

The first PA-11 with a Whitaker duster at Lock Haven, s/n 11-892 registration N4999H. (via W.T. Piper Jr.)

Wagner twin registration N1334N. (P. Bowers collection)

PA-12 Super Cruiser

The post war version of the J-5C Super Cruiser was a development of the 1942 model J-5C Super Cruiser. The differences being that two wing tanks were fitted (with metal wing spars), the interior was updated and a few aerodynamic changes were made to clean up the appearance. The prototype was J-5C s/n 5-1601 with registration NX41561 which had its first flight on the 29th of October 1945. Power unit was the Lycoming O-235-C of 100 hp. The s/n on this aircraft was originally 5-1396, being changed to 5-1601 before its first flight. Production commenced in early 1946, and the first production aircraft was s/n 5-1602 registration NC87800 completed 22nd of February at Lock Haven. In March 1946 Piper decided to change the type designation of the Super Cruiser from the J-5C to the PA-12, the first fifteen aircraft had their serial numbers converted from 5-16xx to 12-x, (e.g. 5-1601 became 12-1). The PA-12 was type approved on A780 on the 24th of March 1946. The utility category version was priced at $2,995 and the normal category version was $3,295.

Piper tested the 108 hp Lycoming O-235-C1 engine in s/n 12-9 registration NC87807 in September 1946, this engine was not available in production aircraft until 1947.

On the 9th of December 1946 s/n 12-4 registration NC87803 was flown experimentally fitted with a 100 hp Franklin engine. This version was not proceeded with.

Piper produced a float equipped PA-12S seaplane, the test aircraft was s/n 12-885 registration NX7874H which first flew on the 29th of May 1947. This was type approved on the 11th August 1948.

With the aircraft business booming in late 1946 the Piper board authorised the production of serial numbers 12-2001 through 12-9000. Three production lines were set up, two at Lock Haven and one at Ponca City. When the aircraft market collapsed at the beginning of 1947, Piper slowed production, then stopping it for many months. Production did start again later but never reached the 9000 units they had planned. The final production aircraft s/n 12-3625 was completed at Lock Haven on the 22nd of May 1948 and was exported to Argentina. This was the third model to be built at Ponca City as well as at Lock Haven, production starting there in January 1947 with s/n 12-1901 registration NC3650N and finishing with s/n 12-4036 registration NC78846 on the 18th of March 1948.

PA-12 PRODUCTION DETAILS

Fiscal Year	Serial Number Range From	To	Type	Total	Comments
Prototype	12-1		PA-12	1	Lock Haven
1946	12-2	12-561 *	PA-12	559	Lock Haven
1947	12-562	12-1900	PA-12	1339	Lock Haven
1947	12-1901	12-2000	PA-12	100	Ponca City
1947	12-2001	12-3553	PA-12	1553	Lock Haven
1947	12-3901	12-3994 *	PA-12	94	Ponca City
1948	12-3554	12-3625	PA-12	72	Lock Haven
1948	12-3995	12-4036	PA-12	42	Ponca City

A total of 2 aircraft in the batches marked * were not delivered, instead they were given a new serial number or not built. See table below.

Total manufactured 3759

PA-12 SERIAL NUMBER CHANGES

Model	Old Serial Number	New Serial Number	New Model (if different)
PA-12	12-68	12-219	
PA-12	12-3964	Not built	

Prototype J-5C Super Cruiser s/n 5-1601 registration NC41561 at Lock Haven in October 1945. (Piper Aircraft Corporation)

PA-12S Super Cruiser Seaplane s/n 12-885 registration NC7874H. (Piper Aircraft Corporation)

PA-12 Super Cruiser s/n 12-353 registration XB-CAR ready for delivery at Lock Haven. (Piper Aviation Museum)

THE 1947
PIPER CUB SUPER CRUISER
FOR 3 PEOPLE

PIPER
brings you a
TWO-WAY RADIO
and an
ELECTRIC STARTER
as standard equipment

TWO-WAY, TWO-BAND RADIO. A complete set, combining transmitter and receiver. Two bands provide both airways and regular broadcast reception. The simple controls are located on instrument panel.

ELECTRIC STARTER. No need to have anyone out front to "spin the prop" when you start your new Super Cruiser. It's as safe and easy as starting your car. Just press the handy instrument panel button.

"IT has everything!"... that describes the three-passenger Piper Cub Super Cruiser. Although it is moderately priced, the Super Cruiser includes a two-way, two-band radio and an electric starter as *standard equipment!* Now you can fly cross-country by radio beam, talk with airport control towers, enjoy favorite programs in flight. The electric starter eliminates hand-cranking the propeller. You simply press a button on the instrument panel. It's safer . . . more convenient!

A full hundred-horsepower engine, quieted by a muffler, gives the Super Cruiser a top speed of 115 miles per hour. And you can travel more than 600 miles at a hop, thanks to the 38-gallon gas capacity! All this in a *three*-passenger plane—for the price of many two-passenger ships.

Have your Piper Cub Dealer give you a free flight demonstration now. See him, too, for the full-color Piper Cub literature and the popular books . . . *How to Fly a Piper Cub* and *What Your Town Needs for the Coming Air Age.* Remember—only Piper makes the Cub, that good, safe plane. Piper Aircraft Corporation, Lock Haven, Penna., U.S.A. . . . In Canada: Cub Aircraft Corporation, Ltd., Hamilton.

LOOK TO THE LEADER FOR GOOD SAFE PLANES
YOU CAN AFFORD TO BUY AND FLY

PIPER

POST*....March 22, 1947 **COLLIER'S***....March 15, 1947 **COUNTRY GENTLEMAN***....March, 1947 **FARM JOURNAL***....March, 1947

Air Force** .... January	American Exporter..... January (English and Spanish)	Flying .... January	Skyways............. January (English)
American Aviation.... January 1	Aviation .... January	Revista Aerea .... January (Spanish)	Skyways............. January (Spanish)

*Full page in four colors. **Full page in two colors. All others, listed above, full page in black and white.

Aerial view of the Piper factory at Lock Haven in 1947. (via W.T. Piper Jr.)

The two PA-12 Super Cruisers on their round the world flight caught at Croydon, England in 1947, s/n 12-1618 registration NX2365M and s/n 12-2623 registration NX3671M. (T. Hooton)

PA-12 SPECIFICATION & PERFORMANCE		
SPECIFICATION	12 'Utility'	12 'Normal'
Engine	100 hp Lycoming O-235-C later 108 hp Lycoming O-235-C1	100 hp Lycoming O-235-C later 108 hp Lycoming O-235-C1
Engine TBO (hrs)		
No of seats	3	3
Wing Span (ft/ins)	35/6	35/6
Length (ft/ins)	23/1	23/1
Height (ft/ins)	6/10	6/10
Useable fuel capacity (US gal)	19 (34 optional)	19 (34 optional)
Gross weight (lbs)	1500 (100 hp), 1550 (108 hp)	1750
Empty weight (lbs)	855 (100 hp), 900 (108 hp)	950
Useful load (lbs)	645 (100 hp), 650 (108 hp)	800
Propeller	Sensenich	Sensenich
Floats available	Edo 2000	
PERFORMANCE		
Max speed	115 mph	114 mph
Cruise speed	105 mph	103 mph
Efficiency (gph)	6.0	6.0
Stall speed - flaps / gear down	42 mph	49 mph
Climb @ sea level (fpm)	650	510
Range with reserves	300 sm	600 sm (optional fuel)
Service ceiling (ft)	15,700	12,600
Take off (Ground run)(ft)	480	640
Take off (over 50ft obst)(ft)		720
Landing (Ground roll)(ft)	360	410
Landing (over 50ft obst)(ft)		470

Between the 9th of August and the 10th of December 1947 George Truman and Clifford Evans flew around the world in two specially fitted Super Cruisers, the first in their class to do so. These were s/n 12-1618 registration NX2365M and s/n 12-2623 registration NX3671M. They took off and landed at Teterboro, New Jersey and flew 22,500 miles.

PA-13

This designation was not used.

PA-14 Family Cruiser

The Family Cruiser was a 4 seat development of the PA-12 Super Cruiser. The cabin was widened by five inches at the instrument panel allowing one extra seat at the front. The first PA-14 with s/n 14-1 registration NX2658M first flew on the 21st of March 1947. It consisted of a modified Super Cruiser fuselage and standard Super Cruiser wings without flaps and it was fitted with a 115 hp Lycoming O-235-C1 engine. A new fuselage and slotted flaps were added during development. It first flew with these on the 23rd of June 1947. Development was delayed due to the virtual shut down of the company in the second half of 1947. A second aircraft was completed on the 6th February 1948, this was s/n 14-2 registration NX4117H. The first production aircraft with s/n 14-3 registration NC4200H was completed on the 10th of March. Production commenced in May, but the Approved Type Certificate A797 was not granted until the 26th of August. The PA-14 cost $3,825. Production of the 1948 model year finished in December.

PA-14 PRODUCTION DETAILS

Model Year	Serial Number Range From	To	Type	Total	Comments
Prototypes	14-1	14-2	PA-14	2	
1948	14-3	14-204	PA-14	202	
1949	14-490	14-523	PA-14	34	
Total manufactured 238 (All built at Lock Haven)					

PA-14 Family Cruiser s/n 14-2 registration NC4117H. (via W.T. Piper Jr.)

The first production PA-14 Family Cruiser s/n 14-3 registration NC4200H with W.T. Piper Sr. at Lock Haven. (via W.T. Piper Jr.)

PA-14S Family Cruiser Seaplane s/n 14-47 registration CF-NRX at Peterborough, Ontario. (J. McNulty)

The 1949 model PA-14 Family Cruiser s/n 14-496 registration N5193H at Lock Haven. (Piper Aircraft Corporation)

PA-14 SPECIFICATION & PERFORMANCE	
SPECIFICATION	14
Engine	115 hp Lycoming O-235-C1
Engine TBO (hrs)	
No of seats	4
Wing Span (ft/ins)	35/6
Length (ft/ins)	23/2
Height (ft/ins)	6/5
Useable fuel capacity (US gal)	35
Gross weight (lbs)	1850
Empty weight (lbs)	1020
Useful load (lbs)	830
Propeller	Sensenich or Kypers Aeromatic (1949)
Floats available	
PERFORMANCE	
Max speed	123 mph
Cruise speed	110 mph @ 80%
Efficiency (gph)	7 @ 80%
Stall speed - flaps / gear down	46 mph
Climb @ sea level (fpm)	600
Range with reserves	500 sm @ 80%
Service ceiling (ft)	12,000
Take off (Ground run)(ft)	720
Take off (over 50ft obst)(ft)	1660
Landing (Ground roll)(ft)	470
Landing (over 50ft obst)(ft)	1390

For the 1949 model year the Family Cruiser was updated with a new paint scheme and the serial numbers started with 14-490, completed on the 17th of December 1948.

The float equipped Family Cruiser was the PA-14S seaplane, an example is s/n 14-47 registration CF-NRX.

Production ceased with s/n 14-523 registration N5408H completed on the 9th of September 1949.

The 1947 collapse

In January and February 1947, 30 aircraft a day were being produced by Piper. In the second week of March, sales plummeted to 3 a day and the market collapsed. By the 1st of July, 300 unsold aircraft were sitting at Lock Haven with large stocks of unused components. As mentioned earlier, these were large numbers of PA-11 Cub Specials and PA-12 Super Cruisers. Production had to cease altogether in June whilst attempts were made to sell the existing stocks and then look to the future programme for the company. Since there were large stocks of components the logical thing to do was to build an aircraft that could make use of the stocks and so be cheap in price. The resulting aircraft was the PA-15 Vagabond. Production of Super Cruisers started again in February 1948 and Cub Specials in April.

PA-15 Vagabond

The Vagabond was designed during 1947 as a side-by-side two-seater and followed the usual pattern in being a high wing design and fabric covered, but with a reduced span (6 feet shorter than the J-3 / PA-11). It was powered by a 65hp Lycoming O-145-B2, and had a rigid suspension. The prototype was s/n 15-1 registration NX5000H which first flew on the 29th of October 1947. It was followed by s/n 15-2 registration NX4906M completed on the 5th of January 1948. Type Approval A800 was granted on the 7th of January 1948. Production commenced early in 1948 with s/n 15-3 registration NC4120H completed on the 30th January. It was priced at $1,990.

Production ceased with s/n 15-387 on the 14th of July 1948, but one more was completed on the 12th of April 1949 which was the conversion of s/n 17-176 to s/n 15-388 registered N4877H.

PA-15 PRODUCTION DETAILS					
Fiscal Year	Serial Number Range From	To	Type	Total	Comments
Prototype	15-1	15-2	PA-15	2	
1948	15-3	15-387 *	PA-15	384	
1949	15-388		PA-15	1	
One aircraft in the batch marked * was not delivered, instead it was updated to a different model and given a new serial number. See table below. Total manufactured 387 - (All built at Lock Haven)					

PA-15 SERIAL NUMBER CHANGES			
Model	Old Serial Number	New Serial Number	New Model (if different)
PA-15	15-36	17-1	PA-17

PA-15 Vagabond s/n 15-2 registration NC4906M at Lock Haven. (Piper Aircraft Corporation)

PA-15 SPECIFICATION & PERFORMANCE	
SPECIFICATION	**15**
Engine	65 hp Lycoming O-145-B2
Engine TBO (hrs)	
No of seats	2
Wing Span (ft/ins)	29/3
Length (ft/ins)	18/8
Height (ft/ins)	6/0
Useable fuel capacity (US gal)	12
Gross weight (lbs)	1100
Empty weight (lbs)	620
Useful load (lbs)	480
Propeller	Sensenich
Floats available	
PERFORMANCE	
Max speed	102 mph
Cruise speed	92 mph @ 80%
Efficiency (gph)	4 @ 80%
Stall speed - flaps / gear down	45 mph
Climb @ sea level (fpm)	510
Range with reserves	255 sm @ 80%
Service ceiling (ft)	12,500
Take off (Ground run)(ft)	900
Take off (over 50ft obst)(ft)	1570
Landing (Ground roll)(ft)	300
Landing (over 50ft obst)(ft)	1280

In the field several PA-15 aircraft have had PA-17 type shock-chord suspension fitted. An example is s/n 15-156 registration N4372H. Another modification is an extra small window on each side (similar to the PA-16). An example is s/n 15-307 registration N4534H.

Aircraft s/n 15-36 registration NX4153H, which was completed on the 10th of March, was later converted to the PA-17 Vagabond prototype. Another aircraft s/n 15-304 registration NC4526H completed on the 12th of May had a 65 hp Continental engine installed and became NX4526H on the 17th of August.

PA-15 Vagabond s/n 15-6 registration NC4123H. (Piper Aircraft Corporation)

PA-16 Clipper

The PA-16 Clipper was a four seater version of the PA-15 Vagabond, with the same short span wing, but with the fuel tank placed in the left wing and dual controls fitted as standard, and also cord gear suspension. The engine fitted was a 115 hp Lycoming O-235-C1. The prototype was s/n 16-01 registration NX4000H which was completed on the 23rd of January 1948. During development a redesigned wing was fitted. A little while later it became s/n 16-1. The Approved Type Certificate 1A1 was granted on the 18th of October.

Production commenced at Lock Haven at the beginning of 1949 with s/n 16-2 registration N5200H completed on the 25th January.

PA-16 PRODUCTION DETAILS					
Fiscal Year	Serial Number Range From	To	Type	Total	Comments
Prototype	16-01		PA-16	1	to 16-1
1949	16-2	16-672	PA-16	671	
1950	16-673	16-736	PA-16	64	
Total manufactured 736 (All built at Lock Haven)					

The first float equipped PA-16S seaplane completed was s/n 16-110 registration N5306H on the 14th of April 1949.

Prototype PA-16 Clipper s/n 16-01 registration NX4000H at Lock Haven. (via C. Smith Jr.)

PA-16 SPECIFICATION & PERFORMANCE	
SPECIFICATION	16
Engine	115 hp Lycoming O-235-C1
Engine TBO (hrs)	
No of seats	4
Wing Span (ft/ins)	29/4
Length (ft/ins)	20/0
Height (ft/ins)	6/2.5
Useable fuel capacity (US gal)	36
Gross weight (lbs)	1650
Empty weight (lbs)	850
Useful load (lbs)	800
Propeller	Sensenich
Floats available	Edo 1650
PERFORMANCE	
Max speed	125 mph
Cruise speed	112 mph
Efficiency (gph)	
Stall speed - flaps / gear down	50 mph
Climb @ sea level (fpm)	600
Range with reserves	480 sm
Service ceiling (ft)	11,000
Take off (Ground run)(ft)	720
Take off (over 50ft obst)(ft)	1910
Landing (Ground roll)(ft)	600
Landing (over 50ft obst)(ft)	1440

Pan American Airways were unhappy with Piper using the name Clipper, but before the issue reached the law courts Piper replaced the Clipper with the PA-20 Pacer. Production terminated with s/n 16-736 registration N6888K completed on the 2nd of November 1949.

PA-16 Clipper s/n 16-2 registration N5200H at Lock Haven. (Piper Aircraft Corporation)

PA-16S Clipper Seaplane s/n 16-110 registration N5306H on the Susquehanna River at Lock Haven. (Piper Aircraft Corporation)

The prototype PA-17 Vagabond s/n 17-1 registration N4153H caught in the 1960s after it was sold. (J.M. Gradidge)

PA-17 Vagabond Trainer s/n 17-152 registration N4852H at Lock Haven. (Piper Aircraft Corporation)

PA-17 Vagabond

The PA-17 Vagabond (also known as the Vagabond Trainer) was similar to the PA-15 apart from being fitted with dual controls, shock-cord suspension and a 65 hp Continental A65-8 engine instead of the Lycoming. All PA-17 aircraft were built using a PA-15 fuselage and wings. The prototype was s/n 17-1 registration NX4153H converted from PA-15 s/n 15-36 and completed on the 4th of May 1948. It first flew on the following day, the 5th. Aircraft s/n 15-2 registration NX4906M first flew with a 65 hp Continental A65 engine on the 24th of May. The approved type certificate A805 was granted on the 1st of July 1948. It was priced at $2,195.

PA-17 PRODUCTION DETAILS

Fiscal Year	Serial Number Range From	To	Type	Total	Comments
Prototype	17-1		PA-17	1	
1948	17-2	17-214 *	PA-17	212	
1949	17-215		PA-17	1	
One aircraft in the batch marked * was not delivered, instead it was updated to a different model and given a new serial number. See table below. Total manufactured 214 - (All built at Lock Haven)					

PA-17 SERIAL NUMBER CHANGES

Model	Old Serial Number	New Serial Number	New Model (if different)
PA-17	17-176	15-388	PA-15

All production took place during 1948 and began with s/n 17-2 registration NC4586H, completed on the 27th May, and ceased with s/n 17-214 completed 19th of August which was an export to South Africa. One more was completed on the 19th of October which was s/n 17-215 registration N5056H.

In the field, one PA-17 aircraft, s/n 17-157 registration N4857H, has been fitted with tri-cycle undercarriage (similar to the J-3 / PA-11 tri-cycle conversion). Also several Vagabonds have had an extra small window fitted on each side (similar to the PA-16). An example is s/n 17-94 registration G-BSMV.

SPECIFICATION & PERFORMANCE	
SPECIFICATION	17
Engine	65 hp Continental A65-8
Engine TBO (hrs)	
No of seats	2
Wing Span (ft/ins)	29/4
Length (ft/ins)	18/8
Height (ft/ins)	6/1
Useable fuel capacity (US gal)	12
Gross weight (lbs)	1150
Empty weight (lbs)	650
Useful load (lbs)	500
Propeller	Sensenich
Floats available	
PERFORMANCE	
Max speed	102 mph
Cruise speed	90 mph
Efficiency (gph)	
Stall speed - flaps / gear down	45 mph
Climb @ sea level (fpm)	530
Range with reserves	250 sm
Service ceiling (ft)	10,500
Take off (Ground run)(ft)	800
Take off (over 50ft obst)(ft)	1572
Landing (Ground roll)(ft)	300
Landing (over 50ft obst)(ft)	1280

PA-18 (Vagabond)

In the Spring of 1948 Piper started to develop a remodelled PA-17 Vagabond with PA-16 wings and lift trusses and extra equipment under the designation PA-18. On the 13th of May a prototype s/n 15-306 registration NX4532H was completed with a 65 hp Lycoming engine. This was changed to a 90 hp Continental C90-12F engine. Gross weight was increased to 1325 pounds and the top speed increased to 110 mph. This aircraft was to be launched for the 1949 model year, but was cancelled in early 1949 in favour of updating the PA-11 Cub Special into the Super Cub for the Piper 2-seater aircraft.

Stinson

Piper purchased the assets of the Stinson Division of the Consolidated Vultee Aircraft Corporation of San Diego, California on the 1st of December 1948. These assets included about 200 Stinson 108-3 Voyagers and Station Wagons and the drawings of the Twin Stinson. The Station Wagon was a general utility or light freight version of the Voyager with the two rear seats removed. Piper built 125 aircraft at the Stinson factory at Wayne, Michigan from components that were included in the assets between the end of 1949 and the end of 1950. Piper sold 184 108-3 aircraft between December 1948 and the end of 1949. Consolidated retained the marketing rights of the 108-3 outside the U.S.A. They sold 48 aircraft for foreign distribution and Piper sold 141 aircraft in 1950. A number of the aircraft in the Stinson inventory lacked rudders, and as the dies for forming the skins had been scrapped, the skins were re-designed at Piper and tested to satisfy airworthiness standards. Aircraft s/n 108-4695 registration N6695M was used for this at Lock Haven in May 1950. Aircraft were either delivered via Lock Haven or direct from Michigan. The last Piper Stinson 108-3 built at the factory at Wayne was s/n 108-5260 registration N4260C.

Stinson 108-3 PRODUCTION DETAILS					
Model Year	Serial Number Range From	To	Type	Total	Comments
1949 / 50	108-5135	108-5260	108-3	125	
Total manufactured 125 (all at Wayne, Michigan) - total sold 373 (325 by Piper)					

Piper Stinson 108-3 SPECIFICATION & PERFORMANCE	
SPECIFICATION	108-3
Engine	165 hp Franklin 6A4-150-B3
Engine TBO (hrs)	
No of seats	4
Wing Span (ft/ins)	33/11
Length (ft/ins)	25/2
Height (ft/ins)	7/6
Useable fuel capacity (US gal)	50
Gross weight (lbs)	2400
Empty weight (lbs)	1295
Useful load (lbs)	1105
Propeller	
Floats available	Edo 2425
PERFORMANCE	
Max speed	130 mph
Cruise speed	125 mph
Efficiency (gph)	10 @ 83%
Stall speed - flaps / gear down	55 mph
Climb @ sea level (fpm)	770
Range with reserves	600 sm @ 83%
Service ceiling (ft)	14,000
Take off (Ground run)(ft)	525
Take off (over 50ft obst)(ft)	1400
Landing (Ground roll)(ft)	
Landing (over 50ft obst)(ft)	1500

1949 model Piper Stinson 108-3 with cowling inscription 'Piper Stinson 49'.
This one is s/n 108-5019 registration N4019C. (E. Lundahl NASM Smithsonian Institution SI Neg No 95-8805)

PA-18 Super Cub 95 s/n 18-20 registration N5429H at Lock Haven. (via C. Smith Jr.)

PA-18 Super Cub

Since the updated PA-18 (Vagabond) was cancelled, the now vacant PA-18 designation was assigned to the civilian version of the PA-19. This was type certificated 1A2 on the 18th of November 1949 using the PA-19 as the test aircraft. The PA-18 replaced the PA-11 on the production line during November 1949, commencing with s/n 18-1 registration N5410H which first flew on the 23rd of November. This was powered by a 95 hp Continental C90-8F engine. It had no flaps, straight elevator hinge with no horn balance, an enlarged rudder compared to the PA-11. It was fitted with one wing fuel tank, a second tank on the right side was available as an optional extra. This version cost $5,850. Later production is sometimes referred to as the PA-18 '95' to distinguish this variant from the later alternatives. Production of the 95 hp version continued until 1961.

In 1950 the PA-18 '105' appeared, commencing with s/n 18-33 registration N5450H completed on the 9th of January. This was similar to the Continental powered version except for the engine, the 108 hp Lycoming O-235-C1, flaps and a larger horizontal tail with horn balanced elevators.

Late in 1950, the PA-18 '105' was replaced by the PA-18 '125', powered by a 125 hp Lycoming O-290-D engine, but the second wing tank still remained optional. The approved type certificate was granted on the 1st September 1950 using the PA-19 as the test aircraft. Aircraft s/n 18-83 registration N5492H was also converted from a '105' on the 30th of August 1950. The first production aircraft s/n 18-550 registration N7179K was completed on the 10th of October 1950.

Two years later in 1952, the PA-18 '125' was available with either a wooden fixed-pitch propeller ('125') or a metal controllable-pitch propeller ('135'). Production of the '135' commenced with s/n 18-1654 registration N1785A.

Later in 1952, the PA-18 '125' was replaced by the 135 hp Lycoming O-290-D2 powered PA-18-135. The addition of an oil cooler air scoop at the bottom of the nose cowling distinguished this version from the '125'. This version received its approved type certificate on the 25th of April 1952. Production commencing with s/n 18-1810 registration N1986A completed on the 23rd of May. This was very similar to the 125 hp variant but all were now fitted with two wing tanks as standard.

1952 saw the start of a special version for the Civil Air Patrol, the PA-18-105 Special. This was used for training purposes by the CAP, U.S. Army and Air Force flying clubs as well as for some actual military pilot training, and was referred to as the PA-18T. It had the Lycoming O-235-C1 of 108 hp and provision for seat parachutes, no flaps but it had horn balanced elevators. The first was s/n 18-2214 registration N100T completed on the 25th of September 1952. The Approved Type Certificate was granted on the 24th of November 1952. Production was built in a continuous block ending with s/n 18-2456 registration N342T, completed on the 12th of March 1953.

Late 1954 for the 1955 model year saw the emergence of the PA-18-150 with 150 hp Lycoming O-320 engine, being otherwise identical to the 135 hp variant. The experimental aircraft was s/n 18-3771 registration N1656P completed on the 26th of August 1954. The Approved Type Certificate was granted on the 1st of October. Production commenced with s/n 18-3781 registration N1659P in October 1954. The 150 hp version cost $7,450. The engine fitted in later production aircraft was the O-320-A2A and finally the O-320-A2B.

As was the case with earlier models, the PA-18 was available on floats. The first example of the Super Cub Seaplane was s/n 18-33 registration N5450H which first flew with floats on the 3rd of April 1950. The Approved Type Certificate for both the PA-18S and the PA-19S was granted on the 9th of May. The PA-18S '125' and PA-19S '125' was approved on the 25th of October, the PA-18S-135 was approved on the 15th of May 1952 and the PA-18S-150 was approved on the 1st of October 1954. Some examples of PA-18S seaplane:

PA-18S	N7265K	18-158
PA-18S '125'	N1123A	18-716
PA-18S-135	N2483A	18-1951
PA-18S-150	N1757P	18-4077

PA-18 Super Cub 105 s/n 18-79 registration N5488H with Whitaker tandem wheels. (Piper Aircraft Corporation)

PA-18 Super Cub 125 s/n 18-549 registration N7178K at Lock Haven. (via W.T. Piper Jr.)

The 1953 PA-18-135 Super Cub s/n 18-1972 registration N2515A at Lock Haven. (Piper Aircraft Corporation)

PA-18S Super Cub 105 Seaplane s/n 18-79 registration N5488H on the Susquehanna River at Lock Haven. (Piper Aircraft Corporation)

1956 model PA-18 Super Cub on Edo 399 amphibious floats at College Point, N.Y. in 1957. (Piper Aircraft Corporation)

The experimental 150 hp 1955 model PA-18-150 Super Cub s/n 18-3771 registration N1656P at Lock Haven. (Piper Aircraft Corporation)

PA-18 PRODUCTION DETAILS

Model Year	Serial Number Range From	To	Type	Total	Comments
1950	18-1	18-548 *	'95','105', L-18C	548	
1951	18-549	18-1214 *	'95','125', L-18C, L-21A, YL-21	666	
1952	18-1215	18-1969 *	'95','125','135',135, L-18C	))	
1952	18-1262	18-2146	A-'125',A-'135',A-135	) 756)	
1953	18-1970	18-3010 *	'95','105',135,L-18C, L-21B	))1043	
1953	18-2147	18-3013	A-135	)	
1954	18-3014	18-3444 (1) *	'95', 135, A-135, L-18C, L-21B	431	18-3443 (1) & 18-3444 (1) w/o
1954	18-3443 (2) & 18-3444 (2) *		L-18C	2	
1954	18-3445	18-3780 *	'95',135,A-135,L-18C, L-21B	336	18-3771 to 150 hp 1955 model
1955	18-3781	18-4617	'95',135,A-135,150,A-150, L-21B, L-21C	837	
1956	18-4618	18-5294	'95',150,A-150	677	
1957	18-5295	18-6115 *	'95',150,A-150,L-21B	821	18-5804 to 1958 model
1958	18-6116	18-6684	'95',150,A-150	569	
1959	18-6685	18-7172	'95',150,A-150	488	
1960	18-7173	18-7520	'95',150,A-150	348	
1961	18-7521	18-7746 *	'95',150, L-21B	226	
1962	18-7747	18-7871	150	125	
1963	18-7872	18-8045	150	174	
1964	18-8046	18-8199	150	154	
1965	18-8200	18-8338	150	139	
1966	18-8339	18-8464	150	126	
1967	18-8465	18-8601	150	137	
1968	18-8602	18-8743	150	142	
1969	18-8744	18-8851	150	108	
1970	18-8852	18-8919	150	68	
1971	18-8920	18-8963	150	44	
1972	18-8964	18-9004	150	41	
-	18-9005	18-9015	150		Not built, see Appendix B
1973	18-7309016	18-7309025	150	10	
1974	18-7409026	18-7409151	150	126	
1975	18-7509001	18-7509142	150	142	
1976	18-7609001	18-7609157	150	157	
1977	18-7709001	18-7709198	150	198	
1978	18-7809001	18-7809188	150	188	
1979	18-7909001	18-7909200	150	200	
1980	18-8009001	18-8009061	150	61	
1981	18-8109001	18-8109086	150	86	
1982	18-8209001	18-8209025	150	25	
1983	18-8309001	18-8309025	150	25	

PA-18 PRODUCTION DETAILS (continued)

Model Year	Serial Number Range From	To	Type	Total	Comments
1988	1809002	1809003	150	2	Vero Beach
1989	1809001		150	1	Vero Beach
1989	1809004	1809052	150	49	Vero Beach
1990	1809053	1809057	150	5	Vero Beach
1990	1809060		150	1	Vero Beach
1991	1809089	1809099	150	0	Chincul, s/n assigned by Piper, no kit
1992	1809058		150	1	Vero Beach
1993	1809059		150	1	Vero Beach
1993	1809061	1809078	150	18	Vero Beach
1994	1809079	1809088	150	10	Vero Beach
1994	1809100	1809113	150	14	Vero Beach

* The model year assignment does not apply to the military variants whose serial numbers fall within these blocks.

Total manufactured 10,326 (All built at Lock Haven unless stated otherwise)

The Super Cub was also available on amphibious floats, designated PA-18AS. Both the 125 hp and the 135 hp versions were certified on the 1st of July 1953. The PA-18AS-150 was approved on the 1st of October 1954. Two examples of these:

PA-18AS-135	N2134A	18-1856
PA-18AS-150	N2798P	18-4433

Piper first experimented in early 1950 with an agricultural variant of the PA-18. A sprayer unit and chemical tank were installed in aircraft s/n 18-68 registration N5475H in February. Piper went on to develop the PA-18A in early 1951. The following changes were made: hopper door aft of rear wing fitting, removable rear seat substituted with chemicals tank, rudder travel increased, re-routed flap cables, fuselage substantiated for rear seat load of 230 pounds. The experimental aircraft was s/n 18-677 registration N1099A completed on the 16th of February 1951 and was a PA-18A '125'. The Approved Type Certificate was granted on the 21st of September. The first production PA-18A was s/n 18-1262 registration N1600A completed on the 10th of December 1952. The PA-18A-135 was approved on the 25th of April 1952 and the PA-18A-150 was approved on the 1st of October 1954. Production of the PA-18A ceased in 1960 following the introduction of the PA-25 Pawnee to the product range. Two examples of PA-18A aircraft:

PA-18A-135	N1987A	18-1812
PA-18A-150	ZS-DKK	18-3786

In 1951 Caro Bayley set a category III world altitude record of 30,000 feet in a Super Cub.

The experimental PA-18 sprayer at Lock Haven. (via W.T. Piper Jr.)

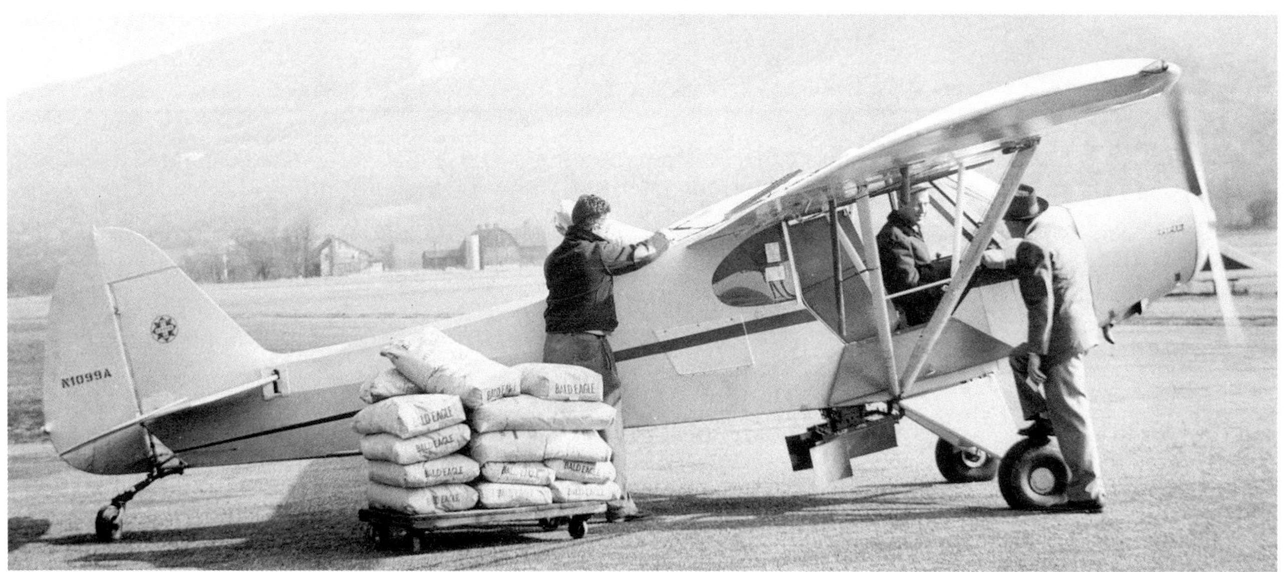

The experimental PA-18A Super Cub s/n 18-677 registration N1099A with a duster unit at Lock Haven. (via W.T. Piper Jr.)

The experimental PA-18A s/n 18-677 registration N1099A with sprayer unit at Lock Haven. (Piper Aircraft Corporation)

PA-18-105 Super Cub s/n 18-2214 registration N100T with W.T. Piper Sr. (Piper Aircraft Corporation)

YL-21 s/n 18-750 U.S. Army serial 51-6496 at Lock Haven. (Piper Aircraft Corporation)

L-18C s/n 18-999 U.S. Army serial 51-15302 at Lock Haven. (Piper Aviation Museum)

PA-18 SPECIFICATION & PERFORMANCE

SPECIFICATION	18 95'	18 '105'	18 '125' / L-21A
Engine	95 hp Continental C90-12F	108 hp Lycoming O-235-C1	125 hp Lycoming O-290-D
Engine TBO (hrs)			
No of seats	2	2	2
Wing Span (ft/ins)	35/4	35/4	35/4
Length (ft/ins)	22/5	22/5	22/5
Height (ft/ins)	6/8	6/8	6/8
Useable fuel capacity (US gal)	18, optional 36		
Gross weight (lbs)	1500	1500	1500
Empty weight (lbs)	800	825	845
Useful load (lbs)	700	675	655
Propeller	Sensenich	Sensenich	Sensenich
Floats available	Edo 1400		
PERFORMANCE			
Max speed	112 mph	115 mph	123 mph
Cruise speed	100 mph	105 mph	108 mph
Efficiency (gph)	5	7	
Stall speed - flaps / gear down	42 mph	38 mph	42 mph
Climb @ sea level (fpm)	710	780	875
Range with reserves	360 sm	270 sm	270 sm
Service ceiling (ft)	15,750	15,750	17,100
Take off (Ground run)(ft)	390	350	210
Take off (over 50ft obst)(ft)	750		510
Landing (Ground roll)(ft)	385		300
Landing (over 50ft obst)(ft)	800		600

Whilst the production of the civil aircraft was taking place, the PA-18 in several variations was being supplied to the U.S. Army and for the U.S.A.F., often for transfer elsewhere under the MDAP (Mutual Defence Aid Pact). The prototype was PA-19 s/n 19-3 registration N5417H. The first of these variants was the Continental powered L-18C, the engine being the O-205-1 as the C90-8F was known in military circles. This variant had no wing flaps and a glass-house type cabin glass similar to that fitted to the L-4 versions of the earlier J-3 Cub. The first batch of sixty eight L-18C aircraft was delivered starting in September 1950 with s/n 18-401 and were for Turkey and Greece.

Lycoming powered variants were to follow soon after the L-18C. The prototype L-21 was PA-19 s/n 19-1 registration N5011H. Thirty aircraft starting with s/n 18-550 registration N7179K were delivered to the U.S. Army at Fort Sill in late October / early November 1950. Initially they were owned by Piper, later on the 6th of April 1951 the 30 aircraft were sold to the U.S. Army with serial numbers starting 51-15654. Two YL-21 aircraft were supplied, with 125 hp Lycoming O-290-D engine and wing flaps. These were s/n 18-749 U.S. Army serial 51-6495 and s/n 18-750 U.S. Army serial 51-6496 completed on the 2nd and 3rd of April 1951 respectively. The second production batch being of the L-21A, the first was s/n 18-849 US Army serial 51-15684 completed on the 20th of July 1951. The main Lycoming version being the 135 hp Lycoming O-290-D2 powered L-21B. The experimental aircraft was s/n 18-2182 registration N2660A completed on the 10th of December 1952. The first production was s/n 18-2738 US Army serial 53-3738 completed on the 7th of April 1953. This version was supplied from 1953 to 1957, with an extra two added in 1962. (See Appendix A). Some L-21A aircraft were converted by the U.S. Army into TC-21A trainers. In 1962 all L-21B survivors were re-designated U-7A.

In 1955 Piper worked on an L-21C (short range observation liaison aircraft), an improved version of the L-21B with a 150 hp Lycoming O-320 engine, improved panel and a 36 gallon reserve tank in the baggage compartment. This aircraft had the conventional civil windows and Whitaker tandem wheels. Aircraft s/n 18-4470 U.S. Army serial (X)55-4749 was completed on the 13th of July 1955. Piper didn't get a contract so no production was carried out.

L-21A s/n 18-860 U.S. Army 51-15695 at Lock Haven. (Piper Aircraft Corporation)

Experimental L-21B s/n 18-2182 registration N2660A at Lock Haven. (Piper Aircraft Corporation)

YL-21 s/n 18-750 U.S. Army serial 51-6496 with nose wheel and boundary layer control. (H. Levy)

PA-18 SPECIFICATION & PERFORMANCE			
SPECIFICATION	**18-135 / L-21B**	**18-150**	**18A-150**
Engine	135 hp Lycoming O-290-D2	150 hp Lycoming O-320 / O-320-A2A / O-320-A2B	150 hp Lycoming O-320
Engine TBO (hrs)			
No of seats	2	2	2
Wing Span (ft/ins)	35/3	35/3	35/3
Length (ft/ins)	22/5	22/5	22/6
Height (ft/ins)	6/7.5	6/8	6/8
Useable fuel capacity (US gal)	36	36	36
Gross weight (lbs)	1500	1750	2070
Empty weight (lbs)	895	930	960
Useful load (lbs)	605	820	1110
Propeller	Sensenich	Sensenich	Sensenich
Floats available	Edo 650A		
PERFORMANCE			
Max speed	127 mph	130 mph	128 mph
Cruise speed	112 mph	115 mph	113 mph
Efficiency (gph)		9@75%	9@75%
Stall speed - flaps / gear down	38 mph	43 mph	45 mph
Climb @ sea level (fpm)	870	960	760
Range with reserves	500 sm	460 sm	360 sm
Service ceiling (ft)	17,100	19,000	17,000
Take off (Ground run)(ft)	700	200	300
Take off (over 50ft obst)(ft)	990	500	950
Landing (Ground roll)(ft)	430	350	410
Landing (over 50ft obst)(ft)	730	725	875

Details of U.S.A.A.F. designations of PA-18 variants were:

U.S.A.A.F.	Piper	Number built	Contract Numbers (See Appendix A for further details)
L-18B	PA-11*	105	6658
L-18C	PA-18 '95'	68	14950
L-18C	PA-18 '95'	58	25908
L-18C	PA-18 '95'	324	27014 & 25908
L-18C	PA-18 '95'	164	23949
L-18C	PA-18 '95'	40	26431
YL-21	PA-18-125	2	unknown
L-21A	PA-18-125	150	24719
L-21B	PA-18-135	75	15480
L-21B	PA-18-135	138	23116
L-21B	PA-18-135	369	27008
* For details of these see the PA-11 section.			

Later the Mississippi State College converted YL-21 51-6496 into a tricycle aircraft and added boundary layer control (perforated wing, double windshield serving as duct from wing to blower, engine driven blower above engine - cooling the engine). The tricycle gear gave greater incidence at take-off.

Production of the Super Cub series was split into model year groups, but since the military variants were built in blocks within the main s/n blocks, these model years do not apply to the military aircraft.

In 1977 Piper proposed using all metal wing flaps and ailerons on the Super Cub. This was not proceeded with.

French Army L-21B modified s/n 18-5322 at Lock Haven. (Piper Aviation Museum)

L-21C s/n 18-4470 U.S. Army serial X55-4749. (P. Bowers collection)

L-21B s/n 18-3443 (1) U.S. Army serial 54-743 written off in a wind storm at Lock Haven, (P. Everly)

PA-18 SPECIFICATION & PERFORMANCE

SPECIFICATION	18S-150	18A '125'	L-18C
Engine	150 hp Lycoming O-320	125 hp Lycoming O-290-D	95 hp Continental O-205-I
Engine TBO (hrs)			
No of seats	2	2	2
Wing Span (ft/ins)	35/3	35/4	35/2.5
Length (ft/ins)	23/11	22/5	22/4.5
Height (ft/ins)	10/4	6/8	
Useable fuel capacity (US gal)	36		
Gross weight (lbs)	1760	2070	1500
Empty weight (lbs)	1190	1110	800
Useful load (lbs)	570	960	700
Propeller	Sensenich	Sensenich	Sensenich
Floats available	Edo 2000 / Edo 650A / Edo 2250		
PERFORMANCE			
Max speed	115 mph	108 mph	110 mph
Cruise speed	103 mph	95 mph	100 mph
Efficiency (gph)			
Stall speed - flaps / gear down	42 mph	45 mph	
Climb @ sea level (fpm)	830	680	624
Range with reserves	412 sm	220 sm	
Service ceiling (ft)	17,500	13,800	
Take off (Ground run)(ft)	700		
Take off (over 50ft obst)(ft)	990	950	
Landing (Ground roll)(ft)	430		
Landing (over 50ft obst)(ft)	730	875	

In August 1981 Piper sold the marketing rights of the Super Cub to WTA of Lubbock, Texas together with 15 unsold 1981 model Super Cubs. Production ended at Lock Haven in 1982 with s/n 18-8309025 registration N91293 completed on the 22nd of November 1982.

Piper restarted production of the Super Cub at Vero Beach in 1988. They purchased s/n 18-8109032 registration N6691A as a test aircraft. The first aircraft off the Vero Beach production line was s/n 1809001 registration N4150H. It first flew on the 26th of July 1988. It was planned to offer the Super Cub as a kit either with or without engine and propeller, but Piper's financial crisis prevented implementation, but not before s/n 1809033 and s/n 1809060 were test built as kits at the factory in 1989 and 1990 respectively. The Super Cub was offered at $45,000 complete or $21,000 in kit form less engine and propeller. Production continued until 1994, the last production aircraft was s/n 1809113 registration N41594 completed in December 1994. The last few aircraft were all sold to Muncie Aviation, one of Piper's dealers.

A number of aircraft have been converted with a 180 hp engine, one example being s/n 18-8337 registration HB-OLW.

The Aeromod 100 was a field conversion to fit a small lower wing the PA-18 to make it into a bi-plane. Examples are s/n 18-8669 registration N4351Z, s/n 18-1739 registration N1906A and s/n 18-6874 registration N9797D (later to N200TD). Another conversion was by Jack Yentzer of the General Aircraft Service (of Buffalo, Wyoming) with their Model 11 for agricultural use. This also had a smaller lower wing, 200 hp Ranger engine in a PT-19 cowl, revised wing struts, Whitaker tandem wheels and used a 1953 Super Cub with a new s/n 1-11 and registration N202A.

PA-18-150 Super Cub s/n 18-8357 registration TG-HIQ-F awaiting delivery at Lock Haven. (P.R. Keating)

The rebuilt PA-18-150 Super Cub s/n 18-8109032 registration N6691A at Vero Beach. (R.W. Peperell)

The first of the new production PA-18-150 Super Cub at Oshkosh, s/n 1809001 registration N4150H. (J.M. Gradidge)

PA-18 SPECIFICATION & PERFORMANCE

SPECIFICATION	18-150 (1988-1994)
Engine	150 hp Lycoming O-320-A2B
Engine TBO (hrs)	
No of seats	2
Wing Span (ft/ins)	35/4
Length (ft/ins)	22/6
Height (ft/ins)	6/8
Useable fuel capacity (US gal)	35.8
Gross weight (lbs)	1750
Empty weight (lbs)	1062
Useful load (lbs)	688
Propeller	Sensenich
Floats available	Edo 2000
PERFORMANCE	
Max speed	130 mph
Cruise speed	115 mph
Efficiency (gph)	9
Stall speed - flaps / gear down	43 mph
Climb @ sea level (fpm)	960
Range with reserves	374 sm
Service ceiling (ft)	19,000
Take off (Ground run)(ft)	200
Take off (over 50ft obst)(ft)	500
Landing (Ground roll)(ft)	350
Landing (over 50ft obst)(ft)	885

PA-18 Super Cub s/n 18-1739 registration N1906A with the smaller lower wings fitted at Wenatchee, Wash. (K. Donald)

PA-19 Super Cub

At the end of 1948 Piper designed the PA-19 for the U.S. Army. This was a PA-11 with rectangular wing centre section, PA-14 rudder and a 90 hp Continental engine. The first experimental aircraft s/n 19-1 registration N5011H first flew on the 25th of March 1949 with the C90-12F engine. Glazing was added to the fuselage and this design was submitted to the US Army for the L-18 short range observation liaison aircraft on the 1st April. On the same day Piper received approval 1A2 for the PA-19 with the C90 engine. The Army reviewed this aircraft at Lock Haven in early April, suggesting several improvements to Piper. In the meantime Piper developed the L-18B, based on the PA-11, for the U.S. Army (for Turkey) during the summer. Piper continued to develop the PA-19, installing a 108 hp Lycoming O-235-C1 engine in N5011H in July. Type approval for this configuration, the PA-19 '105', was granted on the 19th of August. The second experimental PA-19 s/n 19-2 registration N5572H first flew on the 31st of August. Meanwhile the 1949 PA-18 (Vagabond) was cancelled and Piper decided to civilianize the PA-19 Super Cub using the now vacant designation PA-18. The third and final PA-19 s/n 19-3 registration N5417H was completed on the 29th of November 1949. This was a special for the U.S. Department of the Interior with a 90 hp Continental C90-12F engine. Piper went on to develop the PA-19 by installing PA-20 flaps and a larger horizontal tail in combination with the Lycoming engine. The flaps were installed in N5011H on the 17th November. This combination of wing flaps and Lycoming engine went into production with the PA-18 '105' in January 1950.

In March 1950 Piper proposed the PA-19 observation reconnaissance aircraft with 125 hp Lycoming O-290-D engine, slotted flaps and glazing. These were fitted to the experimental N5572H on the 29th / 30th of March. Between April and June it competed with other manufacturers for a U.S. Army contract, which was won by Cessna with the L-19 Bird Dog. The 125 hp Lycoming O-290-D engine was fitted to N5011H on the 25th of August and Type Approval for the PA-18 '125' and PA-19 '125' (and L-21) was granted on the 1st of September. Production of the PA-18 '125' / L-21 started in October 1950.

In August 1950 Piper was awarded the first L-18C contract. The first production aircraft was s/n 18-401 completed on the 1st of September.

Later in October the 125 hp experimental N5011H was converted to a seaplane with Edo 92-1400 floats. The PA-18S '125' and PA-19S '125' Type Approval was granted on the 25th of October.

Only three PA-19 aircraft were built. They were used as Army experimentals and development aircraft for Piper. The PA-19 and PA-18 were the same designs. All production used the PA-18 designation.

Later in October 1950 a Nazir slotted wing was fitted to N5572H and was tested against the standard PA-19 N5011H by Piper. This was found to give a little increase in performance, but more cost, weight and complexity.

PA-19 PRODUCTION DETAILS

Model Year	Serial Number Range From	To	Type	Total	Comments
Experimental	19-1	19-2	PA-19	2	
Special	19-3		PA-19	1	
Total manufactured 3 (All built at Lock Haven)					

PA-19 SPECIFICATION & PERFORMANCE			
SPECIFICATION	19 (L-18C)	19 '105'	19 '125'
Engine	95 hp Continental C90-12F	108 hp Lycoming O-235-C1	125 hp Lycoming O-290-D1
Engine TBO (hrs)			
No of seats	2	2	2
Wing Span (ft/ins)	35/3	35/3	35/3
Length (ft/ins)	22/7	22/7	22/7
Height (ft/ins)	6/8	6/8	6/8
Useable fuel capacity (US gal)			
Gross weight (lbs)	1500	1500	1750
Empty weight (lbs)			
Useful load (lbs)			
Propeller	Sensenich	Sensenich	Sensenich
Floats available			
PERFORMANCE			
Max speed			
Cruise speed	90 mph		107 mph
Efficiency (gph)			
Stall speed - flaps / gear down			
Climb @ sea level (fpm)			800
Range with reserves			
Service ceiling (ft)	18,000		16,000
Take off (Ground run)(ft)			
Take off (over 50ft obst)(ft)	650		600
Landing (Ground roll)(ft)			
Landing (over 50ft obst)(ft)	600		600

PA-19 Super Cub s/n 19-2 registration N5572H at Lock Haven. (via W.T. Piper Jr.)

PA-20 Pacer

The Pacer was a PA-16 Clipper with a redesigned tail and cabin interior, wing flaps were fitted, two wing fuel tanks were fitted as standard and the gear was wider. The prototype was s/n 20-01 registration N7000K completed on the 13th of July 1949. Power was supplied by a 115 hp Lycoming O-235-C1 engine. A second aircraft s/n 20-1 registration N7100K first flew on the 4th of October 1949 with a 125 hp Lycoming O-290-D engine. The Approved Type Certificate 1A4 was granted on the 21st of December. Production of the PA-20 commenced in January 1950 with the 125 hp Lycoming engine, the first production aircraft being s/n 20-3 registration N6901K completed on the 6th of January (there was no s/n 20-2). The PA-20 Pacer was available as a '125' with a wooden fixed pitch propeller or as a '135' with a metal controllable pitch propeller. In 1950 the 115 hp Lycoming O-235-C1 engine was made available as well as the 125 hp version. This version was approved on the 22nd of March. Production of the 115 hp PA-20-115 commenced with s/n 20-330 registration N7420K completed on the 26th of March 1950.

In 1950 Piper promoted the PA-20 as an air ambulance with the ability to load a person on a stretcher into the aircraft. Aircraft s/n 20-5 registration N6910K was used to publicise this at Lock Haven.

Floats were available and the first example of the PA-20S Seaplane was on N7100K which first flew on the 1st of May 1950. This was approved on the 18th of May.

In 1950 Max Conrad flew Pacer s/n 20-231 registration N7330K from Minneapolis to Rome and back. For a aircraft of this size, it was a monumental achievement. In 1952 it was again flown across the Atlantic and back again.

In the middle of 1950 Piper carried out some flight comparisons between a production Pacer '125' s/n 20-278 registration N7369K (with the Lycoming engine) and the prototype Pacer N7100K fitted with a 145 hp Continental C-145 engine. Piper decided to stay with the Lycoming engine.

For the 1952 model year the gear width was increased by 12 inches, a new bubble windshield, an improved heater, better cabin airflow and sound-proofing were fitted.

It was not until 1952 that the engine power was next raised, this time to the 135 hp Lycoming O-290-D2. This version was approved on the 5th of May. The first production aircraft being s/n 20-877 registration N1960A completed on the 13th of June.

For the 1953 model year the fuselage was widened at the rear near the baggage compartment.

In January 1953 Piper experimented with a 185 hp Continental O-315-A engine (taken from the Sky Sedan s/n 6-01) installed in aircraft s/n 20-959 registration N1133C. It is not known why this was done.

PA-20 PRODUCTION DETAILS

Model Year	Serial Number Range From	To	Type	Total	Comments
Prototype	20-01		115	1	
Prototype	20-1		115	1	
1950	20-3	20-552 *	'125','135'	549	
1951	20-553	20-811	115,'125','135'	259	
1952	20-812	20-933	115,'125','135',135	122	
1953	20-934	20-1083	135	150	
1954	20-1084	20-1121	135	38	

A total of 1 aircraft in the batch marked * was updated to another model and given a new serial number. See table below.

Total manufactured 1120 (All built at Lock Haven)

PA-20 Pacer s/n 20-1 registration N7100K at Lock Haven. (via W.T. Piper Jr.)

PA-20 Pacer 125 s/n 20-813 registration N1579A at Lock Haven. (via W.T. Piper Jr.)

PA-20S Pacer 125 Seaplane s/n 20-826 registration N1590A on the Susquehanna River at Lock Haven. (Piper Aircraft Corporation)

PA-20 SERIAL NUMBER CHANGES

Model	Old Serial Number	New Serial Number	New Model (if different)
PA-20-125	20-432	22-666	PA-22-135

PA-20 SPECIFICATION & PERFORMANCE

SPECIFICATION	20-115	20 '125'
Engine	115 hp Lycoming O-235-C1	125 hp Lycoming O-290-D
Engine TBO (hrs)		
No of seats	4 (3 seaplane)	4(3 seaplane)
Wing Span (ft/ins)	29/4	29/4
Length (ft/ins)	20/5	20/5
Height (ft/ins)	6/2.5	6/2.5
Useable fuel capacity (US gal)	36	36
Gross weight (lbs)	1750	1800
Empty weight (lbs)	920	970
Useful load (lbs)	830	830
Propeller	Sensenich	Sensenich or Kypers Aeromatic
Floats available	Edo 1650	
PERFORMANCE		
Max speed	125	135
Cruise speed	112	125
Efficiency (gph)	7	7.7
Stall speed - flaps / gear down	50	48
Climb @ sea level (fpm)	600	810
Range with reserves	580 sm	580 sm
Service ceiling (ft)	11,000	14,250
Take off (Ground run)(ft)	1290	1210
Take off (over 50ft obst)(ft)	1910	1788
Landing (Ground roll)(ft)	780	780
Landing (over 50ft obst)(ft)	1440	1187

Production ended at Lock Haven with s/n 20-1121 registration N1605P completed on the 9th of September 1954.

A number of PA-20 aircraft have had their engines exchanged for the 150 hp Lycoming O-320-A2B, one such being s/n 20-961 registration N1148C.

PA-20 SPECIFICATION & PERFORMANCE		
SPECIFICATION	20 '135'	20-135
Engine	125 hp Lycoming O-290-D	135 hp Lycoming O-290-D2
Engine TBO (hrs)		
No of seats	4 (3 seaplane)	4 (3 seaplane)
Wing Span (ft/ins)	29/4	29/4
Length (ft/ins)	20/5	20/5
Height (ft/ins)	6/2.5	6/2.5
Useable fuel capacity (US gal)	36	36
Gross weight (lbs)	1800	1950
Empty weight (lbs)	970	
Useful load (lbs)	830	
Propeller	Sensenich	Sensenich
Floats available		Edo 2000 / Edo 2200
PERFORMANCE		
Max speed	135	139
Cruise speed	134	134
Efficiency (gph)	7.7	7.7
Stall speed - flaps / gear down	48	48
Climb @ sea level (fpm)	850	850
Range with reserves	580	530
Service ceiling (ft)	15,500	15,500
Take off (Ground run)(ft)	1210	1220
Take off (over 50ft obst)(ft)	1788	1600
Landing (Ground roll)(ft)	780	500
Landing (over 50ft obst)(ft)	1187	1280

Experimental PA-20 s/n 20-959 registration N1133C with a 185 hp Continental engine at Lock Haven. (via C. Smith Jr.)

The Baumann Brigadier under conversion to the Piper PA-21 at Lock Haven. (via W.T. Piper Jr.)

The PA-21 airframe hung in the roof of the Engineering Building at Lock Haven in 1952. (Piper Aircraft Corporation)

PA-21

In July 1949 Piper purchased the four seat twin-engined Baumann B-250 Brigadier s/n 1 registration N30025 from the Baumann Aircraft Corporation of Santa Barbara, California with a view to putting the type into production. (This was originally NX30025 which first flew in June 1947). They purchased the manufacturing rights not the design, with Piper agreeing not to manufacture the design with pusher engines and Baumann agreeing not to produce it with tractor engines. The PA-21 model designation was assigned to the Baumann on the 30th August 1949. Between October and December Piper re-designed the wings for standard (tractor) engine layout and work started on the aircraft. The engineer on the project, Essenwein unfortunately left Piper in January 1950 and the project was cancelled because of high predicted production costs. The prototype was sold to a local college. In the meantime Baumann was developing the Brigadier into the model B-290 with 145 hp Continental engines, flying with s/n 102 registration N90616. Baumann subsequently supplied the airframe that was to be used to build the prototype CCW-5 Custer Channel-Wing aircraft with s/n CCW5X registration N6257C.

Baumann B-250 SPECIFICATION & PERFORMANCE

SPECIFICATION	Baumann B250
Engines	125 hp Continental C-125 pusher
No of seats	5
Wing Span (ft/ins)	41/0
Length (ft/ins)	27/5
Height (ft/ins)	10/2
Useable fuel capacity (US gal)	76
Gross weight (lbs)	3500
Empty weight (lbs)	2150
Useful load (lbs)	1350
Propellers	
PERFORMANCE	
Max speed	170 mph
Cruise speed	160 mph
Efficiency (gph)	
Stall speed - flaps / gear down	55 mph
Climb @ sea level (fpm)	1250
Range with reserves	750 sm
Service ceiling (ft)	18,000

Baumann B-250 Brigadier s/n 1 registration NX30085. (via J. Taylor)

PA-22 Tri-Pacer / Caribbean / Colt

This was an updated version of the PA-20 Pacer in which the main undercarriage legs had been moved rearwards to enable a nose-wheel to be fitted. It was the first aircraft to have the rudder / aileron interconnect system fitted and retained the fabric covering. The first PA-22 Tri-Pacer was s/n 22-1 registration N7700K completed on the 27th May 1950 and was fitted with a 125 hp Lycoming O-290-D engine. It was followed by a second test aircraft s/n 22-2 registration N7777K completed on the 15th of November. The Approved Type Certificate 1A6 was granted on the 20th of December 1950.

Production got underway in December 1950 commencing s/n 22-3 registration N600A completed on the 30th with the 125 hp engine. The PA-22 was built alongside the PA-20 Pacer. The first six aircraft consisted of a PA-22 fuselage and PA-20 wings. Like the Pacer, the Tri-Pacer was available as a '125' with a wooden fixed pitch propeller or as a '135' with a metal Kypers Aeromatic or Sensenich controllable pitch propeller.

For the 1952 model year, a bubble windshield was fitted, improved cabin airflow and sound-proofing was installed and increased heater capacity was available. The experimental model was s/n 22-333 registration N999A converted during September and October 1951. Production started with s/n 22-354 registration N1433A completed on the 21st of November 1951.

The first production PA-22-135 with s/n 22-534 and registration N1962A was completed on the 6th of June 1952. Engine fitted was the 135 hp Lycoming O-290-D2. Approval for this version was received on the 5th of May. It is likely that N7700K was the experimental aircraft, fitted with the 135 hp engine in early 1952. Production of the PA-20 Pacer continued alongside the Tri-Pacer until it was phased out during July 1954. One PA-22-135 was converted by Safir Flying Service at Teterboro, New Jersey, a Piper dealer, from an earlier PA-20 '125', this was N7615K s/n 20-432, becoming s/n of 22-666 (which was assigned by Piper) but retaining its original registration.

For the 1953 model year the fuselage was widened at the rear near the baggage compartment. The experimental model was s/n 22-714 registration N2333A converted on the 1st of August 1952. Production started with s/n 22-807 registration N2470A completed on the 30th of October 1952.

For the 1954 model year, special windows, improved panel and new bottom engine cowl were fitted. The experimental aircraft was s/n 22-1285 registration N8539C completed on the 8th of June 1953. Production for 1954 commenced with s/n 22-1760 registration N3488A completed on the 6th of November 1953.

Higher power was again introduced for the 1955 model year when production of the PA-22-150 commenced with the 150 hp Lycoming O-320-A2B engine. There were two experimental aircraft, N600A fitted with a 150 hp engine in late 1953 and s/n 22-2000 registration N3767A completed with a 150 hp engine on the 28th of December 1953. A third aircraft s/n 22-2378 registration N1555P was completed on the 12th of August 1954 and was used for show purposes. Approval for this version was granted on the 3rd of September. The first production aircraft s/n 22-2425 registration N1611P was delivered in November.

The experimental aircraft for the 1956 model year was s/n 22-3218 registration N3500P completed on the 15th of July 1955. It had a new rear window and door seal, new door latches, the rudder pedals were moved forward, new instrument panel and hydrasoft landing gear. Production started with s/n 22-3387 completed on the 28th of October 1955, exported to South Africa on the 15th of November.

In May 1956 Piper experimented with a Tri-Pacer with two 90 hp Continental C90 engines mounted one above the other in the nose, driving separate propellers. Aircraft s/n 22-2948 registration N2613P was used. No production was contemplated as it was purely a development programme.

For the 1957 model, the baggage space was increased to 18 cubic feet and an auxiliary 8 gallon fuel tank was available as an option. The experimental aircraft was s/n 22-4143 registration N6844B converted on the 16th of July 1956. Production started with s/n 22-4460 completed on the 2nd of October 1956 and was exported to South Africa on the 22nd.

Prototype PA-22 Tri-Pacer s/n 22-1 registration N7700K at Lock Haven. (via C. Smith Jr.)

The 1952 model PA-22 Tri-Pacer s/n 22-333 registration N999A with bubble windshield at Lock Haven. (via J. Taylor)

The 1953 model PA-22-135 Tri-Pacer s/n 22-714 registration N2333A at Lock Haven. (Piper Aircraft Corporation)

The 1955 model PA-22-150 Tri-Pacer s/n 22-2378 registration N1555P. (Piper Aircraft Corporation)

The Piper experimental two-engined PA-22 at Lock Haven, s/n 22-2948 registration N2613P. (Aerospace Publishing)

Another view of the Piper experimental two-engined PA-22 s/n 22-2948 registration N2613P at Lock Haven. (Aerospace Publishing)

PA-22 PRODUCTION DETAILS

Model Year	Serial Number Range From	To	Type	Total	Comments
Prototypes	22-1	22-2	125	2	Tri-Pacer
1951	22-3	22-353	125	351	Tri-Pacer
1952	22-354	22-533 *	125	179	Tri-Pacer
1952	22-534	22-806	135	273	Tri-Pacer
1953	22-807	22-1759	135	953	Tri-Pacer
1954	22-1760	22-2424	135	665	Tri-Pacer 22-2378 to 150 hp & 1955 model
1955	22-2425	22-3386	150	962	Tri-Pacer 22-3218 to 1956 model
1956	22-3387	22-4459	150	1073	Tri-Pacer 22-4143 to 1957 model
1957	22-4460	22-5602	150	1143	Tri-Pacer 22-5139 to 1958 model
1958	22-5603	22-6351	150,160	749	Tri-Pacer 22-6216 to 1959 model
1959	22-6352	22-6510	160	159	Tri-Pacer
1959	22-6511	22-6979	160,150	469	Tri-Pacer, Caribbean 22-6785 & 22-6857 to 1960 models
1960	22-6980	22-7630	160,150	651	Tri-Pacer, Caribbean
Prototype	22-8000		108	1	Colt
1961	22-8001	22-9036	108	1036	Colt
1962	22-9037	22-9469	108	433	Colt
1963	22-7631	22-7642	150	12	Tri-Pacer
1963	22-9470	22-9728	108	259	Colt
1964	22-9729	22-9848	108	120	Colt

One aircraft in the batch marked * was not delivered, instead it was updated to the next year's model and given a new serial number. See table below.

Total manufactured 9490 (All built at Lock Haven)

PA-22 SERIAL NUMBER CHANGES

Model	Old Serial Number	New Serial Number	New Model (if different)
PA-22	22-533	22-746	PA-22-135

It was not until October 1957 that the next engine change took place, this was the introduction of the 1958 model 160 hp Lycoming O-320-B powered PA-22-160. The 1958 experimental aircraft was s/n 22-5139 registration N7353D converted in the summer of 1957. Approval for this version was granted on the 27th of August. In addition to a new engine and paint, it had a new interior. The first production aircraft was s/n 22-5603 registration N8113D completed on the 3rd of October. The Tri-Pacer 160 was available with one of three levels of equipment, standard, Super custom or Autoflite. A small number of PA-22-150 aircraft continued to be built alongside the 160 hp variant.

In the autumn of 1958 the original PA-22-150 was phased out and replaced by a cheaper version, this new variant was still designated the PA-22-150 but was given a new name, the Caribbean. The experimental aircraft was s/n 22-6444 registration N9528D converted from a Tri-Pacer on the 20th of October. The Caribbean was specifically created for the airport operator, offering them a 130 mph, four place aircraft at a low cost. The first production aircraft was s/n 22-6511 registration N9602D completed on the 22nd of November.

The PA-22-150 Caribbean experimental aircraft, s/n 22-6444 registration N9528D. (Piper Aircraft Corporation)

The 1958 model PA-22-160 Tri-Pacer s/n 22-5139 registration N7353D at Lock Haven. (Piper Aircraft Corporation)

PA-22S-150 Tri-Pacer Seaplane s/n 22-2000 registration N3767A. (Piper Aviation Museum)

PA-22-108 Colt s/n 22-8001 registration N4501Z. (Piper Aircraft Corporation)

PA-22S-108 Colt Seaplane s/n 22-8839 registration N5175Z. (Piper Aircraft Corporation)

1962 model PA-22-108 Colt s/n 22-8722 registration N5088Z at Lock Haven. (Piper Aircraft Corporation)

PA-22 SPECIFICATION & PERFORMANCE

SPECIFICATION	22 '125'	22 '135'	22-135
Engine	125 hp Lycoming O-290-D	125 hp Lycoming O-290-D	135 hp Lycoming O-290-D2
Engine TBO (hrs)			
No of seats	4	4	4 (Seaplane 3)
Wing Span (ft/ins)	29/4	29/4	29/4
Length (ft/ins)	20/5	20/5	20/5
Height (ft/ins)	8/2.5	8/2.5	8/2.5
Useable fuel capacity (US gal)	36	36	36
Gross weight (lbs)	1800	1800	1950
Empty weight (lbs)	1020	1020	1020
Useful load (lbs)	780	780	930
Propeller	Sensenich or Kypers Aeromatic	Sensenich	Sensenich
Floats available			Edo 2000 / 2200
PERFORMANCE			
Max speed	133 mph	133 mph	137 mph
Cruise speed	123 mph	132 mph	132 mph
Efficiency (gph)	7.7	7.7	
Stall speed - flaps / gear down	48 mph	48 mph	48 mph
Climb @ sea level (fpm)	810	850	800
Range with reserves	580 sm	580 sm	580 sm
Service ceiling (ft)	15,500	15,500	15,500
Take off (Ground run)(ft)	1100	1100	1220
Take off (over 50ft obst)(ft)	1540	1540	1600
Landing (Ground roll)(ft)	780	780	500
Landing (over 50ft obst)(ft)	1260	1260	1280

Production of the Tri-Pacer and Caribbean ceased with s/n 22-7630 completed on the 26th of August 1960 when Piper introduced its new four seater PA-28 Cherokee at its Vero Beach facility. Instead of dismantling the jigs and tooling, they used them to build a two seat version of the PA-22 to be used for training purposes and thus could fit a smaller and therefore cheaper engine of 90 or 100 hp. It had no flaps and only one wing fuel tank. In August 1960 the PA-22-90 was under development. By the time the first aircraft was completed Piper had decided on the 108 hp Lycoming O-235-C1B engine. The prototype aircraft was the PA-22-108 s/n 22-8000 registration N4500Z completed on the 30th of August. Type approval was obtained on the 21st October. Launched on the 1st of November the Colt was available in three options: standard, Custom or Super custom, priced at $4,995, $5,995 and $6,995 respectively.

For the 1962 model year there was a new paint scheme. Aircraft s/n 22-8722 registration N5088Z was the show aircraft. The Colt continued in production until the 26th of March 1964 (the last was s/n 22-9848 registration N5974Z) when Piper introduced the two seat Cherokee 140 at Vero Beach. Whilst the Colt was being built a batch of twelve PA-22-150 aircraft were produced during January and February 1963 on a special order from the French Army (ALAT).

As with most earlier models the PA-22 was available on floats. The following are examples of the PA-22S Seaplane:

PA-22S-150	N6844B	22-4143
PA-22S-160	N9188D	22-6246
PA-22S-108	N5175Z	22-8839

The Approved Type Certificate for the PA-22S-135 was granted on the 14th of May 1952, for the PA-22S-150 on the 3rd of September 1954 and for the PA-22S-160 on the 25th of October 1957. The 150 hp experimental seaplane was N3767A tested by Piper on the Susquehanna River during the summer of 1954.

PA-22 SPECIFICATION & PERFORMANCE

SPECIFICATION	22-150	22-150 Caribbean
Engine	150 hp Lycoming O-320-A2B	150 hp Lycoming O-320-A2B
Engine TBO (hrs)		
No of seats	4 (Seaplane 3)	4 (Seaplane 3)
Wing Span (ft/ins)	29/4	29/4
Length (ft/ins)	20/5	20/6
Height (ft/ins)	8/4	8/4
Useable fuel capacity (US gal)	36, (44 optional)	36, (44 optional)
Gross weight (lbs)	2000	2000
Empty weight (lbs)	1100	1100
Useful load (lbs)	900	900
Propeller	Hartzell	Hartzell
Floats available	Edo 2000 / 2200	Edo 2000 / 2200
PERFORMANCE		
Max speed	139 mph	139 mph
Cruise speed	123 mph	132 mph
Efficiency (gph)		9@75%
Stall speed - flaps / gear down	49 mph	49 mph
Climb @ sea level (fpm)	725	725
Range with reserves	528 sm	528 sm
Service ceiling (ft)	15,000	15,000
Take off (Ground run)(ft)	1220	1220
Take off (over 50ft obst)(ft)	1600	1600
Landing (Ground roll)(ft)	500	500
Landing (over 50ft obst)(ft)	1280	1280

In January 1962 Piper Vero Beach Engineering tested a General Motors Chevrolet Convair air cooled engine in Colt s/n 22-8449 registration N4870Z. General Motors was unwilling to support the engine in an aircraft so the project was dropped.

In the field Univair of Colorado make a taildragger conversion kit for the PA-22. Tail-wheel examples are N4520A s/n 22-3827 in the USA and ZS-CRB s/n 22-7627 in South Africa, there are others known in the USA, Sweden and the U.K. Harold Wagner converted another Piper aircraft into a twin. PA-22 s/n 22-236 registration N932A became a Twin Tri-Pacer with two 85 hp Lycoming engines. This first flew on the 8th February 1952.

The last PA-22-108 Colt s/n 22-9848 registration N5974Z rolls off the production line at Lock Haven on the 26th of March 1964. (Piper Aircraft Corporation)

PA-22 SPECIFICATION & PERFORMANCE

SPECIFICATION	22-160	22-108
Engine	160 hp Lycoming O-320-B	108 hp Lycoming O-235-C1B
Engine TBO (hrs)		
No of seats	4 (Seaplane 3)	2
Wing Span (ft/ins)	29/4	29/3
Length (ft/ins)	20/6	20/2
Height (ft/ins)	8/4	8/3
Useable fuel capacity (US gal)	36 (44 optional)	36
Gross weight (lbs)	2000	1650
Empty weight (lbs)	1110	940
Useful load (lbs)	890	710
Propeller	Hartzell	Hartzell
Floats available	Edo 2000 / 2200	PeeKay 1800 / Edo 2000
PERFORMANCE		
Max speed	141 mph	120 mph
Cruise speed	134 mph	108 mph
Efficiency (gph)	9	
Stall speed - flaps / gear down	49 mph	56 mph
Climb @ sea level (fpm)	800	610
Range with reserves	536 sm (655 sm opt)	648 sm
Service ceiling (ft)	16,500	12,000
Take off (Ground run)(ft)	1120	950
Take off (over 50ft obst)(ft)	1480	1500
Landing (Ground roll)(ft)	500	500
Landing (over 50ft obst)(ft)	1280	1250

PA-22 with tail wheel conversion, PA-22-20 s/n 22-2459 registration N1643P. (J.M. Gradidge)

5
AMERICAN INDIANS

PA-23 Apache

The Apache was the first twin-engined design to emerge from the Piper factory and helped Piper move away from the 'Cub' image. It was developed from a proposal found in the files at the Stinson factory and was originally known as the 'Twin Stinson'. The PA-23 development started in January 1951.

The experimental aircraft was s/n 23-01 registration N1953A and first flew on the 2nd of March 1952. It was a low wing twin-engined four seater, the engines being 125 hp Lycoming O-290-D's. It had a retractable tricycle undercarriage and was of steel tube construction with fabric covered fuselage and outer wing panels. Flight tests showed up a number of problems. Firstly it had single-engine handling problems. This was followed by engine cooling problems which were fixed by cowling and exhaust changes. The aircraft was under powered so full-feathering propellers with 135 hp Lycoming engines were fitted. Also it had a bad case of the 'shakes'. Aircraft N1953A was a twin-finned design, so Piper engineering modified it to the more orthodox single fin-and-rudder layout (from PA-6 s/n 6-1 registration N4000M) in a high configuration to get the tail out of the air-flow. Penn State University wind tunnel tests showed that the airflow was being disrupted over the upper surface of the inboard wing by airflow between the fuselage and engine nacelle. Wing fillets solved this problem, so they put the tail back down in the conventional low position. They added more power by installing 150 hp Lycoming engines.

For the prototype aircraft Piper replaced the fabric covering with metal and re-designed completely from the rear of the cabin backwards. The engines were the 150 hp Lycoming O-320-A with constant speed propellers. The prototype PA-23 Apache s/n 23-1 registration N23P and first flew on the 29th of July 1953. A pre-production aircraft s/n 23-2 registration N1000P was completed on the 21st of December 1953. These two aircraft were used for certification trials and the Type Certificate 1A10 was issued on 29th of January 1954. Deliveries to customers started with s/n 23-4 registration N1002P on the 30th of April. It was priced at $32,000.

PA-23 PRODUCTION DETAILS

Model Year	Serial Number Range From	To	Type	Total	Comments
Experimental	23-01		125	1	later '135', then '150'
Prototype	23-1		'150'	1	
Pre-production	23-2		'150'	1	
1954 & 55	23-3	23-375	'150'	373	
1956	23-376	23-746	'150'	371	
1957	23-747	23-1163	'150'	417	23-1068 to 160 hp
1958	23-1164	23-1176	'150'	13	
1958	23-1177		160	1	
1958	23-1178	23-1182	'150'	5	
1958	23-1183	23-1501	160	319	23-1397 to 1959 model
1959	23-1502	23-1870	160	369	23-1774 to Apache 'G'
1960	23-1871	23-1907	160 'G'	37	
1961	23-1908	23-2012	160 'G'	105	
1962	23-2013	23-2043	160 'H'	31	
1963	23-2044	23-2046	160 'G'	3	for UK
Total manufactured 2047 (All built at Lock Haven)					

Experimental PA-23 s/n 23-01 registration N1953A with twin-fin tail at Lock Haven. (Piper Aircraft Corporation)

Experimental PA-23 s/n 23-01 registration N1953A with single-fin high tail at Lock Haven. (via W.K. Giles)

Experimental PA-23 s/n 23-01 registration N1953A with single-fin low tail. (via J. Myers)

There was no change for the 1955 model year. Thereafter annual detail refinements and colour scheme changes were carried out. The 1956 Apache commenced with s/n 23-376 registration N1331P completed on the 16th of November 1955. The 1956 test aircraft was s/n 23-229 registration N2000P completed on the 13th of May 1955. During December 1955 Piper installed a fifth seat in the Apache, starting with s/n 23-414 registration N1365P. The 1957 Apache test aircraft was s/n 23-2 registration N1000P which was re-built by the factory in August 1956. This aircraft went on to be the experimental Aztec. The 1957 model Apache commenced with s/n 23-747 registration N2145P completed on the 4th of October 1956.

After production of the 1958 Apache had commenced, the engine's power was increased by fitting two 160 hp Lycoming 0-320-B's. The 160 hp test aircraft was s/n 23-1068 registration N3001P converted from a 1957 model. Type approval was granted on the 14th of October 1957. Production of this variant, the PA-23-160, commenced with s/n 23-1183 registration N3238P completed on the 17th of September 1957.

The 1959 Apache was similar but with a new auto control system, commencing with s/n 23-1502 registration N4027P completed on the 6th of October 1958. The test aircraft was s/n 23-1397 registration N4000P converted from a 1958 model. Aircraft s/n 23-1426 registration N3454P was painted in the 1959 colour scheme and used as the show aircraft.

For the Apache G, extra cabin windows were fitted to give the fifth seat passenger a better view. Other improvements included rudder pressure, carburettor heat adjustment, increased generator capacity and higher permissible gear down / flap down speeds. The model 'G' was used as this is what it would have been if they had started in 1954 with the model 'A'. The Apache G test aircraft was s/n 23-1774 registration N4272P converted from a 1959 model and first flew on the 17th of July 1959. The first production aircraft was s/n 23-1871 registration N4370P completed on the 12th of May 1960 and it was launched on the 1st of July.

For the 1962 model year the Apache H was introduced with the new type 'ruggedized' Lycoming O-320-B2B engines commencing s/n 23-2013 registration N4491P completed on the 3rd of October 1961.

Between July and November 1960 Ed Swearingen cleaned up Apache N1000P for Piper with various speed modifications including fillets, nacelle changes and landing gear fairings. Piper did not put these modifications into the production Apache, even though tests showed an increase in speed of 8.5 mph.

Production ceased in early 1962 when it was replaced on the line by the PA-23-235 Apache. Three more 160 hp Apache G were built in September 1962, the last one completed was s/n 23-2046 registration G-ASDI on the 24th of September. These three and six previous Apache G aircraft were delivered to England for Air Service Training Ltd at Hamble, Hampshire.

The Seguin Geronimo package of modifications includes: 180 hp Lycoming O-360-A1D engines, streamlined engine cowls, extended nose cone, fully enclosed gear doors, new wing tips, square tipped fin and rudder, one piece windshield, gross weight increase, new Hartzell props, sixth seat and rear baggage compartment. Examples of the conversation are s/n 23-502 registration TG-JIH and s/n 23-1676 registration N4188P. At least 15 have been reported as having undergone this conversion.

Another known conversion is the Miller Jet Profile, e.g. s/n 23-515 registration N1452P and the Wilson Jet Profile, e.g. s/n 23-1284 registration N3333P. They have 200 hp Lycoming O-360 engines and modifications to the tail.

On the 18th of October 1957 Fairbanks Air Service of Fairbanks, Alaska obtained approval to fit Wesco A-25 skis to the Apache. Aircraft s/n 23-877 registration N2267P was used for this testing.

In early 1962 Piper checked out some field modifications which had been carried out to Apache aircraft. Aircraft s/n 23-2005 registration N4483P with a dorsal fin in January. Aircraft s/n 23-2007 registration N4485P with Rayjay turbo-chargers in May. The turbo-charged Apache had previously been certified by Rayjay Company Inc. in the February 1961. The turbo-chargers improved climb and speed at altitude.

The prototype PA-23 Apache s/n 23-1 registration N23P at Lock Haven. (Piper Aircraft Corporation)

The 1958 model 160 hp Apache, PA-23-160 s/n 23-1068 registration N3001P. (Piper Aircraft Corporation)

PA-23 SPECIFICATION & PERFORMANCE

SPECIFICATION	Experimental 23	23	23-160
Engine	125 hp Lycoming O-290	150 hp Lycoming O-320-A	160 hp Lycoming O-320-B, -B1A, -B1B, -B2B, -B3B
Engine TBO (hrs)		1200	1200
No of seats	4	4	4 - 5
Wing Span (ft/ins)	35/0 then 34/0	37/0	37/0
Length (ft/ins)	23/0	27/1.5	27/1.5
Height (ft/ins)	7/7	9/6	9/6
Useable fuel capacity (US gal)	60	72, 108 optional	90
Gross weight (lbs)	2900 then 3200	3500	3800
Empty weight (lbs)	1700 then 1950	2158-2180	2280-2320
Useful load (lbs)	1200 then 1250	1320-1342	1480-1520
Propellers		Hartzell 2 blade	Hartzell 2 blade
Floats available			
PERFORMANCE			
Max speed	177 mph	180 mph	183 mph
Cruise speed	150 - 158 mph	150 - 170 mph	173 mph
Efficiency (gph)			18 @ 75%
Stall speed - flaps / gear down	52 -58 mph	52 - 59 mph	61 mph
Climb @ sea level (fpm)	1200 - 1227	1350 - 1450	1260
Range with reserves	659 - 720 sm	660 - 720 sm	840 sm
Service ceiling (ft)	21,000	18,500	17,000
Take off (Ground run)(ft)	900	900	1190
Take off (over 50ft obst)(ft)		1150	1550
Landing (Ground roll)(ft)	670	670	750
Landing (over 50ft obst)(ft)			1360

The experimental PA-23-160 Apache G s/n 23-1774 registration N4272P. (Piper Aircraft Corporation)

PA-23 SPECIFICATION & PERFORMANCE		
SPECIFICATION	Seguin Geronimo	Miller Apache
Engine	180 hp Lycoming O-360-A1D	200 hp Lycoming IO-360-C1C
Engine TBO (hrs)	2000	
No of seats	4 - 6	4 - 5
Wing Span (ft/ins)	35/0	
Length (ft/ins)	31/6	
Height (ft/ins)		
Useable fuel capacity (US gal)	108 (156 optional)	
Gross weight (lbs)	4000	4000
Empty weight (lbs)	2500	2400
Useful load (lbs)	1500	1600
Propellers	Hartzell	
Floats available		
PERFORMANCE		
Max speed	200 mph	
Cruise speed	190-196 mph @ 75%	198 mph @ 75%
Efficiency (gph)		
Stall speed - flaps / gear down	54 mph	57 mph
Climb @ sea level (fpm)	2000	2000
Range with reserves	1043 sm @ 75% 1118 sm @ 65%	1556 sm @ 75%* 1643 sm @ 55%*
Service ceiling (ft)	23,000	21,000
Take off (Ground run)(ft)	400	
Take off (over 50ft obst)(ft)	650	
Landing (Ground roll)(ft)	400	
Landing (over 50ft obst)(ft)	675	1100
		* no reserve

Wilson Jet Profile s/n 23-1284 registration N3333P. (Aerospace Publishing)

PA-23 AZTEC

The higher powered Apache development was first discussed by Piper engineering in August 1956. By putting 250 hp Lycoming engines onto the PA-23 Apache and installing a large sweeping vertical tail and a stabilator (all moving horizontal tail), Piper created the PA-23-250 Aztec. The designation PA-27 was allocated to the Aztec and the construction numbers use 27, but the official designation stayed as the PA-23. The experimental department received the rebuilt Apache N1000P in January 1957. Firstly, Piper installed 250 hp Lycoming O-540-A1A engines in extended cowls and fitted a larger tail. (The extra horse-power necessitated a larger tail surface). This first flew on the 13th of June 1957. In the Spring of 1958 Piper installed the new definitive larger tail on Apache s/n 23-1068 registration N3001P. The prototype Aztec s/n 27-1 registration N4250P was produced by the experimental shop and first flew on the 1st of October 1958. Unfortunately it crashed on the 16th of February 1959 due to flutter problems. The first production aircraft s/n 27-2 registration N4500P first flew on the 28th of March and completed the flutter tests in mid May by installing lead balances in the tail. Martin Aircraft helped out on the flutter analysis. Lycoming proposed O-540-E1A supercharged engines for the Aztec in August 1959, Piper stayed with the O-540-A1D5 engines. FAA approval was granted on the PA-23 type approval 1A10 on the 18th of September 1959 and first deliveries of this 5 seater commenced with s/n 27-3 registration N4501P on the 23rd of January 1960. Three levels of equipment were available, standard, Super custom or Autoflite and it had a standard price of $52,000.

In 1960, Piper delivered 20 Aztecs to the U.S. Navy under the designation UO-1 against contract number 60-0063F. The UO-1 test aircraft was s/n 27-134 registration N4800P completed in April. The UO-1 was similar to the civilian Aztec with the exception of radio, oxygen and propeller anti-icing equipment. In 1962 they were re-designated U-11A.

Piper tested Cessna 310D registration N6784T at Lock Haven in May 1960 to compare it with the new Aztec.

In late 1960, aircraft s/n 27-49 registration N4544P was used to develop the de-icing option for the Aztec. Between the 27th of February and the 8th of March 1961 Max Conrad flew Aztec N4544P around the world, starting in Miami, Florida, in 8 days 18 hours, 36 minutes doing 25,946 miles at an average speed of 123.2 mph. He claimed an international Class-C-I-d record for speed.

In 1961 the Aztec B was developed with a longer nose incorporating a 150 pound baggage compartment, 6 seats and modified instruments. The prototype s/n 27-2000 registration N5000Y first flew on the 11th of September 1961. FAA type approval was received on the 15th December 1961. Deliveries commenced with s/n 27-2001 registration N5001Y, which was completed on the 13th of January 1962. It was priced at $52,990 in standard form.

In late 1961 the Apache 235 was developed, using the short-nosed Aztec airframe with 235 hp Lycoming O-540-B1A5 engines. The test aircraft was s/n 27-460 registration N4914P converted from a 250 hp version and first flew on the 11th of December 1961. FAA certification of this version was achieved on the 22nd of January 1962. The first production aircraft s/n 27-505 registration N4915P was completed on the 11th of September 1962. The standard version was priced at $44,990, the Super Custom at $50,790 and the Autoflite at $51,590. It continued in production in parallel to the 250 hp version until June 1966.

Between 1962 and 1964 the Aztec C was developed. Aircraft N5000Y was used as the test aircraft with Lycoming IO-540-C1B5 engines and electric fuel pumps fitted on the 29th of March 1962. Gear doors were fitted on the 3rd of April 1963. This version had an increase in useful load, revised landing gear with new doors, flush flaps, improved sound proofing, a new ventilation system and new luxurious interior styling. It was available with Lycoming IO-540-C4B5 engines or TIO-540-C1A turbo charged engines in 'Tiger Shark' engine nacelles. Aircraft N5000Y was also fitted with the turbo-charged Lycoming engines. The first production aircraft s/n 27-2505 registration N5427Y was completed on the 20th of February 1964. The first turbo-charged production aircraft was s/n 27-2911 registration N5781Y completed on the 26th of April. This had the AiResearch turbo on the Lycoming engine. Piper announced the Aztec C on the 2nd of April. Three levels of equipment were available, Custom, Sportsman or Professional, priced at $54,990.

The experimental PA-23 Apache s/n 23-2 registration N1000P with 250 hp engines and a bigger tail.
(Piper Aircraft Corporation)

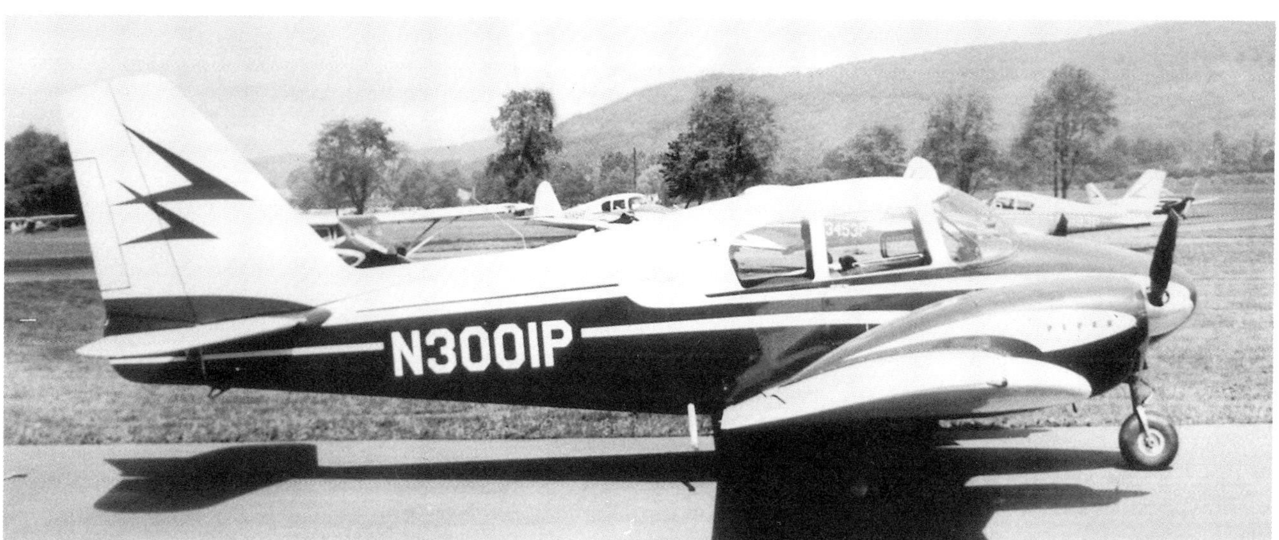

Another experimental PA-23 Apache s/n 23-1068 registration N3001P with the definitive Aztec tail at Lock Haven.
(Piper Aircraft Corporation)

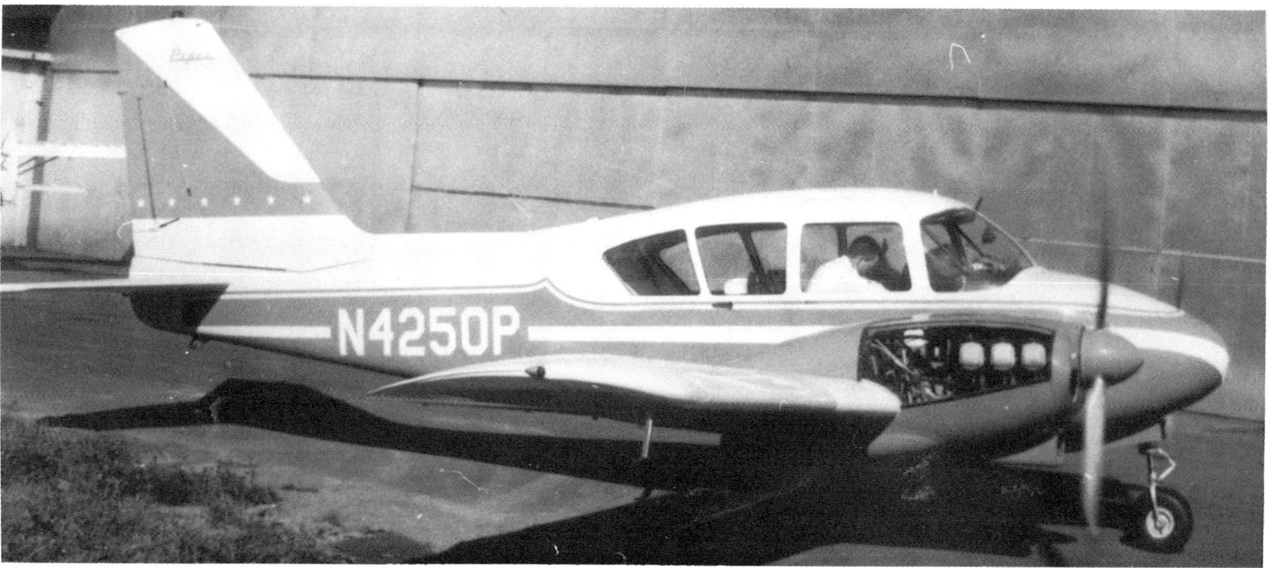

The prototype PA-23-250 Aztec s/n 27-1 registration N4250P at Lock Haven. (via W.T. Piper Jr.)

The first production Aztec s/n 27-2 registration N4500P in final assembly at Lock Haven. (Piper Aircraft Corporation)

The experimental UO-1 s/n 27-134 registration N4800P at Lock Haven. (Piper Aircraft Corporation)

The first two UO-1 aircraft flying in formation, s/n 27-259 U.S. Navy serial 149050 and s/n 27-264 U.S. Navy serial 149051. (Piper Aircraft Corporation)

The PA-23-235 Apache test aircraft s/n 27-460 registration N4919P. (Piper Aircraft Corporation)

The prototype PA-23-250 Aztec B s/n 27-2000 registration N5000Y. (Piper Aircraft Corporation)

PA-23-250 Turbo Aztec C s/n 27-2505 registration N5427Y. (Piper Aircraft Corporation)

PA-23-250 / 235 PRODUCTION DETAILS

Model / Fiscal Year	Serial Number Range From	To	Type	Total	Comments
Experimental	23-2		250	0	
Prototype	27-1		250	1	
1960	27-2	27-366	250	365	
1961	27-367	27-504	250	138	27-460 to 235 hp
Prototype	27-2000		250 'B'	1	
1962	27-505	27-506	235	2	
1962	27-2001	27-2231	250 'B'	231	
1963	27-507	27-587	235	81	
1963	27-2232	27-2436	250 'B'	205	
1964	27-588	27-603	235	16	
1964	27-2437	27-2504	250 'B'	68	
1964	27-2505	27-2690	250 'C'	186	
1965	27-604	27-616	235	13	
1965	27-2691	27-3070	250 'C'	380	
1966	27-617	27-622	235	6	
1966	27-3071	27-3508	250 'C'	438	
1967	27-3509	27-3759	250 'C'	251	
1967	27-3762		250 'C'	1	
1968	27-3760	27-3761	250 'C'	2	
1968	27-3763	27-3943	250 'C'	181	27-3837 TO 250 'D'
1968	27-3944	27-4042	250 'D'	99	
1969	27-4043	27-4399	250 'D'	357	
1970	27-4400	27-4564	250 'D'	165	27-4426 TO 250 'E'
1970	27-4574	27-4575	250 'E'	2	
1971	27-4565	27-4573	250 'D'	9	
1971	27-4576	27-4755	250 'E'	180	
1972	27-4756	27-4866	250 'E'	111	
-	27-4867	27-4916	250 'E'		Not built, see Appendix B
1973	27-7304917	27-7305234	250 'E'	318	
1974	27-7405235	27-7305476	250 'E'	242	
1975	27-7554001	27-7554168 *	250 'E'	167	
1976	27-7654001	27-7654203	250 'F'	203	
1977	27-7754001	27-7754163	250 'F'	163	
1978	27-7854001	27-7854139 *	250 'F'	138	
1979	27-7954001	27-7954121	250 'F'	121	
1980	27-8054001	27-8054059	250 'F'	59	
1981	27-8154001	27-8154030	250 'F'	30	

The experimental aircraft 23-2 has been included in the PA-23 manufactured total.
Two aircraft in the batches marked * were not delivered, instead they were updated to another year's model and given new serial numbers. See table below.
Total manufactured 4930 (All built at Lock Haven)

PA-23-250 SERIAL NUMBER CHANGES

Model	Old Serial Number	New Serial Number	New Model (if different)
PA-23-250 'E'	27-7554123	Built as 27-7654001	PA-23-250 F
PA-23-250 'F'	27-7854017	27-7754163	

PA-23-250 Aztec C s/n 27-2507 registration N5430Y. (Piper Aircraft Corporation)

PA-23S-250 Aztec Seaplane s/n 27-3411 registration N6185Y. Note additional port side door. (via J. Taylor)

PA-23-250 / 235 SPECIFICATION & PERFORMANCE

SPECIFICATION	23-235	23-250	23-250 'B'
Engine	235 hp Lycoming O-540-B1A5	250 hp Lycoming O-540-A1D5	250 hp Lycoming O-540-A1D5
Engine TBO (hrs)			
No of seats	5	5	6
Wing Span (ft/ins)	37/0	37/0	37/2
Length (ft/ins)	27/7	27/7	30/3
Height (ft/ins)	10/4	10/4	10/4
Useable fuel capacity (US gal)	137	137	137
Gross weight (lbs)	4800	4800	4800
Empty weight (lbs)	2735	2775	2900
Useful load (lbs)	2065	2025	1900
Propellers	Hartzell 2 blade	Hartzell 2 blade	Hartzell 2 blade
Floats available			
PERFORMANCE			
Max speed	202 mph	215 mph	215 mph
Cruise speed	191 mph @ 75%	205 mph @ 75%	205 mph
Efficiency (gph)	28 @ 75%	28 @ 75%	28 @ 75%
Stall speed - flaps / gear down	62 mph	62 mph	66 mph
Climb @ sea level (fpm)	1450	1650	1650
Range with reserves	980-1185 sm	1025-1200 sm	1025-1200 sm
Service ceiling (ft)	17,200	22,500	21,000
Take off (Ground run)(ft)	830	750	750
Take off (over 50ft obst)(ft)	1520	1100	1100
Landing (Ground roll)(ft)	880	900	900
Landing (over 50ft obst)(ft)	1280	1360	1260

For the UK market, the Aztec was approved with a gross weight of 4995 instead of 5200 pounds. Designated the PA-E23-250, this type was certified on the 21st of June 1965.

Piper made further improvements in 1968, designating it the Aztec D. It had a new instrument panel and a new cruise power concept. The test aircraft for the new interior was s/n 27-3837 registration N6540Y converted from a 'C' first flying with the new panel on the 17th of January. The first production aircraft was s/n 27-3944 registration N6632Y completed on the 11th of June 1968.

At the end of 1969 Lycoming started to use Lycoming turbos in place of AiResearch in the Turbo Aztec. This engine had first flown in aircraft s/n 27-3636 registration N6496Y on the 26th of December 1967.

Max Conrad claimed more world records in 1969. He took off in aircraft s/n 27-3530 registration N123LF from St. Louis Woman airport flying round the world and over both poles covering 33,985 miles starting on the 30th of November. He claimed three world records; equator to equator over a pole, South pole to North pole and round the world over both poles. In June 1971 Sheila Scott was the first woman to fly solo over the North Pole in Aztec s/n 27-4568 registration G-AYTO, named 'Mythre'. By August of that year she claimed her 100th air record.

An improved Aztec D programme was initiated in early 1969 as the Aztec F. Piper wanted to increase the horse-power to 260 hp Lycomings, increase the baggage compartments, increase the gross weight to 5400 pounds, fit wing tip fuel tanks and change the flap planform. Unfortunately the tip tanks were not available and the engines didn't give any real increase in performance. Aircraft N6496Y was testing the 260 hp Lycoming engine in April and flap extensions in November and December 1969. Piper cancelled the programme in March 1970 and created an 'interim Aztec' called the Aztec E. This had the nose lengthened by one foot (with increased baggage space) and a new flight director system and no other change. The test aircraft was s/n 27-4426 registration N13775 converted from Model 'D' and first flew on the 21st of November 1969. The Mitchell Altimatic V flight director and panel improvements were tested in aircraft N6540Y between April and November 1969. The first production model 'E' s/n 27-4574 registration N13922 was completed on the 14th of May 1970 and volume production was underway at the end of October. Piper announced the model 'E' in November.

Max Conrad's 'Lets Fly' PA-23-250 s/n 27-3530 registration N123LF. (Piper Aircraft Corporation)

PA-23-250 Aztec D s/n 27-3837 registration N6540Y. (Piper Aircraft Corporation)

PA-23-250 Turbo Aztec D s/n 27-3636 registration N6496Y. (Piper aircraft Corporation)

PA-23-250 / 235 SPECIFICATION & PERFORMANCE			
SPECIFICATION	23-250 'C' & 23-250 'D'	23-250 'Turbo C' & 23-250 'Turbo D'	23-250 'E'
Engine	250 hp Lycoming IO-540-C4B5	250 hp Lycoming TIO-540-C1A	250 hp Lycoming IO-540-C4B5
Engine TBO (hrs)	1800	1500	1800
No of seats	6	6	6
Wing Span (ft/ins)	37/2	37/2	37/2
Length (ft/ins)	30/3	30/3	31/3
Height (ft/ins)	10/4	10/4	10/4
Useable fuel capacity (US gal)	137	137	137
Gross weight (lbs)	4400, 4800, 5200	5200	5200
Empty weight (lbs)	2933	3123	3042
Useful load (lbs)	1467, 1867, 2267	2077	2158
Propellers	Hartzell 2 blade	Hartzell 2 blade	Hartzell 2 blade
Floats available			
PERFORMANCE			
Max speed	220, 218, 216 mph	256 mph	216 mph
Cruise speed	210, 205, 206 mph @ 75%	236 mph @ 75% 224 mph @ 65%	210 mph @ 75% 204 mph @ 55%
Efficiency (gph)	27.4 @ 75%	27.4 @ 75% 24.8 @ 65%	34 @ 75% 25 @ 55%
Stall speed - flaps / gear down	64, 66, 68 mph	68 mph	68 mph
Climb @ sea level (fpm)	1490	1490	1490
Range with reserves	1075, 1065, 1055 sm @ 75%	1215 sm @ 75% 1265 sm @ 65%	946 sm @ 75% 1265 sm @ 55%
Service ceiling (ft)	22,400, 21,000, 19,800	30,000	21,100
Take off (Ground run)(ft)	820	820	820
Take off (over 50ft obst)(ft)	1250	1250	1250
Landing (Ground roll)(ft)	860	860	850
Landing (over 50ft obst)(ft)	1250	1250	1250

In May 1973 Piper resurrected the Aztec F programme with several enhancements including a reduction in control forces, re-shaped stabilitor with tip balances, better brakes, more advanced instruments, 28 volt electrics, more effective fuel system and new optional wing tip fuel tanks (which were now available) of interconnection with flaps with the tailplane. Two experimental aircraft were used in 1974 and early 1975. These were s/n 27-4843 registration N14281 and s/n 27-4864 registration N14301 for testing the new stabilizer and wing tips, first flying on the 25th of April and 14th of November 1974 respectively. FAA approval was granted on the 20th of January 1975. The production prototype s/n 27-7654001 registration N54826 first flew on the 15th of April 1975 and used components of s/n 27-7554123. First deliveries were in October 1975. The base price of the standard Aztec F was $99,600 and $122,500 for the Turbo Aztec F.

In August 1976 Piper initiated the Aztec G project. Aircraft s/n 27-7854084 registration N63953 had an Aztec E horizontal stabilator and first flew as such on the 27th of April 1978. Tolve Inc. of Atlanta, Georgia carried out flutter tests in late May 1978 and FAA tests were done in March and April 1979. Piper launched this model for the 1980 model year, but decided not to change the model name and stayed with the Aztec F name.

All Aztecs were built at Lock Haven and production was discontinued with s/n 27-8154030 registration N2536R completed on the 10th of November 1981.

Melridge Aviation of Vancouver, Washington and Jobmaster Company of Seattle obtained approval for the Aztec on Edo 4930 floats, called the Aztec Nomad. Aircraft s/n 27-3411 registration N6185Y was converted in May 1967. Useful load was still 1800 lbs with the float conversion and as part of the conversion kit an extra door was supplied. An amphibious Aztec conversion was carried out by Wipline at Inver Grove Heights, Minneapolis by fitting 6000A floats. Aircraft s/n 27-4279 registration N14BP was converted in June 1988.

PA-23-250 Aztec E s/n 27-4426 registration N13775. (Piper Aircraft Corporation)

PA-23-250 Aztec F s/n 27-7654001 registration N54826. (Piper Aircraft Corporation)

PA-23-250 Aztec F s/n 27-7754092 registration N63759 in the 1978 paint design at Lock Haven. (Piper Aircraft Corporation)

PA-23-250 / 235 SPECIFICATION & PERFORMANCE

SPECIFICATION	23-250 'Turbo E'	23-250 'F'	23-250 'Turbo F'
Engine	250 hp Lycoming TIO-540-C1A	250 hp Lycoming IO-540-C4B5	250 hp Lycoming TIO-540-C1A
Engine TBO (hrs)	1500	2000	1800
No of seats	6	6	6
Wing Span (ft/ins)	37/2	37/4	37/4
Length (ft/ins)	31/3	31/3	31/3
Height (ft/ins)	10/4	10/1	10/1
Useable fuel capacity (US gal)	137	137, 177 optional	137, 177 optional
Gross weight (lbs)	5200	5200	5200
Empty weight (lbs)	3226-3229	3049-3221	3188-3358
Useful load (lbs)	1971-1974	1979-2151	1842-2012
Propellers	Hartzell 2 blade	Hartzell 2 blade	Hartzell 2 blade
Floats available			
PERFORMANCE			
Max speed	253 mph	204 mph	248 mph
Cruise speed	226 mph @ 75% 200 mph @ 55%	204 mph @ 75%	248 mph @ 75%
Efficiency (gph)	32.6 @ 75% 26 @ 55%		
Stall speed - flaps / gear down	68 mph	69 mph	69 mph
Climb @ sea level (fpm)	1530	1400	1470
Range with reserves	1105 sm @ 75% 1225 sm @ 55%	1122 sm @ 55%	952 sm @ 55%
Optional fuel range with reserves		1390 sm @ 75% 1504 sm @ 55%	1305 sm @ 55%
Service ceiling (ft)	30,000	17,600	24,000
Take off (Ground run)(ft)	820	990	990
Take off (over 50ft obst)(ft)	1250	1980	1980
Landing (Ground roll)(ft)	850	760	760
Landing (over 50ft obst)(ft)	1250	1585	1585

In November 1969 Continental Motors at Mobile, Alabama put two Tiara engines on Aztec s/n 27-4394 registration N6610Y. This was later sold in the UK in November 1973 with standard Lycoming engines fitted.

In the field Robertson offered a STOL conversion to the turbo Aztec, an example is N400PA s/n 27-7405340. Changes were made to the flaps, ailerons and wing tip leading edge. Several agricultural conversions have been made to the Aztec. An example is s/n 27-549 registration N77TA. A large cargo door was fitted to Aztec s/n 27-4502 registration N13864. Clipped wings were fitted to s/n 27-184 registration N4661P and three bladed propellers were fitted to s/n 27-139 registration N4622P.

In November 1956 Piper Lock Haven proposed a PA-29 design which was based on the Apache but enlarged and it was to have 500 hp engines. This design was modified in October 1958 into two proposals. One was an 'Aztec' with two 390 hp Lycoming O-270 engines with more fuel and three-bladed propellers. The second was an executive 'Aztec' with lengthened fuselage, extra door, tapered wings, all sheet metal fuselage structure (not tubular), the 390 hp engines and a separate compartment for the passengers with conference style seating. None of these designs left the drawing board.

After Piper North failed, John Piper formed the Lock Haven Aircraft Company at Lock Haven in 1990 and announced the intention to produce the Empress Aztec SE. This was an Aztec E with new engines, new interior, new avionics and a one piece windshield. None were produced.

1980 model PA-23-250 Aztec F s/n 27-8054001 registration N6843A. (Piper Aircraft Corporation)

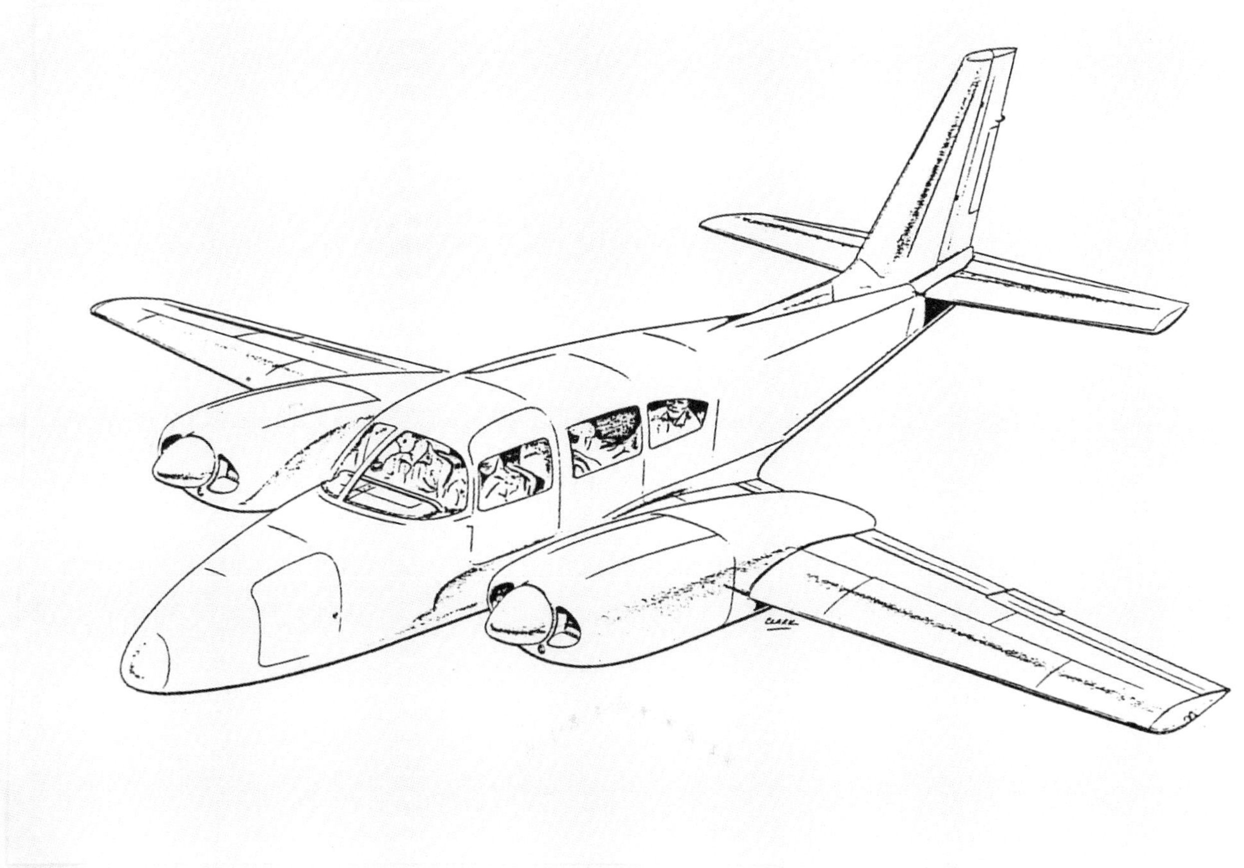

Drawing of the proposed PA-23-390 Executive Aztec. (Piper Aircraft Corporation)

The prototype PA-24-180 Comanche s/n 24-1 registration N2024P with trailing beam gear at Lock Haven. (via W.T. Piper Jr.)

The second prototype PA-24-180 Comanche s/n 24-2 registration N6000D. (Piper Aircraft Corporation)

PA-24 COMANCHE

Development of the Comanche started in 1954. It was an all-metal, four-seat, single-engined, high performance, low-wing monoplane with a 'Mooney' style trailing beam retractable undercarriage. It had a swept tail fin and a stabilator which eliminated the need for an elevator. Schweizer helped in the design and development in late 1955. The prototype s/n 24-1 registration N2024P first flew on the 19th of May 1956. It was followed, also in 1956, by s/n 24-2 registration N6000D which first flew on the 17th of October. Both of these test aircraft were powered by a 180 hp Lycoming O-360-AIA engine with a Hartzell two-blade constant speed propeller.

The PA-24-180 Comanche received its FAA approval 1A15 on the 20th of June 1957. The first production aircraft s/n 24-3 registration N5000P had its first flight on 21st of October 1957. Production aircraft did not have the trailing beam undercarriage. The first customer delivery was s/n 24-13 registration N5010P on the 6th of January 1958. It was priced at $14,500.

Shortly afterwards a higher powered model appeared, the PA-24-250 with a 250 hp Lycoming O-540-A1A5 engine. This was to be the PA-26 but Piper decided to keep to the PA-24 designation. The 250 hp engine was installed in prototype N2024P and first flew on the 18th of June 1957, followed by s/n 24-47 registration N5044P in early 1958. FAA approval of the 250 hp version was granted on the 16th of April. Production commenced with s/n 24-105 registration N5100P completed on the 12th of April. The Comanche was made to three levels of equipment, standard, Custom or Super Custom.

PA-24 PRODUCTION DETAILS

Model / Fiscal Year	Serial Number Range From	To	Type	Total	Comments
Prototypes	24-1	24-2	180	2	
1958	24-3	24-336	180, 250	334	
1959	24-337	24-1476	180, 250	1140	
1960	24-1477	24-2298	180, 250	822	
1961	24-2299	24-2843	180, 250	545	
1962	24-2844	24-3284	180, 250	441	
1963	24-3285	24-3557	180, 250	273	
1964	24-3558	24-3687	180, 250	130	24-3642 to 260 hp
1965	24-3688 *		260	0	
1965	24-4000	24-4042	260	43	
1965	24-4043	24-4299	260	257	24-4247 to 260 'B'
1966	24-4300	24-4336	260 'B'	37	
1966	24-4337	24-4593	260 'B'	257	
1967	24-4594	24-4716	260 'B'	123	
1967	24-4718	24-4720	260 'B'	3	
1967	24-4724		260 'B'	1	
1968	24-4717		260 'B'	1	
1968	24-4721	24-4723	260 'B'	3	
1968	24-4725	24-4803	260 'B'	79	24-4783 to 260 'C'
1969	24-4804	24-4908	260 'C', Turbo 260 'C'	105	
1970	24-4909	24-4963	260 'C', Turbo 260 'C'	55	
1971	24-4964	24-5002	260 'C', Turbo 260 'C'	39	
1972	24-5003	24-5028	260 'C', Turbo 260 'C'	26	
-	24-5029	24-5041	260 'C', Turbo 260 'C'		Not completed, see Appendix B
Prototype	24-6000		300	1	

One aircraft in the batch marked * was not delivered, instead it was given a new serial number. See table below.

Total manufactured 4717 (All built at Lock Haven)

The first production PA-24-180 Comanche s/n 24-3 registration N5000P. (Piper Aircraft Corporation)

PA-24S-250 Comanche Seaplane s/n 24-310 registration N888Z on the Susquehanna River at Lock Haven. (via W.T. Piper Jr.)

The experimental PA-24 Comanche s/n 24-2003 registration N6868P. (C. Wilson)

SERIAL NUMBER CHANGES			
Model	Old Serial Number	New Serial Number	New Model (if different)
PA-24-260	24-3688	24-4000	

Several engines were tested by Piper in N2024P. Between October and December 1959 a 265 hp Lycoming was installed. In September 1960 a 180 hp fuel injected Lycoming was tested. The 265 hp engine continued to be tested in aircraft s/n 24-2003 registration N6868P during 1960.

Two records were set by Max Conrad in Comanches in 1959. Between the 2nd and the 4th of June he flew from Casablanca, Morocco to Los Angeles, a distance of 7,668 miles in 58.6 hours in Comanche 250 N110LF - a class IV record. In November he flew from Casablanca to El Paso, a distance of 6,967 miles in a Comanche 180 - a class III record. Fuel capacity was 720 gallons instead of the standard 90.

The Comanche 250 has also been approved for floats. The only example known was s/n 24-310 registration N888Z fitted with floats by Edo during late 1958. It was based at Lock Haven in November 1959.

For the model years 1959 through 1961 improvements were made and the following show aircraft were used:

Model Year	180 hp Registration	s/n	250 hp Registration	s/n	Improvements
1959	N5100P	24-105	N5165P	24-181	Autoflite model equipped with the Piper AutoControl electronic automatic flight system tied in with the artificial horizon and directional gyro.
1960	N6026P	24-1121	N6016P	24-1111	Seats with tilting backs, cabin air system
1961	N7100P	24-2203	N6961P	24-2099	Instrument panel, Climate control system, 90 gallon fuel capacity, Autonav radio direction finder, AltiMatic automatic pilot

A Herman engine (later known as the Dyna-Cam engine) was fitted to the second prototype N6000D by AirMotive at Lock Haven in 1960. It only made one short flight with 'Pug' Piper at the controls.

During 1961 Piper developed a fuel injected Comanche with a 250 hp Lycoming IO-540-C engine. The experimental aircraft with the Bendix fuel injected engine was s/n 24-2088 registration N6953P. This was used for hot weather trials in Dallas, Texas. The prototype was s/n 24-2563 registration N8250P and first flew on the 27th of February 1961. Two more aircraft were used for service testing, s/n 24-2929 registration N7716P and s/n 24-2949 registration N7735P between December 1961 and February 1962. The first production fuel injected Comanche with the Lycoming IO-540-C1B5 engine was s/n 24-3205 registration N7968P completed on the 2nd of April 1962. The injected engine was offered as an option.

For the 1962 model, new electrically operated 'max-lift' slotted flaps and controls were fitted. Also the landing gear was improved and the interior was restyled. The test aircraft was s/n 24-2621 registration N7432P and first flew on the 20th of March 1961. Unfortunately, during testing it crashed on the 1st September 1961. Aircraft N8250P first flew with the slotted flaps in early July 1961. In 1961 aircraft N6868P was used to check out improved main gear with doors. Two pre-production aircraft were used as show aircraft by Piper. These were s/n 24-2833 registration N7622P, a 250 hp version and s/n 24-2834 registration N7623P, a 180 hp version, both completed between June and August 1961.

In 1962 Ed Swearingen cleaned-up the Comanche with various speed modifications, i.e. automatic cooling air-inlet shutters, aileron and flap gap sealing, single fork main gear, new ventilator inlets, double plexiglas windshield and forward side windows, revised oil cooler location. Aircraft s/n 24-3101 registration N7875P was converted. This was tested by Piper in the summer of 1962. Compared to the standard Comanche it was 4 mph faster.

For the 1963 model, aircraft s/n 24-3286 registration N8040P and s/n 24-3285 registration N8141P were used as the show aircraft.

Inside the Experimental building at Lock Haven showing in the background the experimental fuel injected Comanche s/n 24-2563 registration N8250P and both Comanche 400 prototypes s/n 26-1 registration N8380P and s/n 26-2 registration N7511P. (Piper Aviation Museum)

The experimental fuel injected PA-24-250 s/n 24-2563 registration N8250P with engineering staff at Lock Haven. (Piper Aircraft Corporation)

The experimental PA-24-260 Comanche s/n 24-3642 registration N8383P. (Piper Aircraft Corporation)

PA-24 SPECIFICATION & PERFORMANCE

SPECIFICATION	24-180	24-250	24-260
Engine	180 hp Lycoming O-360-A1A	250 hp Lycoming O-540-A1A5, IO-540-C1B5	260 hp Lycoming O-540-E4A5, IO-540-D4A5
Engine TBO (hrs)			
No of seats	4	4	4
Wing Span (ft/ins)	36/0	36/0	36/0
Length (ft/ins)	24/8	24/11	25/3.5
Height (ft/ins)	7/4	7/4	7/4
Useable fuel capacity (US gal)	60	60, 90 optional	60, 90 optional
Gross weight (lbs)	2550	2800	2900
Empty weight (lbs)	1455-1475	1600	1628
Useful load (lbs)	1075-1095	1200	1172
Propeller	Hartzell 2-blade	Hartzell 2-blade	Hartzell 2-blade
Floats available		Edo 2700	
PERFORMANCE			
Max speed	167 mph	190 mph	194 mph
Cruise speed	160 mph @ 75% 134 mph @ 55%	181 mph @ 75% 161 mph @ 55%	182 mph @ 75% 163 mph @ 55%
Efficiency (gph)	10 @ 75%	14 @ 75%	14 @ 75%
Stall speed - flaps / gear down	61 mph	61 mph	61 mph
Climb @ sea level (fpm)	910	1350-1400	1370
Range with reserves	900 sm @ 75% 1100 sm @ 55%	750 sm @ 75% 1100 sm @ 55%	728 sm @ 75% 800 sm @ 55%
Range with optional fuel reserves		1100 sm @ 75% 1650 sm @ 55%	1120 sm @ 75% 1265 sm @ 55%
Service ceiling (ft)	18,500	20,000	20,000
Take off (Ground run)(ft)	750	750	760
Take off (over 50ft obst)(ft)	2240	1650	1400
Landing (Ground roll)(ft)	600	650	655
Landing (over 50ft obst)(ft)	1025	1280	1290

In March 1964 aircraft s/n 24-3642 registration N8383P was fitted with a 260 hp Lycoming O-540-E4A5 engine to become the test vehicle for a new version of the Comanche. It first flew on the 20th. Later in May the injected IO-540-D4A5 engine was fitted and flew on the 25th. Approval for this version was granted on the 19th of June. The new model was the PA-24-260 and entered production in the summer of 1964, commencing with s/n 24-4000 registration N8499P (which changed serial number from 24-3688) completed on the 11th of August. The 260 had a redesigned interior, double paned windows and double sound proofing, new seats, new high capacity fresh air system, improved cabin heating, single fork gear, re-arranged full IFR instrumentation and a new electric trim.

Between 1958 and 1964 the 180 hp accounted for 30% of the Comanche sales, the majority being the 250 hp version. Production of the 180 hp and 250 hp versions stopped in May 1964 when replaced by the 260 hp version.

In 1965 the Comanche B was introduced, differing from the previous model in having optional fifth and sixth seats available where the baggage compartment used to be and extra cabin windows. The test aircraft was s/n 24-4247 registration N8794P converted on the 12th of March. First production aircraft was s/n 24-4300 registration N8845P. It had new soundproofing and increased useful load and was available in one of two operational groups, Custom or Sportsman.

In 1966 Piper contracted Lock Haven AirMotive to put a twisted wing onto the Comanche to see if improved stall characteristics could be achieved. Aircraft N8499P was used and first flew on the 29th of January 1966. The tests were inconclusive.

In 1966 Sheila Scott circled the world in Comanche s/n 24-4346 registration G-ATOY, named Myth Too, claiming several records.

PA-24 SPECIFICATION & PERFORMANCE

SPECIFICATION	24-260 'B'	24-260 'C'	24-260 'Turbo C'
Engine	260 hp Lycoming O-540-E4A5	260 hp Lycoming IO-540-E4A5	260 hp Lycoming IO-540-R1A5
Engine TBO (hrs)	1200	1200, 2000 (1971-72)	2000
No of seats	6	6	6
Wing Span (ft/ins)	36/0	36/0	36/0
Length (ft/ins)	25/3.5	25/8	25/8
Height (ft/ins)	7/4	7/4	7/4
Useable fuel capacity (US gal)	60, 90 optional	60, 90 optional	90
Gross weight (lbs)	3100	3200	3200
Empty weight (lbs)	1728	1773	1810
Useful load (lbs)	1372	1427	1390
Propeller	Hartzell 2-blade	Hartzell 2-blade	Hartzell 2-blade
Floats available			
PERFORMANCE			
Max speed	194 mph	195 mph	242 mph
Cruise speed	182 mph @ 75% 163 mph @ 55%	185 mph @ 75% 166 mph @ 55%	227 mph @ 75%
Efficiency (gph)	14.1 @ 75% 12.7 @ 65%	14.1 @ 75% 12.7 @ 65%	15.2 @ 75% 12.1 @ 55%
Stall speed - flaps / gear down	61 mph	61 mph	61 mph
Climb @ sea level (fpm)	1370	1320	1320
Range with reserves	722 sm @ 75% 775 sm @ 65%	735 sm @ 75% 800 sm @ 65%	1150 sm @ 75% 1290 sm @ 55%
Range with optional fuel with reserves	1108 sm @ 75% 1190 sm @ 65%	1130 sm @ 75% 1225 sm @ 65%	
Service ceiling (ft)	20,000	19,500	25,000
Take off (Ground run)(ft)	760	820	820
Take off (over 50ft obst)(ft)	1400	1400	1400
Landing (Ground roll)(ft)	655	690	690
Landing (over 50ft obst)(ft)	1290	1320	1320

In 1967 a single aircraft with the designation PA-24-300 appeared with a 300 hp Lycoming IO-540-L1A5 engine in a special cowling, this was s/n 24-6000 registration N9300P. This had the Comanche 400 fuselage with 6 seats, the -400 main gear and the Twin Comanche 200 tail and wings. It first flew on the 21st of April 1967, but there was not enough of an increase in performance to replace the 260 model. No production of this model took place.

For the 1969 model, the Comanche C had an increase in gross weight, new instrument panel, new reclining seats, optional wing tip fuel tanks, extended propshaft, 'Tiger Shark' cowl and fuel injection engine, the 260 Lycoming I0-540-EA45. The test aircraft was s/n 24-4783 registration N9283P converted from a Comanche 'B' in March 1968. Also converted was s/n 24-4661 registration N9172P. The first production 'C' was s/n 24-4804 registration N9308P completed on the 23rd of January 1969. Volume production started in April 1969 and it was launched on the 2nd of June.

On the 1st of May 1970, Piper introduced the Turbo Comanche C with the 260 hp Lycoming IO-540-R1A5 engine. The test aircraft N9308P first flew on the 3rd of March 1969 with the turbocharged engine. The first production aircraft s/n 24-4904 registration N9400P was completed on the 18th of September 1969. This version was approved on the 21st November.

No more Comanche aircraft were produced at Lock Haven after the June 1972 flood. The last built was s/n 24-5028 registration N9510P completed on the 7th of June 1972.

The PA-24-260 Comanche B test aircraft s/n 24-4247 registration N8794P. (Piper Aircraft Corporation)

Sheila Scott with PA-24-260 Myth Too s/n 24-4346 registration G-ATOY at Lock Haven.
Max Conrad's PA-24 s/n 24-695 registration N110LF is behind. (Piper Aviation Museum)

The PA-24-260 Comanche C test aircraft s/n 24-4783 registration N9283P. Note non standard nose.
(Piper Aviation Museum)

PA-24-260 Turbo Comanche C s/n 24-4804 registration N9308P. (Piper Aircraft Corporation)

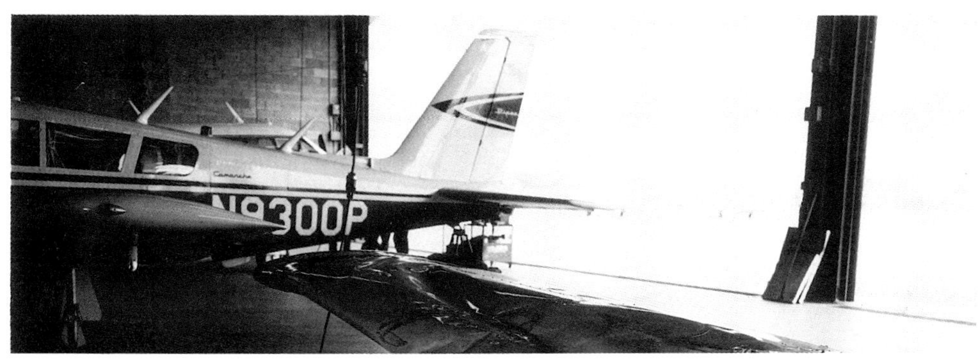

PA-24-300 Comanche s/n 24-6000 registration N9300P at Lock Haven. (Piper Aircraft Corporation)

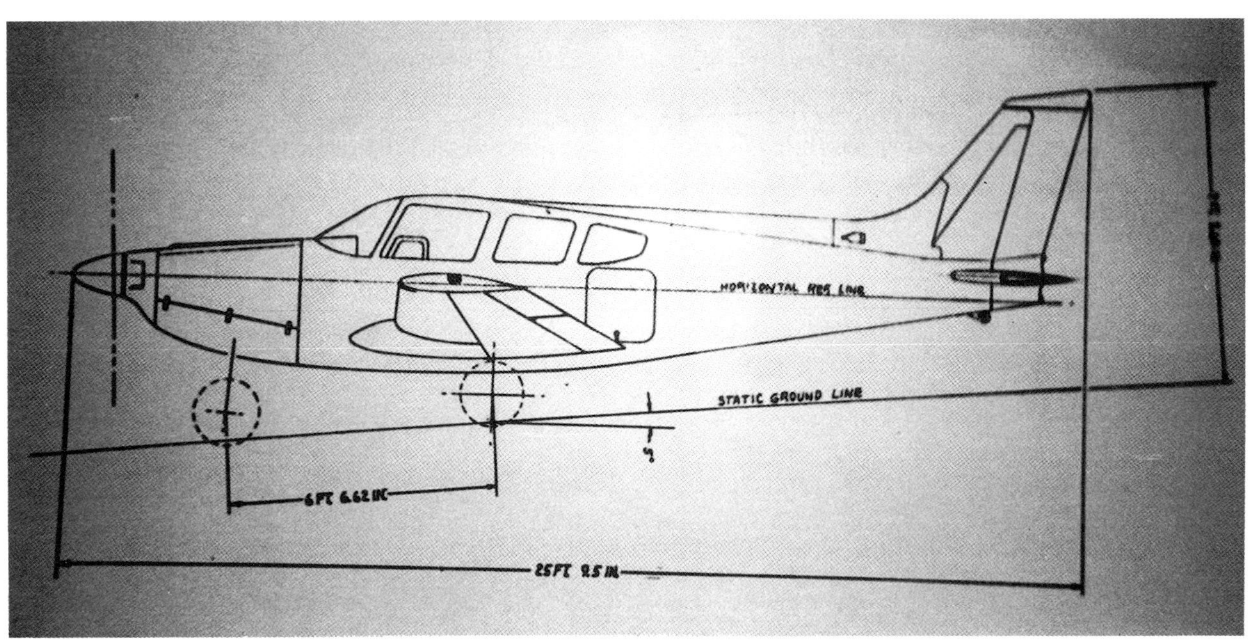

Drawing of the proposed PA-24 Comanche to be launched with the Arapaho. (Piper Aircraft Corporation)

PA-24 SPECIFICATION & PERFORMANCE

SPECIFICATION	24-300
Engine	300 hp Lycoming IO-540-L1A5
Engine TBO (hrs)	
No of seats	6
Wing Span (ft/ins)	35/10
Length (ft/ins)	24/10.5
Height (ft/ins)	7/10.5
Useable fuel capacity (US gal)	
Gross weight (lbs)	3400
Empty weight (lbs)	1700
Useful load (lbs)	1700
Propeller	
Floats available	
PERFORMANCE	
Max speed	204 mph
Cruise speed	184 mph @ 75%
Efficiency (gph)	
Stall speed - flaps / gear down	
Climb @ sea level (fpm)	
Range with reserves	
Service ceiling (ft)	
Take off (Ground run)(ft)	
Take off (over 50ft obst)(ft)	
Landing (Ground roll)(ft)	
Landing (over 50ft obst)(ft)	

In late 1972 Piper started to develop an improved Comanche which was to be common with the PA-40 Arapaho with longer landing gear legs (1.5 inches longer), larger windows, one piece windshield, larger vertical tail fairing, revised instrument panel and revised stabilator trim system. The engine was to be the 260 hp Lycoming IO-540-N1A5. In early 1973 Lock Haven Engineering obtained a flood damaged fuselage s/n 24-5039 for the development. It was to be launched with the PA-40 Arapaho for the 1974 model year. This updated Comanche would have been prohibitively expensive in relation to the Cherokee Arrow, hence a very restricted market which resulted in little justification to proceed with certification. The project was cancelled.

At the same time Piper tested stabilizer tip balance weights on the Comanche which increased maximum permissible speed for the 250 and 260 hp models. Aircraft s/n 24-5028 registration N9510P flew in September 1972 and aircraft s/n 24-4963 registration N9455P between February and May 1973. Piper received approval for this from the FAA.

At the end of 1972 Piper carried out a preliminary study on a pressurised Comanche designated the PA-24-350P. This was to have a pressurized PA-24-260 fuselage, a 350 hp Lycoming TIO-540 engine, -400 wings and a new entrance door similar to the PA-41P. This was not proceeded with.

Like many other aircraft manufacturers Piper tested competitive models to compare flight characteristics, sound levels, etc. to their own models. The following models were tested at Lock Haven in the 1960s in order to compare with the Comanche:- Beechcraft K35 Bonanza registration N6009E in February 1960, Cessna 210 registration N7444E in May 1960, Navion G registration N2407T in September 1962, Cessna 182E registration N2852Y in October 1962, Beechcraft S35 registration N7972K in November 1964, Mooney 20C registration N78864 in November 1964, Cessna 210D registration N3850Y in November 1964 and Mooney 20E registration N6968U in March 1966.

PA-24-400 COMANCHE

In 1959 Piper initiated design of the Comanche 400. A 380 hp Lycoming IO-720 engine was installed in Comanche s/n 24-357 registration N5316P. This first flew on the 22nd of February 1960. Later, in 1961, a prototype and a service test aircraft were built with the designation PA-24-380 with the larger Aztec tail (needed because of the extra horse-power), longer modified engine cowl and a Hartzell three-blade propeller. The prototype was s/n 26-1 registration N8380P which first flew on the 7th of March with the refurbished engine from N5316P and the service test was s/n 26-2 registration N7511P which was completed on the 2nd of June and first flew on the 8th. These two aircraft used standard Comanche airframes but each were powered by a 380 hp Lycoming IO-720-A1A engine. Unfortunately N8380P was damaged in a forced landing on the 11th of July 1962 with engine problems and was scrapped. FAA certification was granted on the 27th of December 1963.

Piper announced the Comanche 400 on the 16th of March 1964 as the worlds fastest single engine production aircraft. It was available at a list price of $28,750 with one of three operational packages: Custom, Sportsman, Professional. Production commenced in mid 1963 as the PA-24-400 powered by the 400 hp Lycoming IO-720-A1A. The first production aircraft s/n 26-3 registration N8400P was completed on the 15th of August. Production ended with s/n 26-148 registration N8629P completed on the 11th of November.

PA-24-400 PRODUCTION DETAILS

Model Year	Serial Number Range From	To	Type	Total	Comments
Experimental	24-357		380	0	
Prototype	26-1		380	1	
Service test	26-2		380	1	
1964	26-3	26-148	400	146	

The experimental aircraft 24-357 has been included in the PA-24 manufactured total.
Total manufactured 148 (All built at Lock Haven)

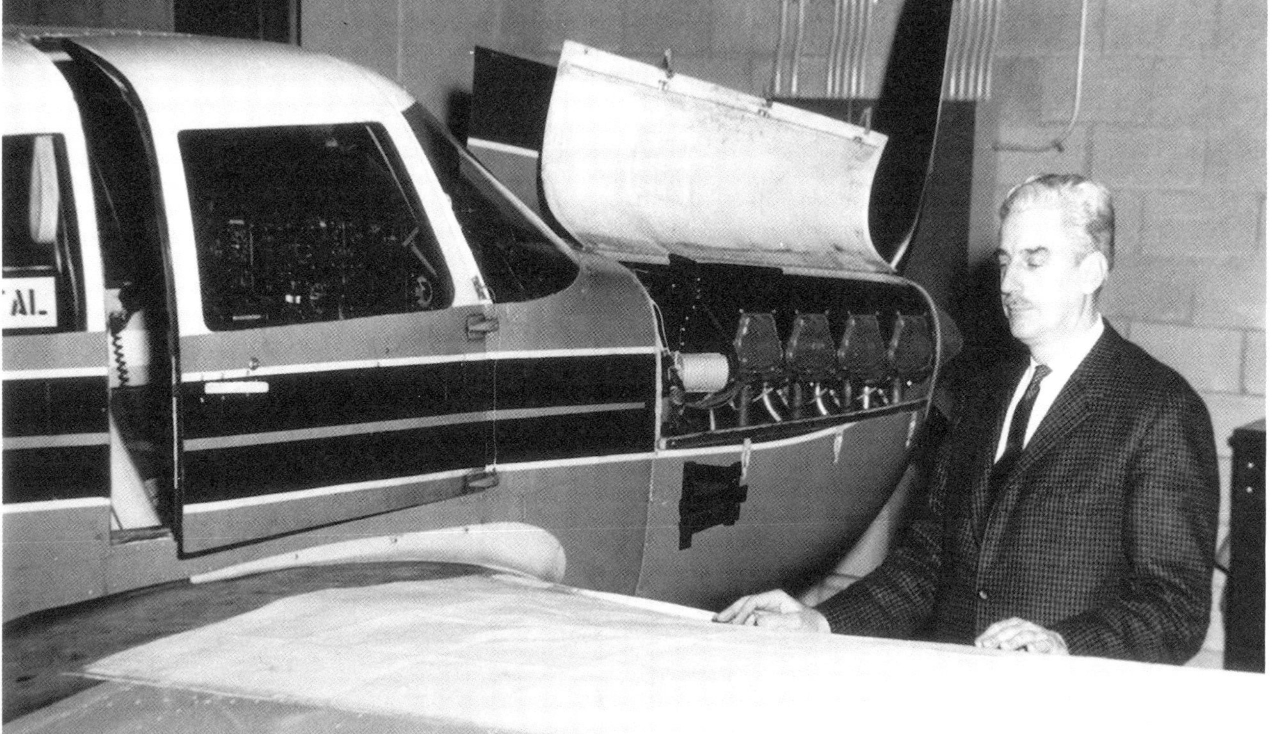

PA-24-380 s/n 26-2 registration N7511P with W. Jamouneau at Lock Haven. (Piper Aircraft Corporation)

The first production PA-24-400 Comanche s/n 26-3 registration N8400P. (Piper Aircraft Corporation)

PA-24-600 Turbine Comanche s/n 26-4 registration N8401P. (via J. Taylor)

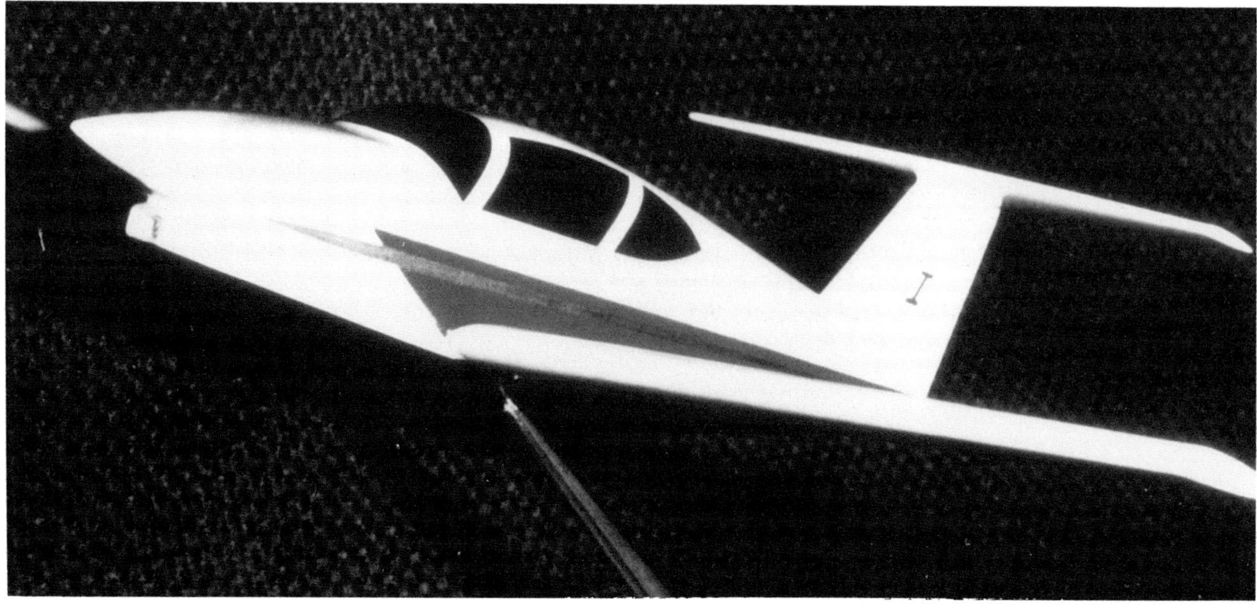

Model of the ACT-1. (J. Bryerton)

PA-24-400 SPECIFICATION & PERFORMANCE

SPECIFICATION	24-400
Engine	400 hp Lycoming IO-720-A1A
Engine TBO (hrs)	
No of seats	4
Wing Span (ft/ins)	36/0
Length (ft/ins)	25/8
Height (ft/ins)	7/10
Useable fuel capacity (US gal)	130
Gross weight (lbs)	3600
Empty weight (lbs)	2110
Useful load (lbs)	1590
Propeller	Hartzell 3-blade
Floats available	
PERFORMANCE	
Max speed	223 mph
Cruise speed	213 mph @ 65% 195 mph @ 45%
Efficiency (gph)	
Stall speed - flaps / gear down	68 mph
Climb @ sea level (fpm)	1600
Range with reserves	958 sm @ 65% 1700 sm @ 45%
Service ceiling (ft)	19,500
Take off (Ground run)(ft)	980
Take off (over 50ft obst)(ft)	1500
Landing (Ground roll)(ft)	1180
Landing (over 50ft obst)(ft)	1820

Many aircraft were unsold at the end of 1964 and they were re-certified in 1965 and then sold. These were s/n 26-97, 99, 100, 101, 102, 103, 104, 105, 107, 108, 110, 111, 112, 113, 114, 115, 117, 118, 119, 122 and 123.

During 1968, AiResearch of Phoenix, Arizona installed a 605 shp AiResearch TPE-331 turboprop engine in Comanche s/n 26-4 registration N8401P and used it as a flying test-bed. On the 31st of May this Comanche 600 attained a height of 42,560 feet, a class c-1c group 11 record.

ACT

The ACT design was to be the ultimate single engined aircraft, drawn up by Lock Haven Engineering in 1972. This Advanced Concept Testbed had a high aspect ratio wing, spoilers, large single air in-take and a T-tail. The experimental ACT-1 aircraft was to use a Comanche airframe, still with low tail with a 260 hp Lycoming IO-540-D4A5 engine with Fowler flaps and spoilers. An SSSA (Separate Surface Stability Augmentation) was also proposed but was not to be installed on the first experimental aircraft. This project was never accepted by Piper senior management.

PA-25 PAWNEE

Up to 1949, aircraft used for agricultural purposes had frequently been converted from surplus military types, but they were not as safe or efficient as they should have been.

In August 1949, Fred Weick started to design a new agricultural aircraft at Texas A & M College, named AG-1. The AG-1, registration N222, with a 225 hp Continental E-225 engine first flew on 1st December 1950. It crashed during a demonstration at Lubbock, Texas in June 1953. George Wing purchased the remains of the AG-1 and set up the Transland Company in Torrance, California to manufacture a larger version, the AG-2. This was powered by a 600 hp Pratt & Whitney R-1340 engine and had a much higher gross weight in excess of 7000 pounds.

In the early 1950s the only aircraft being built for agricultural purposes was the PA-18A Super Cub, but this was a modification of an existing aircraft. In July 1953, Mr. Piper visited Fred Weick at Texas A & M to ask him to consult for Piper to design, build and test a distributor for dust and seeds for the PA-18A. A few weeks later, Piper sponsored the Texas A & M Research Centre to develop a new agricultural aircraft. It was to be similar to the AG-1 but smaller, and instead of being mainly made of aluminium alloys it was to have steel tube fuselage and fabric covering. Another Piper requirement was that it be built with as many standard PA-18A and PA-22 components as possible without compromising the design. The resulting aircraft was the Texas AG-3, with registration N888B, with a 135 hp Lycoming O-290 engine. It was a single-seat low-wing design with a US35B airfoil and a tail-down undercarriage. The wings were braced to the fuselage with struts. The hopper, made of fibreglass and plastic with 800 pound capacity, situated in front of the pilot who sat in a big 'Apache' type seat and the cockpit, which was full of safety features, was situated high in the fuselage to give maximum visibility. This first flew in November 1954.

Following satisfactory flight tests, Piper invited Fred Weick to join them in November 1956, and formed the new Piper development centre at Vero Beach, Florida in April 1957. The design was given the Piper number PA-25, the prototype the s/n 25-01 and it was called the Pawnee. It was refitted with a 150 hp Lycoming O-320-A1A engine. Two pre-production aircraft were produced at Vero Beach in 1957, these were s/n 25-1 and 25-2 with registrations N9100D and N9101D respectively. FAA approval was granted on the 6th of January 1959 (2A8 - normal) and on the 20th of May 1959 (2A10 - restricted). Production commenced at Lock Haven in early 1959 with s/n 25-3 registration N6000Z completed on the 21st of May. The first five production aircraft were delivered in August. The Pawnee cost $8,995. The first aircraft were fitted with spray units only. The duster unit was tested on aircraft s/n 25-124 registration N6107Z in February. The first production duster was s/n 25-247 registration N6209Z completed on the 26th of April.

In 1961 Piper experimented with a 235 hp Lycoming engine in a Pawnee at the Vero Beach Development Centre. The definitive Pawnee 235 prototype appeared in 1962 with s/n 25-02 registration N74829, fitted with a 235 hp Lycoming O-540-B2B5 engine. FAA approval for the PA-25-235 was granted on the 14th of March 1962 (restricted) and on the 12th of October 1962 (normal). Production of this variant started at Lock Haven with s/n 25-2000 registration 4X-APA completed on the 16th of March 1962. Changes for the 1962 model for both the 150 hp and 235 hp were new double tail-brace wires, new swept-back leading edge wing root, new eye-brow cool air vent above the windshield and a side exhaust. The 1962 show aircraft was s/n 25-601 registration N6451Z. Piper tested a new bottom cowl on aircraft s/n 25-2165 registration N6697Z on the 15th of August 1962, but this was not proceeded with. Production of the 150 hp version continued until September 1963.

As was normal, updated versions appeared. In September 1964, the Pawnee B appeared, the test aircraft was s/n 25-2711 registration N6966Z and production commenced with s/n 25-2986 registration HK-1173X completed on the 25th of August. This version was fitted with a larger hopper, improved dispersal gear, improved ventilation, double tail braces and a new propeller.

During 1965 Piper changed the nose cowl landing light from s/n 25-3436 onwards.

The 1967 model did not appear until the 2nd of January of that year, this was the Pawnee C, with oleo shock-absorbers, better cockpit comfort and ventilation, removable fuselage rear decking, improved oil cooler and alternator. The test aircraft was s/n 25-4068 registration N4437Y converted from a model 'B' and the first production aircraft was s/n 25-4172 registration N4523Y completed on the 16th of January 1967. With standard equipment it was priced at $19,990.

AG-1 registration N222. (Aerospace Publishing)

AG-3 registration N888B with F. Weick. (via F. Weick)

Aerial view of the Piper factory at Vero Beach in the early 1960s. (Piper Aircraft Corporation)

The prototype PA-25 Pawnee s/n 25-1 registration N9100D at Vero Beach. (via W.K. Giles)

The second prototype PA-25 Pawnee s/n 25-2 registration N9101D. (Piper Aircraft Corporation)

The first five PA-25 Pawnees on delivery at Lock Haven. At the front is PA-25 s/n 25-3 registration N6000Z. (Piper Aircraft Corporation)

The prototype PA-25-235 Pawnee s/n 25-02 registration N74829. (Piper Aircraft Corporation)

The PA-25-235 Pawnee B test aircraft s/n 25-2711 registration N6966Z at Vero Beach. (Piper Aircraft Corporation)

PA-25-235 Pawnee B s/n 25-3959 registration OH-PIG on skis. (Piper Aircraft Corporation)

PA-25 PRODUCTION DETAILS

Model / Fiscal Year	Serial Number Range From	To	Type	Total	Comments
Experimental	25-01		AG-3	1	Built Texas A&M College
Prototypes	25-1	25-2	'150'	2	Built Vero Beach
1959	25-3	25-97	'150'	34	
1960	25-98	25-443	'150'	407	
1961	25-444	25-655	'150'	212	
1962	25-656	25-717	'150'	62	
Prototype	25 02		235	1	Built Vero Beach
1962	25-2000	25-2195	235	196	
1963	25-718	25-731	'150'	14	
1963	25-2196	25-2532	235	337	
1964	25-2533	25-2985	235	453	
1964	25-2986	25-3016	235 'B'	31	
1965	25-3017	25-3658	235 'B'	642	
1966	25-3659	25-4171	235 'B'	513	
1967	25-4172	25-4435	235 'C'	264	
1968	25-4436	25-4452	235 'C'	17	
1968	25-4453	25-4793	235 'C', 260 'C'	341	
1969	25-4794	25-5149	235 'C', 260 'C'	356	
1970	25-5150	25-5289	235 'C', 260 'C'	140	
1971	25-5290	25-5412	235 'C', 260 'C'	123	
1972	25-5413	25-5498	235 'C', 260 'C'	86	
-	25-5499	25-5521	235 'C', 260 'C'		Not completed, see Appendix B
1973	25-7305522	25-7305554	235 'C', 260 'C'	33	
1974	25-7405555	25-7405572	235 'C', 260 'C'	18	
1974	25-7405573	25-7405821	235 'D', 260 'D'	249	
1975	25-7556001	25-7556233	235 'D', 260 'D'	233	
1976	25-7656001	25-7656122 *	235 'D', 260 'D'	120	
1977	25-7756001	25-7756095 *	235 'D'	93	
1978	25-7856001	25-7856072	235 'D'	72	
1979	25-7956001	25-7956042	235 'D'	42	
1980	25-8056001	25-8056051	235	51	
1981	25-8156001	25-8156024	235	24	

A total of 4 aircraft in the batches marked * were not completed. See table below.
Total manufactured 5167 (All built at Lock Haven unless stated otherwise)

PA-25 SERIAL NUMBER CHANGES

Model	Old Serial Number	New Serial Number	New Model (if different)
PA-25	25-7656092	Kit not completed	
PA-25	25-7656093	Kit not completed	
PA-25	25-7756025	Kit not completed	
PA-25	25-7756027	Kit not completed	

PA-25 SPECIFICATION & PERFORMANCE

SPECIFICATION	AG-1	AG-3
Engine	225 hp Continental E-225	135 hp Lycoming O-290
Engine TBO (hrs)		
No of seats	1	1
Wing Span (ft/ins)	39/10	36/2
Length (ft/ins)	29/8	23/7
Height (ft/ins)	8/7	6/10
Useable fuel capacity (US gal)	48	40
Gross weight (lbs)	3400	2300
Empty weight (lbs)	1900	1035
Useful load (lbs)	1500	1265
Propeller		
Hopper Load (lbs)		800
Hopper capacity (gals / cu.ft)		
PERFORMANCE		
Max speed	115 mph	124 mph
Cruise speed	100 mph	
Efficiency (gph)	12 @ 75%	
Stall speed - flaps / gear down	45 mph	
Climb @ sea level (fpm)	600	
Range with reserves	400 sm	
Service ceiling (ft)	12,000	
Take off (Ground run)(ft)		
Take off (over 50ft obst)(ft)	1300	920
Landing (Ground roll)(ft)		
Landing (over 50ft obst)(ft)		

On the 23rd of October 1967, Piper introduced the alternative 260 hp Lycoming O-540-E engine with a controllable pitch propeller to produce the PA-25-260. The 260 hp Lycoming engine was installed in N4437Y and first flew at Vero Beach on the 23rd November 1966. FAA approval was granted on the 19th April 1967 for both normal and restricted categories. Also available with the 260 hp engine was a constant speed propeller. This was tested on N4437Y in August and September. The 260 hp engine could be fitted to the Pawnee from s/n 25-4415 onwards, but the first production aircraft was s/n 25-4453 registration N4716Y completed on the 27th of October. With standard equipment it was priced at $20,700.

A further update, the Pawnee D, appeared in early 1974. The main enhancement was moving the fuel tank from the fuselage to the wing. The test aircraft s/n 25-7305529 registration N8925L first flew with the wing tank installation on the 13th of July 1973 at Lock Haven. A second aircraft was converted by Engineering and this was s/n 25-7405573 registration N54000 which first flew on the 27th of November. The first production aircraft was s/n 25-7405574 registration N6837L completed on the 18th of March 1974.

Piper tested a new rudder and trim on aircraft s/n 25-7556188 registration N9864P in October 1975. This was not proceeded with.

Piper revised the fuselage top and side panels and fitted plastic front lift strut fairings on aircraft s/n 25-7656061 registration N82306 at Lock Haven in April 1976. These changes were not put on production aircraft.

For the 1977 model year and beyond, the 260 hp model was only available on special request. The flaps and ailerons were changed to metal at the end of 1977 from s/n 25-7856005 onwards. These were first tested on aircraft s/n 25-7756039 registration N82508 on the 25th of August 1977. For the final model year, 1981, the letter 'D' was dropped, the type reverting simply to the Pawnee 235.

The final production aircraft s/n 25-8156024 registration N91070 was completed at Lock Haven on the 22nd of March 1981. Since introduction of the 260 hp version in 1967, just over one third of the Pawnees sold had this engine version.

The PA-25-235 Pawnee C test aircraft s/n 25-4068 registration N4437Y at Vero Beach. (Piper Aircraft Corporation)

PA-25-260 Pawnee s/n 25-5181 registration HI-188 on delivery at Baltimore. Note damaged propeller. (P.R. Keating)

The PA-25-235 Pawnee D test aircraft s/n 25-7305529 registration N8925L at Lock Haven. (Piper Aircraft Corporation)

PA-25 SPECIFICATION & PERFORMANCE

SPECIFICATION	25	25-235	25-235 'B'
Engine	150 hp Lycoming O-320-A1A	235 hp Lycoming O-540-B2B5	235 hp Lycoming O-540-B2B5
Engine TBO (hrs)	1200	1200	1200
No of seats	1	1	1
Wing Span (ft/ins)	36/2.5	36/3	36/3
Length (ft/ins)	24/0	24/8	24/8
Height (ft/ins)	6/9.5	7/3	7/3
Useable fuel capacity (US gal)	38.5	38.5	38.5
Gross weight (lbs)	2300	2900	2900
Empty weight (lbs)	1220	1420 (no equip) 1479 (dust) 1488 (spray)	1479 (dust) 1488 (spray)
Useful load (lbs)	1080	1480 (no equip) 1421 (dust) 1412 (spray)	1421 (dust) 1412 (spray)
Propeller	Sensenich 2-blade	McCauley 2-blade	McCauley 2-blade
Hopper Load (lbs)	800	1200	1200
Hopper capacity (gals / cu.ft)		145/20	150/21
PERFORMANCE			
Max speed	113 mph	110 mph (dust) 117 mph (spray)	110 mph (dust) 117 mph (spray)
Cruise speed	95 mph	100 mph (dust) 105 mph (spray)	100 mph (dust) 105 mph (spray)
Efficiency (gph)	9 @ 75%	14 @ 75%	14 @ 75%
Stall speed - flaps / gear down	45 mph	61 mph	61 mph
Climb @ sea level (fpm)	510	630	500 (dust) 630 (spray)
Range with reserves	440 sm	285 sm (dust) 300 sm (spray)	285 sm (dust) 300 sm (spray) @ 75%
Service ceiling (ft)	10,000	13,000	13,000
Take off (Ground run)(ft)	695	800	956 (dust) 800 (spray)
Take off (over 50ft obst)(ft)	1375	1370	1470 (dust) 1370 (spray)
Landing (Ground roll)(ft)	440	850	850
Landing (over 50ft obst)(ft)			

A number of Pawnee aircraft have been modified into two seat trainers. One of these conversions was the Fledgling AP-1 from Aerophase Products Corporation, Eaton Rapids, Michigan, with the second pilot seat in the hopper area. They brought the aircraft s/n 25-66 registration N6059Z to Lock Haven in October 1971 to try to get Piper to manufacture it and / or produce a conversion kit. Another one, but a side-by-side conversion was developed by Agricultural Aviation Pty Ltd, Brisbane, Queensland, Australia. The fuselage was widened by 10 inches, new wider windscreen and bulged windows in the doors, all flying controls duplicated. Aircraft s/n 25-2824 registration VH-PEG was converted in 1970. Another two seat conversion was s/n 25-2835 registration VH-SMR, this was given a new designation PA-25-235/A6. Chincul in Argentina also developed a two-seat Pawnee in 1985 (see Chapter 15).

The Gippsland GA-200 is a modified Pawnee to improve handling and performance, making changes to the tail. Aircraft s/n 25-3729 registration VH-BCE was modified in April 1991 and was given a new serial number 200-9101.

PA-25 SPECIFICATION & PERFORMANCE

SPECIFICATION	25-235 'C', 25-235 'D'	25-260 'C', 25-260 'D' fixed pitch prop	25-260 'C', 25-260 'D' constant speed prop
Engine	235 hp Lycoming O-540-B2B5	260 hp Lycoming O-540-E	260 hp Lycoming O-540-E
Engine TBO (hrs)	1200	1200	
No of seats	1	1	1
Wing Span (ft/ins)	36/3	36/3	36/3
Length (ft/ins)	24/8	24/8	24/8
Height (ft/ins)	7/3	7/3	7/3
Useable fuel capacity (US gal)	38.5	38.5	38.5
Gross weight (lbs)	2900	2900	2900
Empty weight (lbs)	1420 (no equip) 1479 (dust) 1488 (spray)	1472 (no equip) 1531 (dust) 1540 (spray)	1488 (no equip) 1547 (dust) 1556 (spray)
Useful load (lbs)	1480 (no equip) 1421 (dust) 1412 (spray)	1428 (no equip) 1369 (dust) 1360 (spray)	1412 (no equip) 1353 (dust) 1344 (spray)
Propeller	McCauley Fixed pitch 2-blade	McCauley or Hartzell Fixed pitch 2-blade	Hartzell Constant speed 2-blade
Hopper load (lbs)	1200	1200	1200
Hopper capacity (gals / cu.ft)	150/21	150/21	150/21
PERFORMANCE			
Max speed	124 mph (no equip) 110 mph (dust) 117 mph (spray)	128 mph (no equip) 113 mph (dust) 120 mph (spray)	128 mph (no equip) 113 mph (dust) 120 mph (spray)
Cruise speed	114 mph (no equip) 100 mph (dust) 105 mph (spray)	115 mph (no equip) 100 mph (dust) 106 mph (spray)	116 mph (no equip) 100 mph (dust) 106 mph (spray)
Efficiency (gph)	14 @ 75%	14.1 @ 75%	14.1 @ 75%
Stall speed - flaps / gear down	61 mph	61 mph	61 mph
Climb @ sea level (fpm)	700 (no equip) 500 (dust) 630 (spray)	755 (no equip) 555 (dust) 685 (spray)	775 (no equip) 575 (dust) 705 (spray)
Range with reserves	290 sm (no equip) 255 sm (dust) 270 sm (spray)	285 sm (no equip) 230 sm (dust) 265 sm (spray)	290 sm (no equip) 230 (dust) 265 sm (spray)
Service ceiling (ft)			
Take off (Ground run)(ft)	956 (dust) 785-800 (spray)	890 (dust) 740 (spray)	830 (dust) 680 (spray)
Take off (over 50ft obst)(ft)	1470 (dust) 1350-1370 (spray)	1420 (dust) 1270 (spray)	1370 (dust) 1220 (spray)
Landing (Ground roll)(ft)	850	850	850
Landing (over 50ft obst)(ft)			

Fledgling two-seat PA-25 Pawnee s/n 25-66 registration N6059Z. (Aerospace Publishing)

Gippsland GA-200 s/n 200-9101 registration VH-BCE at Innisall, Queensland.
Note this was previously PA-25 Pawnee s/n 25-3729. (P.R. Keating)

PA-26 COMANCHE

This was the drawing board design number for a higher powered version of the PA-24 Comanche. (See PA-24 section).

PA-27 AZTEC

This was the drawing board design number for the higher powered version of the PA-23 Apache, named the Aztec. (See PA-23 section).

6
THE CHEROKEE

The Cherokee is divided into six sections:

1) The first Cherokees were the 150, 160 and 180 hp versions, followed by the Archer II (and later Archer III) with tapered wings which replaced the 180 hp version.

2) The Cherokee 140 with the 150 hp engine initially with two seats, later with four seats.

3) The Warrior with tapered wings and 150 hp engine and Warrior II and III and Cadet with 160 hp engine.

4) The Cherokee 235 followed by the Dakota with tapered wings which replaced the 235 version and Turbo Dakota with 200 hp engine.

5) The retractable gear Cherokee Arrow and Arrow II, followed by the Arrow III and IV with tapered wings.

6) Lastly the PA-28R-300 trainer or T-35 Pillan.

PA-28 CHEROKEE

In the early 1950's Piper wanted a four seat, metal, low wing, single engined aircraft to replace the Tri-Pacer. In 1952, Piper proposed buying a Mooney design (later the Mooney 20), but Mooney wouldn't sell. Piper looked again at John Thorp's Sky Skooter but backed off probably because the Sky Skooter aircraft was tied up in law suits. In 1955 the project was revived. The Comanche was too expensive to fill the role and the Super Cub wasn't acceptable either. Piper looked at the Ercoupe, but decided not to buy it. In 1957 Piper decided to build its own aircraft, but at a new research / production centre outside Lock Haven. Vero Beach and Venice, both in Florida, had been visited by W. Piper Senior in late 1956 as possible venues for the new Piper development centre. Vero Beach was selected and Fred Weick joined Piper in April 1957 to head up the centre reporting to Howard 'Pug' Piper. In January 1957, Piper engaged Thorp to do the preliminary design study on the new aircraft (to be called the PA-28 Cherokee). Karl Bergey joined Piper in September 1957 and immediately started on the project. The Cherokee was a modern, all metal design, with a low-wing and wide-track tricycle gear. The overall structure had less than half the number of parts of the Comanche, which was being manufactured at Lock Haven. The experimental aircraft with a 150 hp Lycoming O-320-A2A engine s/n 28-01 registration N9315R first flew on the 10th of January 1960.

The prototype aircraft s/n 28-03 registration N2800W with a 160 Lycoming O-320-D2A engine was registered later in 1960. Certification 2A13 for the 160 hp version was gained on the 31st of October 1960. The first production model s/n 28-1 registration N5000W first flew on the 10th of February 1961.

The first Cherokee type available for delivery, in 1961, was the 160 hp version priced at $11,500. Certification of the 150 hp version was gained on 2nd of June 1961 and was available starting with s/n 28-70 priced at $10,900. They were made to four levels of equipment, standard, Custom, Super Custom or Autoflite.

In 1961 Piper created an Electronics Division at Vero Beach. Their first design was the AutoNav radio compass. In 1962 they developed the PTR-1 transceiver radio and the O-1 Omni navigation indicator. The division was closed down, as specialist manufacturers like King, Collins, Narco, etc. were able to develop more advanced products more quickly for a larger market.

In 1962 Piper improved the Cherokee to create the Cherokee B for the 1963 model year. Dynaflair wheel fairings were fitted, an alternator was standard and three different engines were now available, the 150, 160 and 180 horse power. Aircraft s/n 28-524 registration N5312W was also converted to a Cherokee B. The first production model 'B' was s/n 28-671 registration N7000W which went to the experimental shop in May 1962. In late 1961 N2800W had been fitted with a 180 hp Lycoming O-360-A2A engine and was used for certification testing. The 180 hp version was approved on the 3rd August. Piper announced the Cherokee B on the 15th of August 1962. The 180 hp standard version was priced at $12,900.

The experimental PA-28 Cherokee s/n 28-01 registration N9315R at Vero Beach. (via W.T. Piper Jr.)

The prototype PA-28 Cherokee s/n 28-03 registration N2800W. (via J. Taylor)

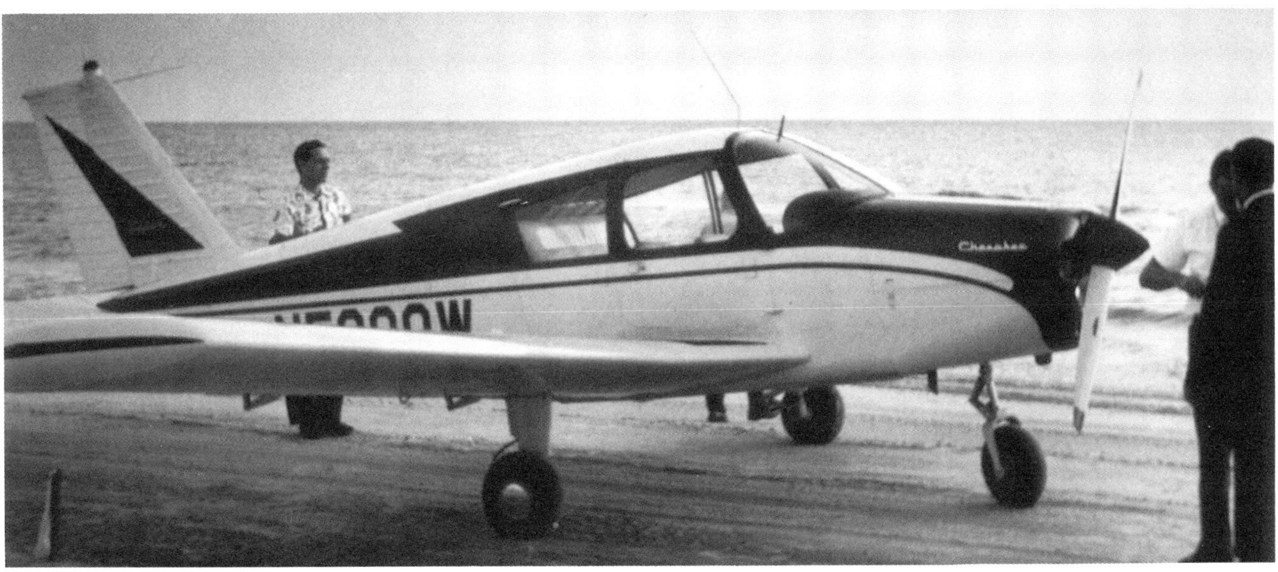

The first production PA-28-160 Cherokee s/n 28-1 registration N5000W on a beach at a Piper Distributors meeting. (Piper Aircraft Corporation)

PA-28S-160 Cherokee Seaplane s/n 28-102 registration N5093W. (Piper Aircraft Corporation)

PA-28-160 Cherokee B s/n 28-524 registration N5447W. (Piper aircraft Corporation)

PA-28 PRODUCTION DETAILS

Model / Fiscal Year	Serial Number Range From	To	Type	Total	Comments
Experimental	28-01		150	1	later 160
Prototype	28-03		160	1	later 180
1961	28-1	28-100	150, 160	100	
1962	28-101	28-820	150, 160	720	
1963	28-821	28-1440	150, 160, 180 'B'	620	
1964	28-1441	28-1760 & 28-1760A	150, 160, 180 'B'	321	
1964	28-1761	28-1891	150, 160, 180 'B'	131	
1965	28-1892	28-2792	150, 160, 180 'C'	901	
1966	28-2793	28-3674	150, 160, 180 'C'	882	
1967	28-3675	28-4377	150, 160, 180 'C'	703	
1968	28-4378	28-5279	180 'D'	902	
1969	28-5280	28-5499	180 'D'	220	
1970	28-5601	28-5859	180 'E'	259	
1971	28-7105001	28-7105234	180 'F'	234	
1972	28-7205001	28-7205318	180 'G'	318	
Prototype	28-E10		180 Challenger	1	
Prototype	28-E13		180 Challenger	1	
1973	28-7305001	28-7305601	180 Challenger	601	
1974	28-7405001	28-7405280	180 Archer	280	
1975	28-7505001	28-7505260*	180 Archer	259	
One aircraft in the batch marked * was not delivered, instead it was updated to the next year's model and given a new serial number. See table below. Total manufactured 7455 (All built at Vero Beach)					

SERIAL NUMBER CHANGES

Model	Old Serial Number	New Serial number	New Model (if different)
PA-28-180	28-7505143	28-7690001	PA-28-181

The Cherokee B was approved on Edo 2000 floats, designated PA-28S-160 and PA-28S-180 seaplane. The seaplane test aircraft were s/n 28-102 registration N5093W, a 160 hp version and s/n 28-1257 registration N7375W, a 180 hp version. They were certified on the 25th of February and the 10th of May 1963 respectively.

In early 1964 Sorensen Aircraft of Minnesota offered spray equipment to convert the Cherokee into an agricultural aircraft. Aircraft s/n 28-712 registration N7028W was used to develop this option.

The Cherokee B was developed into the Cherokee C in mid 1964. The test aircraft were s/n 28-1571 registration N7611W and s/n 28-1573 registration N7613W. The Cherokee C was available with three levels of equipment, Custom, Executive or Sportsman. The Cherokee C had a new interior, new instrument panel, increased baggage allowance, new step, new soundproofing, a new fibreglass engine cowl, new propeller spinner, new exhaust system and more rear seat leg room. The first production model 'C' was s/n 28-1761 registration N7762W.

The Cherokee C was approved on Edo 2000 floats, designated PA-28S-160 and PA-28S-180. A seaplane example of the Cherokee C was the N7375W converted from a Cherokee B.

In 1966 the time between overhauls (TBO) of the Lycoming engines was increased to 2000 hours.

PA-28 SPECIFICATION & PERFORMANCE

SPECIFICATION	28-150 & 28-150 'B'	28-160 & 28-160 'B'	28S-160 'B'
Engine	150 hp Lycoming O-320-A2B	160 hp Lycoming O-320-B2B	160 hp Lycoming O-320-B2B
Engine TBO (hrs)	1200	1200	1200
No of seats	4	4	4
Wing Span (ft/ins)	30/0	30/0	30/0
Length (ft/ins)	23/3.5	23/3.5	23/3.5
Height (ft/ins)	7/3.5	7/3.5	11/1
Useable fuel capacity (US gal)	48	48	48
Gross weight (lbs)	2150	2200	2140
Empty weight (lbs)	1205	1215	1370
Useful load (lbs)	945	985	780
Propeller	Sensenich	Sensenich	Sensenich
Floats available			Edo 2000
PERFORMANCE			
Max speed	136 mph	138 mph	126 mph
Cruise speed	123 mph @ 75% 105 mph @ 55%	125 mph @ 75% 115 mph @ 55%	117 mph
Efficiency (gph)	9 @ 75%	9.6 @ 75%	9
Stall speed - flaps / gear down	55 mph	56 mph	55 mph
Climb @ sea level (fpm)	660	690	600
Range with reserves	725 sm @ 75% 839 sm @ 55%	730 sm @ 75% 810 sm @ 55%	706 sm
Service ceiling (ft)	14,300	15,000	10,000
Take off (Ground run)(ft)	800	780	
Take off (over 50ft obst)(ft)	1700	1650	
Landing (Ground roll)(ft)	535	550	
Landing (over 50ft obst)(ft)	890	890	

In 1967 the Cherokee D was developed which had the third fuselage window (originally used for the Arrow), an elongated propeller spinner, improved instrument panel in preferred 'T' section layout and a 180 hp engine. The first model 'D' was s/n 28-4378 registration N4845L. Announced on the 1st of November 1967, deliveries started for the 1968 model year. By 1967 very few of the 150 and 160 hp versions were being sold, so Piper didn't offer these engines as options on the Cherokee D. Three hundred 150 hp and eight hundred and ten 160 hp Cherokees were sold between 1961 and 1967.

During 1967 Piper tested the Cherokee 180 in order to obtain spinning approval from the British CAA. Aircraft N7613W was used during June. Approval was not obtained.

Piper improved the Cherokee 180 each year between 1970 and 1972:

PA-28 IMPROVEMENTS

Model Year	Type	Improvements	Development / Show aircraft s/n	Registration	1st Production aircraft s/n	Registration
1970	180 'E'	Ventilation Instrument panel improved engine mount	28-5318 28-5417	N7860N N7978N	28-5601	N2385R
1971	180 'F'	Separate rear seats Fuel selector system	28-5663 28-5796	N4036R N4035R	28-7105001	N5147S
1972	180 'G'	Instrument panel	28-7105164 28-7105165	N2172T N2150T	28-7205001	N2151T

PA-28-180 Cherokee C s/n 28-1571 registration N7611W at Vero Beach. (Piper Aircraft Corporation)

PA-28-180 Cherokee D s/n 28-4378 registration N4845L. (Piper Aircraft Corporation)

1972 model PA-28-180 Cherokee s/n 28-7105164 registration N2172T. (Piper Aircraft Corporation)

PA-28 SPECIFICATION & PERFORMANCE

SPECIFICATION	28-180 'B'	28S-180 'B'	28-150 'C'
Engine	180 hp Lycoming O-360-A2A	180 hp Lycoming O-360-A2A	150 hp Lycoming O-320-E2A
Engine TBO (hrs)	1200	1200	1200 (64-65) 2000 (66 & later)
No of seats	4	4	4
Wing Span (ft/ins)	30/0	30/0	30/0
Length (ft/ins)	23/3.5	23/3.5	23/6
Height (ft/ins)	7/3.5	11/1	7/3.5
Useable fuel capacity (US gal)	48	48	48
Gross weight (lbs)	2400	2222	2150
Empty weight (lbs)	1225	1385	1250
Useful load (lbs)	1135	835	900
Propeller	Sensenich	Sensenich	Sensenich
Floats available		Edo 2000	
PERFORMANCE			
Max speed	150 mph	131 mph	141-144 mph
Cruise speed	141 mph @ 75%	122 mph	132-135 mph @ 75%
Efficiency (gph)	10 @ 75%	10	9 @ 75%
Stall speed - flaps / gear down	57 mph	56 mph	54 mph
Climb @ sea level (fpm)	720	640	690
Range with reserves	695 sm @ 75% 750 sm @ 55%	655 sm	725 sm @ 75% 800 sm @ 55%
Service ceiling (ft)	15,700	11,000	14,900
Take off (Ground run)(ft)	720		800
Take off (over 50ft obst)(ft)	1620		1700
Landing (Ground roll)(ft)	600		535
Landing (over 50ft obst)(ft)	1150		890

For the 1972 model year 'Piperaire' air conditioning was available. Aircraft s/n 28-5653 registration N180AC was used to certify this option in July 1971.

Between 1970 and 1972 Piper developed the 'stretched Cherokee'. The Cherokee Challenger had the five inch increase in fuselage length (as used in the Arrow II) between the front and rear seats, resulting in a roomier rear cabin. Other changes included a two foot increase in wing span (as used on the 235), a larger, all moving horizontal tailplane, a wider door, a higher gross weight (up 50 lbs), new seats and a padded instrument panel. A prototype s/n 28-E10 registration N4273T had been flying since 1971. A second prototype s/n 28-E13 registration N4373T first flew in 1972 and type approval was gained on 22nd of May 1972. The first production aircraft s/n 28-7305001 registration N15020 was completed in the summer of 1972 and deliveries began later that year. Price was $16,990.

During the 1960s Piper continued to lobby the US armed forces for them to use modified Piper production aircraft in various roles. In the early 1960s Piper did some initial design work on a modified PA-28 liaison aircraft with the engine placed in the middle of the fuselage to enable vastly improved visibility for the crew. This never left the drawing board.

For the 1974 model year the Cherokee Challenger was renamed the Cherokee Archer. This had restyled window lines, improved nose wheel steering, improved interior and adjustable front seats. The first production Cherokee Archer was s/n 28-7405001 registration N15264 completed in 1973.

Improvements for the 1975 model year included a new vertically adjustable seat and optional 'quietized' sound proofing.

In the field there are various conversions available including wing-tip modifications. An example of a tail-wheel and wing-tip modification is the Cherokee Chief 180TG, s/n 28-2660 registration N8430W.

PA-28 SPECIFICATION & PERFORMANCE

SPECIFICATION	28-160 'C'	28S-160 'C'	28-180 'C'
Engine	160 hp Lycoming O-320-D2A	160 hp Lycoming O-320-D2A	180 hp Lycoming O-360-A3A
Engine TBO (hrs)	1200 (64-65) 2000 (66 & 67)	1200 (64-65) 2000 (66 & 67)	1200 (64-65) 2000 (66 & 67)
No of seats	4	4	4
Wing Span (ft/ins)	30/0	30/0	30/0
Length (ft/ins)	23/6	23/6	23/6
Height (ft/ins)	7/3.5	11/1	7/3.5
Useable fuel capacity (US gal)	48	48	48
Gross weight (lbs)	2200	2140	2400
Empty weight (lbs)	1255	1375	1270
Useful load (lbs)	945	765	1130
Propeller	Sensenich	Sensenich	Sensenich
Floats available		Edo 2000	
PERFORMANCE			
Max speed	143-146 mph	128 mph	152 mph
Cruise speed	134-137 mph	119 mph	143 mph @ 75%
Efficiency (gph)	9 @ 75%	9	10 @ 75%
Stall speed - flaps / gear down	55 mph	55 mph	57 mph
Climb @ sea level (fpm)	730	630	750
Range with reserves	735 sm @ 75% 815 sm @ 55%	716 sm	725 sm @ 75% 760 sm @ 55%
Service ceiling (ft)	15,800	10,000	16,400
Take off (Ground run)(ft)	780		720
Take off (over 50ft obst)(ft)	1650		1620
Landing (Ground roll)(ft)	550		600
Landing (over 50ft obst)(ft)	890		1150

The experimental stretched PA-28-180 Cherokee s/n 28-E10 registration N4273T. (Piper Aircraft Corporation)

The second experimental stretched Cherokee, PA-28-180 Cherokee Challenger s/n 28-E11 registration N4373T. (Piper Aircraft Corporation)

The first production PA-28-180 Cherokee Archer s/n 28-7405001 registration N15264. (Piper Aircraft Corporation)

PA-28-180 sprayer s/n 28-712 registration N7028W. (Piper Pilot)

PA-28 SPECIFICATION & PERFORMANCE

SPECIFICATION	28S-180 'C'	28-180 'D'	28-180 Challenger
Engine	180 hp Lycoming O-360-A3A	180 hp Lycoming O-360-A3A	180 hp Lycoming O-360-A3A
Engine TBO (hrs)	1200 (64-65) 2000 (66 & 67)	2000	2000
No of seats	4	4	4
Wing Span (ft/ins)	30/0	30/0	32/0
Length (ft/ins)	23/6	23/6	24/0
Height (ft/ins)	11/1	7/3.5	7/10
Useable fuel capacity (US gal)	48	48	48
Gross weight (lbs)	2222	2400	2450
Empty weight (lbs)	1390	1300	1386
Useful load (lbs)	832	1100	1064
Propeller	Sensenich	Sensenich	Sensenich
Floats available	Edo 2000		
PERFORMANCE			
Max speed	133 mph	152 mph	148 mph
Cruise speed	124 mph	143 mph @ 75% 126 mph @ 60%	141 mph @ 75%
Efficiency (gph)	10	10 @ 75%	10 @ 75% 8.8 @ 55%
Stall speed - flaps / gear down	56 mph	56 mph	61 mph
Climb @ sea level (fpm)	670	750	725
Range with reserves	665 sm	725 sm @ 75% 760 sm @ 60%	686 sm @ 75%
Service ceiling (ft)	11,700	16,400	14,150
Take off (Ground run)(ft)		720	720
Take off (over 50ft obst)(ft)		1620	1625
Landing (Ground roll)(ft)		600	635
Landing (over 50ft obst)(ft)		1150	1185

Drawing of the proposed PA-28 modified liaison aircraft. (Piper Aviation Museum)

PA-28 SPECIFICATION & PERFORMANCE

SPECIFICATION	28-180 Archer	28-180 Archer Seaplane
Engine	180 hp Lycoming O-360-A4A	180 hp Lycoming O-360-A4A
Engine TBO (hrs)	2000	2000
No of seats	4	4
Wing Span (ft/ins)	32/0	32/0
Length (ft/ins)	24/0	24/0
Height (ft/ins)	7/10	
Useable fuel capacity (US gal)	48	48
Gross weight (lbs)	2450	2222
Empty weight (lbs)	1390-1395	1385
Useful load (lbs)	1055-1060	837
Propeller	Sensenich	Sensenich
Floats available		Edo 2000
PERFORMANCE		
Max speed	148 mph	
Cruise speed	141 mph @ 75%	
Efficiency (gph)	8.6 @ 75%	
Stall speed - flaps / gear down	61 mph	
Climb @ sea level (fpm)	725	640
Range with reserves	710 sm @ 75% 750 sm @ 55%	
Service ceiling (ft)	14,150	11,000
Take off (Ground run)(ft)	720	1450
Take off (over 50ft obst)(ft)	1625	
Landing (Ground roll)(ft)	635	
Landing (over 50ft obst)(ft)	1185	

PA-28-160 s/n 28-123 registration N5106W with tail wheel conversion. (R.W. Peperell)

PA-28-181

During 1975 Piper developed the PA-28-181 Cherokee Archer II. It was an Archer with the semi-tapered wing and tail of the Warrior, but structurally upgraded and hinged ailerons instead of aerodynamically balanced ones. It had a 3 mph increase in speed a 100 pound increase in gross weight over the Archer and a 180 hp Lycoming O-360-A4M engine. The prototype s/n 28-7690001 registration N33413 was converted from s/n 28-7505143 and first flew on the 28th of March 1975. The first production aircraft s/n 28-7690002 N4319X was registered in 1975. FAA type approval was granted on 8th of July 1975. It was priced at $23,170.

Since 1975 the Archer II has seen a series of minor improvements. For the 1977 model year it had new seats, new door latch, new ventilation and new panel. For the 1979 model year the name 'Cherokee' was dropped, becoming the Archer II. It had new, larger landing gear fairings which increased cruise speed and range. For the 1980 model year it received a new interior and quick change wheel fairings. Each year the exterior colour scheme changed.

In 1994 Piper developed the Archer III with Saratoga II HP type modifications. Aircraft s/n 2890196 registration N9181J had the new cowl fitted with circular inlets and first flew on the 25th of April. The production prototype was s/n 2890206 registration N92474 completed in June 1994. This had the new window line, new interior and panel. Production got underway with s/n 2890207 registration N92500 in September for the 1995 model year. Initially it was priced at $144,900.

The Archer III was in production at Vero Beach in December 1996.

The prototype PA-28-181 Cherokee Archer II s/n 28-7690001 registration N33413. (Piper Aircraft Corporation)

PA-28-181 PRODUCTION DETAILS

Model Year	Serial Number Range From	To	Type	Total	Comments
Prototype	28-7690001		Archer II	1	
1976	28-7690002	28-7690467	Archer II	466	
1977	28-7790001	28-7790607 *	Archer II	606	
1978	28-7890001	28-7890551	Archer II	551	
1979	28-7990001	28-7990594 *	Archer II	589	
1980	28-8090001	28-8090372	Archer II	372	
1981	28-8190001	28-8190318 *	Archer II	305	
1982	28-8290001	28-8290178 *	Archer II	169	
1983	28-8390001	28-8390090	Archer II	90	
1984	28-8490001	28-8490112	Archer II	112	
1985	28-8590001	28-8590092	Archer II	92	
1986	28-8690001	28-8690008	Archer II	8	
1986	28-8690010	28-8690011	Archer II	2	
1986	28-8690014	28-8690017	Archer II	4	
1986	28-8690019	28-8690062 *	Archer II	40	
1986	2890001	2890008	Archer II	8	
1986	2890010	2890021	Archer II	12	
1986	2890023	2890025	Archer II	3	
1987	28-8690009 & 28-8690012		Archer II	2	
1987	28-8690013 & 28-8690018		Archer II	2	
1987	2890009 & 2890022		Archer II	2	
1987	2890026	2890048	Archer II	25	
1988	2890049	2890099	Archer II	51	
1989	2890100	2890136	Archer II	37	
1989	2890140	2890147	Archer II	8	
1989	2890149	2890153	Archer II	5	
1990	2890137	2890139	Archer II	3	
1990	2890148 & 2890154		Archer II	2	
1990	2890168	2890169	Archer II	2	
1992	2890155	2890167	Archer II	13	
1992	2890170		Archer II	1	
1993	2890171	2890195	Archer II	25	
1994	2890196	2890205	Archer II	10	
1995	2890206	2890239 *	Archer III	26	
1995	2843001	2843020	Archer III	20	
1996	2843021	2843066	Archer III	46	
1997	2843067		Archer III		

A total of 40 aircraft in the batches marked * were not delivered, instead they were updated to the next year's model and given new serial numbers or not built. See table below.
Total manufactured 3710 (All built at Vero Beach)

PA-28-181 SERIAL NUMBER CHANGES

Model	Old Serial Number	New Serial Number	New model (if different)
PA-28-181	28-7790569	28-7921001	PA-28-201T
PA-28-181	28-7990590-594	28-8090002-006	
PA-28-181	28-8190191	28-8290052	
PA-28-181	28-8190244	28-8290036	
PA-28-181	28-8190258	28-8290028	
PA-28-181	28-8190260	28-8290033	
PA-28-181	28-8190265	28-8290017	
PA-28-181	28-8190266	28-8290018	
PA-28-181	28-8190273	28-8290034	
PA-28-181	28-8190284	28-8290019	
PA-28-181	28-8190303	28-8290030	
PA-28-181	28-8190309	28-8290029	
PA-28-181	28-8190314-316	Not built	
PA-28-181	28-8290103	28-8390073	
PA-28-181	28-8290117	28-8390075	
PA-28-181	28-8290118	28-8390020	
PA-28-181	28-8290128	28-8390035	
PA-28-181	28-8290142	28-8390018	
PA-28-181	28-8290150	28-8390019	
PA-28-181	28-8290159	28-8390017	
PA-28-181	28-8290164	28-8390074	
PA-28-181	28-8290167	28-8390036	
PA-28-181	28-8690057	2890001	
PA-28-181	28-8690058	2890002	
PA-28-181	28-8690059	2890003	
PA-28-181	28-8690060	2890004	
PA-28-181	2890232	2843001	
PA-28-181	2890233	2843002	
PA-28-181	2890234	2843003	
PA-28-181	2890235	2843004	
PA-28-181	2890236	2843005	
PA-28-181	2890237	2843006	
PA-28-181	2890238	2843007	
PA-28-181	2890239	2843008	

1980 model PA-28-181 Archer II s/n 28-7990368. (Piper Aircraft Corporation)

PA-28-181 Archer II test aircraft s/n 2890196 registration N9181J with the new Archer III cowling at Vero Beach. (R.W. Peperell)

PA-28-181 SPECIFICATION & PERFORMANCE

SPECIFICATION	28-181 'II'	28-181 'III'
Engine	180 hp Lycoming O-360-A4M	180 hp Lycoming O-360-A4M
Engine TBO (hrs)	2000	2000
No of seats	4	4
Wing Span (ft/ins)	35/0	35/6
Length (ft/ins)	24/0	24/0
Height (ft/ins)	7/4	7/4
Useable fuel capacity (US gal)	48	48
Gross weight (lbs)	2550-2558	2550
Empty weight (lbs)	1390-1421	1639
Useful load (lbs)	1137-1160	919
Propeller	Sensenich	Sensenich
Floats available		
PERFORMANCE		
Max speed	133 kts	129 kts
Cruise speed	126-129 kts @ 75%	129 kts @ 75% 111 kts @ 55%
Efficiency (gph)	8.8 @ 75%	10.5 @ 75% 7.8 @ 55%
Stall speed - flaps / gear down	53 kts	52 kts
Climb @ sea level (fpm)	740	667
Range with reserves	590 nm @ 75% 670 nm @ 55%	520 nm @ 75% 580 nm @ 55%
Service ceiling (ft)	13,650	13,236
Take off (Ground run)(ft)	740	870
Take off (over 50ft obst)(ft)	1625	1210
Landing (Ground roll)(ft)	925	925
Landing (over 50ft obst)(ft)	1390	1390

The first PA-28-181 Archer III s/n 2890206 registration N92474 at Vero Beach. (R.W. Peperell)

PA-28-140 CHEROKEE

In 1961 Piper inaugurated a new idea - an introductory flying lesson for five dollars. Anyone could walk into a Piper dealer and pay five dollars and be taken for a trial lesson. Cessna copied the idea two years later. After reviewing various aircraft in 1963 as potential flying trainers, Piper developed the PA-28-140 Cherokee as a trainer. They copied the Tri-Pacer Colt experience by stripping a four place Cherokee 150 down to a two place trainer. The prototype s/n 28-20000 registration N6000W was registered in November 1963 with a 150 hp Lycoming O-320-A2A engine (but with a higher pitch propeller as compared to the Cherokee 150 which reduced rpm and effective power to 140 hp).

The first production aircraft s/n 28-20001 registration N6001W was registered in early 1964 and FAA approval was granted on the 14th of February. It was launched on the 15th of February and deliveries started in March priced at $8,500. Three levels of equipment were available, Custom, Executive or Sportsman.

In the Autumn of 1965 the Cherokee 140-4 was announced, a 4 seater version of the Cherokee 140 with a 150 hp Lycoming O-320-A2B engine. The test aircraft was s/n 28-20730 registration N6632W converted in the Spring of 1965. Piper removed the rpm restriction on the engine enabling the full 150 hp to be available. Certification was gained on 17th of June. Production of the 2 or 4 seat 150 hp Cherokee 140 started for the 1966 model year.

PA-28-140 PRODUCTION DETAILS

Model / Fiscal Year	Serial Number Range From	To	Type	Total	Comments
Prototype	28-20000		140	1	
1964	28-20001	28-20391	140	391	
1965	28-20392	28-21161	140	770	
1966	28-21162	28-22200	140	1039	
1967	28-22201	28-23792	140	1592	
1968	28-23793	28-24945	140	1153	
1969	28-25001	28-26331	140 'B'	1331	
1970	28-26401	28-26946	140 'C'	546	
1971	28-7125001	28-7125641	140 'D' / Fliteliner	641	
1972	28-7225001	28-7225602	140 'E' / Cruiser / Fliteliner	602	
1973	28-7325001	28-7325674	140 'F' / Cruiser / Fliteliner	674	
1974	28-7425001	28-7425444	Cruiser / Fliteliner	444	
1975	28-7525001	28-7525340	Cruiser / Fliteliner	340	
1976	28-7625001	28-7625275	Cruiser	275	
1977	28-7725001	28-7725290	Cruiser	290	
Total manufactured 10,089 (All built at Vero Beach)					

Many aircraft were unsold at the end of 1967 and they were re-licensed in 1968 and then sold. These were s/n: 28-23902, 23938, 23953, 23995, 24001, 24004, 24011, 24021, 24032, 24038, 24039, 24044, 24056, 24062, 24068, 24069, 24072, 24073, 24078, 24081, 24089, 24094.

The prototype PA-28-140 Cherokee s/n 28-20000 registration N6000W. (Piper Aircraft Corporation)

The four seat Cherokee 140-4 with 150 hp engine, PA-28-140 s/n 28-20730 registration N6632W. (Piper Aircraft Corporation)

1969 model PA-28-140 Cherokee B s/n 28-24006 registration N1595J. (Piper Aircraft Corporation)

In July 1968 Piper experimented with a 115 hp Lycoming engine in the Cherokee 140. The test PA-28-115 aircraft was s/n 28-22120 registration N7557R. It is thought (though not confirmed) that a second aircraft, s/n 28-25001 registration N7378J was tested between October 1968 and January 1969. The derivative never went into production. The training schools wanted a 100 hp trainer, but Piper couldn't get the Cherokee to perform with such low power. Later in 1970 Piper continued to look for a direct competitor to the Cessna 150. A 125 hp Lycoming engine was fitted to s/n 28-26554 registration N5738U and this PA-28-125 first flew on the 24th November. Performance was still not good enough.

Between 1969 and 1973 Piper improved the Cherokee 140 each year:

PA-28-140 IMPROVEMENTS

Model Year	Type	Improvements	Development / Show aircraft s/n	Registration	1st Production aircraft s/n	Registration
1969	140 'B'	Dynafocal engine mount	28-24006 28-24588	N1595J N7303J	28-25001	N7378J
1970	140 'C'	Interior Instrument Panel	28-25890 28-26062	N95394 N98079	28-26401	N5615U
1971	140 'D'	Cabin heating system minor changes	28-26729 28-26737	N6002U N6001U	28-7125001	N1684T
1972	140 'E'	Interior Fin leading edge fillet	28-7125501 28-7125505	N5272S N1872T	28-7225001	N1852T
1973	140 'F'	Padded instrument panel, Seats	28-7225022 28-7225318	N1873T N5373T	28-7325001	N3079T

In 1968 Piper set up 425 'Flite Centers' across the U.S.A and Canada using a new audio visual Piper instructional program to teach flying principles on the ground. It was the first factory-originated standardised flight education program in the history of general aviation. In 1969 the 'Flite Centers' were extended to the rest of the world. By 1974 there were 500. In 1970 Piper developed the PA-28-140 Cherokee Flite Liner. This was a low cost two seater trainer based on the Cherokee 140 for the 'Flite Center' flying schools. The experimental Flite Liner, s/n 28-7125111 registration N140FL was completed in December 1970 and deliveries commenced with s/n 28-7125174 registration N400FL in March 1971.

For the 1972 model year two operational groups were available, Custom or Executive and the four seat version was named the Cherokee Cruiser with baggage compartment and modified ventilation. The base price of the Cherokee Cruiser was $12,530.

For the 1972 model year 'Piperaire' air conditioning was available. Aircraft s/n 28-25001 registration N140AC was used to certify this option in March 1971.

In 1973 production of the basic 140 was terminated in favour of the Cherokee Cruiser and in 1975 production of the Cherokee Flite Liner was stopped at Vero Beach. For the 1975 model year the Cherokee Cruiser had new vertically adjustable seats and optional 'quietized' sound proofing. For the 1977 model year there was a new panel, new seats, new door latch and new ventilation.

Production of the Cherokee Cruiser at Vero Beach terminated in September 1977 with s/n 28-7725290 registration N38760 as it was to be replaced as a trainer by the Tomahawk.

In the field Avcon offered a conversion, with a 180 hp Lycoming O-360 engine which increased rate of climb and improved field distances. For many years in the mid 1970s, Cherokee 140 s/n 28-7325406 registration N55449 was used by the EAA for auto fuel tests.

PA-28-140 SPECIFICATION & PERFORMANCE

SPECIFICATION	28-140	28-140 (1966 onwards), 'B', 'C', 'D', 'E', 'F'	Fliteliner
Engine	140 hp Lycoming O-320-A2A	150 hp Lycoming O-320-A2B	150 hp Lycoming O-320-E3D
Engine TBO (hrs)	1200	2000	2000
No of seats	2	2 4 (140-4 / Cruiser)	2
Wing Span (ft/ins)	30/0	30/0	30/0
Length (ft/ins)	23/4	23/4	23/4
Height (ft/ins)	7/4	7/4	7/4
Useable fuel capacity (US gal)	48	48	48
Gross weight (lbs)	1950	2150	2150
Empty weight (lbs)	1180	1180-1245	1305
Useful load (lbs)	770	905-970	845
Propeller	Sensenich	Sensenich	Sensenich
Floats available			
PERFORMANCE			
Max speed	141 mph	139-142 mph	139 mph
Cruise speed	131 mph @ 75%	130-135 mph @ 75%	132 mph @ 75%
Efficiency (gph)	5.3 @ 50%	9 @ 75% 5.5 @ 50%	8.4 @ 75%
Stall speed - flaps / gear down	54 mph	54 mph	55 mph
Climb @ sea level (fpm)	660	660	631
Range with reserves	780 sm @ 75%	725 sm @ 75% 950 sm @ 50%	495 sm @ 75% 705 sm @ 55%
Service ceiling (ft)	14,300	14,300	10,950
Take off (Ground run)(ft)	800	800	800
Take off (over 50ft obst)(ft)	1700	1700	1700
Landing (Ground roll)(ft)	535	535	535
Landing (over 50ft obst)(ft)	1080	1080	1080

PA-28-140 Cherokee Fliteliner s/n 28-7125111 registration N140FL. (Piper Aircraft Corporation)

PA-28-140 SPECIFICATION & PERFORMANCE

SPECIFICATION	28-140 Cruiser (1974-77)	28-115
Engine	150 hp Lycoming O-320-E3D	115 hp Lycoming O-235
Engine TBO (hrs)	2000	
No of seats	4	2
Wing Span (ft/ins)	30/0	30/0
Length (ft/ins)	23/4	23/4
Height (ft/ins)	7/4	7/4
Useable fuel capacity (US gal)	48	20
Gross weight (lbs)	2150	1750
Empty weight (lbs)	1274-1283	1193
Useful load (lbs)	867-876	557
Propeller	Sensenich	Sensenich
Floats available		
PERFORMANCE		
Max speed	142 mph	124 mph
Cruise speed	135 mph @ 75%	112 mph @ 75%
Efficiency (gph)	8.4 @ 55%	
Stall speed - flaps / gear down	55 mph	51 mph
Climb @ sea level (fpm)	631	590
Range with reserves	510 sm @ 75% 780 sm @ 55%	299 sm
Service ceiling (ft)	10,950	
Take off (Ground run)(ft)	800	
Take off (over 50ft obst)(ft)	1700	
Landing (Ground roll)(ft)	535	
Landing (over 50ft obst)(ft)	1080	

1973 model PA-28-140 Cherokee Cruiser s/n 28-7225318 registration N5373T. (Piper Aircraft Corporation)

PA-28-151 / 161 WARRIOR / CADET

Piper announced the PA-28-151 Cherokee Warrior on the 26th of October 1973. It was originally to be named the Cherokee Lance but Piper marketing decided the retractable Cherokee Six should be named the Lance. So the Warrior it was, using the longer fuselage and large all-moving horizontal tail aircraft of the Cherokee Challenger with a 150 hp Lycoming O-320-E2D engine and a new wing. The wing was not constant chord plan form as used on the other Cherokees, but a taper on the outer panels and large ailerons to improve pilot control in cross winds and slow speed flight. It also had a streamlined engine cowl and a smaller nose wheel. Piper saw the Warrior as a direct competitor to the Cessna 172 Skyhawk. Design began in early 1972, the Challenger prototype s/n 28-E10 registration N4273T first flew with the new tapered wing and 150 hp Lycoming engine on the 17th of October 1972. The prototype and the first production aircraft s/n 28-7415001 registration N55151 (which first flew on the 19th of July 1973) were involved in the certification flying with type approval being gained on 9th of August 1973. First deliveries of the Cherokee Warrior took place in late 1973, priced at $14,990.

For the 1975 model year the seats were improved to give vertical height adjustment and optional 'quietized' sound proofing was available. The first aircraft of the 1976 model year s/n 28-7615001 registration N1190X was converted from s/n 28-7515400. This was used to develop new wheel speed fairings. The 1977 model year had a new panel, new ventilation and a new door latch.

In 1976 the PA-28-161 Cherokee Warrior II was developed with a 100 Octane 160 hp Lycoming O-320-D3G engine. The experimental aircraft N4273T first flew with the 160 hp engine. The prototype s/n 28-7716001 registration N6938J was previously s/n 28-7615402, and first flew with the 160 hp engine on the 27th of August 1976. FAA approval was granted on the 22nd of November. The first production aircraft s/n 28-7716002 registration N1190H was registered in January 1977.

The 1978 model had new high speed fairings increasing speeds by 5% over the 1977 model Warrior II and was priced at $22,360.

For the 1979 model year the name 'Cherokee' was dropped, becoming just the Warrior II. It had new larger landing gear fairings which increased cruise speed and range and a new propeller spinner. For the 1983 model year the gross weight and useful load were increased by over 100 lbs. Each year the exterior colour scheme was changed.

In April 1985 Piper continued to search for a lower powered PA-28 to be used by training schools. A PA-28-115 based upon the PA-28-161 airframe was considered with a 115 hp Lycoming O-235 engine, but not proceeded with. Gross weight was to be restricted to 1800 pounds and the maximum speed would be reduced to 108 knots.

Piper announced the PA-28-161 Cadet in April 1988. This was created specifically for the training market with only two side windows but still with the 160 hp Lycoming O-320-D3G engine. The experimental aircraft was s/n 2816066 registration N9142S built by production and first flew on the 24th of June 1988. This aircraft was later changed to s/n 2841061. The first production aircraft was s/n 2841001 registration N9201Z completed on the 28th of October 1988 and was the first of a large order for Flight Safety. The basic VFR equipped price was $45,000. Production of the Cadet finished when Piper's cash problems forced them into Chapter 11. Some nearly complete aircraft were finished in 1993, followed by nine unfinished aircraft that were converted to Warrior II and III and Archer II aircraft, finally the last six were built in 1994.

In 1995 Piper introduced the Warrior III by adding 28 volt electrics and a new panel to the Warrior II in support of all the advanced avionics used by training schools. The first aircraft was s/n 2816110 registration N9249J completed on the 16th of June 1994.

The Warrior III was in production at Vero Beach in December 1996.

The experimental stretched PA-28-151 Cherokee s/n 28-E10 registration N4273T now with the tapered wing and 150 hp engine. (Piper Aircraft Corporation)

PA-28-151 / 161 PRODUCTION DETAILS

Model Year	Serial Number Range From	To	Type	Total	Comments
Experimental	28-E10		151	1	later to 161
1974	28-7415001	28-7415703	151	703	
1975	28-7515001	28-7515449 *	151	448	
Prototype	28-7615001		151	1	
1976	28-7615001	28-7615435 *	151	433	
1977	28-7715001	28-7715314	151	314	
Prototype	28-7716001		161 'II'	1	
1977	28-7716002	28-7716323	161 'II'	322	
1978	28-7816001	28-7816680	161 'II'	680	
1979	28-7916001	28-7916598	161 'II'	598	
1980	28-8016001	28-8016373	161 'II'	373	
1981	28-8116001	28-8116322 *	161 'II'	313	
1982	28-8216001	28-8216226	161 'II'	226	
1983	28-8316001	28-8316112	161 'II'	112	
1984	28-8416001	28-8416131 *	161 'II'	129	
1985	28-8516001	28-8516099	161 'II'	99	
1986	28-8616001	28-8616062 *	161 'II'	57	
1986	2816001		161 'II'	1	
1986	2816003	2816010	161 'II'	8	
1987	2816002		161 'II'	1	
1987	2816011	2816036	161 'II'	27	
1988	2816037	2816075 *	161 'II'	38	
1988	2841001	2841036	161 Cadet	36	
1988	2841038	2841040	161 Cadet	3	
1989	2816076	2816094	161 'II'	19	
1989	2841037		161 Cadet	1	
1989	2841041	2841289	161 Cadet	249	
1989	2841294	2841300	161 Cadet	7	
1989	2841304	2841314	161 Cadet	11	
1990	2816095	2816099	161 'II'	5	
1990	2841290	2841293	161 Cadet	4	
1990	2841301	2841303	161 Cadet	3	
1990	2841315	2841320	161 Cadet	6	
1990	2841322		161 Cadet	1	
1990	2841325	2841330	161 Cadet	6	
1992	2816100	2816103	161 'II'	4	
1992	2841321		161 Cadet	1	
1992	2841323	2841324	161 Cadet	2	
1992	2841331	2841350	161 Cadet	20	
1993	2816104	2816109	161 'II'	6	
1994	2816110		161 'III'	1	
1994	2841351	2841365 *	161 Cadet	6	
1995	2816111	2816125 *	161 'III'	9	
1995	2842001	2842009	161 'III'	9	
1996	2842010	2842018	161 'III'	9	
1997	2842019		161 'III'		

The Experimental aircraft 28-E10 has been included in the PA-28 manufactured total and a total of 34 aircraft in the batches marked * were not delivered, instead they were updated to the next year's model and given new serial numbers or not built. See table below.
Total manufactured 5303 (All built at Vero Beach)

PA-28-151 / 161 SERIAL NUMBER CHANGES

Model	Old Serial Number	New Serial Number	New Model (if different)
PA-28-151	28-7515400	28-7615001	
PA-28-151	28-7615402	28-7716001	PA-28-161
PA-28-161	28-8116126	28-8216019	
PA-28-161	28-8116139	28-8216021	
PA-28-161	28-8116148	28-8216017	
PA-28-161	28-8116248	28-8216007	
PA-28-161	28-8116253	28-8216014	
PA-28-161	28-8116272	28-8216015	
PA-28-161	28-8116277	28-8216006	
PA-28-161	28-8116287	28-8216027	
PA-28-161	28-8116314	28-8216016	
PA-28-161	28-8416095	28-8516007	
PA-28-161	28-8416112	28-8516008	
PA-28-161	28-8616058	2816001	
PA-28-161	28-8616059	2816002	
PA-28-161	28-8616060	2816003	
PA-28-161	28-8616061	2816004	
PA-28-161	28-8616062	2816005	
PA-28-161	2816066	2841061	PA-28-161 Cadet
PA-28-161 Cadet	2841351-359	Not built, major components used in Warrior II / III & Archer II production	
PA-28-161	2816120	2842001	
PA-28-161	2816121	2842002	
PA-28-161	2816122	2842003	
PA-28-161	2816123	2842004	
PA-28-161	2816124	2842005	
PA-28-161	2816125	2842006	

PA-28-161 Cherokee Warrior II show plane s/n 28-7615137 registration N8500E. (Piper Aircraft Corporation)

PA-28-151 / 161 SPECIFICATION & PERFORMANCE

SPECIFICATION	28-151	28-161 'II'	28-161 Cadet
Engine	150 hp Lycoming O-320-E3D	160 hp Lycoming O-320-D3G	160 hp Lycoming O-320-D3G
Engine TBO (hrs)	2000	2000	2000
No of seats	4	4	2-4
Wing Span (ft/ins)	35/0	35/0	35/0
Length (ft/ins)	23/10	23/10	23/10
Height (ft/ins)	7/4	7/4	7/4
Useable fuel capacity (US gal)	48	48	48
Gross weight (lbs)	2325	2325 (77-82) 2440-2447 (83 & later)	2335
Empty weight (lbs)	1301-1315	1344-1348	1390
Useful load (lbs)	1010-1024	972-1099	942
Propeller	Sensenich	Sensenich	Sensenich
Floats available			
PERFORMANCE			
Max speed	118 kts	127 kts	121 kts
Cruise speed	117 kts	126-127 kts @ 75% 94 kts @ 55%	119 kts @ 75% 101 kts @ 55%
Efficiency (gph)	9.2 @ 75% 8.4 @ 55%	10 @ 75% 7.8 @ 55%	8.5 @ 75% 6.6 @ 55%
Stall speed - flaps / gear down	51 kts	50 kts	50 kts
Climb @ sea level (fpm)	649	644-710	670
Range with reserves	605 nm @ 75% 632 nm @ 55%	525 nm @ 75% 640 nm @ 55%	550 @ 75% 600 @ 55%
Service ceiling (ft)	12,700	11,000 - 14,000	11,600
Take off (Ground run)(ft)	1065-1410	975	950
Take off (over 50ft obst)(ft)	1760	1490-1650	1500
Landing (Ground roll)(ft)	595	595	590
Landing (over 50ft obst)(ft)	1115	1115	1050

The experimental PA-28-161 Cadet s/n 2816066 registration N9142S in final assembly at Vero Beach. (Piper Aircraft Corporation)

PA-28-161 SPECIFICATION & PERFORMANCE

SPECIFICATION	28-161 'III'
Engine	160 hp Lycoming O-320-D3G
Engine TBO (hrs)	2000
No of seats	4
Wing Span (ft/ins)	35/0
Length (ft/ins)	23/10
Height (ft/ins)	7/4
Useable fuel capacity (US gal)	48
Gross weight (lbs)	2447
Empty weight (lbs)	1491
Useful load (lbs)	956
Propeller	Sensenich
Floats available	
PERFORMANCE	
Max speed	127 kts
Cruise speed	126 kts @ 75% 118 kts @ 65%
Efficiency (gph)	
Stall speed - flaps / gear down	44 kts
Climb @ sea level (fpm)	644
Range with reserves	
Service ceiling (ft)	11,000
Take off (Ground run)(ft)	
Take off (over 50ft obst)(ft)	1650
Landing (Ground roll)(ft)	
Landing (over 50ft obst)(ft)	1160

The first PA-28-161 Warrior III s/n 2816110 registration N9249J at Vero Beach. (R.W. Peperell)

PA-28-235 / 236 CHEROKEE / DAKOTA

Piper announced the PA-28-235 Cherokee in August 1963. It was a Cherokee with the wing span increased by two feet, a fuel tank in each wing tip (an extra 34 U.S. gallons) and a 235 hp Lycoming O-540-B2B5 engine. It was designed to carry more than its empty weight, having the highest useful load in its class. The prototype was again N2800W converted from a Cherokee 180 in 1962 and first flew on 9th of May 1962. The first production aircraft was s/n 28-10001 registration N8500W registered in February 1963. FAA approval was granted on 15th of July 1963 and deliveries began immediately afterwards. This was priced at $15,900.

In October 1964 for the 1965 model year Piper launched the 235 'mid model' using s/n 28-10100 registration N8588W as the show aircraft. This had new engine mounts, shock mounted cowl, added insulation, centre mounted hand brake and an improved panel.

At the end of 1964 Piper experimented with a 3-bladed propeller in aircraft N8500W.

In 1965 Franklin fitted a 220 hp Franklin engine in Cherokee 235 s/n 28-10339 registration N8791W. This was a Franklin promotion and was test flown by Piper between October 1965 and January 1966.

In 1966 Piper introduced the improved 235 'B'. It had a longer propeller spinner, improved fuel system and an optional constant speed propeller in place of the standard fixed pitch one. The 235B test aircraft was N8500W converted from a 235. Aircraft s/n 28-10676 registration N9076W was also converted to a 235 'B'.

During March 1967 Piper tested a Cherokee with a single on / off fuel system using aircraft N2800W. Piper was trying to make fuel management easier, but it was not a success.

In 1967 the PA-28-235 Cherokee C was developed which had the third fuselage window (originally used for the Arrow), restyled interior, striking exterior paint scheme and a new panel and power console. The first model 'C' was s/n 28-11040 registration N9352W. Deliveries started for the 1968 model year.

Pug Piper wanted an inexpensive four seat twin keeping costs to a minimum. In 1968 a twin Cherokee 235 was drawn up and both a scale model and full scale mock-up were made. Nothing came of this. Eight years later, in 1974, Piper started development of a four seat twin Cherokee, the PA-44.

Between 1970 and 1972 Piper improved the Cherokee 235 each year:

PA-28-235 / 236 IMPROVEMENTS

Model Year	Type	Improvements	Development / Show aircraft s/ n	Registration	1st Production aircraft s/n	Registration
1970	235 'D'	Minor changes	28-11165 28-11216	N9446W N9481W	28-11301	N8512N
1971	235 'E'	Interior	28-11317	N8580N	28-7110001	N8581N
1972	235 'F'	Interior, Panel	28-7110024	N5125S	28-7210001	N2653T

For the 1972 model year two operational groups were available, Custom or Executive.

During 1971 and 1972 Piper developed the PA-28-235 Cherokee Charger, which had a five inch increase in fuselage length (as used in the Arrow II) between the front and rear seats, resulting in a roomier rear cabin. Other changes included a larger all moving horizontal tail aircraft, a wider door, an increased gross weight and useful load (up 100 lbs), new seats and a padded instrument panel. The engine was a 235 hp Lycoming O-540-B4B5. The prototype s/n 28-E11 registration N2673T first flew in 1972. The Charger was certified on 9th June 1972. The first production aircraft s/n 28-7310001 registration N3078T was completed in the summer of 1972 and deliveries began later that year. The suggested base price was $24,390.

The experimental PA-28-235 s/n 28-03 registration N2800W and PA-28-235 s/n 28-10002 registration N8501W. (Piper Aircraft Corporation)

PA-28-235 Cherokee B s/n 28-10676 registration N9076W at Vero Beach. (Piper Aircraft Corporation)

The first PA-28-235 Cherokee C s/n 28-11040 registration N9352W at Lock Haven. (via J. Taylor)

Model of the proposed twin PA-28-235. (G.K. Gates)

Drawing of the proposed twin PA-28-235. (D. Clark)

PA-28-235 / 236 / 201T PRODUCTION DETAILS					
Model / Fiscal Year	Serial Number Range From	To	Type	Total	Comments
Prototype	28-03		235	0	
1964	28-10001	28-10505	235	505	
1965	28-10506	28-10715	235	210	
1966	28-10716	28-10755	235 'B'	40	
1967	28-10756	28-11039	235 'B'	284	
1968	28-11040	28-11226	235 'C'	187	
1969	28-11227	28-11255	235 'C'	29	
1970	28-11301	28-11378	235 'D'	78	
1971	28-7110001	28-7110028	235 'E'	28	
1972	28-7210001	28-7210023	235 'F'	23	
Experimental	28-E11		235 Charger	1	
1973	28-7310001	28-7310176	235 Charger	176	
1974	28-7410001	28-7410110	235 Pathfinder	110	
1975	28-7510001	28-7510135	235 Pathfinder	135	
1976	28-7610001	28-7610181	235 Pathfinder	181	
1977	28-7610182	28-7610202	235 Pathfinder	21	
1977	28-7710001	28-7710089	235 Pathfinder	88	
Experimental	28-7911001		236 Dakota	1	
Experimental	28-7921001		201T Turbo Dakota	1	
1979	28-7911002	28-7911335	236 Dakota	334	
1979	28-7921002	28-7921095 *	201T Turbo Dakota	90	
1980	28-8011001	28-8011151	236 Dakota	151	
1981	28-8111001	28-8111097 *	236 Dakota	95	
1982	28-8211001	28-8211050 *	236 Dakota	45	
1983	28-8311001	28-8311026 *	236 Dakota	25	
1984	28-8411001	28-8411031	236 Dakota	31	
1985	28-8511001	28-8511020	236 Dakota	20	
1986	28-8611001	28-8611009 *	236 Dakota	8	
1986	2811001	2811004	236 Dakota	4	
1987	2811005	2811016	236 Dakota	12	
1988	2811017	2811022	236 Dakota	6	
1989	2811023	2811032	236 Dakota	10	
1990	2811033		236 Dakota	1	
1993	2811034	2811037	236 Dakota	4	
1994	2811038	2811050	236 Dakota	13	

The Experimental aircraft 28-03 has been included in the PA-28 manufactured total and 14 aircraft in the batches marked * were not delivered, instead they were updated to the next year's model and given new serial numbers or not built. See table below.

Total manufactured 235 / 236 2856 201T 91 (All built at Vero Beach)

The third experimental stretched Cherokee, PA-28-235 Cherokee Charger s/n 28-E13 registration N2673T. (Piper Aircraft Corporation)

The first PA-28-235 Cherokee Pathfinder s/n 28-7410001 registration N15474. (Piper Aircraft Corporation)

The experimental PA-28-236 Dakota s/n 28-7911001 registration N38505. (Piper Aircraft Corporation)

PA-28-235 / 236 / 201T SERIAL NUMBER CHANGES

Model	Old Serial Number	New Serial Number	New Model (if different)
PA-28-235	28-7710056	28-7911001	PA-28-236
PA-28-201T	28-7921092-095	Not built	
PA-28-236	28-8111076	28-8211015	
PA-28-236	28-8111097	Not built	
PA-28-236	28-8211025	28-8311008	
PA-28-236	28-8211034	28-8311010	
PA-28-236	28-8211042	28-8311018	
PA-28-236	28-8211043	28-8311022	
PA-28-236	28-8211050	28-8311001	
PA-28-236	28-8311026	28-8411001	
PA-28-236	28-8611009	2811001	

For the 1974 model year it was named the Cherokee Pathfinder commencing with s/n 28-7410001 registration N15474. It had restyled window lines, improved nose wheel steering, improved interior and adjustable front seats. For the 1975 model year it had new vertically adjustable seats and optional 'quietized' sound proofing was available.

During 1977/1978 Piper developed the PA-28-236 Dakota. It was a Pathfinder with the semi tapered wing of the Warrior and with increased fuel capacity. It had revised undercarriage fairings which increased speed and range and revised engine cowl. The prototype s/n 28-7911001 registration N38505 was registered in late 1977 and was converted from s/n 28-7710056. The first production aircraft s/n 28-7911002 registration N39500 was registered in 1978 and the Dakota was certified on 1st of June. Deliveries began in the summer of that year with a basic price of $36,750.

At the same time as developing the Dakota, Piper developed the PA-28-201T Turbo Dakota. When this model was first discussed at Vero Beach in late 1976, it was to be T-tailed, but when the Arrow III stayed with the low-tail so did the Turbo Dakota. It used the Archer II fuselage, the Dakota wing and a 200 hp Continental TS10-360-FB engine. The prototype s/n 28-7921001 registration N38600 was registered in late 1977 and was converted from s/n 28-7790069. The Turbo Dakota received FAA approval on the 14th of December 1978. The first production aircraft s/n 28-7921002 registration N2173K was registered in early 1979. Piper announced the model in March priced at $41,980. Production of the Turbo Dakota at Vero Beach was discontinued in the Summer of 1979, but not before s/n 28-7921004 registration N2121V was painted in the 1980 colour scheme and promotion for the 1980 model year had started.

For the 1980 model year the Dakota had improved cabin ventilation, a radio master switch and quick change wheel fairings. Each year exterior colour scheme was changed.

In late 1993 Piper proposed a Dakota II with modifications similar to the Saratoga II HP. Lack of money also prevented this being a reality.

Production of the Dakota terminated at Vero Beach at the end of 1994 with s/n 2811050 registration N9251H.

PA-28-235 / 236 / 201T SPECIFICATION & PERFORMANCE			
SPECIFICATION	28-235 & 28-235 'B'	28-235 'C', 'D', 'E', 'F'	28-235 Charger
Engine	235 hp Lycoming O-540-B2B5	235 hp Lycoming O-540-B4B5	235 hp Lycoming O-540-B4B5
Engine TBO (hrs)	1200 (64-67) 2000 (68)	2000	2000
No of seats	4	4	4
Wing Span (ft/ins)	32/0	32/0	32/0
Length (ft/ins)	23/8.5	23/8.5	24/1
Height (ft/ins)	7/1	7/1, 7/4 (E & F)	7/10
Useable fuel capacity (US gal)	83.3	83.3	82
Gross weight (lbs)	2900	2900	3000
Empty weight (lbs)	1410, 1435 (B)	1467 (FP), 1491 (CS)	1550
Useful load (lbs)	1490, 1465 (B)	1433 (FP), 1491 (CS)	1450
Propeller	Sensenich or McCauley Fixed pitch or Constant speed	Sensenich or McCauley Fixed pitch or Constant speed	Sensenich Fixed pitch or Hartzell Constant speed
Floats available			
PERFORMANCE			
Max speed	146 kts	144 kts (FP) 143 kts (CS)	141 kts
Cruise speed	137 kts @ 75%	135 kts (FP) @ 75% 134 kts (CS) @ 55%	133 kts @ 75%
Efficiency (gph)	14 @ 75%	14 @ 75% 10.3 @ 55%	13 @ 75%
Stall speed - flaps / gear down	53 kts	52 kts	57 kts
Climb @ sea level (fpm)	825	825 (FP), 900 (CS)	800
Range with reserves	820 nm @ 75% 991 nm @ 55%	812 nm (FP) @ 75% 800 nm (CS) @ 75%	739 nm @ 75% 912 nm @ 55%
Service ceiling (ft)	14,500	14,500 (FP), 16,500 (CS)	12,000
Take off (Ground run)(ft)	800	800 (FP), 750 (CS)	800
Take off (over 50ft obst)(ft)	1360	1360 (FP), 1220 (CS)	1260
Landing (Ground roll)(ft)	680	680	1040
Landing (over 50ft obst)(ft)	1300	1300	1740

The experimental PA-28-201T Turbo Dakota s/n 28-7921001 registration N38600. (Piper Aircraft Corporation)

PA-28-235 / 236 / 201T SPECIFICATION & PERFORMANCE

SPECIFICATION	28-235 Pathfinder	28-236 Dakota	28-201T Turbo Dakota
Engine	235 hp Lycoming O-540-B4B5	235 hp Lycoming O-540-J3A5D	200 hp Continental TSIO-360-FB
Engine TBO (hrs)	2000	2000	1400
No of seats	4	4	4
Wing Span (ft/ins)	32/0	35/5	35/0
Length (ft/ins)	24/1	24/8.5	25/0
Height (ft/ins)	7/10	7/2	7/7
Useable fuel capacity (US gal)	82	80	72
Gross weight (lbs)	3000	3000-3011	2900
Empty weight (lbs)	1550-1565	1581-1610	1563
Useful load (lbs)	1435-1450	1390-1419	1337
Propeller	Hartzell Constant speed	Hartzell Constant speed	Hartzell Constant speed
Floats available			
PERFORMANCE			
Max speed	141 kts	148 kts	162 kts
Cruise speed	134 kts @ 75%	144 kts @ 75% 130 kts @ 55%	156 kts @ 75%
Efficiency (gph)	13 @ 75%	12.7 @ 75%	12 @ 75%
Stall speed - flaps / gear down	57 kts	56 kts	59 kts
Climb @ sea level (fpm)	800	1000-1110	902
Range with reserves	803 nm @ 75% 974 nm @ 55%	650 nm @ 75% 795-810 nm @ 55%	715 nm @ 75% 795 nm @ 55%
Service ceiling (ft)	13,550	17,000-20,000	20,000
Take off (Ground run)(ft)	850	886	963
Take off (over 50ft obst)(ft)	1410	1216	1402
Landing (Ground roll)(ft)	1040	640-825	861
Landing (over 50ft obst)(ft)	1740	1530-1725	1697

PA-28-236 Dakota s/n 28-8011024 registration N8239V at Lock Haven. (R.W. Peperell)

PA-28R ARROW

Originally known as the Cherokee 180 retractable, the prototype s/n 28-30000 registration N9997W first flew on the 1st of February 1966. This had the Cherokee 180 fuselage with the two side windows and was followed by s/n 28-30002 registration N9996W which had a third window on each side of the fuselage, which first flew on the 11th of July. The third prototype s/n 28-30003 first flew on the 8th of September. All had the 180 hp Lycoming IO-360 engine, a constant speed propeller, retractable gear with automatic gear extension. Whereas the Cherokee 180 had the O-360 engine with a carburettor that hung below the engine, the IO-360 engine allowed room under the engine for retraction of the nose gear within the cowling but it was necessary to reduce the nose wheel size to 500 X 5 inches. The construction numbers were changed to 28R in 1967. The Arrow 180 was certified on 8th of June 1967 and Piper announced the PA-28R-180 Cherokee Arrow on the 19th. The first production aircraft s/n 28R-30004 registration N3700T was registered in 1967 and deliveries began later that year. It was priced at $16,900. N9997W was cancelled from the U.S. register in 1968 when it was donated to a local community organisation.

In 1968 Piper developed the PA-28R-200 Cherokee Arrow with a 200 hp Lycoming engine IO-360-C1C engine. The test aircraft was s/n 28R-30482 registration N4603J converted from an Arrow 180 and first flew on 12th of July 1968. The 200 hp show aircraft was s/n 28R-31007 registration N7626J completed in September. The Arrow 200 was certified on 16th January 1969. The first production aircraft was s/n 28R-35001 registration N9301N and deliveries began in early 1969.

Also in early 1969 Teledyne fitted a 265 hp Continental Tiara engine in Arrow N9996W. This was test flown by Piper between June 1969 and January 1970 and was a Continental promotion.

In August 1969 Piper looked at a lower cost Cherokee Arrow, the PA-28R-C180 with an O-360 engine (with a carburettor not fuel injection) and a fixed pitch propeller. This was not proceeded with.

During 1970 Piper developed the Cherokee Arrow B with minor improvements which was sold for the 1971 model year. The test aircraft was s/n 28R-30489 registration N4608J converted from an ordinary Arrow. The first production aircraft were s/n 28R-713001 registration CF-ZJK (180 hp) registered in March 1971 and s/n 28R-7135001 registration N2064T (200 hp version) registered in October 1970. In September 1971 the 180 hp version was dropped.

In 1970 and 1971 Piper developed the 'stretched Cherokee'. The Cherokee Arrow II had a 5 inch increase in fuselage length between the front and rear seats resulting a more spacious rear cabin and a wider door. Also a larger all moving horizontal tail aircraft, improved ventilation system, improved seat adjustment, an increase in gross weight (up 150 lbs), new flared fibreglass wing tips increasing span by 24 inches, new interior and 'Piperaire' air conditioning available as an option. The test aircraft was s/n 28R-35768 registration N7696J converted from a 'B' and first flew on 29th of September 1970. The first production Cherokee Arrow II s/n 28R-7235001 registration N2272T was completed in November 1971. It was certified on the 2nd December 1971 and deliveries commenced for the 1972 model year. The base price was $23,500. Aircraft s/n 28R-35656 registration N200AC was used to certify the 'Piperaire' air conditioning installation during 1971.

Devore Aviation had obtained a supplementary type certificate for a turbocharger on the engine in an Arrow. Aircraft s/n 28R-30337 registration N3986T was tested by Piper in February 1970. Piper considered producing a Turbocharged Arrow designated the PA-28R-T200, but the project was dropped later in February. They eventually produced the Turbo Arrow in 1977.

For the 1973 model year the Cherokee Arrow II had new seats and a padded instrument panel. For the 1974 model year it had rounded window lines and improved nose gear steering. For the 1975 model year new vertically adjustable seats and optional 'quietized' sound proofing were available. For 1976 the engine TBO was increased to 1600 hours.

The prototype PA-28-180 retractable s/n 28-30001 registration N9997W at Vero Beach. Note only two side windows. (P. Peck)

The second prototype PA-28-180 retractable s/n 28-30002 registration N9996W. (G.K. Gates)

PA-28R s/n 28R-30002 registration N99996W with Tiara engine and three blade propeller at Vero Beach. (C. Diefendorf)

PA-28R-180 Cherokee Arrow s/n 28R-30003 registration N9995W at Vero Beach. (Piper Aircraft Corporation)

The Cherokee Arrow 200 test aircraft s/n 28R-30482 registration N4603J in 1970 colour scheme. (Piper Aircraft Corporation)

1969 model Cherokee Arrow 200, PA-28R-200 s/n 28R-31007 registration N7626J. (Piper Aircraft Corporation)

PA-28R-200 Cherokee Arrow B s/n 28R-35753 registration N5020S. (Piper Aircraft Corporation)

The PA-28R-200 Cherokee Arrow II test aircraft s/n 28R-31076 registration N7696J at Vero Beach. (Piper Aircraft Corporation)

PA-28R PRODUCTION DETAILS

Model / Fiscal Year	Serial Number Range From	To	Type	Total	Comments
Prototype	28-30000		180	1	to 28R-
Prototypes	28-30002	28-30003	180	2	to 28R-
1967	28R-30004	28R-30097	180	94	
1968	28R-30098	28R-31087	180	990	28R-30482 to 200 hp
1969	28R-31088	28R-31135*	180	47	
1969	28R-35001	28R-35392	200	392	
1970	28R-31251	28R-31270	180	20	
1970	28R-35601	28R-35820	200	220	
1971	28R-7130001	28R-7130013	180 'B'	13	
1971	28R-7135001	28R-7135229	200 'B'	229	
1972	28R-7235001	28R-7235320	200 'II'	320	
1973	28R-7335001	28R-7335446	200 'II'	446	
1974	28R-7435001	28R-7435323	200 'II'	323	
1975	28R-7535001	28R-7535383 *	200 'II'	382	
1976	28R-7635001	28R-7635473 *	200 'II'	471	28R-7635243 to T-tail
1977	28R-7635474	28R-7635545	200 'II'	72	Kits
Prototype	28R-7737001		201 'III'	1	T-tail
Prototype	28R-7737002		201 'III'	1	
Prototype	28R-7703001		201T 'III'	1	
1977	28R-7737003	28R-7737178	201 'III'	176	
1977	28R-7703002	28R-7703427	201T 'III'	426	
1978	28R-7837001	28R-7837317 *	201 'III'	316	
1978	28R-7803001	28R-7803373 *	201T 'III'	372	
Prototype	28R-7918001		201 'IV'	1	
Prototype	28R-7931001		201T 'IV'	1	
1979	28R-7918002	28R-7918267	201 'IV'	266	
1979	28R-7931002	28R-7931310	201T 'IV'	309	
1980	28R-8018001	28R-8018106	201 'IV'	106	
1980	28R-8031001	28R-8031178	201T 'IV'	178	
1981	28R-8118001	28R-8118082 *	201 'IV'	81	
1981	28R-8131001	28R-8131208	201T 'IV'	208	
1982	28R-8218001	28R-8218026	201 'IV'	26	
1982	28R-8231001	28R-8231081 *	201T 'IV'	77	
1983	28R-8331001	28R-8331051	201T 'IV'	51	
1984	28R-8431001	28R-8431032	201T 'IV'	32	
1985	28R-8531001	28R-8531015	201T 'IV'	15	
Prototype	28R-8626001		221T	1	
1986	28R-8631001		201T 'IV'	1	
1986	285-8631005	28R-8631006 *	201T 'IV'	1	
1987	28R-8631002	28R-8631004	201T 'IV'	3	
1987	2831001	2831033	201T 'IV'	33	
1988	2831034	2831038	201T 'IV'	5	
1988	2837001	2837010	201	10	
1989	2837011	2837035	201	25	
1989	2837038	2837049	201	12	
1989	2803001	2803012	201T	12	
1990	2837036	2837037	201	2	
1990	2837050	2837054	201	5	
1990	2803013		201T	1	kit
1991	2803014	2803015	201T	2	kits

PA-28R PRODUCTION DETAILS (continued)

Model Year	Serial Number Range From	To	Type	Total	Comments
1994	2837061		201	1	
1995	2837062 *		201	0	
1995	2844001	2844003	201	3	
1996	2844004	2844011	201	8	
1997	2844012		201		
A total of 13 aircraft in the batches marked * were not delivered, instead they were updated to the next year's model and given new serial numbers or not built. See table below. Total manufactured 6791 (All built at Vero Beach)					

PA-28R SERIAL NUMBER CHANGES

Model	Old Serial Number	New Serial Number	New Model (if different)
PA-28R-180	28R-31089	28R-31266	
PA-28R-200	28R-7535264	28R-7737001	PA-28RT-201
PA-28R-200	28R-7635018	28R-7703001	PA-28R-201T
PA-28R-200	28R-7635375	28R-7737002	PA-28R-201
PA-28R-201	28R-7837107	28R-7918001	PA-28RT-201
PA-28R-201T	28R-7803114	28R-7931001	PA-28RT-201T
PA-28RT-201	28R-8118036	28R-8218007	
PA-28RT-201T	28R-8231037	28R-8331011	
PA-28RT-201T	28R-8231042	28R-8331051	
PA-28RT-201T	28R-8231050	28R-8331012	
PA-28RT-201T	28R-8231081	Not built	
PA-28RT-201T	28R-8631006	2831001	
PA-28R-201	2837062	2844001	

The Cherokee Arrow III was to be similar to the Arrow II but with the semi-tapered wing of the Warrior, an all moving tailplane mounted at the top of the fin (T-tail) and an increase in fuel capacity (72 U.S. gallons instead of 48). The prototype with the T-tail, but still with the standard rectangular wing, was s/n 28R-7535264 registration N1169X which first flew at Lakeland on the 9th of July 1975. The semi-tapered wing was fitted and it first flew in this configuration as the PA-28RT-201 on the 9th of January 1976. It's construction number was changed to 28R-7737001. Unfortunately this aircraft was written off during spin tests on 14th May 1976. A second prototype was developed by Piper, with semi-tapered wing but with the standard low tail. This was s/n 28R-7737002 registration N3895F, having been converted from s/n 28R-7635375 in mid 1976. This version, the PA-28R-201, was certified on the 2nd of November. Piper went on to develop the T-tail Arrow in the Arrow IV during 1978. The first production aircraft s/n 28R-7737003 registration N1412H first flew on the 7th of January 1977. Deliveries began shortly afterwards.

During 1976 Piper developed the Turbo Cherokee Arrow III. It was similar to the Arrow II (new wing but with low tail) but with a turbo-charged 200 hp Continental TSIO-360-F engine in a modified cowl and an increase in gross weight (up 250 pounds). The prototype s/n 28R-7635018 registration N3918X first flew on the 14th of January 1976 with the turbocharger, its construction number was changed to 28R-7703001 later in 1976. This version was certified on the 8th of October. The first production PA-28R-201T aircraft s/n 28R-7703002 registration N4949F first flew on the 1st of December 1976 and deliveries began in January 1977.

For the 1978 model year the name 'Cherokee' was dropped, becoming just the Arrow III and Turbo Arrow III.

PA-28R-200 Cherokee Arrow II s/n 28R-7235002 registration N1972T. (Piper Aircraft Corporation)

The spin chute installation on the prototype PA-28RT-201 Cherokee Arrow III s/n 28R-7737001 registration N1169X at Lakeland. (K. Rooke)

The 2nd prototype PA-28R-201 Cherokee Arrow III s/n 28R-7737002 registration N3895F. (Piper Aircraft Corporation)

PA-28R-201T Turbo Cherokee Arrow III s/n 28R-7703002 registration N4949F. (Piper Aircraft Corporation)

The experimental Cherokee Arrow s/n 28R-7635243 registration N9465K with T-tail at Vero Beach. (H.W. Barnhouse)

The experimental Cherokee Arrow s/n 28R-7635243 registration N519NA owned by NASA. (J.M. Gradidge)

PA-28R SPECIFICATION & PERFORMANCE			
SPECIFICATION	28R-180 & 28R-180 'B'	28R-200 & 28R-200 'B'	28R-200 'II'
Engine	180 hp Lycoming IO-360	200 hp Lycoming IO-360-C1C	200 hp Lycoming IO-360-C1C
Engine TBO (hrs)	2000	1200	1600
No of seats	4	4	4
Wing Span (ft/ins)	30/0	30/0	32/0
Length (ft/ins)	24/2.5	24/2.5	24/7
Height (ft/ins)	8/0	8/0	8/0
Useable fuel capacity (US gal)	48	48	48
Gross weight (lbs)	2500	2600	2650
Empty weight (lbs)	1380-1431	1459-1470	1508-1531
Useful load (lbs)	1069-1120	1130-1141	1119-1142
Propeller	Hartzell 2-blade	Hartzell 2-blade	Hartzell 2-blade
Floats available			
PERFORMANCE			
Max speed	149 kts	154 kts	153 kts
Cruise speed	141 kts @ 75%	146 kts @ 75%	148 kts @ 75%
Efficiency (gph)	9.4 @ 75%	10.2 @ 75%	10.2 @ 75%
Stall speed - flaps / gear down	53 kts	56 kts	56 kts
Climb @ sea level (fpm)	875	910	900
Range with reserves	743 nm @ 75% 864 nm @ 55%	710 nm @ 75% 833 nm @ 55%	740 nm @ 75% 850 nm @ 55%
Service ceiling (ft)	15,000	16,000	15,000
Take off (Ground run)(ft)	820	770	1025
Take off (over 50ft obst)(ft)	1665		1800
Landing (Ground roll)(ft)	776	780	780
Landing (over 50ft obst)(ft)	1340		1380

In order to try to determine the cause of the N1169X spin problem, Piper modified aircraft s/n 28R-7635243 registration N9465K with a T-tail in place of the low tail and kept the straight wing. This first flew at Lakeland on the 21st of June 1976. Later the tapered wing was added and the tail was stretched (known as the PA-28R-201S) by 27 inches. This configuration was first flown on the 26th January 1977. Two tail tops were tried, one forged, the other sheet metal. Piper management were offered either the 27 inch or 18 inch stretch for the Arrow IV. During 1978 Piper developed the Arrow IV with T-tail and an increase in gross weight (up 100 pounds over the Arrow III). The fuselage was increased in length by 18 inches at the tail cone. The normally aspirated prototype s/n 28R-7918001 (previously 28R-7837107) registration N2970M first flew on the 20th of March 1978. The turbo charged prototype s/n 28R-7931001 (previously 28R-7803114) registration N2251M first flew on the 14th of March. N9465K was eventually sold to NASA in 1979 for various tests including vortex tests and gained discontinuous leading edge wings and its registration was changed to N519NA.

FAA approval for PA-28RT-201 and PA-28R-201T was granted on the 13th of November 1978. The Arrow IV was priced at $44,510 and the Turbo Arrow IV at $49,150. Deliveries began in early 1979, the first production examples were s/n 28R-7918002 registration N2136E and s/n 28R-7931002 registration N2079B.

During early 1978 Piper initiated design of a 310 hp turbocharged Continental TSIO-520-L powered Arrow with a T-tail, designated the PA-28RT-310T. The gross weight was increased to 3320 pounds and the Saratoga SP wing was to be used. A maximum speed of 250 knots at 20,000 feet was predicted. This never left the drawing board.

The word 'turbo' was not painted on the Turbo Arrow aircraft from the 1981 model year onwards, in order not to confuse fuel operators with jet fuel for Turboprop engines. Production of the normally aspirated Arrow stopped at the end of 1982.

The prototype PA-28RT-201 Arrow IV s/n 28R-7918001 registration N2970M. (Piper Aircraft Corporation)

The prototype PA-28RT-201T Turbo Arrow IV s/n 28R-7931001 registration N2251M. (Piper Aircraft Corporation)

PA-28R SPECIFICATION & PERFORMANCE

SPECIFICATION	28R-201 'III'	28R-201T 'Turbo III'	28RT-201 'IV'
Engine	200 hp Lycoming IO-360-C1C6	200 hp Continental TSIO-360-F	200 hp Lycoming IO-360-C1C6
Engine TBO (hrs)	1600	1400	1600
No of seats	4	4	4
Wing Span (ft/ins)	35/0	35/0	35/5
Length (ft/ins)	25/0	25/0	27/0
Height (ft/ins)	8/0	8/0	8/3
Useable fuel capacity (US gal)	72	72	72
Gross weight (lbs)	2750	2900	2750
Empty weight (lbs)	1601	1663	1593-1641
Useful load (lbs)	1149	1237	1109-1157
Propeller	Hartzell 2-blade	Hartzell constant speed	Hartzell 2-blade
Floats available			
PERFORMANCE			
Max speed	152 kts	178 kts	152 kts
Cruise speed	143 kts @ 75% 122 kts @ 55%	172 kts @ 75% 154 kts @ 55%	143 kts @ 75%
Efficiency (gph)		14 @ 75%	10 @ 75%
Stall speed - flaps / gear down	55 kts	58 kts	55 kts
Climb @ sea level (fpm)	831	940	831
Range with reserves	810 nm @ 75% 980 nm @ 55%	675 nm @ 75% 860 nm @ 55%	720-810 nm @ 75%
Service ceiling (ft)	16,200	20,000	17,000
Take off (Ground run)(ft)	1025	1110	1025
Take off (over 50ft obst)(ft)	1600	1620	1600
Landing (Ground roll)(ft)	615	645	615
Landing (over 50ft obst)(ft)	1525	1555	1525

During 1984 / 1985 Piper designed a new Arrow. It had a one piece windshield, a 220 hp Continental TSIO-360-KB2A engine and a conventional low tail. The prototype PA-28R-221T was s/n 28R-8626001 registration N9286T and it first flew on the 3rd of September 1985. It was known internally as the Arrow V and at one time was to be called the Monterey. This derivative was cancelled in October 1986 as a casualty of Lear Siegler's lack of money for Piper and it was dismantled at the end of the year.

In the field Turboplus in Washington make a Turbo Arrow conversion with engine modifications and cowl flaps. Robertson offer a modification with spoilers and slotted flaps. An example is s/n 28R-35708 registration N4987S.

In 1987 a Dyna-Cam engine was installed in Arrow s/n 28R-7703152 registration N5743V by a Fixed Based Operator in California. Piper were very interested in this engine and at one time in 1988 had an option to purchase Dyna-Cam.

The low tailed Arrow was revived in 1988 with both the normally aspirated PA-28R-201 and the turbo PA-28R-201T replacing the T-tailed Turbo Arrow IV which was in production. The first aircraft off the line were s/n 2837001 registration N9621N and s/n 2803001 registration N9626N in October and November respectively. Production of the Turbo Arrow was discontinued in 1991, the last three were delivered to Chincul as kits.

In late 1992 Piper looked at producing the PA-28R-250 Dakota SP, a retractable Dakota (to replace the Arrow) with Saratoga II HP modifications and a 250 hp Lycoming IO-540 engine. Lack of money prevented it being anything more than a marketing proposal.

The normally aspirated Arrow was in production at Vero Beach in December 1996.

The prototype PA-28R-221T Arrow s/n 28R-8626001 registration N9286T at Vero Beach. (C. Diefendorf)

PA-28R-201T Turbo Arrow s/n 2803005 registration N9178N at Vero Beach. (R.W. Peperell)

PA-28R-201 Arrow s/n 2837061 registration N9249C at Vero Beach. (R.W. Peperell)

PA-28R SPECIFICATION & PERFORMANCE			
SPECIFICATION	28RT-201T 'Turbo IV'	28R-201 (1988-1996)	28R-221T
Engine	200 hp Continental TSIO-360-FB	200 hp Lycoming IO-360-C1C6	220 hp Continental TSIO-360-PB
Engine TBO (hrs)	1800	1600	
No of seats	4	4	4
Wing Span (ft/ins)	35/5	35/5	35/5
Length (ft/ins)	27/3.5	24/8	25/0
Height (ft/ins)	8/3	7/11	8/0
Useable fuel capacity (US gal)	72	72	72
Gross weight (lbs)	2900-2912	2750	2900
Empty weight (lbs)	1638-1704	1798	
Useful load (lbs)	1208-1262	952	
Propeller	Hartzell 2 or 3-blade	Hartzell 2 or 3-blade	
Floats available			
PERFORMANCE			
Max speed	178 kts	152 kts	187 kts
Cruise speed	172 kts @ 75%	143 kts @ 75%	
Efficiency (gph)	12 @ 75%		
Stall speed - flaps / gear down	56 kts	55 kts	58 kts
Climb @ sea level (fpm)	940	831	
Range with reserves	695-790 nm @ 75%		
Service ceiling (ft)	20,000	16,200	20,000
Take off (Ground run)(ft)	1110		
Take off (over 50ft obst)(ft)	1620	1600	
Landing (Ground roll)(ft)	645		
Landing (over 50ft obst)(ft)	1555	1525	

PA-28RT-201T s/n 28R-8631006 registration N9524N at Vero Beach. The s/n was later changed to 2831001 before delivery. (R.W. Peperell)

PA-28R-300

In mid 1980 Piper started to develop the PA-28R-300 at Lakeland for ENAER of Chile to assemble as the T-35 Pillan (Devil). It was a two seat military trainer based on the Saratoga fuselage with a new cockpit section and an aerobatic wing based on the Cherokee with a 300 hp Lycoming IO-540-K1K5 engine. The first prototype marked 'XBT' (experimental basic trainer) s/n 28R-300-01 registration N300BT first flew on the 6th of March 1981. During development the all-moving tailplane was replaced by an electrically trimmable tailplane with a conventional elevator. The second prototype marked 'YBT' s/n 28R-300-02 registration N40898 which first flew on the 31st of August 1981 was shipped to Chile. N300BT was delivered to ENAER in January 1982 but was written off in an accident on the 10th March 1982. Three pre-production kits were assembled by ENAER in 1982, the first of these was s/n 10182 registration CC-EFP which first flew on the 30th of January. The second, Chile A.F. serial 102 was assembled in Chile and returned to Vero Beach to have a new canopy, windshield, a fully castoring nose-wheel and new seats fitted. It was registered N43612 for test flights at Vero Beach in August 1984 and subsequently became s/n 10484 Chile A.F. serial 104 and later CC-EFS with ENAER. The first production aircraft built to final configuration was assembled in 1984 with s/n 10784 registration CC-EFU and first flew on the 28th of December. Eighty kits were being assembled for the Chile Air Force (T-35A - primary trainer and T-35B - instrument trainer) and 12 for the Panamanian Air Force and the Paraguay Armed Forces as the T-35D. Forty kits were being assembled for the Spanish Air Force by CASA as the T-35C (E.26 Tamiz) starting at the end of 1984. The first delivered to the Air Academy in Chile was s/n 10985 registration FACh101 on the 31st of July 1985.

In May 1993 Piper shipped 18 wing sets to ENAER for a possible order from Argentina, which subsequently did not materialise.

PA-28R-300 PRODUCTION DETAILS

Model Year	Serial Number Range From	To	Type	Total	Comments
Prototypes	28R-300-01	28R-300-02	300	2	Built Lakeland
1982	28R-8319001	28R-8319005	300	5	from Vero Beach
1983	28R-8319006	28R-8319035	300	30	from Vero Beach
1985	28R-2219036	28R-2219086	300	51	from Vero Beach
1986	28R-2219087		300	1	from Vero Beach
1987	28R-2219088	28R-2219098	300	11	from Vero Beach
1988	28R-2219099	28R-2219120	300	22	from Vero Beach
Total manufactured 122 (plus 18 wing sets in 1993)					
Note: Only 2 prototypes built as complete aircraft, all production built as kit.					

Taylor E-2 Cub s/n 12 registration NC10594 in the Piper assembly hall at Vero Beach in 1995. (R.W. Peperell)

Taylor J-2 Cub s/n 1754 registration G-JTWO at Old Warden, England in 1992. (R.W. Peperell)

Piper J-3C-65 Cub s/n 15314 registration NC4218V at Sentimental Journey at Lock Haven in 1989. (R.W. Peperell)

Piper L-4 s/n 8936 U.S. Army serial 236812 (N58347) at Sentimental Journey at Lock Haven in 1989. (R.W. Peperell)

Piper J-4A Cub Coupe s/n 4-1077 registration NC27857 at Sentimental Journey at Lock Haven in 1989. (R.W. Peperell)

Piper HE-1 s/n 5-1483 U.S. Navy serial 30280 (N718E) at Sentimental Journey at Lock Haven in 1989. (R.W. Peperell)

Piper PT-1 s/n 1 registration NX4300 at Oshkosh. (Piper Aviation Museum)

Piper PA-11 Cub Special s/n 11-1420 registration N78659 at Sentimental Journey at Lock Haven in 1989. (R.W. Peperell)

Piper PA-12 Super Cruiser s/n 12-2605 registration NC3648M at Sentimental Journey at Lock Haven in 1989. (R.W. Peperell)

Piper PA-16 Clipper s/n 16-59 registration N5255H at Sentimental Journey at Lock Haven in 1989. (R.W. Peperell)

Piper L-18C s/n 18-1983 U.S. Army serial 52-2383 (N1395R) at Sentimental Journey at Lock Haven in 1989. (R.W. Peperell)

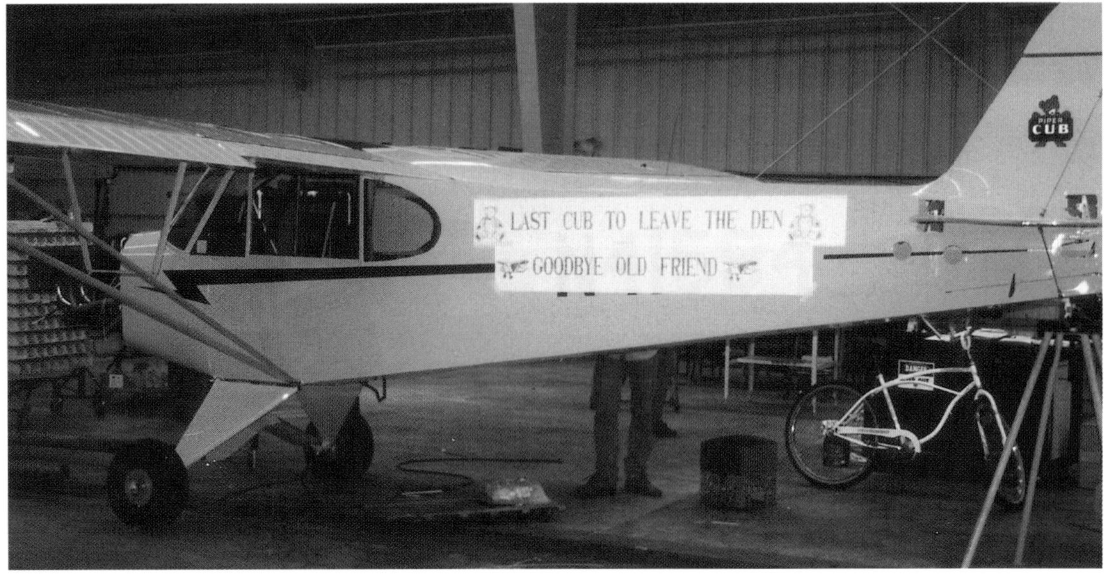

The last Cub, PA-18-150 s/n 1809113 registration N41594 at Vero Beach in December 1994. (R.W. Peperell)

Piper PA-20-135 Pacer s/n 20-887 registration N2107A at Sentimental Journey at Lock Haven in 1989. (R.W. Peperell)

Piper PA-22-160 Tri-Pacer s/n 22-6420 registration N9505D at Sentimental Journey at Lock Haven in 1989. (R.W. Peperell)

Piper PA-23-160 Apache s/n 23-1625 registration HB-LBH at Geneva, Switzerland in 1990. (R.W. Peperell)

Piper PA-23-250 Aztec F s/n 27-8054043 registration ZP-PUS at Lock Haven in 1981. (R.W. Peperell)

Piper PA-24-260 Comanche C s/n 24-4923 registration G-AYED at Kidlington, England in 1994. (R.W. Peperell)

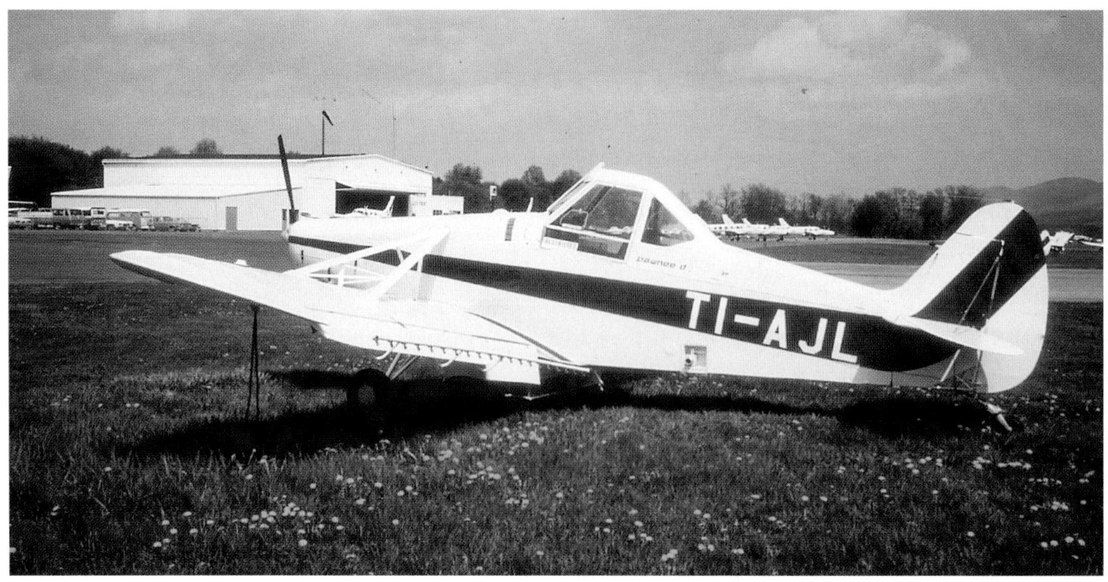

Piper PA-25-260 Pawnee D s/n 25-7656051 registration TI-AJL at Lock Haven in 1976. (R.W. Peperell)

Piper PA-28-181 Archer III s/n 2843015 registration N9260J at Vero Beach in 1995. (R.W. Peperell)

Piper PA-28-161 Warrior III s/n 2842004 registration OK-AKA in the paint-shop at Vero Beach in 1995. (R.W. Peperell)

Piper PA-28-236 Dakota s/n 2811014 registration N9575N (for Indonesia) at Vero Beach in 1987. (R.W. Peperell)

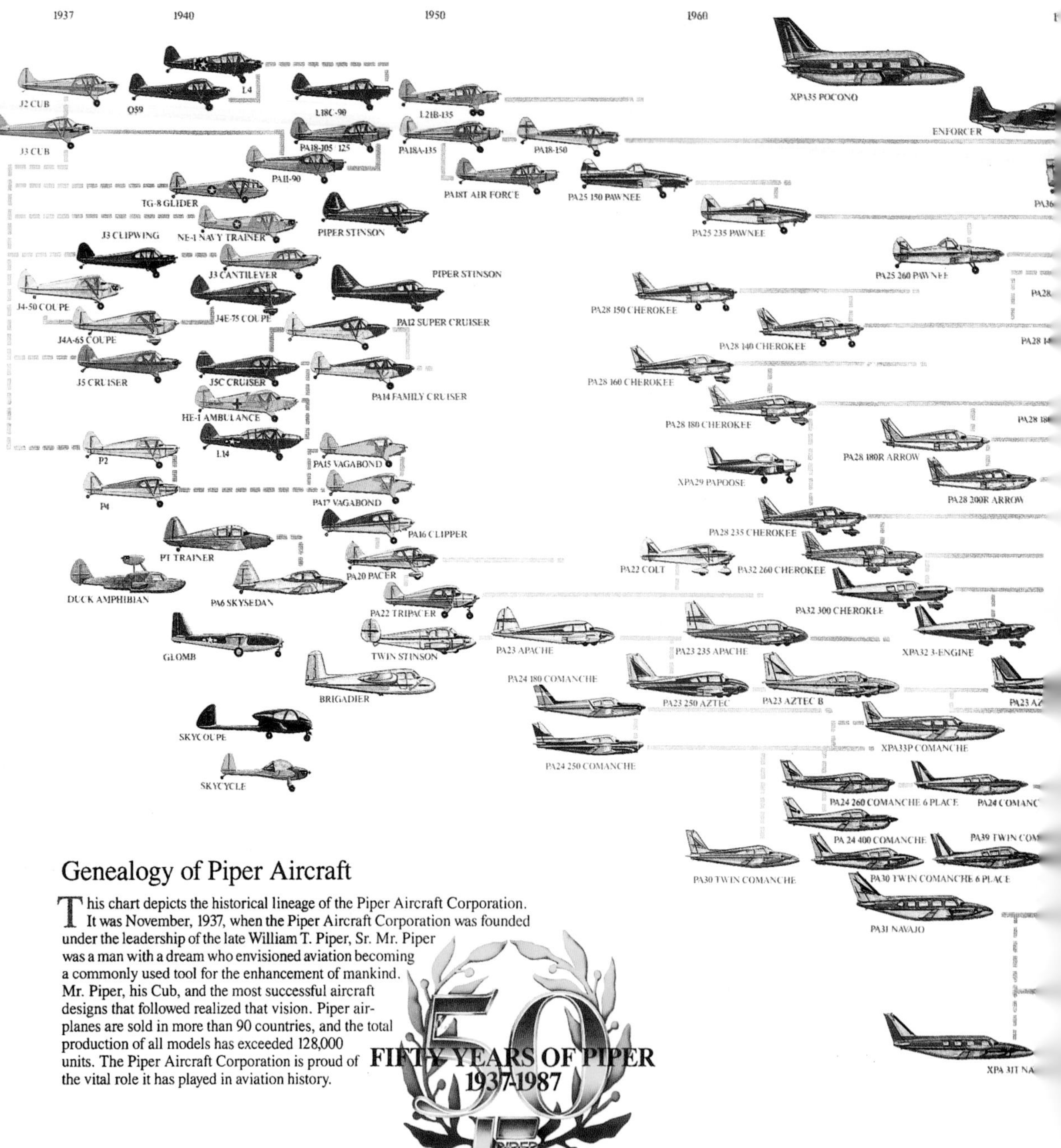
1937
1940
1950
1960
J2 CUB
Q59
L4
L18C-90
L21B-135
XPA35 POCONO
J3 CUB
PA18-105 125
PA18A-135
PA18-150
ENFORCER
PA11-90
PA18T AIR FORCE
PA25 150 PAWNEE
TG-8 GLIDER
J3 CLIPWING
NE-1 NAVY TRAINER
PIPER STINSON
PA25 235 PAWNEE
J3 CANTILEVER
PIPER STINSON
PA25 260 PAWNEE
J4-50 COUPE
J4E-75 COUPE
PA28 150 CHEROKEE
J4A-65 COUPE
PA12 SUPER CRUISER
PA28 140 CHEROKEE
J5 CRUISER
J5C CRUISER
PA14 FAMILY CRUISER
PA28 160 CHEROKEE
HE-1 AMBULANCE
PA28 180 CHEROKEE
L14
P2
PA15 VAGABOND
PA28 180R ARROW
XPA29 PAPOOSE
P4
PA17 VAGABOND
PA28 200R ARROW
PA16 CLIPPER
PA28 235 CHEROKEE
PT TRAINER
PA20 PACER
PA22 COLT
PA32 260 CHEROKEE
DUCK AMPHIBIAN
PA6 SKYSEDAN
PA22 TRIPACER
PA32 300 CHEROKEE
GLOMB
TWIN STINSON
PA23 APACHE
PA23 235 APACHE
XPA32 3-ENGINE
PA24 180 COMANCHE
BRIGADIER
PA23 250 AZTEC
PA23 AZTEC B
SKYCOUPE
XPA33P COMANCHE
PA24 250 COMANCHE
SKYCYCLE
PA24 260 COMANCHE 6 PLACE
PA 24 400 COMANCHE
PA39 TWIN COM
PA30 TWIN COMANCHE
PA30 TWIN COMANCHE 6 PLACE
PA31 NAVAJO
XPA 31T NA
Genealogy of Piper Aircraft
This chart depicts the historical lineage of the Piper Aircraft Corporation. It was November, 1937, when the Piper Aircraft Corporation was founded under the leadership of the late William T. Piper, Sr. Mr. Piper was a man with a dream who envisioned aviation becoming a commonly used tool for the enhancement of mankind. Mr. Piper, his Cub, and the most successful aircraft designs that followed realized that vision. Piper airplanes are sold in more than 90 countries, and the total production of all models has exceeded 128,000 units. The Piper Aircraft Corporation is proud of the vital role it has played in aviation history.
50
FIFTY YEARS OF PIPER
1937-1987
PIPER

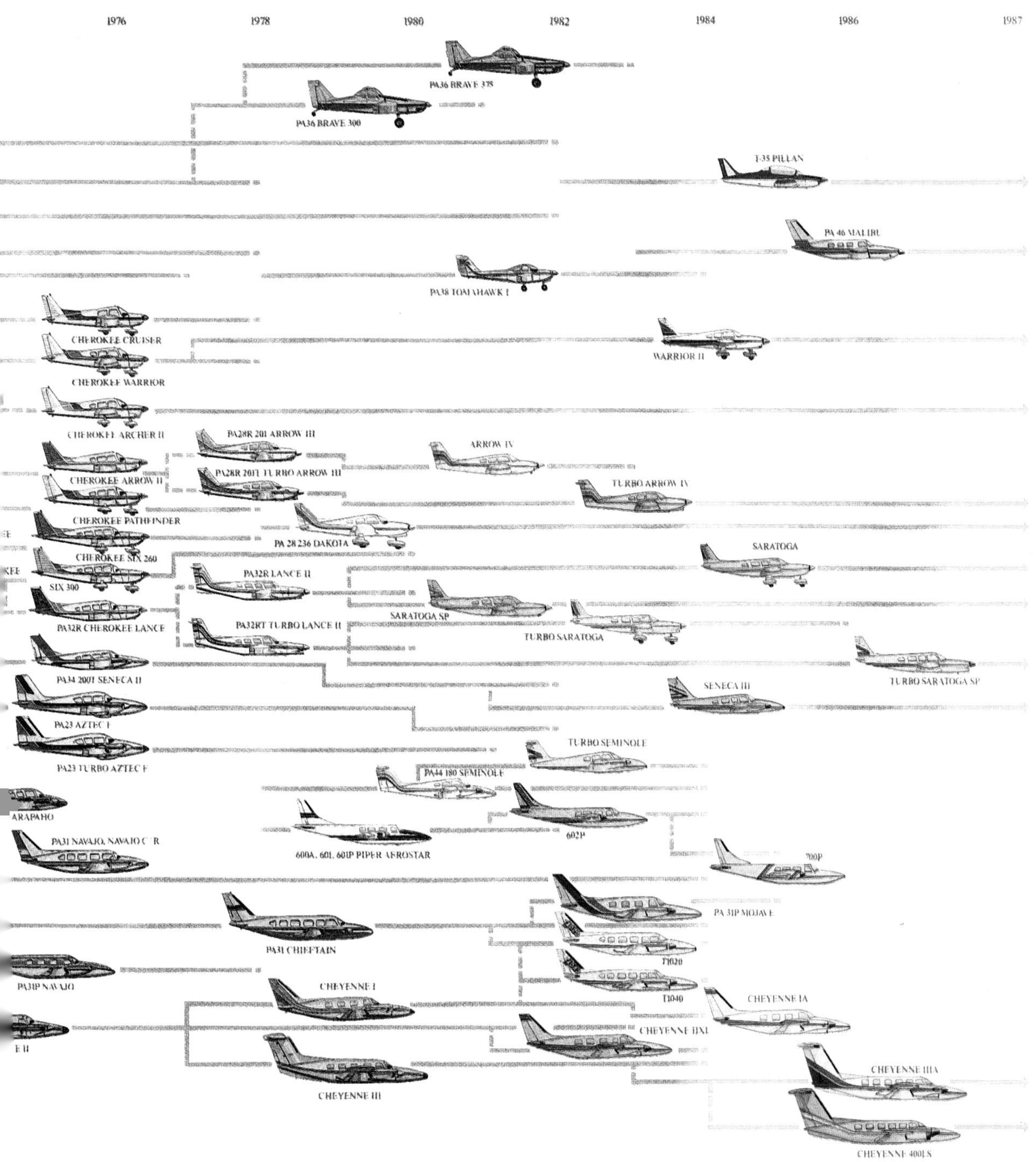
1976
1978
1980
1982
1984
1986
1987
PA36 BRAVE 375
PA36 BRAVE 300
T-35 PILLAN
PA 46 MALIBU
PA38 TOMAHAWK II
CHEROKEE CRUISER
CHEROKEE WARRIOR
WARRIOR II
CHEROKEE ARCHER II
PA28R 201 ARROW III
ARROW IV
CHEROKEE ARROW II
PA28R 201T TURBO ARROW III
TURBO ARROW IV
CHEROKEE PATHFINDER
PA 28 236 DAKOTA
CHEROKEE SIX 260
SARATOGA
SIX 300
PA32R LANCE II
SARATOGA SP
PA32R CHEROKEE LANCE
PA32RT TURBO LANCE II
TURBO SARATOGA
TURBO SARATOGA SP
PA34 200T SENECA II
SENECA III
PA23 AZTEC F
PA23 TURBO AZTEC F
TURBO SEMINOLE
PA44 180 SEMINOLE
ARAPAHO
602P
600A, 601, 601P PIPER AEROSTAR
700P
PA 31P MOJAVE
PA31 CHIEFTAIN
T1020
PA31P NAVAJO
CHEYENNE I
T1040
CHEYENNE IA
CHEYENNE IIXL
CHEYENNE IIIA
CHEYENNE III
CHEYENNE 400LS

Piper PA-28R-201 Arrow s/n 2837051 registration N9219N just after delivery across the Atlantic Ocean at Kildington, England in 1990. Note the extra fuel tank in the back seat. (R.W. Peperell)

Piper PA-30 Twin Comanche B (Miller 200) s/n 30-1363 registration N8237Y at Lock Haven in 1989. (R.W. Peperell)

Piper PA-31 Navajo (Panther conversion) s/n 31-7812035 registration HC-BKP at Lakeland in 1988. (R.W. Peperell)

Piper PA-31-350 Chieftain (Panther conversion) s/n 31-8352037 registration N95TC at Vero Beach in 1992.
(R.W. Peperell)

Piper PA-31T Cheyenne II Maritime s/n 31T-8120026 registration N2483X (for Mauritius) at Lock Haven. (J. Bryerton)

Piper PA-31T2 Cheyenne IIXL s/n 31T-1166008 registration N362AB at Vero Beach in 1987. (R.W. Peperell)

Piper PA-32-300 COIN s/n 32-21 registration N3218W with dummy load at Vero Beach. (G.K. Gates)

The first production Piper PA-32S-300 Cherokee Six Seaplane s/n 32S-40277 registration N4192W. (G.K. Gates)

Piper PA-32-301 Saratoga s/n 3206047 registration N9164B at Vero Beach in 1989. (R.W. Peperell)

Piper PA-32R-301 Saratoga II HP s/n 3213097 registration N495WF at Vero Beach in 1995. (R.W. Peperell)

Piper PA-34-220T Seneca IV s/n 3448072 registration PT-WJB in the paint shop at Vero Beach in 1995. (R.W. Peperell)

Piper PA-35 Pocono s/n 35-E1 registration N3535C in open storage at Widelka, Poland in 1996.
It was sold to Pezetel in 1976. (P. Dunnington)

Piper PA-36 Pawnee Brave s/n 36-7660097 registration N9684N (for export) at Lock Haven in 1976. (R.W. Peperell)

Piper PA-38-112 Tomahawk II s/n 38-81A0093 registration N26006 at Lock Haven in 1981. (R.W. Peperell)

Piper PA-40 Arapaho s/n 40-7400003 registration N9997P with pilot Jack Wetzel (on the right) at Lock Haven. (C. Wilson)

Piper PA-42-720 Cheyenne IIIA s/n 42-5501018 registration N4117V at Lakeland. (Piper Aircraft Corporation)

Piper PA-42-1000 Cheyenne 400LS s/n 42-5527035 registration G-BMVP at Vero Beach in 1986. (R.W. Peperell)

Piper PA-44-180 Seminole s/n 4496002 registration N9256X at Vero Beach in 1995. (R.W. Peperell)

Piper PA-46-350P Malibu Mirage s/n 4636037 registration G-HOOP at Kidlington, England in 1996. (R.W. Peperell)

Piper PA-46T Turbine Malibu s/n 46-8408001 registration N35646 at Vero Beach. (G.K. Gates)

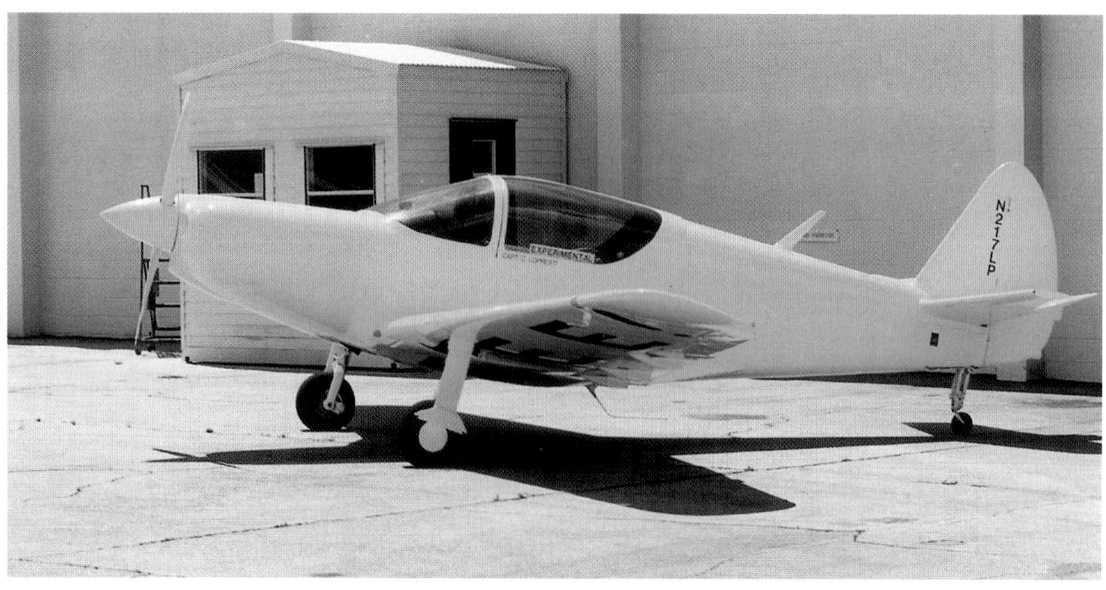

LoPresti-Piper Swiftfury s/n 310 registration N217LP at Vero Beach. (Piper Aircraft Corporation)

The prototype PA-28R-300 experimental basic trainer s/n 28R-300-01 registration N300BT. (G.K. Gates)

*The prototype PA-28R-300 s/n 28R-300-01 registration N300BT painted in Chile A.F. colour scheme.
(Piper Aircraft Corporation)*

The second prototype PA-28R-300 s/n 28R-300-02 marked YBT in the museum at Los Cerrillos, Chile. (G. Ghiretti)

PA-28R-300 SPECIFICATION & PERFORMANCE		
SPECIFICATION	28R-300 T-35 Pillan	T-35TX Aucan
Engine	300 hp Lycoming IO-540-K1K5	420 shp Allison 250B-17D
Engine TBO (hrs)		
No of seats	2	2
Wing Span (ft/ins)	28/11	28/11
Length (ft/ins)	26/3	27/5
Height (ft/ins)	7/8	7/8
Useable fuel capacity (US gal)	74	77
Gross weight (lbs)	2950	3000
Empty weight (lbs)	2050	2307
Useful load (lbs)	900	693
Propeller	Hartzell 3 blade	Hartzell 3 blade
Floats available		
PERFORMANCE		
Max speed	168 kts	198 kts
Cruise speed	161 kts @ 75%	186 kts
Efficiency (gph)		
Stall speed - flaps / gear down	62 kts	59 kts
Climb @ sea level (fpm)	1525	2220
Range with reserves	590 nm @ 75%	620 nm
Service ceiling (ft)	19,100	28,000
Take off (Ground run)(ft)	961	583
Take off (over 50ft obst)(ft)	1660	
Landing (Ground roll)(ft)	797	797
Landing (over 50ft obst)(ft)	1709	

Enaer T-35 s/n 10484 registration N43612 coded 104 with the new larger canopy at Vero Beach. Note this was previously coded 102. (C. Diefendorf)

PA-29 PAPOOSE

In May 1958 Piper started to design a fibreglass aircraft at Vero Beach. Initially a 100 hp Continental engine was proposed but this was later changed to the 108 hp Lycoming O-235-C1B engine. It was to be a 2 place side-by-side low-wing tricycle gear training aircraft. In 1962 the PA-29 Papoose emerged. The airframe was of fibreglass reinforced plastic construction. It incorporated an all moving horizontal tail, full span ailerons which droop to act as flaps and fibreglass sprung main landing gear legs. The prototype s/n 29-01 registration N2900M first flew on the 30th of April 1962. In addition to the flying aircraft a static test wing and fuselage were made. Over time, sun and humidity was damaging the paper honeycomb stabilizing material between the inner and outer honeycomb layers, which had not been treated against humidity. The project was dropped until improved materials became available. The prototype was given to the EAA Museum at Oshkosh, and now resides at Lock Haven in the Piper Aviation Museum.

PA-29 SPECIFICATION & PERFORMANCE

SPECIFICATION	29
Engine	108 hp Lycoming O-235-C1B
No of seats	2
Wing Span (ft/ins)	25/0
Length (ft/ins)	20/8
Height (ft/ins)	7/0
Useable fuel capacity (US gal)	23
Gross weight (lbs)	1500
Empty weight (lbs)	803.5 (planned)
Useful load (lbs)	
Propeller	
PERFORMANCE	
Max speed	130 mph
Cruise speed	
Efficiency (gph)	
Stall speed - flaps / gear down	
Climb @ sea level (fpm)	
Range with reserves	
Service ceiling (ft)	

PA-29 Papoose s/n 29-01 registration N2900M at Vero Beach. (Piper Aviation Museum)

7
THE TWINS

PA-30 TWIN COMANCHE

In November 1956 Piper proposed a Comanche twin with two 150 hp engines, designated the PA-30. Due to commitments to the Aztec and Comanche developments no work was done on this proposal until 1960.

In October 1958 Piper proposed a dual-engined Comanche (driving a single propeller) with the PA-31 designation, which was later to be developed by Bill Lear in California, Piper planned to provide a Comanche and Lycoming would provide two 200 hp IO-360 engines. This development did not take place, and in 1960 Piper decided to use Ed Swearingen for the 'Twin' Comanche using the designation PA-30.

In June 1960 PA-24 Comanche s/n 24-888 registration N5808P was shipped to Ed Swearingen for conversion into a twin Comanche. It had two 160 hp Lycoming IO-320-B1A engines and first flew on the 12th of April 1961 at San Antonio. During development Swearingen fitted propeller hub extensions and the newly developed Lord Dynafocal engine mounts to cure vibrations. It returned to Lock Haven on the 13th of October 1961 and final testing was carried out by Piper until March 1962. This was a success, so Piper built the prototype PA-30 aircraft s/n 30-1 registration N7000Y. This first flew at Lock Haven on the 7th of November 1962. FAA type approval A1EA was granted on the 5th February 1963. Unfortunately deliveries were delayed due to an engine mount problem found in May. Deliveries finally began on the 12th of July 1963. It was priced at $33,900. The experimental N5808P was cancelled from the U.S. Register in late 1963.

Between the 24th and the 26th of December 1964, Max Conrad set a Class 4 World non-stop distance record in Twin Comanche s/n 30-4 registration N7003Y of 7,868 miles from Cape Town, South Africa to St. Petersburg, Florida in 56.8 hours.

PA-30 PRODUCTION DETAILS

Model / Fiscal Year	Serial Number Range From	To	Type	Total	Comments
Experimental	24-888			0	
Prototype	30-1			1	
1963	30-2	30-142		141	
1964	30-143	30-627		485	
1965	30-628	30-901		274	30-853 to B
1966	30-902	30-1329	'B' & 'Turbo B'	428	
1966	30-1331		'B' & 'Turbo B'	1	
1967	30-1330		'B' & 'Turbo B'	1	
1967	30-1332	30-1650	'B' & 'Turbo B'	319	
1968	30-1651	30-1744	'B' & 'Turbo B'	94	30-1717 to C
1969	30-1745	30-1993	'C' & 'Turbo C'	249	
1970	30-1994	30-2000	'C' & 'Turbo C'	7	
Prototype	30-4000		200	1	
The experimental aircraft 24-888 has been included in the PA-24 manufactured total. Total manufactured 2001 (All built at Lock Haven)					

Many aircraft were unsold at the end of 1967 and they were re-licensed (and some were re-registered) in 1968 and then sold. These were s/n: 30-1565, 1568, 1576, 1594, 1606, 1607, 1623, 1624, 1625, 1626, 1635, 1640, 1641, 1645, 1646.

The experimental Twin Comanche being converted by Ed Swearingen at San Antonio, Texas, s/n 24-888 registration N5808P. Note the non standard engine nacelles. (via W.K. Giles)

The experimental Twin Comanche s/n 24-888 registration N5808P at Lock Haven. (via W.K. Giles)

The prototype PA-30 Twin Comanche s/n 30-1 registration N7000Y at Lock Haven. (Piper Aircraft Corporation)

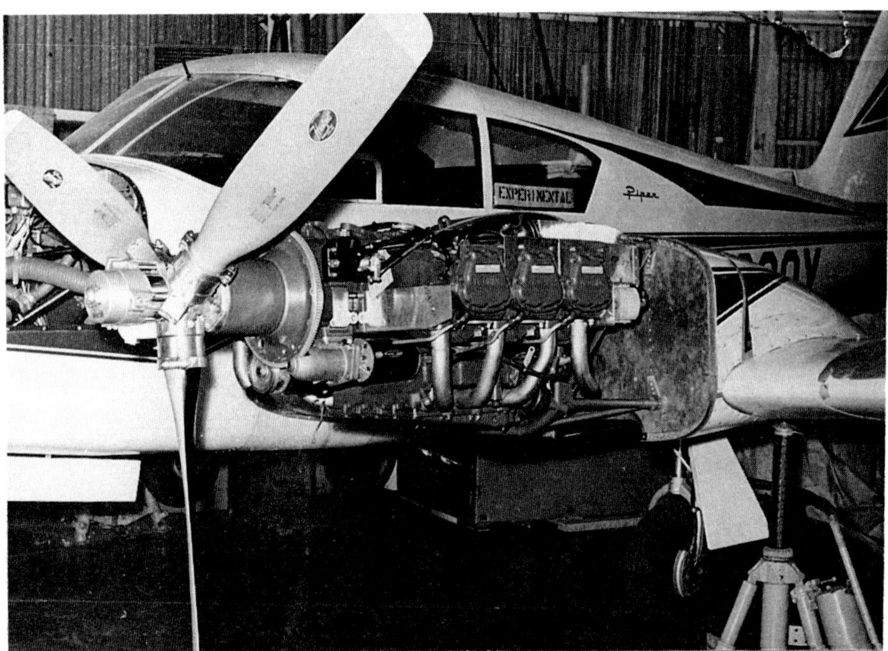

The experimental PA-30-290 being converted by Ed Swearingen, s/n 30-1 registration N7000Y. (via E. Phillips)

The experimental PA-30-290 s/n 30-1 registration N7000Y at Lock Haven. Note larger rudder with trim tab. (P.R. Keating)

PA-30 SPECIFICATION & PERFORMANCE

SPECIFICATION	30	30 'B'	30 'Turbo B'
Engine	160 hp Lycoming IO-320-B	160 hp Lycoming IO-320-B	160 hp Lycoming TIO-320-C1A
Engine TBO (hrs)		2000	1200
No of seats	4	6	6
Wing Span (ft/ins)	36/0	36/0	36/9
Length (ft/ins)	25/2	25/2	25/2
Height (ft/ins)	8/2	8/2	8/2
Useable fuel capacity (US gal)	84	90 + 30 (optional tip tanks)	120 (tip tanks standard)
Gross weight (lbs)	3600	3600	3725
Empty weight (lbs)	2160	2210	2408
Useful load (lbs)	1440	1390	1317
Propellers	Hartzell 2-blade	Hartzell 2-blade	Hartzell 2-blade
Floats available			
PERFORMANCE			
Max speed	205 mph	205 mph	240 mph
Cruise speed	194 mph @ 75%	194 mph @ 75%	223 mph @ 75%
Efficiency (gph)	17.2 @ 75% 14 @ 55%	17.2 @ 75% 15.2 @ 55%	
Stall speed - flaps / gear down	65 mph	69 mph	69 mph
Climb @ sea level (fpm)	1460	1460	1460
Range with reserves	948 sm @ 75%	948 sm @ 75% 1270 sm @ 65%	1425 sm @ 75% 1465 sm @ 65%
Service ceiling (ft)	18,600	18,600	30,000
Take off (Ground run)(ft)	950	950	990
Take off (over 50ft obst)(ft)	1570	1570	1590
Landing (Ground roll)(ft)	700	700	1250
Landing (over 50ft obst)(ft)	1875	1875	1900

In early 1964 Ed Swearingen was asked by Piper to develop a high-speed twin as Lock Haven was too busy. Aircraft N7000Y was used and 290 hp Lycoming IO-540-G engines were installed becoming the PA-30-290. An Aztec tail (bigger than the Twin Comanche's tail) was fitted in April as the aircraft was uncontrollable in single engine operation. Testing was carried out at Lock Haven in May. Later in February 1965 N7000Y was flying with IO-540-H1A5 engines. This was not put into production as it was considered too powerful and there was insufficient directional control and trim.

Piper test flew aircraft s/n 30-7 registration N7005Y with Rayjay turbos on the 27th of January 1965 at Lock Haven. Piper then installed Rayjay turbos on aircraft s/n 30-819 registration N7730Y which first flew on the 6th of April. Rayjay Inc. brought their own converted turbo-charged aircraft s/n 30-123 registration N7105Y to Lock Haven in July. The first two production turbo Twin Comanches were s/n 30-887 and 30-892 delivered in August.

The Twin Comanche B had an extra fuselage side window, 6 seats (the fifth and sixth seats were where the baggage compartment used to be), improved interior and sound proofing. Two operational groups were available, Custom or Sportsman. Also a turbo charged version was available with 160 hp Lycoming TIO-320 engines and standard wing tip fuel tanks which held an extra 30 gallons. The Twin Comanche B test aircraft was s/n 30-853 registration N7750Y converted in 1965. Also converted was s/n 30-790 registration N7758Y. The first model 'B' production aircraft was s/n 30-902 registration N7827Y delivered in November 1965.

In 1966 Piper installed a 200 hp Lycoming IO-360-A engine on aircraft N7005Y and this first flew on the 23rd of February. Piper went on to build a 200 hp Lycoming IO-360-C1C powered Twin Comanche B designated the PA-30-200. This was s/n 30-4000 registration N8300Y and it first flew on the 26th of January 1967. There was not enough performance gain over the 160 hp version to put this into production.

PA-30 Twin Comanche B test aircraft s/n 30-853 registration N7750Y. (Piper Aircraft Corporation)

PA-30 Turbo Twin Comanche B s/n 30-790 registration N7758Y. (Piper Aircraft Corporation)

PA-30 Twin Comanche C test aircraft s/n 30-1717 registration N8568Y. (Piper Aircraft Corporation)

PA-30 SPECIFICATION & PERFORMANCE

SPECIFICATION	30 'C'	30 'Turbo C'
Engine	160 hp Lycoming IO-320-B	160 hp Lycoming TIO-320-C1A
Engine TBO (hrs)	2000	1200
No of seats	6	6
Wing Span (ft/ins)	36/0	36/9
Length (ft/ins)	25/2	25/2
Height (ft/ins)	8/2	8/2
Useable fuel capacity (US gal)	90 + 30 (optional tip tanks)	120 (tip tanks standard)
Gross weight (lbs)	3600	3725
Empty weight (lbs)	2238	2384
Useful load (lbs)	1362	1341
Propellers	Hartzell 2-blade	Hartzell 2-blade
Floats available		
PERFORMANCE		
Max speed	205 mph	246 mph
Cruise speed	198 mph @ 75%	221 mph @ 75%
Efficiency (gph)	19.6 @ 75%	22.6 @ 75%
Stall speed - flaps / gear down	69 mph	69 mph
Climb @ sea level (fpm)	1460	1290
Range with reserves	830 sm @ 75%	1270 sm @ 75%
Service ceiling (ft)	20,000	24,000
Take off (Ground run)(ft)	940	990
Take off (over 50ft obst)(ft)	1530	1590
Landing (Ground roll)(ft)	1215	1250
Landing (over 50ft obst)(ft)	1870	1900

Piper announced the Twin Comanche C on the 15th of August 1968 with further minor improvements including new interior with reclining seats, improved panel and faster cruise speeds obtained from IO-320 engines with higher output. The 'C' test aircraft was s/n 30-1717 registration N8568Y, converted from a 'B' in May 1968 and first flew as such on the 22nd. Turbo Twin Comanche B s/n 30-1567 registration N8416Y was painted in the Twin Comanche C colour scheme. The first production aircraft was s/n 30-1745 registration N8605Y delivered in November 1968.

Production of the PA-30 at Lock Haven was discontinued with s/n 30-2000 registration N8842Y completed on the 5th of November 1969 when the PA-39 replaced it.

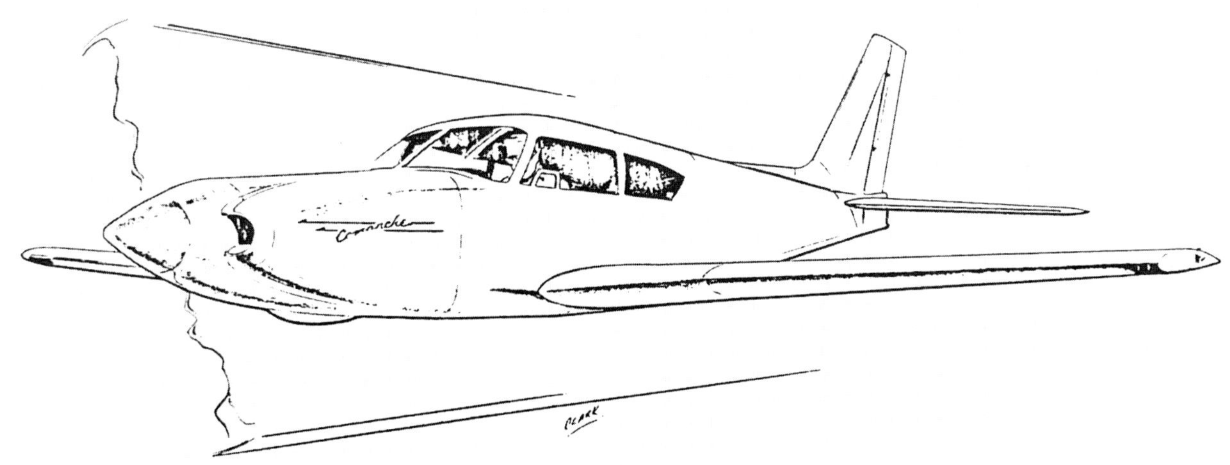

Drawing of the proposed dual engined Comanche (driving one propeller). (Piper Aircraft Corporation)

PA-30 SPECIFICATION & PERFORMANCE		
SPECIFICATION	Miller Twin Comanche 200	Miller Turbo Twin Comanche 200
Engine	200 hp Lycoming IO-360-C1C	200 hp Lycoming TIO-360-C1F
Engine TBO (hrs)		
No of seats	4 / 6	4 / 6
Wing Span (ft/ins)		
Length (ft/ins)		
Height (ft/ins)		
Useable fuel capacity (US gal)		
Gross weight (lbs)	3780	3780
Empty weight (lbs)	2366	2406
Useful load (lbs)	1414	1374
Propellers		
Floats available		
PERFORMANCE		
Max speed		
Cruise speed	217 mph @ 75% 208 mph @ 55%	257 mph @ 75% 242 mph @ 55%
Efficiency (gph)		
Stall speed - flaps / gear down	68 mph	68 mph
Climb @ sea level (fpm)	1900	1900
Range with reserves	1696 sm @ 75% 1811 sm @ 55%	1703 sm @ 75% 1995 sm @ 55%
Service ceiling (ft)	21,000	30,000
Take off (Ground run)(ft)		
Take off (over 50ft obst)(ft)		
Landing (Ground roll)(ft)		
Landing (over 50ft obst)(ft)	1875	1875

In the field two conversions have been offered. The Robertson Twin Comanche has added dorsal fin, drooping ailerons, redesigned leading wing edge and wing fences. An example is s/n 30-1128 registration N8019Y. The Miller Twin Comanche 200 has 200 hp Lycoming IO-360 engines or turbo charged 200 hp Lycoming TIO-360 engines, extended nose, one piece windshield, wing lockers and dorsal fin. Examples of the Miller are s/n 30-992 registration YV-178P, s/n 30-338 registration N7297Y and s/n 30-670 registration XB-WIZ.

Highly modified PA-30 Twin Comanche B s/n 30-1044 registration N7948Y. (R.W. Peperell)

PA-31 NAVAJO

W.T. Piper Senior insisted that Piper design an aircraft in which the tail cone didn't begin tapering until aft of the cabin. So in 1961 at Lock Haven Piper started to develop a new cabin class business twin. Initially it was named the Inca, but before the launch on the 26th of September 1966 the name was changed to Navajo. The prototype s/n 31-1 registration N3100E with 310 hp Lycoming engines first flew on the 30th of September 1964. Originally this aircraft had only two cabin windows, later this was changed to four and the engine nacelles were lengthened. The Navajo was a 6-8 place aircraft with two turbocharged 310 hp Lycoming TIO-540-A engines. The second prototype s/n 31-2 registration N3105E first flew on the 21st of December 1965. Two service test aircraft were produced in 1966, s/n 31-3 registration N3105E first flew on the 8th of June and s/n 31-4 registration N9000Y first flew on the 16th of September. The PA-31 was granted FAA approval A8EA / A20SO on the 24th of February 1966 for 6200 pound gross take-off and landing. After further testing with aircraft N3104E it was re-issued on the 25th of July that same year for 6500 pound take-off and 6200 pound landing. The first production aircraft s/n 31-5 registration N9001Y first flew on the 21st of December. Deliveries commenced with s/n 31-8 registration N9004Y and s/n 31-9 registration N9005Y on the 30th of March 1967. The basic price of the Navajo was $89,500.

The Navajo was also available with a choice of cabin layouts, 6 place standard, 6 place executive or 8 place commuter. To enable Piper to produce the Navajo, a new Navajo flight test building was built in 1968 at Lock Haven. At the same time, a new Corporate Administration headquarters was built there and a new plant making sub-assemblies for Lock Haven was established 60 miles North West of Lock Haven in Quehanna, Pennsylvania.

PA-31 PRODUCTION DETAILS

Model Year	Serial Number Range From	To	Type	Total	Comments
Prototypes	31-1	31-2	31	2	Built Lock Haven
Service test	31-3	31-4	31 / 31-300	2	Built Lock Haven
1967	31-5	31-94	31	90	Built Lock Haven
1968	31-95	31-227	31	133	Built Lock Haven
1968	31-228	31-305	31 / 31-300	78	Built Lock Haven
1969	31-306	31-511	31 / 31-300	206	Built Lock Haven
1969	31-512	31-544	31	33	Built Lock Haven
1970	31-545	31-693	31	149	Built Lock Haven
1971	31-694	31-751	31 'B'	58	Built Lock Haven
1972	31-752	31-861	31 'B'	110	Built Lock Haven
-	31-862	31-900	31 'B'		Not built, see Appendix B
1973	31-7300901	31-7300976	31 'B'	76	Built Lock Haven
1974	31-7400977	31-7400989	31 'B'	13	Built Lock Haven
1974	31-7400990		31-325 'C/R'	1	Built Lock Haven
1974	31-7400991	31-7400996	31 'B'	6	Built Lock Haven
1974	31-7401201	31-7401268	31 'B'	68	Built Lakeland
1975	31-7512001	31-7512072	31 'C' / 31-325 C/R	72	Built Lakeland
1976	31-7612001	31-7612110	31 'C' / 31-325 C/R	110	Built Lakeland
1977	31-7712001	31-7712103	31 'C' / 31-325 C/R	103	Built Lakeland
1978	31-7812001	31-7812129	31 'C' / 31-325 C/R	129	Built Lakeland
1979	31-7912001	31-7912124	31 'C' / 31-325 C/R	124	Built Lakeland
1980	31-8012001	31-8012102 *	31 'C' / 31-325 C/R	94	Built Lakeland
1981	31-8112001	31-8112077	31 'C' / 31-325 C/R	77	Built Lakeland
1982	31-8212001	31-8212036 *	31 'C' / 31-325 C/R	33	Built Lakeland
1983	31-8312001	31-8312019 *	31 'C' / 31-325 C/R	18	Built Lakeland

A total of 12 aircraft in the batches marked * were not delivered, instead they were updated to the next year's model and given new serial numbers or not built. See table below.

Total manufactured 1785

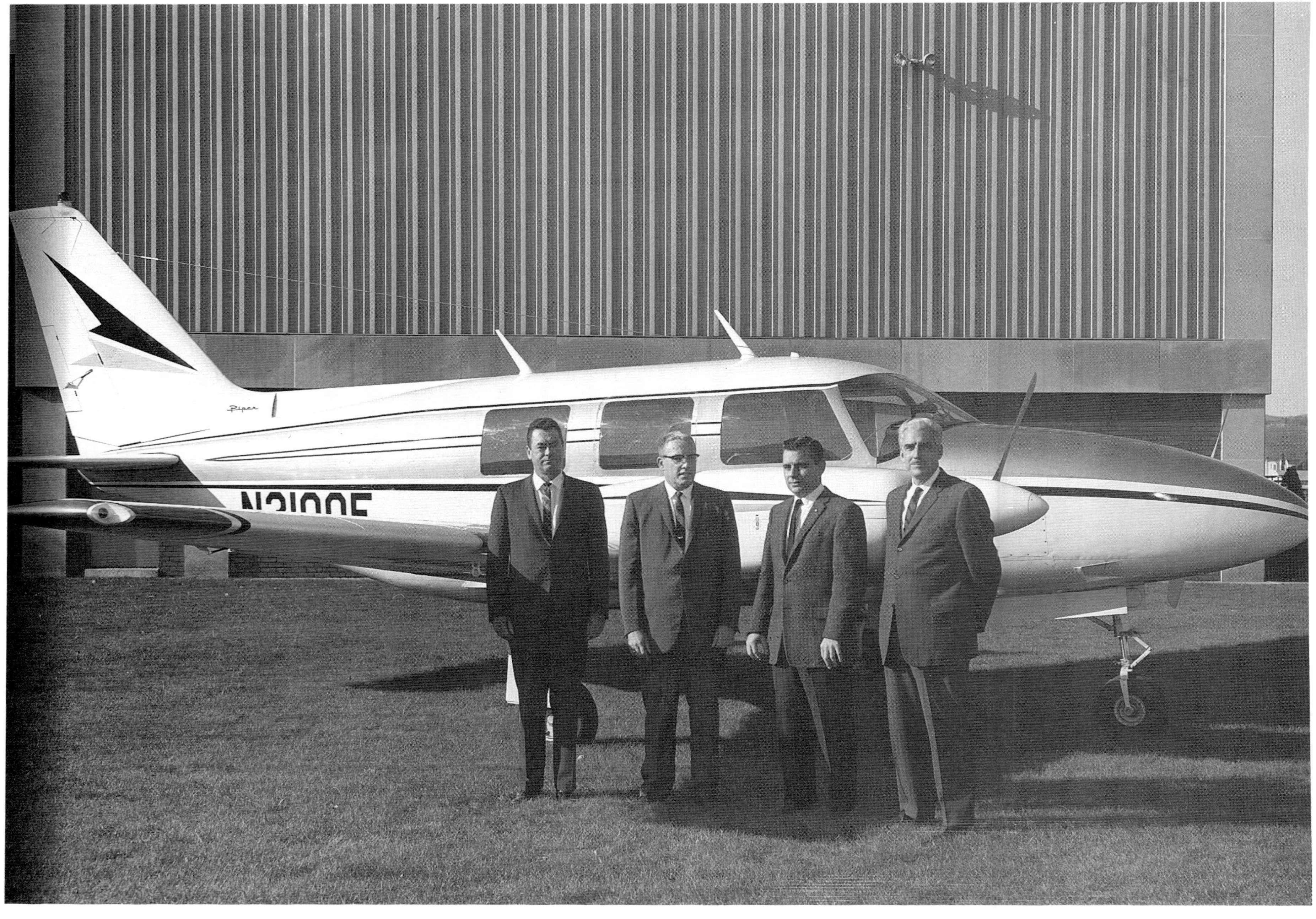

The prototype PA-31 s/n 31-1 registration N3100E at Lock Haven.

The prototype PA-31 s/n 31-1 registration N3100E with four side windows. (Piper Aircraft Corporation)

W.T. Piper Sr. receives FAA certification for the PA-31 Navajo at Lock Haven. Behind is aircraft s/n 31-3 registration N3104E which later became the 300 hp test aircraft. (Piper Aircraft Corporation)

PA-31 Navajo B test aircraft s/n 31-660 registration N6758L with luggage nacelles. (Piper Aircraft Corporation)

PA-31 SERIAL NUMBER CHANGES			
Model	Old Serial Number	New Serial Number	New Model (if different)
PA-31	31-8012093-100	Not built	
PA-31	31-8212022	31-8312009	
PA-31	31-8212026	31-8312008	
PA-31	31-8212035	Not built	
PA-31	31-8312010	Not built	

The Navajo was available with two normally aspirated 300 hp Lycoming IO-540-M1A5 engines in 1967. Aircraft N3104E first flew with the 300 hp engines installed on the 24th of January 1967. The PA-31-300 was FAA approved at 6000 pounds gross on the 12th of June. Only fourteen of the Navajo with the 300 hp engines were built and in 1969 Piper dropped this version.

Piper carried out extensive testing of stalls with and without stall strips during 1969. Aircraft s/n 31-279 registration N9215Y, a 300 hp version and s/n 31-284 registration N9219Y, a 310 hp version were used.

In 1970 Piper developed the improved Navajo B with turbo-charged engines, the 310 hp Lycoming TIO-540-E. It had new air conditioning and electronic systems and optional pilot access door, optional wide utility door and optional nacelle compartments. Aircraft N9001Y was used for baggage nacelle evaluation in March 1969. The two other test aircraft s/n 31-537 registration N6796L and s/n 31-660 registration N6758L were converted from standard Navajos and were registered in 1970. Aircraft N6758L first flew with nacelle lockers in May 1970. Deliveries began with s/n 31-694 registration N366BC in late 1970. In 1973 production of the Navajo was also started at Lakeland, built at both plants for the 1974 model year, before being phased out at Lock Haven.

In October 1972 Lock Haven engineering received an ex flood Navajo s/n 31-861 registration N7463L. This was subsequently used on several minor projects between 1973 and 1975 before being moved to Lakeland.

Between 1972 and 1974 Piper developed the improved Navajo C with 310 hp Lycoming TIO-540-A2C engines and the Navajo C/R with counter rotating 325 hp Lycoming L/TIO-540-F2BD engines. The experimental aircraft, N6758L, with 325 hp counter-rotating engines and wing lockers first flew on the 10th of October 1972. FAA approval was granted on the 31st of May 1974. The first production aircraft s/n 31-7400990 registration N7454L first flew on the 10th November 1974. For those wishing to externally differentiate between the 'C' and the 'C/R', the 'C/R' has engine nacelle luggage compartments which overhang the wings at the trailing edge. These can optionally hold extra fuel tanks. Deliveries of the PA-31 Navajo C and PA-31-325 Navajo C/R commenced with s/n 31-7512001 registration N61481 in December 1974.

Piper tested Cessna 402 registration N3940C at Lock Haven in January 1975 in order to compare it to the new PA-31-325.

Both the Navajo C and Navajo C/R ceased production at Lakeland in September 1983 with s/n 31-8312019 registration N4116K.

Colemill Enterprises of Nashville, Tennessee, U.S.A. obtained a supplemental type certificate in 1982 for the PA-31 Navajo, called the Panther Navajo. It has 350 hp engines, as fitted to the Chieftain, 4 bladed Q-tip Hartzell propellers and zip tips (winglets). An example is s/n 31-7612084 registration N200BE. The Panther Navajo held the FAI Class C1 (d) record between Nashville and England, a distance of 4821 miles in 18 hours 7 minutes. By 1980 Colemill had produced 40 conversions. Other examples are s/n 31-330 registration N2883F, s/n 31-583 registration N7XB, s/n 31-7401254 registration PT-KOD, s/n 31-7812078 registration TI-AMX. Rocket assistance is also available with two 350 pound thrust rockets under the rear fuselage to decrease take-off run and increase climb. An example is s/n 31-186 registration N3ZM.

PA-31 Navajo B test aircraft s/n 31-537 registration N6796L. (Piper Aircraft Corporation)

The experimental PA-31-325 Navajo C/R s/n 31-660 registration N6758L. (Piper Aircraft Corporation)

PA-31 SPECIFICATION & PERFORMANCE

SPECIFICATION	31-300	31	31 'B'
Engine	300 hp Lycoming IO-540-M	310 hp Lycoming TIO-540-A1A	310 hp Lycoming TIO-540-E
Engine TBO (hrs)		1500	1500
No of seats	6-8	6-8	6-8
Wing Span (ft/ins)	40/8	40/8	40/8
Length (ft/ins)	32/8	32/8	32/8
Height (ft/ins)	13/0	13/0	13/0
Useable fuel capacity (US gal)	190	190	190
Gross weight (lbs)	6200	6500	6500
Empty weight (lbs)	3603	3759	3849
Useful load (lbs)	2597	2741	2651
Propellers	Hartzell 2-blade	Hartzell 2-blade	Hartzell 2 or 3-blade
Floats available			
PERFORMANCE			
Max speed	196 kts	228 kts	228 kts
Cruise speed	184 kts @ 75% 171 kts @ 55%	217 kts @ 75% 183 kts @ 55%	220 kts @ 75%
Efficiency (gph)	31.4 @ 75% 24.4 @ 55%	35.6 @ 75% 23.8 @ 55%	37.7 @ 75% 24.8 @ 55%
Stall speed - flaps / gear down	61 kts	62 kts	64 kts
Climb @ sea level (fpm)	1440	1395	1445
Range with reserves	965 nm @ 75% 1193 nm @ 55%	982 nm @ 75% 1316 nm @ 55%	1052 nm @ 75% 1491 nm @ 55%
Service ceiling (ft)	20,500	26,300	26,300
Take off (Ground run)(ft)	930 short 1080 normal	890 short 1066 normal	860 short 1030 normal
Take off (over 50ft obst)(ft)	1950 short 2350 normal	1760 short 2270 normal	1700 short 2190 normal
Landing (Ground roll)(ft)	1115 short 1725 normal	1115 short 1725 normal	1235 short 1915 normal
Landing (over 50ft obst)(ft)	1690 short 2150 normal	1690 short 2150 normal	1810 short 2340 normal

PA-31 Navajo C s/n 31-7512042 at Lock Haven. (R.W. Peperell)

Panther Navajo s/n 31-7401236 registration N61422 at Kidlington, England. (R.W. Peperell)

Aerial view of the Piper factory and the W.T. Piper airport at Lock Haven in 1969. (Piper Aircraft Corporation)

PA-31 SPECIFICATION & PERFORMANCE

SPECIFICATION	31 'C'	31-325 'C/R'	Colemill Panther
Engine	310 hp Lycoming TIO-540-A2C	325 hp Lycoming L/TIO-540-F2BD	350 hp Lycoming TIO-540-J2BD
Engine TBO (hrs)	1800	1600	1600
No of seats	6-8	6-8	6-8
Wing Span (ft/ins)	40/8	40/8	
Length (ft/ins)	32/8	32/8	32/8
Height (ft/ins)	13/0	13/0	13/0
Useable fuel capacity (US gal)	187.3	183.5-190 236 nacelle option	
Gross weight (lbs)	6500 (75) 6536 (80)	6500 (75) 6540 (81)	
Empty weight (lbs)	3930-4003	4000-4099	
Useful load (lbs)	2533-2570	2441-2500	
Propellers	Hartzell 3-blade	Hartzell 3-blade	Hartzell 4-blade Q-tip
Floats available			
PERFORMANCE			
Max speed	228 kts	232 kts	269 kts
Cruise speed	215-217 kts @ 75%	220-221 kts @ 75%	248 kts @ 75%
Efficiency (gph)	37.7 @ 75% 24.8 @ 55%	40.9 @ 75% 25.6 @ 55%	
Stall speed - flaps / gear down	70 kts	64 kts	
Climb @ sea level (fpm)	1220-1445	1220-1500	2000
Range with reserves	935 nm @ 75% 1065 nm @ 55%	940 nm @ 75% 1040 nm @ 55%	
Optional fuel range with reserves		1415 nm @ 55%	
Service ceiling (ft)	24,000-26,300	26,400	
Take off (Ground run)(ft)	860 short 1030 normal	840 short 990 normal	750
Take off (over 50ft obst)(ft)	1700-1720 short 2160-2290 normal	1630 short 2080-2440 normal	1500 750 (rocket assist)
Landing (Ground roll)(ft)	900-1235 short 1915 normal	1235 short 1521 normal	
Landing (over 50ft obst)(ft)	1810 short 2340 normal	1915 short 2340 normal	1400

PA-31-350 CHIEFTAIN

In 1968 Piper started to develop the PA-31 Navajo II at Lock Haven, as a commuter-liner to compete against the Cessna 402 and Beech 99. It was basically a Navajo with a two foot fuselage extension with two extra fuselage windows, large cargo doors, a strengthened floor, an increase in gross weight from 6500 pounds to 7000 pounds, room for 10 seats and initially two 325 hp counter rotating Lycoming L/TIO-540-F2BD engines. Piper realised that it was also a corporate twin winner as well, as the fuselage length would accommodate 6 passengers luxuriously plus the pilot. The experimental aircraft was the Navajo N6758L which was used as a testbed for the more powerful engine requirement. It first flew with a 325 hp counter rotating engine on the 15th of October 1970. The prototype s/n 31-5001 registration N7700L first flew with counter-rotating 325 hp Lycoming TIO-540-F2BD engines on the 22nd of January 1971. During development engine horse-power was increased to meet single engine operation requirements. It first flew with 340 hp on the 14th of April and with 350 hp on the 29th of September. FAA approval using the PA-31 Navajo certificate was granted on the 3rd of May 1972. The first pre-production aircraft was s/n 31-5003 registration N7676L completed in October 1972, delayed by the flood at Lock Haven in June 1972. Static-test fuselage s/n 31-5002 and the first production aircraft s/n 31-5004 registration N7677L were lost in the flood. Piper named it the PA-31-350 Navajo Chieftain with 350 hp Lycoming L/TIO-540-J2BD engines and announced it on the 11th of September 1972. The Type Certificate was re-issued on the 25th October. The first production aircraft s/n 31-7305005 registration N7678L was completed on the 7th of November 1972. Deliveries began in January 1973. The basic price was $141,900 and an IFR equipped Chieftain was priced at $167,045.

Piper retained N7676L for various development tests during 1973, one of these being injector tests for Lycoming engines.

In 1973 production of the Navajo was also started at Lakeland, built at both plants for the 1974 model year, before being phased out at Lock Haven. The first aircraft off the Lakeland Production line was s/n 31-7405401 registration N74999 in June 1973.

In late 1972 Piper initiated design of a PA-31-350P Pressurized Chieftain. In December the design had oval windows, 3.4 psi pressurization and modified Lycoming TIO-540 engines. The project was put on ice for 18 months and then resurrected in July 1974. The pressurization was increased to 3.5 psi and it had PA-31P side windows. This design was developed further and then transferred to Lakeland on the 1st July 1975 as the PA-42, soon after becoming the PA-43.

For the 1980 model year the name 'Navajo' was dropped, becoming just the Chieftain. Production of the PA-31-350 Chieftain ended in October 1984 with s/n 31-8452021 registration N4118B. It was proposed to restart the Chieftain line at the end of 1985, but this suffered from the scaling back of activity by owners Lear Siegler.

Over the years Piper proposed several versions of the Chieftain as an airliner. On 1st September 1981 Piper set up an airline division to deal directly with operators of the new T-1000 (Transport 1000) series aircraft which were to be delivered from April 1982, rather than through its regular distributor network. It offered spare parts sales, 24 hour support and extended warranty on the aircraft. The first of the T-1000 series aircraft was the T-1020 which was a Chieftain derivative aimed at the commuter market. Work had started at Lakeland on this in January 1980. It had improved hard-wearing interior, the landing gear wheel doors were removed (strut doors were kept) and the landing gear was strengthened, new lighter seats enabling 11 seats to be fitted, a simplified fuel system and 350 hp Lycoming TIO-540-J2B engines. The first aircraft was s/n 31-8253001 registration N4120J which first flew on the 25th of September 1981. The T-1020 is certified under the Chieftain type approval. Production at Lakeland ended in 1985 with s/n 31-8553002 registration N41189. Desert Sun Airlines and Air New Orleans operated T-1020's in the late 1980s.

The prototype PA-31 Navajo II s/n 31-5001 registration N7700L. (Piper Aircraft Corporation)

1975 model PA-31-350 Navajo Chieftain s/n 31-7405460 registration N61425. (Piper Aircraft Corporation)

PA-31-350 T-1020 s/n 31-8253001 registration N4120J. (Piper Aircraft Corporation)

For many years Piper had been trying to improve the useful load of the Chieftain. There was a joint Piper and Lycoming programme to develop more powerful engines that were needed for the extra weight. The first proposal was the PA-31-350 SP (also known as the Chieftain II) with a 300 pound increase in useful load, but still with the 350 hp engines. Much testing had taken place during 1977 on 375 hp Lycoming versus 350 hp Lycoming engines. An ex Lock Haven flood damaged Navajo s/n 31-861 registration N7463L had been used by Lock Haven engineering for a few years. It had one foot extended wing tips fitted at Lock Haven during June 1975. It was delivered to Lakeland engineering at the end of January 1976. This aircraft had an experimental 375 hp TIGO-540-E engine installed on the port side and first flew on the 10th of August 1976. Tests continued through to mid 1977. This also supported the PA-43 engine programme. Later, with Lycoming at Williamsport, Pennsylvania it received the new engine on the starboard side. Another option that Piper reviewed was 375 hp engines plus three feet wing tip extensions enabling a 7600 pound gross weight. The wing tip extensions were fitted to N7463L in January 1978.

Wingtip extensions were also fitted to Chieftain s/n 31-7752005 registration N62957 in February. By May there were two alternative designs, the PA-31-350 TF with 350 hp engines, one foot wing tip extensions and 7200 pound gross, and the PA-31-350 ST with 350 hp engines, three feet wing tip extensions and 7600 pound gross. By August these had become the PA-31-351 and PA-31-352 respectively. Aircraft s/n 31-7852121 registration N27722 was to have the three feet wing tip extensions fitted, but it is not known whether this took place. In early 1982 the programme had been developed into the PA-31-350 A as the Chieftain II and T-1020 A.

PA-31-350 PRODUCTION DETAILS

Model Year	Serial Number Range From	To	Type	Total	Comments
Prototype	31-5001		Navajo II	1	Built Lock Haven
Pre-production	31-5003		Chieftain	1	Built Lock Haven
-	31-5004		Chieftain		Not built, see Appendix B
1973	31-7305005	31-7305125	Chieftain	121	Built Lock Haven
1974	31-7405126	31-7405257	Chieftain	132	Built Lock Haven
1974	31-7405401	31-7405497	Chieftain	97	Built Lakeland
1975	31-7552001	31-7552132	Chieftain	132	Built Lakeland
1976	31-7652001	31-7652177	Chieftain	177	Built Lakeland
1977	31-7752001	31-7752192	Chieftain	192	Built Lakeland
1978	31-7852001	31-7852171	Chieftain	171	Built Lakeland
1979	31-7952001	31-7952250	Chieftain	250	Built Lakeland
1980	31-8052001	31-8052221	Chieftain	221	Built Lakeland
1981	31-8152001	31-8152203	Chieftain	203	Built Lakeland
1982	31-8252001	31-8252085 *	Chieftain	69	Built Lakeland
1982	31-8253001	31-8253017 *	T-1020	10	Built Lakeland
1983	31-8352001	31-8352045 *	Chieftain	39	Built Lakeland
1983	31-8353001	31-8353007	T-1020	7	Built Lakeland
1984	31-8452001	31-8452024 *	Chieftain	21	Built Lakeland
1984	31-8453001	31-8453004 *	T-1020	2	Built Lakeland
1985	31-8553001	31-8553002	T-1020	2	Built Lakeland
Prototype	31-8458001 *		353 T-1020	0	Built Lakeland
Prototype	31-8558001		353 T-1020	1	Built Lakeland
Pre-production	31-8557001		353 Chieftain	1	Built Lakeland
1986	31-5557002 *		353 Chieftain	0	
1986	31-8652001	31-8652003 *	Chieftain	0	
A total of 39 aircraft in the batches marked * were not delivered, instead they were updated to the next year's model and given new serial numbers or not built. See table below. Total manufactured -350 1827 T-1020 21 -353 2					

PA-31-350 SERIAL NUMBER CHANGES			
Model	Old Serial Number	New Serial Number	New Model (if different)
PA-31-350	31-8252033	31-8352015	
PA-31-350	31-8252041	31-8352011	
PA-31-350	31-8252051	31-8352012	
PA-31-350	31-8252052	31-8352017	
PA-31-350	31-8252054	31-8352018	
PA-31-350	31-8252057	31-8352013	
PA-31-350	31-8252059	31-8352014	
PA-31-350	31-8252060	31-8352008	
PA-31-350	31-8252064	31-8352020	
PA-31-350	31-8252067	31-8352021	
PA-31-350	31-8252068	31-8352022	
PA-31-350	31-8252073	Not built	
PA-31-350	31-8252078	31-8352004	
PA-31-350	31-8252079	31-8252081	
PA-31-350	31-8252080	31-8252083	
PA-31-350	31-8252082	Not built	
PA-31-350 T-1020	31-8253004	31-8353001	
PA-31-350 T-1020	31-8253011	31-8353002	
PA-31-350 T-1020	31-8253013	31-8353003	
PA-31-350 T-1020	31-8253014	31-8353004	
PA-31-350 T-1020	31-8253015	31-8353005	
PA-31-350 T-1020	31-8253016	31-8353006	
PA-31-350 T-1020	31-8253017	31-8353007	
PA-31-350	31-8352016	Not built	
PA-31-350	31-8352019	Not built	
PA-31-350	31-8352040	31-8452004	
PA-31-350	31-8352043	31-8452006	
PA-31-350	31-8352044	31-8452005	
PA-31-350	31-8352045	31-8452007	
PA-31-350	31-8452022-024	Not built	
PA-31-350 T-1020	31-8453003	31-8553001	
PA-31-350 T-1020	31-8453004	31-8553002	
PA-31-353	31-8458001	31-8558001	
PA-31-353	31-5557002	Not built	
PA-31-350	31-8652001-003	Not built	

The design again changed to the PA-31-353, now with Mojave wings (4 feet bigger span than the Chieftain), 340 pound increased gross weight, Chieftain fuselage, vertical tail and engine nacelles, T-1040 horizontal tail and 350 hp Lycoming L/TIO-540-X48 engines counter rotating away from the fuselage. The prototype s/n 31-8458001 registration N353PA was registered in December 1982. The pre-production aircraft s/n 31-8557001 registration N353PX first flew on the 18th of May 1984 but now with -W2A engines. This aircraft was re-registered N353PA in June and was to be the new Chieftain. The prototype aircraft was re-registered N353PX with s/n changed to 31-8558001 also in June and was the new T-1020. In 1985 the project was put on ice due to a decline in Chieftain sales, the first production aircraft s/n 31-5557002 was left on the production line unfinished. The prototype and first production aircraft were dismantled at Vero Beach in February 1987 and were given to the Piper Aviation Museum at Lock Haven.

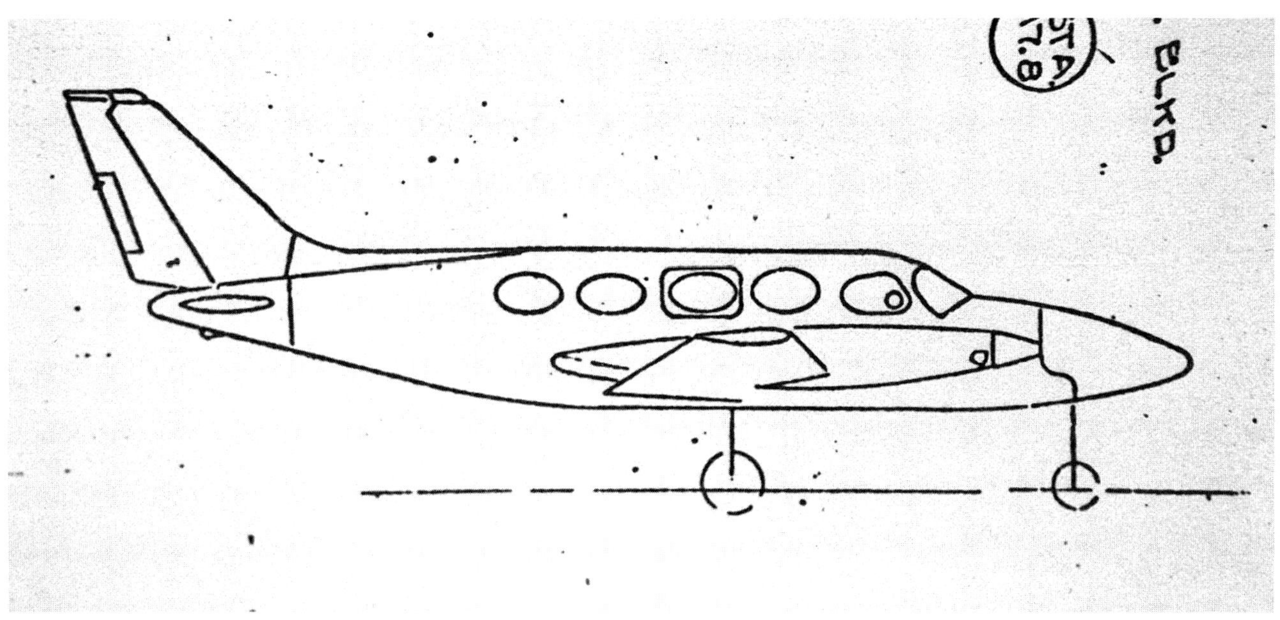

Drawing of the proposed PA-31-350P Pressurized Chieftain. (Piper Aircraft Corporation)

The prototype PA-31-353 s/n 31-8557001 registration N353PX at Vero Beach. (R.W. Peperell)

The pre-production PA-31-353 s/n 31-8558001 registration N353PA at Vero Beach. (R.W. Peperell)

PA-31-350 SPECIFICATION & PERFORMANCE

SPECIFICATION	31-350 Chieftain	31-350 T-1020	Schafer Comanchero 500A / 500B
Engine	350 hp Lycoming L/TIO-540-J2BD	350 hp Lycoming L/TIO-540-J2B	550 / 578 shp Pratt & Whitney PT6A-20 / 27
Engine TBO (hrs)	1200 (73-78) 1600 (79 & later)	1800	
No of seats	6-10	11	
Wing Span (ft/ins)	40/8	40/8	40/8
Length (ft/ins)	34/7.5	34/7.5	34/7.5
Height (ft/ins)	13/0	13/0	13/0
Useable fuel capacity (US gal)	182 236 (nacelle option)	106	346
Gross weight (lbs)	7000 (73-80) 7045 (81 & later)	7045	8003
Empty weight (lbs)	3991-4319	4450	4916
Useful load (lbs)	2726-3009	2595	3087
Propellers	Hartzell 3-blade counter rotating	Hartzell 3-blade counter rotating	
Floats available			
PERFORMANCE			
Max speed	231-236 kts	235 kts	240 kts
Cruise speed	221-228 kts @ 75% 210 kts @ 65%	212 kts @ 75% 162 kts @ 55%	234 kts
Efficiency (gph)	43.6 @ 75% 26.3 @ 55%	43.6 @ 75% 26.3 @ 55	
Stall speed - flaps / gear down	74 kts	74 kts	
Climb @ sea level (fpm)	1120-1390	1120	2400-2800
Range with reserves	873 nm @ 75% 950 nm @ 55%	695 nm @ 55%	500-1300 nm
Optional fuel range with reserves	1260 nm @ 65% 1290 nm @ 55%		
Service ceiling (ft)	24,000-27,200	24,000	24,000
Take off (Ground run)(ft)	1050 short 1350 normal	1350	
Take off (over 50ft obst)(ft)	1780-1850 short 2410-2510 normal	2780	2490
Landing (Ground roll)(ft)	1045-1180 short 1575 normal	1045	
Landing (over 50ft obst)(ft)	1880-2150 short 2725 normal	2150	2375

In late 1989 Romeo Charlie Inc., Piper's owners, announced plans to set up a new company Piper North, at Lock Haven with Pennsylvania State Government aid of $72m. Piper North was to initially make the Chieftain, one in 1990 from major sub assemblies stored at Lakeland, rising to 20 in 1991. John Piper, grandson of W.T. Piper Senior would be president of the company. Due to cash flow problems at Piper in 1990 followed by chapter 11 status, Piper North was never established.

Schafer of Clifton, Texas, U.S.A. make a Chieftain conversion called the Comanchero 500 with 550 shp Pratt and Whitney PT6A-20 turbo prop engines. An example is s/n 31-7552106 registration N61392. Also Colemill Enterprises market a chieftain conversion with four-bladed propellers and winglets called the Panther II. An example is s/n 31-8052054 registration N555MP.

PA-31-350 SPECIFICATION & PERFORMANCE	
SPECIFICATION	**31-353**
Engine	350 hp Lycoming L/TIO-540-X48 later 350 hp Lycoming L/TIO-540-W2A
Engine TBO (hrs)	
No of seats	6-10
Wing Span (ft/ins)	44/8
Length (ft/ins)	34/7.5
Height (ft/ins)	13/0
Useable fuel capacity (US gal)	182, 236 (nacelle option)
Gross weight (lbs)	7385
Empty weight (lbs)	4296
Useful load (lbs)	3099
Propellers	Hartzell 3-blade counter rotating
Floats available	
PERFORMANCE	
Max speed	236 kts
Cruise speed	
Efficiency (gph)	
Stall speed - flaps / gear down	76 kts
Climb @ sea level (fpm)	
Range with reserves	
Service ceiling (ft)	24,000
Take off (Ground run)(ft)	
Take off (over 50ft obst)(ft)	
Landing (Ground roll)(ft)	
Landing (over 50ft obst)(ft)	

Panther Chieftain s/n 31-8052054 registration N555MP. (R.W. Peperell)

PA-31P PRESSURIZED NAVAJO / MOJAVE

In January 1966 Piper began development at Lock Haven of a pressurized cabin class twin, the Pressurized Navajo. A pressurized aircraft had been under discussion at Piper since 1962. In 1967 Piper used Navajo N3104E for various tests for the Pressurized Navajo programme. The PA-31P was basically a Navajo which had a pressurized cabin with room for 6 seats with two 425 hp Lycoming TIGO-540-C1A engines. The prototype s/n 31P-1 registration N9200Y first flew on the 26th of March 1968. The engines were updated to -E1A6 and first flew with these on the 4th of October 1968. The pre-production aircraft s/n 31P-2 registration N6800L first flew on the 13th of May 1969. FAA approval A8EA was granted on the 26th November for 7600 pound gross weight. It was re-issued on the 23rd of January 1970 at 7800 pounds. Piper announced the type in March and deliveries began in April priced at $275,000.

In late 1972 Piper initiated two improvement programmes in parallel. The first was a minor upgrade to the PA-31P for 1973, which was a gross weight increase to 7900 pounds, improved interior and a new panel. Aircraft s/n 31P-75 registration N7322L was used to test these changes, which was to be implemented in the middle of the 1973 model year. The gross weight change was not implemented. The second programme was a major upgrade of the PA-31P for 1976, which was increased range, payload, baggage volume and pilot room in an extended fuselage, extended wing tips, simplified fuel management, counter rotating 450 hp engines and a new instrument panel. Prototype N9200Y had 450 hp Lycoming L/TIGO-540-G1AD engines fitted and first flew on the 26th of April 1973. The programme was cancelled in August 1974, in order to concentrate resources on the Cheyenne programme.

In 1973 Piper had looked at producing a Pressurized Navajo with 350 hp engines, designated the PA-31P-350. This had the PA-31P fuselage and the PA-31-350 wings and 350 hp Lycoming L/TIO-540-J2BD engines. The psi pressurization would have been 3.4. The programme was cancelled in 1974.

PA-31P PRODUCTION DETAILS

Model Year	Serial Number Range From	To	Type	Total	Comments
Prototype	31P-1		31P	1	
Pre-production	31P-2		31P	1	
1970	31P-3	31P-30	31P	28	
1971	31P-31	31P-66	31P	36	
1972	31P-67	31P-80	31P	14	
-	31P-81	31P-109	31P		Not built, see Appendix B
1973	31P-7300110	31P-7300172	31P	63	
1974	31P-7400173	31P-7400230	31P	58	
1975	31P-7530001	31P-7530028 *	31P	27	
1976	31P-7630001	31P-7630019	31P	19	
1977	31P-7730001	31P-7730012	31P	12	
Prototypes	31P-8314001	31P-8314002 *	31P-350	0	
Prototypes	31P-8414001	31P-8414002	31P-350	2	
1984	31P-8414003	31P-8414050	31P-350	50	

A total of 3 aircraft in the batches marked * were not delivered, instead they were updated to the next year's model and given new serial numbers or not built. See table below.
Total manufactured 31P 259 31P-350 50 (All built at Lock Haven)

PA-31P SERIAL NUMBER CHANGES

Model	Old Serial Number	New Serial Number	New Model (if different)
PA-31P	31P-7530021	Not built	
PA-31P-350	31P-8314001	31P-8414001	
PA-31P-350	31P-8314002	31P-8414002	

The prototype PA-31P Pressurized Navajo s/n 31P-1 registration N9200Y. (Piper Aircraft Corporation)

The first production PA-31P Pressurized Navajo s/n 31P-2 registration N6800L at Lock Haven. (Piper Aircraft Corporation)

The experimental PA-31P s/n 31P-73 registration N59900 with T-tail at Lakeland. (G.K. Gates)

The prototype PA-31P-350 Mojave s/n 31P-8314001 registration N9087P at Lock Haven. (D. Schwartz)

The second prototype PA-31P-350 Mojave s/n 31P-8314002 registration N9192P at Lock Haven. (D. Schwartz)

The first production PA-31P-350 Mojave s/n 31P-8414003 registration N9198Y. (Piper Aircraft Corporation)

PA-31P SPECIFICATION & PERFORMANCE

SPECIFICATION	31P	31P-350	31P '450'
Engine	425 hp Lycoming TIGSO-540-E1A	350 hp Lycoming L/TIO-540-V2AD	425 hp Lycoming L/TIGO-541-G1AD
Engine TBO (hrs)		2000	
No of seats	6-8	6-7	6-8
Wing Span (ft/ins)	40/8	44/6	44/7
Length (ft/ins)	34/6	34/6	36/7
Height (ft/ins)	13/3	13/0	13/3
Useable fuel capacity (US gal)	192 242 (Nacelle option)	238	
Gross weight (lbs)	7800	7245	8200
Empty weight (lbs)	4842	5070	4744
Useful load (lbs)	2958	2175	2456
Propellers	Hartzell 3-blade	Hartzell 3-blade	
Pressurization (psi)	5.5	5.0	
Floats available			
PERFORMANCE			
Max speed	243 kts	242 kts	245 kts
Cruise speed	233 kts @ 75% 180 kts @ 55%	235 kts @ 75% 195 kts @ 60%	234 kts @ 75%
Efficiency (gph)	54 @ 75% 34 @ 55%		
Stall speed - flaps / gear down	72 kts	70 kts	72 kts
Climb @ sea level (fpm)	1740	1490	1875
Range with reserves	925 nm @ 75% 1260 nm @ 55%	1113 nm @ 75% 1221 nm @ 60%	
Service ceiling (ft)	29,000	30,400	29,000
Take off (Ground run)(ft)	1440	1625	
Take off (over 50ft obst)(ft)	2200	2469	2980
Landing (Ground roll)(ft)	1370	1390	
Landing (over 50ft obst)(ft)	2700	2300	2800

The 1977 model year had the larger crew window.

Production stopped with s/n 31P-7730012 registration N82608 at Lock Haven on the 26th of August 1977.

In 1978 and 1979 Piper experimented with a T-tail on the Navajo series. Aircraft s/n 31P-73 registration N59900 had a T-tail installed that was very similar to the T-tail on the experimental Cheyenne III N7676L. This first flew on the 2nd November 1978, not only to check out the Navajo with a T-tail, but also to prove the new Lakeland CAD capability. Possible T-tail installations were the PA-43 and the Jet Navajo. In the end none were proceeded with. Later, in 1980, it went to San Antonio on another programme for pressurization tests for the survey camera installation in the bottom of the fuselage.

At the end of 1980 Piper started to develop a new pressurized cabin class twin, named the PA-31P-350 Navajo Mojave. It had the Cheyenne I fuselage, 350 hp counter rotating Lycoming L/TIO-540-V2AD engines, the Chieftain's tail unit and the wings from the PA-31-353. Prototype one was s/n 31P-8314001 registration N9087P which first flew on the 20th of April 1982 and the second prototype was s/n 31P-8314002 registration N9092P which first flew on the 26th of May. This was later re-registered N9198Y in October 1982. Whilst reviewing the TCM TP-500 engine, Piper considered putting the engine on the Mojave in January 1983. The serial numbers were changed to 31P-8414001 and 31P-8414002 on the 9th June 1983 when the FAA approval was also granted. Deliveries of the Mojave (Navajo was dropped from the name) began from Lock Haven in July 1983. Price with IFR equipment was $580,900. Production ended with s/n 31P-8414050 registration N2598N on the 26th of June 1984. This was the last aircraft to be built at Lock Haven, the plant was closed in August 1984 after producing aircraft for 47 years.

PA-31P SPECIFICATION & PERFORMANCE	
SPECIFICATION	Schafer Comanchero
Engine	620 shp Pratt & Whitney PT6A-135
Engine TBO (hrs)	
No of seats	6-8
Wing Span (ft/ins)	40/8
Length (ft/ins)	34/6
Height (ft/ins)	13/3
Useable fuel capacity (US gal)	
Gross weight (lbs)	
Empty weight (lbs)	
Useful load (lbs)	
Propellers	
Pressurization (psi)	
Floats available	
PERFORMANCE	
Max speed	
Cruise speed	280 kts
Efficiency (gph)	
Stall speed - flaps / gear down	
Climb @ sea level (fpm)	4500
Range with reserves	1560 nm
Service ceiling (ft)	29,000
Take off (Ground run)(ft)	
Take off (over 50ft obst)(ft)	1750
Landing (Ground roll)(ft)	
Landing (over 50ft obst)(ft)	

Schafer of Clifton, Texas, U.S.A. make a Pressurized Navajo conversion called the Comanchero. It has 620 shp Pratt & Whitney PT6A-135 turbo prop engines. Examples are s/n 31P 7400208 registration N111RQ, s/n 31P-7300124 registration XC-COC, s/n 31P-7300152 registration N7671L, s/n 31P-7300115 registration N9016H, s/n 31P-7400203 registration N222SA and s/n 31P-7400227 registration N900TB.

Schafer Comanchero s/n 31P-7400203 registration N222SA. (Aerospace Publishing)

PA-31T CHEYENNE

Piper first considered a turbine aircraft in July 1965. To prove the concept of turbo-prop engines on a Navajo airframe, Piper used s/n 31-1 registration N3100E as a test aircraft. The aircraft was delivered to Swearingen Aircraft, Texas on the 6th of October 1966 with the normal Lycoming engines fitted. Swearingen fitted 550 shp Pratt & Whitney PT-6A-20 engines on the 15th of March 1967 and new Hartzell propellers on the 13th of April. It first flew as such on the 18th April and flew back to Lock Haven on 8th of May 1967. The concept proved feasible and Piper went on to develop the Pressurized Navajo with turbo-prop engines. By the 23rd of January 1969 updated -27 engines had been fitted and in March the engines were removed and the aircraft donated to the local fire department.

In 1969 Piper put two Pratt and Whitney 620 shp PT6A-28 turbo-prop engines on the Pressurized Navajo airframe and added wing tip fuel tanks. The new aircraft was initially called the PA-31T Turbine Navajo and had seating for 2 crew and 6 passengers. The prototype s/n 31T-1 registration N7500L first flew on the 20th of August 1969. FAA certification was received on the 3rd of May 1972. Unfortunately the aircraft was restricted to 550 shp on the PT6A-28 engines plus centre of gravity and climb limitations. After the big flood at Lock Haven in June 1972 Piper rebuilt the prototype aircraft by November. Pratt & Whitney rebuilt the engines by September. Installing 1240 hp onto the Pressurized Navajo airframe which was designed to accept 850 hp necessitated a re-design of the flight control system to meet the required stability criteria. Piper installed a relatively simple stability augmentation system (SAS) which varies the tension in the aircraft's elevator downspring as a function of the aircraft's angle of attack. This was installed in the prototype in July 1973. Various tests took place between November 1972 and June 1973. The first production aircraft s/n 31T-7400002 registration N131PT was completed on the 5th of October 1973. Both aircraft were used to re-certify the type with the SAS system at the end of January 1974 at Lakeland, without the previous restrictions. It was licensed at 620 shp, 9000 pound gross and 138.0 inches aft centre of gravity. Also Pressurized Navajo N7322L was used during June 1973 to check out various PA-31T features, e.g. overhead pilot window, Sperry autopilot. Deliveries commenced in the middle of 1974, now named the Cheyenne. The base price was $429,000 and IFR equipped it cost $536,760.

In 1972 Piper started to design a PA-31T 'II' but the project was cancelled in mid 1973. It is not known what the changes were, but it could have been a longer fuselage.

AiResearch proposed a TPE-331 engined Cheyenne to Piper in August 1974, but even though the Pratt & Whitney engines were in short supply at the time Piper wished to stay with the approved configuration.

Piper first started working on the U.S. Navy VTAM(X) programme to replace the Grumman S-2 aircraft fleet in early 1973. This was an advanced multi-engine training mission system for the Air Training Command. Most of the work was carried out by Piper during 1975, proposing the PA-31T in response to the T-44A trainer requirement. The proposal was submitted in February 1976, but the contract was awarded to Beechcraft with their B90 King Air in June.

From 1976 the gross weight was increased to 9050 pounds and the service ceiling was increased to 31,000 feet.

In April 1976 Piper produced its 100,000th aircraft, a Cheyenne s/n 31T-7620023 registration N100MP painted in hunting stripes and dubbed Heritage of 1976 by Piper. The ceremonies at Lock Haven included the 99,999th aircraft, a Super Cub s/n 18-7609073 registration N999MP, and the first aircraft, a J-2 Cub s/n 1937 registration N20137.

The 1977 model year had the larger crew window.

The experimental Turbine Navajo s/n 31-1 registration N3100E. (via H.W. Barnhouse)

The prototype Turbine Navajo s/n 31T-1 registration N7500L. (Piper Aircraft Corporation)

The first production PA-31T Cheyenne s/n 31T-740002 registration N131PT. (Piper Aircraft Corporation)

The blueprint PA-31T Cheyenne s/n 31T-7400004 registration N331PT. (Piper Aircraft Corporation)

Drawing of the Piper proposed PA-31T VTAM(X) for the U.S. Navy. (Piper Aircraft Corporation)

PA-31T Cheyenne II s/n 31T-7820054 registration VH-MWT awaiting delivery at Lock Haven. (Piper Aircraft Corporation)

PA-31T PRODUCTION DETAILS

Model Year	Serial Number Range From	To	Type	Total	Comments
Experimental	31-1			0	
Prototype	31T-1		31T	1	
1974	31T-7400002	31T-7400009	31T	8	
1975	31T-7520001	31T-7520043	31T	43	
1976	31T-7620001	31T-7620057	31T	57	
1977	31T-7720001	31T-7720069	31T	69	
Pre-production	31T-7804001		31T1 'I'	1	
1978	31T-7804002	31T-7804011	31T1 'I'	10	
1978	31T-7820001	31T-7820092	31T 'II'	92	
1979	31T-7904001	31T-7904057	31T1 'I'	57	
1979	31T-7920001	31T-7920094	31T 'II'	94	
1980	31T-8004001	31T-8004057	31T1 'I'	57	
1980	31T-8020001	31T-8020095 *	31T 'II'	92	
1981	31T-8104001	31T-8104041	31T1 'I'	41	
1981	31T-8104043	31T-8104046	31T1 'I'	4	
1981	31T-8104048 & 31T-8104050		31T1 'I'	2	
1981	31T-8104051		31T1 'I'	1	
1981	31T-8104053	31T-8104058	31T1 'I'	6	
1981	31T-8104060	31T-8104061	31T1 'I'	2	
1981	31T-8120001	31T-8120059	31T 'II'	59	
Prototype	31T-8166001		31T2 'IIXL'	1	
1981	31T-8166002	31T-8166039	31T2 'IIXL'	38	
1982	31T-8104042 & 31T-8104047		31T1 'I'	2	
1982	31T-8104049 & 31T-8104052		31T1 'I'	2	
1982	31T-8104059		31T1 'I'	1	
1982	31T-8104062	31T-8104073 *	31T1 'I'	11	
1982	31T-8120060	31T-8120072 *	31T 'II'	7	
1982	31T-8166040	31T-8166063	31T2 'IIXL'	24	
Prototype	31T-8275001		31T3 T-1040	1	
1982	31T-8275002	31T-8275025 *	31T3 T-1040	17	
1983	31T-8104101		31T1 'I'	1	
Prototype	31T-8304001		31T1 'IA'	1	
1983	31T-8304002	31T-8304003	31T1 'IA'	2	
1983	31T-1104004	31T-1104010	31T1 'IA'	7	
1983	31T-8120101	31T-8120104	31T 'II'	4	
1983	31T-8166064	31T-8166076 *	31T2 'IIXL'	11	
1983	31T-8375001	31T-8375005 *	31T3 T-1040	4	
1984	31T-1104011	31T-1104017	31T1 'IA'	7	
1984	31T-1166001	31T-1166006	31T2 'IIXL'	6	
1984	31T-8475001		31T3 T-1040	1	
1985	31T-5575001	31T-5575002 *	31T3 T-1040	1	
Prototypes	31T-1122001	31T-1122002 *	31T2 'IIXLa'	0	
1985	31T-1166007	31T-1166008	31T2 'IIXL'	2	

The experimental aircraft 31-1 has been included in the PA-31 manufactured total.
A total of 22 aircraft in the batches marked * were not delivered, instead they were updated to the next year's model and given new serial numbers or not built. See table below.

Total manufactured 'II' 526 'I/IA' 215 'IIXL' 82 T-1040 24

(All built at Lock Haven)

The experimental PA-31T1 Cheyenne I s/n 31T-1 registration N7500L. (Piper Aircraft Corporation)

PA-31T1 Cheyenne I s/n 31T-8104053 registration N2468Y (in wash-off paint) at Lock Haven. (R.W. Peperell)

The PA-31T Tanker s/n 31T-1 registration N7500L on a test flight. (J. Bryerton)

PA-31T SERIAL NUMBER CHANGES

Model	Old Serial number	New Serial Number	New Model (if different)
PA-31T	31T-8020093-095	31T-8020002-004	
PA-31T	31T-8120065	31T-8120103	
PA-31T	31T-8120066	31T-8120101	
PA-31T	31T-8120067	31T-8120102	
PA-31T	31T-8120069	31T-8120104	
PA-31T	31T-8120071-072	Not built	
PA-31T1	31T-8104069	31T-8104101	
PA-31T2	31T-8166072	31T-1166002	
PA-31T2	31T-8166074	31T-1166003	
PA-31T2 a	31T-1122001	31T-1166007	PA-31T2
PA-31T2 a	31T-1122002	31T-1166008	PA-31T2
PA-31T T-1040	31T-8275018	31T-8375001	
PA-31T T-1040	31T-8275019	31T-8375002	
PA-31T T-1040	31T-8275020	31T-8375003	
PA-31T T-1040	31T-8275021	31T-8375004	
PA-31T T-1040	31T-8275022	31T-8375005	
PA-31T T-1040	31T-8275023	31T-5575001	
PA-31T T-1040	31T-8275024	31T-5575002	
PA-31T T-1040	31T-5575002	Not completed	
PA-31T T-1040	31T-8375004	31T-8475001	

In 1978 Piper introduced the lowest priced turbo-prop on the market, a lower powered version of the Cheyenne, named the Cheyenne I. The original Cheyenne was renamed the Cheyenne II. The PA-31T1 Cheyenne I has two Pratt and Whitney 500 shp PT6A turbo-prop engines. Aircraft N7500L had its SAS removed and a bob-weight installed. The engines were replaced by two 500 shp P&W PT6A-11 engines. This first flew on the 11th of August 1977 and was followed by the pre-production aircraft s/n 31T-7804001 registration N6600A which first flew on the 20th of October 1977. The first production aircraft s/n 31T-7804002 registration N301PT first flew on the 24th of February 1978. FAA certification was granted on the 6th of March. Deliveries began in May with an IFR equipped aircraft costing $810,885. Piper set up eleven Corporate Aircraft Centres (CORPACs) across North America to support the Cheyenne models with financing, tax information, pilot familiarisation, aircraft maintenance and spare parts. At the end of 1978 Piper certified optional wing tip fuel tanks on the Cheyenne I. These were first tested on aircraft N6600A on the 3rd of October.

When Piper wanted to certify the Navajo for flight into known icing, they had to use the Cessna owned icing tanker, a converted Cessna KC-411 registration N7368U. In 1978 Piper converted the prototype Cheyenne N7500L into their own Tanker. A water tank was installed in the fuselage and a spray boom was attached to the bottom of the fuselage. It first flew in this configuration on the 29th of September and first sprayed water on the 9th of October. It's first job was for icing tests for the Aerostar. Aerostar 601P s/n 61P-0266-054 registration N76TS was tested in California on the 29th / 30th of November.

In 1979 Piper developed a maritime surveillance Cheyenne based on the Cheyenne II. A fifty gallon fuel tank was added in the nose and an 18 inch radar antenna replaced the existing radar. Forward Looking Infra Red (FLIR) was also an option as was an underwing pod containing two Vinters cameras for shipping observation. Aircraft s/n 31T-7920002 registration N431PC carried out a World sales tour in October 1979. Two aircraft were delivered to Mauritius in 1980.

At the end of 1978 Piper started to design the PA-31T2 Cheyenne II, which was a Cheyenne with a 24 inch fuselage stretch and PT6A-135 engines. The experimental aircraft was N6600A with -135 engines fitted which first flew on the 17th of September 1979. The prototype s/n 31T-8166001 registration N2446X first flew on the 29th of February 1980. FAA certification was granted on the 12th of February 1981. First customer deliveries commenced with s/n 31T-8166004 registration N2517X in June 1981 now named the Cheyenne IIXL. It went on sale priced at $946,440. At the end of 1981 Piper increase the zero fuel weight by 500 pounds allowing greater payload / range flexibility.

PA-31T Maritime s/n 31T-7920002 registration N431PC. (Piper Aircraft Corporation)

The prototype PA-31T2 Cheyenne IIXL s/n 31T-8166001 registration N2446X taxying out for its first flight at Lock Haven on the 29th of February 1980. (J. Bryerton)

PA-31T2 Cheyenne IIXL s/n 31T-8166003 registration N31XL. (Piper Aircraft Corporation)

The prototype PA-31T3 T-1040 s/n 31T-8275001 registration N2489Y preparing for its first flight at Lock Haven on the 17th of July 1981. (J. Bryerton)

The PA-31T3 T-1040 was launched at the Hannover Air Show, s/n 31T-8375001 registration N9174C. (J.M. Gradidge)

PA-31T SPECIFICATION & PERFORMANCE			
SPECIFICATION	31T1 'I'	31T1 'IA'	31T 'II'
Engine	500 shp Pratt & Whitney PT6A 11	500 shp Pratt & Whitney PT6A-11	620 shp Pratt & Whitney PT6A-28
Engine TBO (hrs)	3,500	3,500	3,500
No of seats	6-7	6-7	6-8
Wing Span (ft/ins)	40/8	42/8	42/8
Length (ft/ins)	34/8	34/8	34/8
Height (ft/ins)	12/9	12/9	12/9
Useable fuel capacity (US gal)	314 (78), 300 (80) 374 (78), 382 (80) with tip tanks	366	382
Gross weight (lbs)	8750	8750	9000 (75) 9050 (76-83)
Empty weight (lbs)	4900	5110	4870 (75) 4976 (76-83)
Useful load (lbs)	3850	3640	4180 (75) 4074 (76-83)
Propellers	Hartzell 3-blade	Hartzell 3-blade	Hartzell 3-blade
Pressurization (psi)	5.5	5.5	5.5
PERFORMANCE			
Max speed	249 kts	261 kts	283 kts
Cruise speed	252 kts (78) 249 kts (79)	247-261 kts	283 kts @ 75%
Efficiency (gph)			81
Stall speed - flaps / gear down	68 kts	72 kts	75 kts
Climb @ sea level (fpm)	2000	1750	2800
Range with reserves	1260 nm 1400 nm (tip tanks)	935-1255 nm	905 nm @ 75% 1510 nm @ 55%
Service ceiling (ft)	27,000 (78) 29,000 (80)	28,200	31,600
Take off (Ground run)(ft)	1350	1429	1410
Take off (over 50ft obst)(ft)	2000	2444	1980
Landing (Ground roll)(ft)	900	921	955
Landing (over 50ft obst)(ft)	1600	1663	1860

For the 1980 model year Piper increased the windscreen area on the Cheyenne I and II by 20% to improve pilot visibility.

A Cheyenne without pressurization was considered in March 1980, but was rejected by Piper management.

In early 1980 Piper started to develop the second aircraft of the T-1000 airline series, the PA-31T3 T-1040. The T-1040 had the fuselage of the Chieftain and the engines, wings, nose and tail of the Cheyenne II. The experimental aircraft was N6600A fitted with the new T-1040 cowls and first flew on the 15th May 1980. Aircraft N7500L was used to evaluate the T-1040 air conditioner in September 1980. The prototype s/n 31T-8275001 registration N2389Y first flew on the 17th of July 1981. FAA certification was granted on the 25th of February 1982 and Piper launched T-1040 at the Hannover Air Show in June 1982. The T-1040 was built at Lock Haven and flown to Lakeland to be customised. First customer deliveries commenced with s/n 31T-8275004 registration N9152Y in July 1982. It was priced at $800,000. The T-1040 can seat 2 crew and 9 passengers and a fuselage cargo pod is available as an option. The Foster cargo pod was first tested on the 27th of April 1982 on the T-1040 s/n 31T-8275003 registration N4140T. During 1982 tip tanks were approved for the T-1040 increasing fuel capacity and range. South Central Air and Atlantis Airlines were operating T-1040's in 1986.

In 1982 Piper reviewed the Butler cargo pod on the Cheyenne IIXL for which Butler had obtained a Supplementary Type Certificate. Aircraft s/n 31T-8166033 registration N59WA was tested at Lock Haven in August. This had a 300 lb capacity, but reduced rate of climb by 7% and reduced cruise speed by 3%. This was offered as an option by Piper.

Federal Express approached Piper in 1981 seeking a new aircraft for small package transportation. Piper initially offered the T-1040 in November. By April 1983 Piper were proposing adding 11 feet 6 inches to the fuselage of T-1040 for cargo use or 15 passengers and increasing the gross weight by 650 pounds, but this derivative, the T-1050 (initially called the Super T-1040) was cancelled when Federal Express purchased the Cessna Caravan in mid 1983 instead.

Piper installed a modified cowl (similar to the new T-1040 cowl) on Cheyenne I s/n 31T-8104068 registration N9088Y which first flew on the 25th of August 1981. This update was abandoned and the standard cowl re-installed. Piper went on to improve the Cheyenne I cowls in the IA. Between late 1981 and 1983 an updated version of the Cheyenne I was developed, the IA, with a 4% increase in engine power at altitude, a lowered panel glare shield, improved engine cowl design and improved interior. The prototype s/n 31T-8304001 registration N9183C first flew on the 2nd of February 1983. FAA certification was granted on the 6th of May. Deliveries began in June 1983. The IFR equipped price was $974,140.

In January 1983 Piper looked at putting wing lockers on the Cheyenne IA. This was not done.

At the end of 1983 the serial number series were changed on the Cheyenne IA and IIXL models to remove the model year from the series and replace it with the Lock Haven plant code (1) repeated. Thus the Cheyenne IA s/n 8304xxx became 1104xxx and Cheyenne IIXL s/n 8166xxx became 1166xxx.

In October 1981 Piper looked at extending the Cheyenne IIXL fuselage and making a 10 or 11 seat commuter in the T-1000 airline series. In early 1982 Piper started to design an improved Cheyenne IIXL, the PA-31T5 at Lock Haven. It was to have 650 shp PT6A-135 engines, new nacelles, new propellers, modified wings, tail and fuselage, a possible 12 inch fuselage extension aft of the wing spar, psi up to 6.3, gross weight up to 9700 pounds and cruise up to 247 knots. Piper could not afford such major changes so in October 1983 they decided to stay with the standard engines but with a 6% increase in power at altitude in modified cowls, the interior was improved, engine nacelle lockers were fitted and extra fuel capacity was available (increased to 422 gallons). This was the PA-31T5 Cheyenne IIXLa. The first prototype s/n 31T-1122001 registration N2428V first flew on the 2nd of February 1984 and the second prototype s/n 31T-1122002 registration N2433V first flew on the 16th of April. Both aircraft were moved to Lakeland on the 3rd August. Piper continued to develop them, then in 1985 the project was cancelled due to Lear Siegler's lack of money for Piper. The two prototypes were converted back to PA-31T2 Cheyenne IIXL standard at Vero Beach during 1986, changing their serial numbers to 31T-1166007 and 1166008 respectively.

Production of the Cheyenne II ended in early 1983 with s/n 31T-8120104 registration N9162Y and the T-1040 ended in late 1984 with s/n 31T-5575001 registration N41202. Production of the Cheyenne IIXL ended (except the previously mentioned two conversions) with s/n 31T-1166006 registration N2409W in May and the Cheyenne IA ended with s/n 31T-1104017 registration N91204 completed on the 11th of June 1984.

Piper and TCM initiated a joint programme in October 1980 to use the TCM TP-500 turbine engine on a Piper twin engined aircraft. In 1982 Piper initiated the PA-31TX programme. TCM installed a 530 shp TCM TP-500 engine (derated to 375 shp) and a new gearbox on aircraft N6600A (keeping the PT-6 on the starboard side) at Mobile, Alabama. This first flew on the 29th of September and the design was developed into the PA-31T4 at the end of September. It had a Chieftain fuselage and Mojave wings. It was proposed to market this in both the T series commuter and as an executive aircraft. By April 1984 the design had developed into using the PA-31-353 fuselage, the Cheyenne I wing, Mojave wing tip extensions and 400 shp TCM TP-500 engines. There were also new nacelles with wing lockers. Unfortunately the programme was cancelled. TCM kept N6600A and installed another TP-500 engine on the starboard side.

In 1989 Soloy put two TCM TPE-500E turboprop engines on s/n 31-7852108 registration N83CF. They planned to certify this configuration by the end of 1990.

In October 1981 Piper initiated the design of a 17 place commuter, designated the PA-31C-850. This was a T-1040 with a three feet extension and PA-42 wings and 850 shp Pratt & Whitney PT6 engines in new nacelles. The design was further developed in mid 1983. This was not produced.

At the end of 1994 Piper carried out a study on bringing to market an updated Cheyenne IA, the Cheyenne IB. The engines were PT6A-135, improved cowls, new props, improved instrument panel and interior and updated avionics. It was predicted that top speed would increase by 19 knots. The project was put on hold due to cost.

Schafer of Clifton, Texas, U.S.A. make a Cheyenne II conversion called the Comanchero 750. It has 750 shp Pratt and Whitney PT6A-135 turbo prop engines. An example is s/n 31T-7720038 registration N77NL.

PA-31T3 T-1040 s/n 31T-8275013 registration N9189Y on a test flight with cargo pod. (via D. Schwartz)

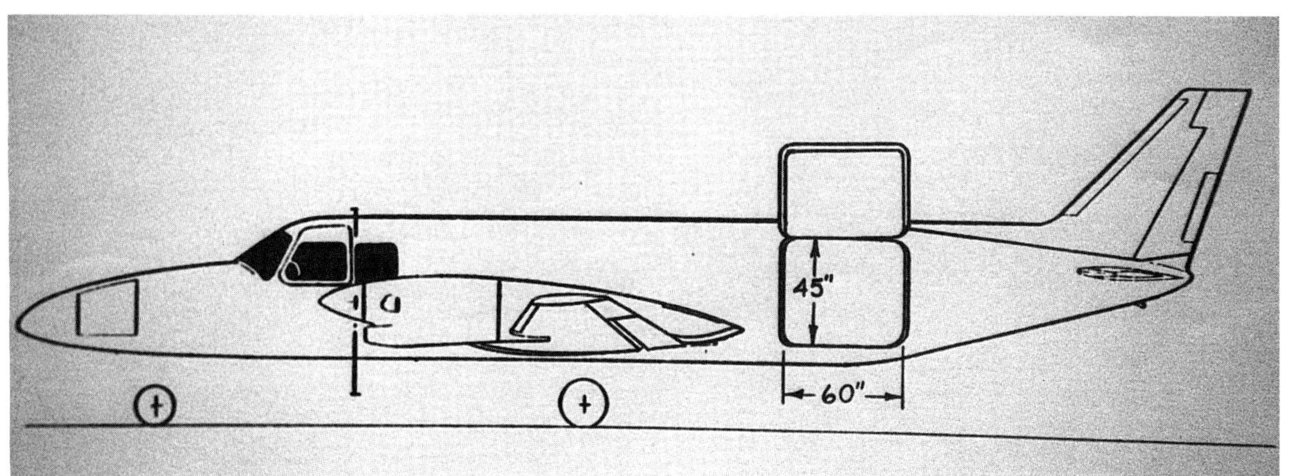

Drawing of the Piper proposed T-1050. (Piper Aircraft Corporation)

The prototype PA-31T1 Cheyenne IA s/n 31T-8304001 registration N9183C at Vero Beach. (R.W. Peperell)

The prototype PA-31T5 Cheyenne IIXLa s/n 31T-1122001 registration N2428V. Note baggage nacelles. (via D. Schwartz)

PA-31T2 Cheyenne IIXL registration N2428V after conversion to standard and to s/n 31T-1166007 at Vero Beach. (R.W. Peperell)

The experimental PA-31T4 s/n 31T-7804001 registration N6600A with TCM TP-500 engine. (Piper Aircraft Corporation)

PA-31T SPECIFICATION & PERFORMANCE

SPECIFICATION	31T2 'IIXL'	31T3 T-1040
Engine	620 shp Pratt & Whitney PT6A-135	500 shp Pratt & Whitney PT6A-11
Engine TBO (hrs)	3500	3500
No of seats	6-8	11
Wing Span (ft/ins)	42/8	41/1
Length (ft/ins)	36/8	36/8
Height (ft/ins)	12/9	12/9
Useable fuel capacity (US gal)	382 (82), 366 (84)	292 366 (optional with tip tanks)
Gross weight (lbs)	9540	9050
Empty weight (lbs)	5164 (82), 5487 (84)	4800
Useful load (lbs)	4376 (82), 4053 (84)	4250
Propellers	Hartzell 3-blade	Hartzell 3-blade
Pressurization (psi)	5.5	
PERFORMANCE		
Max speed	275 kts	244 kts
Cruise speed	255-275 kts	238 kts @ 75%
Efficiency (gph)		
Stall speed - flaps / gear down	77 kts	78 kts
Climb @ sea level (fpm)	1750	1610
Range with reserves	775-1336 nm	624 nm @ 75% 1000 nm with tip tanks
Service ceiling (ft)	32,400	24,000
Take off (Ground run)(ft)	2042	1400
Take off (over 50ft obst)(ft)	2940	2512
Landing (Ground roll)(ft)	1080	
Landing (over 50ft obst)(ft)	1773	1900

Chieftain s/n 31-7852108 registration N83CF with TCM TP-500 engines converted by Soloy. (Aerospace Publishing)

PA-31T SPECIFICATION & PERFORMANCE		
SPECIFICATION	31T4	31T5
Engine	375-400 shp TCM TP-500	650 shp Pratt & Whitney PT6A-135
Engine TBO (hrs)		
No of seats		
Wing Span (ft/ins)	44/6	44/6
Length (ft/ins)	34/7	37/8
Height (ft/ins)	13/0	13/0
Useable fuel capacity (US gal)	260	
Gross weight (lbs)	7350	9700
Empty weight (lbs)	4502	
Useful load (lbs)	2748	
Propellers		
Pressurization (psi)		6.3
PERFORMANCE		
Max speed	230 kts	247 kts
Cruise speed		
Efficiency (gph)		
Stall speed - flaps / gear down	76 kts	
Climb @ sea level (fpm)		
Range with reserves		
Service ceiling (ft)		
Take off (Ground run)(ft)		
Take off (over 50ft obst)(ft)	2900	
Landing (Ground roll)(ft)		
Landing (over 50ft obst)(ft)	1950	

Drawing of the proposed PA-31C-850. (Piper Aircraft Corporation)

PA-31J JET NAVAJO

There were several designs for a Jet Navajo in 1970. They used the basic Pressurized Navajo fuselage with jet engines mounted on the rear of the fuselage and a small T-tail. This programme was a stop / go programme for many years. As late as 1978, Piper were going to use the T-tail design that was fitted to Pressurized Navajo N59900 which was based at Lakeland for the Jet Navajo. At one time Lock Haven engineering had named this design the Cochise. It was never produced.

In 1969 and again in 1982 Piper Lock Haven engineering drew up a single-engined jet (with the jet engine in the rear fuselage) using the Navajo fuselage and drooped wing tip fuel tanks. It never reached the design stage.

Drawing of the proposed PA-31J Jet Navajo. (via J. Bryerton)

Model of the proposed PA-31J Jet Navajo. (J. Bryerton)

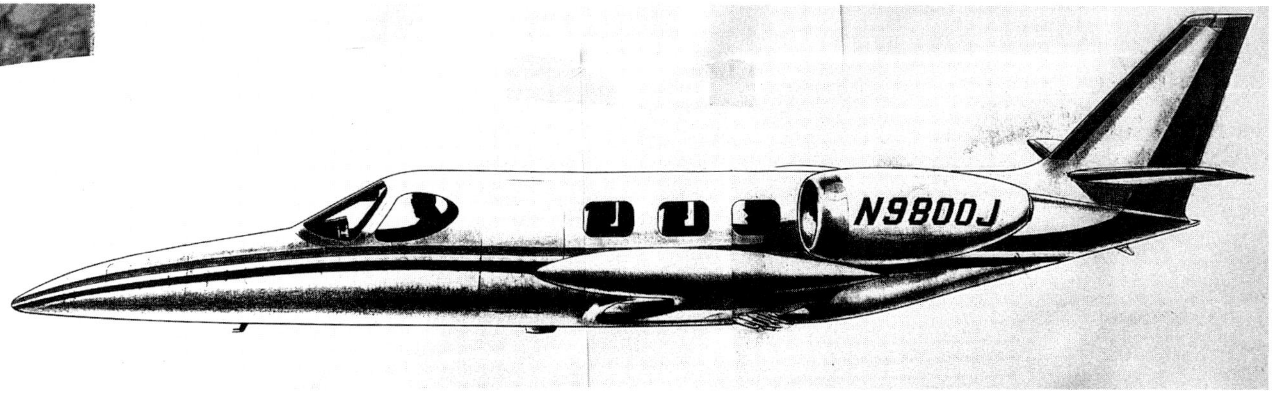

Drawing of the proposed PA-31J Jet Navajo with mid horizontal tail. (via J. Bryerton)

8
FURTHER DEVELOPMENT

PA-32 CHEROKEE SIX

In the early 1960's Howard Piper had the idea of expanding the Cherokee series to include a six place multi-engine model. The first step towards his goal was to produce the single engined six-place PA-32 Cherokee Six. Piper took a Cherokee fuselage and added six inches to the width. The fuselage, behind the cabin, was moved back 30 inches and a new tapered section was added. An additional 18 inch baggage compartment was placed between the firewall and cabin to balance the extended rear fuselage. The wing and tail surfaces were from the Cherokee 235. A 250 hp Lycoming O-540 engine was used and an extra door at the back of the cabin was provided. The first prototype s/n 32-01 registration N9999W first flew on the 6th of December 1963. The second prototype s/n 32-03 registration N9998W first flew on the 17th of September 1964. This had a 260 hp Lycoming O-540 engine and was an extra inch wider so that a second stack of radios could be installed in the panel. The third prototype s/n 32-04 registration N3200W with a 260 hp Lycoming O-540-E engine was registered in 1964. The PA-32-260 was certified A3SO on 4th of March 1965. Deliveries began shortly afterwards commencing with s/n 32-1 registration N3201W. It was priced at $18,500 and three optional groups were available, Custom, Executive or Sportsman. Unfortunately N9998W crashed at Vero Beach on the 1st of July 1965 and was destroyed.

In 1965 Piper developed the PA-32-300 Cherokee Six with a 300 hp Lycoming IO-540-K engine. Two aircraft were used in the development, s/n 32-15 registration N3214W which first flew on the 8th of October with the bigger engine. An additional door was installed next to the existing rear door in order to make loading and unloading cargo easier. Aircraft N3200W was also converted to 300 hp in early 1966. The 300 hp version was certified on 27th of May 1966. Deliveries commenced with s/n 32-40000 registration N4001W in late 1966. The 300 hp version had a 7th optional seat, as did the 260 hp version from 1967 onwards.

In February 1967 Piper delivered its 10,000th export aircraft, s/n 32-40042 registration 5Y-AEH, to Wilken Air Services of Nairobi, Kenya.

Aircraft N3214W was used as the PA-32S seaplane prototype at Vero Beach. Edo 582-3430 floats were installed with a modified engine cowl. First flight was on the 20th of June 1966. All floats are fitted to Pipers in the field, the 'S' designation means factory zinc chromate treatment and stainless steel cables. Modifications were also made to the cowling. The 300 hp version of the Cherokee Six was certified for float operation with Edo floats on the 14th of February 1967. Unfortunately N3214W was damaged in an accident later in the year. The first production example of a PA-32S-300 is s/n 32-40265 registration N4183W. Approximately ten PA-32S aircraft were produced by the factory, some not flying on floats but were ordered by customers wishing to have the extra corrosion protection. No more were produced after the 1972 model year.

In August 1968 s/n 32-21 registration N3218W was used for the U.S.A.F. COIN (Counter Insurgency) development aircraft. A 300 hp Lycoming IO-540-K engine was installed and there were four wing hardpoints for bombs or guns and it was designated the PA-32-300M. This derivative was not proceeded with as no contract was forthcoming from the U.S.A.F.

On the 8th of August 1969, Cherokee Six 300 s/n 32-40853 registration N300AC went into the experimental shop starting the development of the 'Piperaire' air-conditioning option, which was first seen on the whole Cherokee range for the 1972 model year.

The prototype PA-32-250 s/n 32-01 registration N9999W at Vero Beach. (P. Peck)

The second prototype PA-32-260 Cherokee Six s/n 32-03 registration N9998W. (Piper Aircraft Corporation)

PA-32-260 Cherokee Six s/n 32-04 registration N3200W. (Piper Aircraft Corporation)

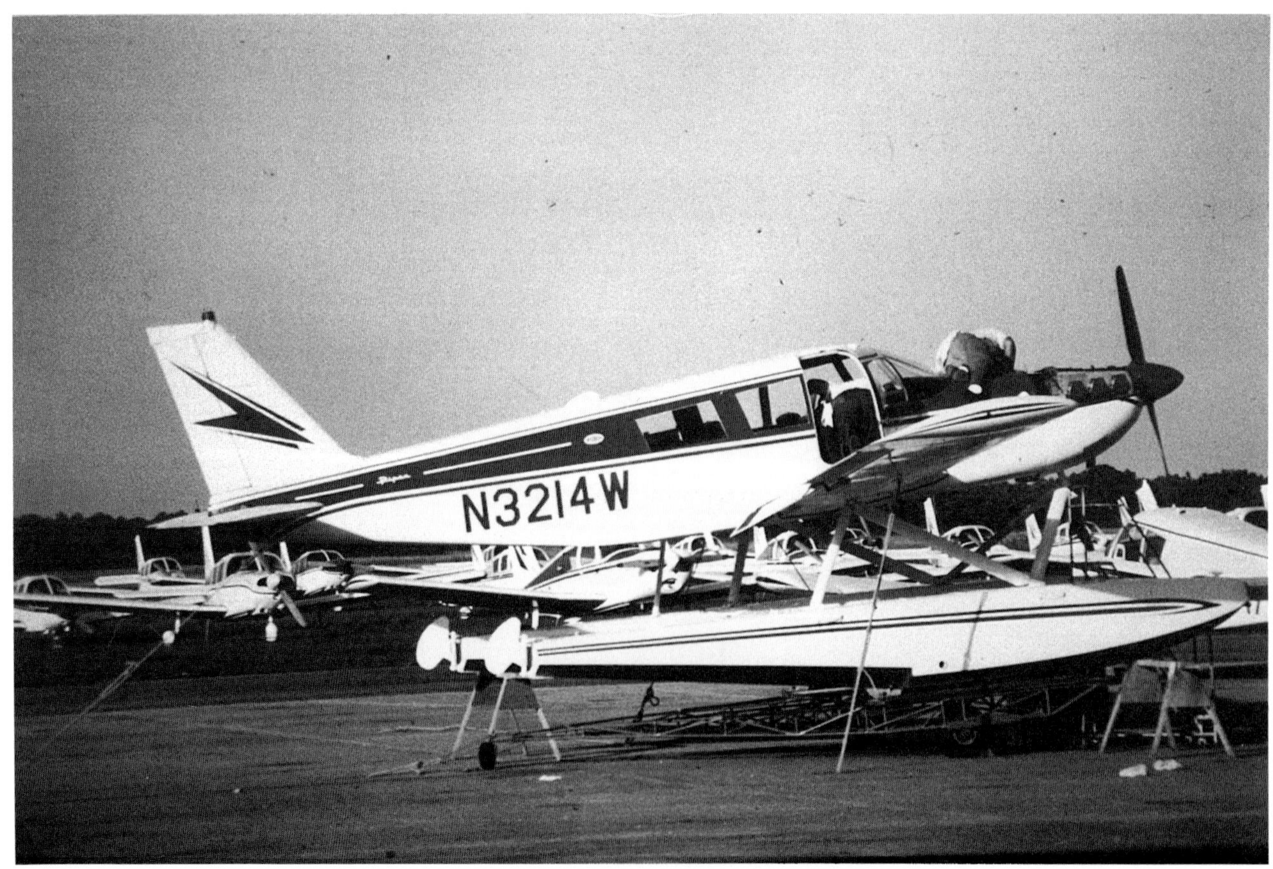

The experimental PA-32S-300 Cherokee Six seaplane s/n 32-15 registration N3214W at Vero Beach.
Note the dolly for taxying and take-off. (G.K. Gates)

PA-32 PRODUCTION DETAILS					
Model / Fiscal Year	Serial Number Range From	To	Type	Total	Comments
Prototype	32-01		250	1	
Prototypes	32-03	32-04	260	2	
1965	32-1	32-115	260	115	
1966	32-116	32-823	260	708	
1966	32-40000		300	1	
1967	32-824	32-972	260	149	
1967	32-40001	32-40337	300	337	
1968	32-973	32-1075	260	103	
1968	32-40338	32-40545	300	208	
1969	32-1111	32-1194	260 'B'	84	
1969	32-40566	32-40777	300 'B'	212	
1970	32-1251	32-1297	260 'C'	47	
1970	32-40851	32-40974	300 'C'	124	
1971	32-7100001	32-7100028	260 'D'	28	
1971	32-7140001	32-7140078	300 'D'	78	
1972	32-7200001	32-7200045	260 'E'	45	
1972	32-7240001	32-7240137	300 'E'	137	
1973	32-7300001	32-7300065	260	65	
1973	32-7340001	32-7340191	300	191	
1974	32-7400001	32-7400051	260	51	
1974	32-7440001	32-7440172	300	172	
1975	32-7500001	32-7500043	260	43	
1975	32-7540001	32-7540188 *	300	187	
1976	32-7600001	32-7600024	260	24	
1976	32-7640001	32-7640130	300	130	
1977	32-7700001	32-7700023	260	23	
1977	32-7740001	32-7740113	300	113	
1978	32-7800001	32-7800008	260	8	
1978	32-7840001	32-7840202 *	300	201	
1979	32-7940001	32-7940290 *	300	288	
Prototype	32-7845001		300L	1	
Prototype	32-7924001 *		300T	0	
A total of 5 aircraft in the batches marked * were not delivered, instead they were updated to the next year's model and given new serial numbers. See table below. Total manufactured 3876 (All built at Vero Beach)					

Many aircraft were unsold at the end of 1967 and they were re-licensed in 1968 and then sold. These were s/n: 32-963, 970, 973, 978, 986, 990, 995, 1001, 1002, 1003, 32-40340, 40360, 40371, 40377, 40381, 40383, 40386, 40387, 40389, 40390, 40393, 40406, 40407, 40409, 40411, 40412, 40413, 40414, 40415, 40418, 40421, 40423, 40424, 40425, 40427.

PA-32 SERIAL NUMBER CHANGES			
Model	Old Serial Number	New Serial number	New Model (if different)
PA-32-300	32-7540069	32-7845001	PA-32-300L
PA-32-300	32-7840094	32-7924001	PA-32-300T
PA-32-300T	32-7924001	32-8024001	PA-32-301T
PA-32-300	32-7940002	32-8006001	PA-32-301
PA-32-300	32-7940118	32-8006002	PA-32-301

Between 1969 and 1972 Piper improved the aircraft each year:

PA-32 IMPROVEMENTS						
Model Year	Type	Improvements	Development / Show aircraft s/n	Registration	1st production aircraft s/n	Registration
1969	260 'B'	Increased cabin space	32-1027	N5585J	32-1111	N5596J
	300 'B'	Instrument panel	32-40455	N4137R	32-40566	N4169R
1970	260 'C'	Minor changes	32-1157	N4704S	32-1251	N4820S
	300 'C'		32-40741	N8939N	32-40851	N8975N
1971	260 'D'	Minor changes	32-1280	N4875S	32-7100001	N4877S
	300 'D'		32-40932	N5250S	32-7140001	N8611N
1972	260 'E'	Instrument panel			32-7200001	N8656N
	300 'E'	Interior	32-7140054	N4872S	32-7240001	N8651N
			32-7140062	N8672N		

For the 1972 model year two operational groups were available, Custom or Executive.

In March 1970 Teledyne fitted a 285 hp Continental Tiara engine in Cherokee Six s/n 32-1275 registration N4815S. This was test flown by Piper throughout 1970 as part of the evaluation of the engine.

For the 1973 model year the letter was dropped, just being named the Cherokee Six 260 or 300. It had a padded instrument panel and new seats. Deliveries commenced with the s/n 32-7300001 registration N15039 and s/n 32-7340001 registration N3076T.

The 1974 model year had two extra fuselage windows, a thicker windscreen to reduce engine noise and a new nose wheel steering system. The new nose wheel steering system was subsequently deleted a year later because of shimmy problems. The 1975 model year saw a new vertically adjustable seat and optional 'quietized' sound proofing.

Between 1975 and 1977 Piper worked on improving the fuel efficiency of the Cherokee Six. They installed a 300 hp Lycoming IO-540-U1A5D engine in a newly designed low drag cowl in aircraft s/n 32-7540069 registration N32834. This first flew on the 16th of May 1975 at Lakeland. By 1976 Piper created the PA-32-300L (L= low drag) by adding low drag wheel fairings and it first flew in this configuration on the 20th of October. Its s/n was changed to 32-7845001. This was provisionally type certified in 1976. This was to be introduced to the market in April 1978 as the Six II 300, but was cancelled in favour of the Saratoga. Major developments emanated from this program:

- new style wheel speed fairings which were first seen on the 1978 model Six 300,
- a new nose (9 inches longer) for the turbocharged engine installation which was first seen in
  - the Turbo Lance II for the 1978 model year,
  - (the Lance II with low drag nose which was not produced),
  - the experimental Turbo Cherokee Six.

The PA-32-300 Cherokee Six s/n 32-18 registration N3218W used for the COIN development. (D.H. Smith)

PA-32-300 Cherokee Six s/n 32-40000 registration N4000W. (Piper Aircraft Corporation)

The experimental PA-32-300L s/n 32-7845001 registration N32834 at Lakeland. (G.K. Gates)

PA-32 SPECIFICATION & PERFORMANCE

SPECIFICATION	32-260, 'B', 'C', 'D'	32-260 (1974)	32-300, 'B', 'C', 'D'
Engine	260 hp Lycoming O-540-E	260 hp Lycoming O-540-E4B5	300 hp Lycoming IO-540-K
Engine TBO (hrs)	1200 (64-67) 1800 (68 & later)	1800	1800
No of seats	6	6	6/7
Wing Span (ft/ins)	32/9	32/9	32/9
Length (ft/ins)	27/8.5	27/8.5	27/8.5
Height (ft/ins)	7/11	7/11	7/11
Useable fuel capacity (US gal)	83.3	83.3	83.3
Gross weight (lbs)	3400	3400	3400
Empty weight (lbs)	1655-1724	1754-1767	1738-1799
Useful load (lbs)	1676-1745	1633-1646	1601-1662
Propeller	Hartzell Fixed pitch or Constant speed	Hartzell Fixed pitch or Constant speed	Hartzell Constant speed
Floats available			
PERFORMANCE			
Max speed	168 mph (FP) 166 mph (CS)	164 mph	174 mph
Cruise speed	158-160 mph @ 75%	153 mph @ 75%	168 mph @ 75%
Efficiency (gph)	14 @ 75%	14 @ 75%	16 @ 75%
Stall speed - flaps / gear down	63 mph	63 mph	63 mph
Climb @ sea level (fpm)	760 (FP) 850 (CS)	775	1050
Range with reserves	950-960 sm @ 75% 1110-1170 sm @ 55%	835-890 sm @ 75% 1035 sm @ 55%	880 sm @ 75% 1060 sm @ 55%
Service ceiling (ft)	13,000 (FP) 14,500 (CS)	12,800	16,250
Take off (Ground run)(ft)	740-810	1325	700
Take off (over 50ft obst)(ft)	1240-1360	1900	1140
Landing (Ground roll)(ft)	630	630	630
Landing (over 50ft obst)(ft)	1000	1000	1000

In early 1978 Piper developed a turbocharged version of the Cherokee Six 300 with a 300 hp Lycoming TIO-540-SIAD engine in a modified engine cowling. The prototype PA-32-300T s/n 32-7924001 registration N9326C was converted from s/n 32-7840094 and was to be called the Turbo Six II. This was cancelled in favour of the Turbo Saratoga.

For the 1978 model year the Cherokee Six 260 and 300 received the new style wheel speed fairings which improved speed by 6 knots and range by 4% over the 1977 model. Aircraft N2932Q s/n 32-7740055 was also used for this development. Production of the 260 hp version ended in 1978.

The 1979 model year saw the name 'Cherokee' dropped, becoming the Six 300 with conference style seating available as an option. Production of the Six ended in December 1979 when the Saratoga series replaced it on the production line.

Sierra Industries (previously R/STOL & Robertson) offer a modification for the Cherokee Six with spoilers and full-span single slotted flaps. An example is s/n 32-7540077 registration N32979.

In Mexico the IA company has been refurbishing Piper aircraft for many years. Once completed they carry new serial numbers. An example is a PA-32 with the s/n IAPA-7870.

PA-32 SPECIFICATION & PERFORMANCE

SPECIFICATION	32S-300	32-300 (1974)	32-300 (1978 & 79)
Engine	300 hp Lycoming IO-540-K	300 hp Lycoming IO-540-K1A5	300 hp Lycoming IO-540-K1G5D
Engine TBO (hrs)	1800	1800	2000
No of seats	6/7	6/7	6/7
Wing Span (ft/ins)	32/9	32/9	32/9
Length (ft/ins)	27/8.5	27/8.5	27/8.5
Height (ft/ins)	11/3.5	7/11	8/2.5
Useable fuel capacity (US gal)	83.3	83.3	83.6 (78) 98 (79)
Gross weight (lbs)	3400	3400	3400
Empty weight (lbs)	2089-2140	1818-1824	1837-1846
Useful load (lbs)	1260-1311	1576-1582	1554-1563
Propeller	Hartzell Constant speed	Hartzell Constant speed	Hartzell Constant speed
Floats available	Edo 3430		
PERFORMANCE			
Max speed	153 mph	174 mph	178 mph
Cruise speed	147 mph @ 75%	168 mph @ 75%	174 mph @ 75%
Efficiency (gph)	16 @ 75%	16 @ 75%	18 @ 75%
Stall speed - flaps / gear down	66 mph	63 mph	63 mph
Climb @ sea level (fpm)	750	1050	1050
Range with reserves	775 sm @ 75% 920 sm @ 55%	850 sm @ 75% 1030 sm @ 55%	752 sm @ 75% (78) 856 sm @ 75% (79)
Service ceiling (ft)	12,100	16,250	16,250-17,100
Take off (Ground run)(ft)	1430	1050	900
Take off (over 50ft obst)(ft)		1500	1350
Landing (Ground roll)(ft)		630	630
Landing (over 50ft obst)(ft)		1000	1000

1978 model PA-32-300 s/n 32-7740055 registration N2932Q. (Piper Aircraft Corporation)

PA-32-301 SARATOGA

During 1978 and 1979 Piper developed the new PA-32-301 Saratoga series which was basically a Cherokee Six 300 with the semi-tapered wing initially developed for the Warrior, with a 4 foot increase in span and an increase of over 200 lbs in gross weight. Two Saratogas were developed, one with a normally aspirated engine and one with a turbocharged engine. The first PA-32-301 Saratoga prototype (normally aspirated) with a Lycoming IO-540-K1G5 engine was s/n 32-8006001 registration N2114C converted from s/n 32-7940002. This aircraft first flew with the new wing on the 1st of November 1978 but unfortunately it crashed near Vero Beach on the 9th of March 1979 and was destroyed. This was replaced by a second prototype with s/n 32-8006002 registration N28216 converted from s/n 32-7940118 in April 1979.

The PA-32-301T Turbo Saratoga prototype was the previously mentioned N9326C but now with the new wing and a new serial number 32-8024001. It first flew with the new wing on the 15th March 1979. FAA approval for the PA-32-301 and PA-32-301T was granted on the 9th of January 1980. Deliveries from Vero Beach commenced with s/n 32-8006003 registration N8144P and s/n 32-8024002 registration N8108W in early 1980.

Production of the Turbo Saratoga ended at Vero Beach in mid 1984, the normally aspirated Saratoga ended in May 1991.

PA-32-301 PRODUCTION DETAILS

Model Year	Serial Number Range From	To	Type	Total	Comments
Prototype	32-8006001	32-8006002	301	2	
Prototype	32-8024001		301T	1	
1980	32-8006003	32-8006106	301	104	
1980	32-8024002	32-8024052	301T	51	
1981	32-8106001	32-8106100	301	100	
1981	32-8124001	32-8124036	301T	36	
1982	32-8206001	32-8206043 *	301	37	
1982	32-8224001	32-8224014	301T	14	
1983	32-8306001	32-8306033 *	301	32	
1983	32-8324001	32-8324016 *	301T	14	
1984	32-8406001	32-8406019	301	19	
1984	32-8424001	32-8424002	301T	2	
1985	32-8506001	32-8506021	301	21	
1986	32-8606001	32-8606023	301	23	
1986	3206001	3206003	301	2	
1986	3206005		301	1	
1987	3206004		301	1	
1987	3206006	3206033	301	29	
1988	3206034	3206044	301	11	
1989	3206045	3206060	301	16	
1990	3206061	3206078	301	18	
1991	3206079	3206098 *	301	10	kits

A total of 19 aircraft in the batches marked * were not delivered, instead they were updated to the next year's model and given new serial numbers or not built. See table below.
Total manufactured 544 (All built at Vero Beach)

PA-32-301 Saratoga s/n 32-8006002 registration N28216. (Piper Aircraft Corporation)

The prototype PA-32-301T Turbo Saratoga s/n 32-8024001 registration N9236C. (Piper Aircraft Corporation)

PA-32-301 SERIAL NUMBER CHANGES

Model	Old Serial Number	New Serial number	New Model (if different)
PA-32-301	32-8206021	32-8306031	
PA-32-301	32-8206025	32-8306030	
PA-32-301	32-8206028	32-8306032	
PA-32-301	32-8206041-043	Not built	
PA-32-301	32-8306033	Not built	
PA-32-301T	32-8324015-016	Not built	
PA-32-301	3206089-098	kits not completed	

PA-32-301 SPECIFICATION & PERFORMANCE

SPECIFICATION	32-301	32-301T
Engine	300 hp Lycoming IO-540-K1G5	300 hp Lycoming TIO-540-S1AD
Engine TBO (hrs)	2000	1800
No of seats	6/7	6/7
Wing Span (ft/ins)	36/5	36/5
Length (ft/ins)	27/8	28/6
Height (ft/ins)	8/3	8/3
Useable fuel capacity (US gal)	102	102
Gross weight (lbs)	3615	3617
Empty weight (lbs)	1935	1998-2000
Useful load (lbs)	1680	1617-1619
Propeller	Hartzell Constant speed 2 or 3 blade	Hartzell Constant speed 2 or 3 blade
Floats available		
PERFORMANCE		
Max speed	152 kts	182 kts
Cruise speed	150 kts @ 75% 146 kts @ 65%	165 kts @ 75% 154 kts @ 65%
Efficiency (gph)	18 @ 75%	19.9 @ 75%
Stall speed - flaps / gear down	58 kts	58 kts
Climb @ sea level (fpm)	990	1075
Range with reserves	745 nm @ 75% 849 nm @ 55%	684 nm @ 75% 772 nm @ 55%
Service ceiling (ft)	16,000	20,000
Take off (Ground run)(ft)	1183 / 1013	1110 / 960
Take off (over 50ft obst)(ft)	1759 / 1573	1590 / 1420
Landing (Ground roll)(ft)	732 / 650	732 / 650
Landing (over 50ft obst)(ft)	1612 / 1530	1725 / 1640

Performance data included for both the 2 and 3-blade propeller versions. For example: The take off ground run of the Saratoga is 1183 feet with a 2-blade and 1013 feet with a 3-blade propeller.

PA-32R LANCE / SARATOGA SP / II HP

In the Spring of 1970 Piper proposed a Cherokee Six with retractable gear with TCM Tiara 6-320 engine, designated the PA-32R-320 and a turbocharged version designated the PA-32R-T320. Problems with the Tiara engine prevented development. Piper went on to develop the retractable Six in late 1973. It had the same main gear as the Seneca II and the same retraction system as the Arrow II which extends automatically (at 115 mph). It was named the PA-32R-300 Cherokee Lance. The first prototype s/n 32R-7680001 registration N44256 first flew on the 30th of August 1974. FAA approval was granted on the 25th of February 1975. The second prototype s/n 32R-7580002 registration N1512X was registered in mid 1975. The first production aircraft s/n 32R-7680003 was registered in late 1975. Deliveries from Vero Beach began in October of that year with a standard equipped price of $48,300.

For the 1977 model year the name 'Cherokee' was dropped, to give the 'Lance'.

During 1975/1976 Piper developed a T-tailed version of the Lance, the PA-32RT-300 Lance II. The stabilitor of reduced size (35 inches) was positioned high on the vertical fin, away from propeller wash, resulting in a smoother, quieter ride. The experimental aircraft was a N44256 and first flew with the stabilator T-tail on the 28th of August 1975 at Lakeland. Another prototype PA-32RT-300 s/n 32R-7885001 registration N9648K was converted from s/n 32R-7680237 and first flew on the 15th of September 1976 at Vero Beach, but with a fixed horizontal stabilizer - elevator combination. After considerable testing (in November 1976 the rear fuselage section and tail were temporarily swapped between N44256 and N9648K), Piper decided to use the stabilator T-tail. The engine fitted was a Lycoming IO-540-K1G5. Another Lance was converted to a Lance II. This was s/n 32R-7780441 registration N38560 which became 32R-7885002 in November 1977. The FAA approval of the PA-32RT-300 was received on the 13th of December 1977. Deliveries of the Lance II from Vero Beach commenced with s/n 32R-7885003 registration N9800K in February 1978. It was priced at $58,990.

During 1976 Piper developed a turbo-charged version of the Lance, the PA-32R-300T. The prototype s/n 32-7680056 registration N7660C was first modified with a T-tail and first flew on the 31st of August at Lakeland. It was re-serialised to 32R-7787001 also in August. The low drag engine installation with a 300 hp Lycoming TIO-540-S1AD was installed and this first flew on the 19th of November 1976. This was the PA-32RT-300T Turbo Lance II. FAA approval was received on the 20th of April 1977. Deliveries of the Turbo Lance II from Vero Beach commenced with s/n 32R-7887002 registration N3078M in April 1978. It was priced at $67,000.

During 1976 and 1977 Piper developed the PA-32RT-300L, which was the Lance II with the low drag nose and low drag 300 hp Lycoming IO-540-U1A5D engine. The engine and nose cowling were installed on aircraft N44256 and it first flew in this configuration on the 24th of March 1976. This model was to be launched in August 1978 replacing the PA-32RT-300 Lance II. This did not go into production. (Aircraft N44256 was used as the PA-32RT-300T show aircraft in early 1978 even though it was a PA-32RT-300L).

Conference style seating was an available option for the 1979 model year for both Lance II models. Production ended in the summer of 1979.

In early 1978 Piper started to develop the Lance III and Turbo Lance III which was the Lance II with semi-tapered wing and a larger stabilator (35 inches wider than the Lance II and the same size as the original Lance) on the T-tail. The PA-32RT-301 prototype with a 300 hp Lycoming IO-540-K1G5D engine was s/n 32R-8013001 registration N9223C. This first flew on the 3rd of November 1978 and was converted from s/n 32R-7885037. The PA-32RT-301T prototype s/n 32R-8029001 registration N20816 was converted from s/n 32R-7887178 and first flew on the 29th of January 1979. During the summer Piper tried to improve the spin characteristics by putting wing tip end-plates on aircraft N9223C. The PA-32RT-301T was actually certified on the 16th of August 1979. Later in 1979, Piper decided that they would like to use the same tail across the PA-32 / 32R range, resulting in the new low-tailed (and reduced span ailerons) Saratoga series. N9223C and N20816 were converted to low tails, thus becoming the PA-32R-301 Saratoga SP (SP stands for Special Performance) and the PA-32R-301T Turbo Saratoga SP respectively. Aircraft N9223C first flew with the low tail on the 1st of October 1979. The two Saratoga SP's received FAA approval on the 7th of November 1979. This change was made after Piper had put the two Lance III models into production and a total of 35 finished and unfinished aircraft had to be converted to low-tail configuration / Saratoga SP in the last few months of 1979. Deliveries from Vero Beach commenced with s/n 32R-8013002 registration N2880W and s/n 32R-8029002 registration N2422U in early 1980. The Saratoga SP sold for $80,200 in standard form.

The prototype PA-32R-300 Cherokee Lance s/n 32R-7680001 registration N44256. (Piper Aircraft Corporation)

The experimental PA-32RT-300 s/n 32R-7680237 registration N9648K with stabilizer / elevator. (via H.W. Barnhouse)

The prototype PA-32RT-300 Lance II s/n 32R-7885001 registration N9648K. (Piper Aircraft Corporation)

The experimental PA-32R-300T s/n 32R-7680056 registration N7660C prior to the T-tail installation at Lakeland. (K. Rooke)

The experimental PA-32RT-300L s/n 32R-7680001 registration N44256. Note this was shown by Piper as the PA-32RT-300T. (Piper Aircraft Corporation)

PA-32RT-300T s/n 32R-7887197 registration G-IFLY at Cranfield, England. (J.M. Gradidge)

The experimental PA-32RT-301 Lance III s/n 32R-8013001 registration N9223C. (W. Moreu)

The experimental PA-32RT-301 Lance III s/n 32R-8013001 registration N9223C with wing tip end plates at Vero Beach. (W. Moreu)

Piper publicity shot of the PA-32RT-301T Turbo Lance III s/n 32R-8029001 registration N20816 and PA-32RT-301 Lance III s/n 32R-8013001 registration N9223C. (Piper Aircraft Corporation)

The prototype PA-32R-301 Saratoga SP s/n 32R-8013001 registration N9223C landing at Vero Beach. (W. Moreu)

PA-32R PRODUCTION DETAILS

Model Year	Serial Number Range From	To	Type	Total	Comments
Prototype	32R-7680001		300	1	
Pre-production	32R-7580002		300	1	
1976	32R-7680003	32R-7680525 *	300	523	
1977	32R-7780001	32R-7780549 *	300	548	
1978	32R-7880001	32R-7880068	300	68	
Prototype	32R-7885001		300 'II'	1	
Prototype	32R-7887001		300T 'II'	1	
1978	32R-7885002	32R-7885285 *	300 'II'	284	
1978	32R-7887002	32R-7887289 *	300T 'II'	288	
1979	32R-7985001	32R-7985106 *	300 'II'	105	
1979	32R-7987001	32R-7987126	300T 'II'	126	
Prototype	32R-8013001		301 'III'	1	to 301 'SP'
Prototype	32R-8029001		301T 'III'	1	to 301T 'SP'
1980	32R-8013002	32R-8013139	301 'SP'	138	
1980	32R-8029002	32R-8029121 *	301T 'SP'	111	
1981	32R-8113001	32R-8113123	301 'SP'	123	
1981	32R-8129001	32R-8129114	301T 'SP'	114	
1982	32R-8213001	32R-8213061 *	301 'SP'	51	
1982	32R-8229001	32R-8229071 *	301T 'SP'	64	
1983	32R-8313001	32R-8313030 *	301 'SP'	29	
1983	32R-8329001	32R-8329040	301T 'SP'	40	
1984	32R-8413001	32R-8413024	301 'SP'	24	
1984	32R-8429001	32R-8429028 *	301T 'SP'	27	
1985	32R-8513001	32R-8513016	301 'SP'	16	
1985	32R-8529001	32R-8529020	301T 'SP'	20	
1986	32R-8613001	32R-8613006 *	301 'SP'	5	
1986	3213001	3213002	301 'SP'	2	
1986	32R-8629001	32R-8629005	301T 'SP'	5	
1986	32R-8629007	32R-8629008 *	301T 'SP'	0	
1986	3229001	3229002	301T 'SP'	2	
1987	3213003	3213008	301 'SP'	6	
1987	32R-8629006		301T 'SP'	1	
1987	3229003		301T 'SP'	1	
1988	32130009	3213019	301 'SP'	11	
1989	3213020	3213033	301 'SP'	14	
1989	3213035		301 'SP'	1	
1990	3213034		301 'SP'	1	
1990	3213036	3213037	301 'SP'	2	
1992	3213038	3213041	301 'SP'	4	
1994	3213042	3213084	301 'II HP'	43	
1995	3213085	3213108 *	301 'II HP'	18	
1995	3246001	3246017	301 'II HP'	17	
1996	3246018	3246059	301 'II HP'	42	
Prototype	3257001		301 'II TC'	1	
1997	3246060		301 'II HP'		
1997	3257002		301 'II TC'		

A total of 45 aircraft in the batches marked * were not delivered, instead they were updated to the next year's model and given new serial numbers or not built. See table below.
Total manufactured 2881 (All built at Vero Beach)

PA-32R-301 Saratoga SP s/n 32R-8013003 registration N2966Y. (Piper Aircraft Corporation)

The prototype PA-32R-301T Turbo Saratoga SP s/n 32R-8029001 registration N20816 at Vero Beach. (R.W. Peperell)

1982 model PA-32R-301T Turbo Saratoga SP s/n 32R-8129069 registration N8388P with de-icing boots. (Piper Aircraft Corporation)

PA-32R SERIAL NUMBER CHANGES

Model	Old Serial Number	New Serial Number	New Model (if different)
PA-32R-300	32R-7680056	32R-7787001	PA-32RT-300T
PA-32R-300	32R-7680237	32R-7885001	PA-32RT-300
PA-32R-300	32R-7780441	32R-7885002	PA-32RT-300
PA-32RT-300	32R-7885037	32R-8013001	PA-32RT-301 then PA-32R-301
PA-32RT-300	32R-7985106	Not built	
PA-32RT-300T	32R-7887178	32R-8029001	PA-32RT-301T then PA-32R-301T
PA-32R-301T	32R-8029111-120	Not built	
PA-32R-301	32R-8213019	32R-8313008	
PA-32R-301	32R-8213031	32R-8313007	
PA-32R-301	32R-8213039	32R-8313013	
PA-32R-301	32R-8213044	32R-8313014	
PA-32R-301	32R-8213050	32R-8313015	
PA-32R-301	32R-8213052	32R-8313019	
PA-32R-301	32R-8213054	32R-8313005	
PA-32R-301	32R-8213057	32R-8313029	
PA-32R-301	32R-8213058	32R-8313006	
PA-32R-301	32R-8213061	32R-8313030	
PA-32R-301	32R-8313018	32R-8413006	
PA-32R-301T	32R-8229036	32R-8829003	
PA-32R-301T	32R-8229037	32R-8329005	
PA-32R-301T	32R-8229040	32R-8329009	
PA-32R-301T	32R-8229061	32R-8329004	
PA-32R-301T	32R-8229069-071	Not built	
PA-32R-301T	32R-8429028	32R-8529001	
PA-32R-301	32R-8513015	32R-8613003	
PA-32R-301	32R-8613006	3213001	
PA-32R-301T	32R-8629007	3229001	
PA-32R-301T	32R-8629008	3229002	
PA-32R-301	3213098	3257001	PA-32R-301T
PA-32R-301	3213104	3246001	
PA-32R-301	3213105	3246002	
PA-32R-301	3213106	3246003	
PA-32R-301	3213107	3246004	
PA-32R-301	3213108	3246005	

De-icers were available as an option on the Turbo Saratoga SP for the 1982 model year.

In January 1987 Piper briefly looked at putting the TCM TP-500 engine on the Saratoga SP. This was not done.

Production of the Turbo Saratoga SP ended in April 1987 with s/n 3229003 registration N9123X and the Saratoga SP ended in 1992 when it was replaced by the Saratoga II HP.

PA-32R SPECIFICATION & PERFORMANCE			
SPECIFICATION	32R-300	32RT-300	32RT-300T
Engine	300 hp Lycoming IO-540-K1A5	300 hp Lycoming IO-540-K1G5	300 hp Lycoming TIO-540-S1AD
Engine TBO (hrs)	2000	2000	1800
No of seats	6/7	6/7	6/7
Wing Span (ft/ins)	32/11	32/11	32/11
Length (ft/ins)	27/8	28/1	28/11
Height (ft/ins)	8/3	9/6	9/6
Useable fuel capacity (US gal)	94	94	94
Gross weight (lbs)	3600	3600	3600
Empty weight (lbs)	1910	1968-2011	2065-2071
Useful load (lbs)	1690	1589-1632	1529-1535
Propeller	Hartzell 2-blade constant speed	Hartzell 2-blade constant speed	Hartzell 2-blade constant speed
Floats available			
PERFORMANCE			
Max speed	167 kts	165 kts	193 kts
Cruise speed	160 kts	156-158 kts @ 75%	172-183 kts @ 75%
Efficiency (gph)	16 @ 75%	16 @ 75%	16 @ 75%
Stall speed - flaps / gear down	61 kts	59 kts	60 kts
Climb @ sea level (fpm)	1000	1000	1000
Range with reserves	925 nm @ 75% 1105 nm @ 55%	730-782 nm @ 75% 864 nm @ 55%	740 nm @ 75% 815 nm @ 55%
Service ceiling (ft)	14,600	14,600	20,000
Take off (Ground run)(ft)	960	960	960
Take off (over 50ft obst)(ft)	1660	1690	1660
Landing (Ground roll)(ft)	880	880	880
Landing (over 50ft obst)(ft)	1670	1710	1710

At the end of 1992 Piper leased back a customer Saratoga SP s/n 3213029 registration N777TH for development of an improved version. They fitted a new cowl designed by Mississippi State University and NASA which has circular inlets. This first flew on the 18th of February 1993. The prototype aircraft s/n 3213042 registration N9197X first flew on the 27th of March. The window line was modified, various aerodynamic clean-ups were installed, a new leather interior with windows blinds and new table and a new panel. The engine used was the 300 hp Lycoming IO-540-K1G5D with different magnetos and a propeller extension. The aircraft was re-named the Saratoga II HP. The first production aircraft was s/n 3213043 registration N9202Q completed on the 8th of June. The standard equipped price was $309,800.

For the 1996 model year Piper updated the Saratoga II HP with 28 volt electrics and an overhead switch panel. They used aircraft s/n 3213098 registration N9296Z in 1995 for this development. The Saratoga II HP was in production at Vero Beach in December 1996.

In late 1993 Piper started to look at a turbo charged model, to be called the Turbo Saratoga II. This was cancelled due to the cash crisis in the company. It was resurrected in 1995 as the PA-32R-301T Saratoga II TC. A turbocharged 300 hp Lycoming TIO-540-X120 engine was installed in a modified cowl on aircraft N9296Z and first flew on the 13th of July 1996. N9296Z is to be re-serialised to 3257001 when certified in early 1997. Production will commence for the 1997 model year with the 300 hp Lycoming TIO-540-AH1A engine. The standard cabin interior will be configured for five, an entertainment console replacing the starboard aft-facing seat, but a six-seat interior is optional. It is planned to cruise at 184 knots.

PA-32R-301 Saratoga SP test aircraft s/n 3213029 registration N777TH with II HP cowling at Vero Beach. (M. Halcomb)

The production prototype PA-32R-301 Saratoga II HP s/n 3213042 registration N9197X at Vero Beach. (D. Schwartz)

PA-32-301 Saratoga II HP s/n 3246014 registration N92610 awaiting delivery at Vero Beach. (R.W. Peperell)

PA-32R SPECIFICATION & PERFORMANCE

SPECIFICATION	32R-301 'SP'	32R-301T 'Turbo SP'	32R-301 'II HP'
Engine	300 hp Lycoming IO-540-K1G5D	300 hp Lycoming TIO-540-S1AD	300 hp Lycoming IO-540-K1G5D
Engine TBO (hrs)	2000	2000	2000
No of seats	6/7	6/7	6
Wing Span (ft/ins)	36/5	36/5	36/3
Length (ft/ins)	27/8	28/6	27/0
Height (ft/ins)	8/6	8/6	8/6
Useable fuel capacity (US gal)	102	102	102
Gross weight (lbs)	3615	3617	3600
Empty weight (lbs)	1999	2078	2364 (equipped)
Useful load (lbs)	1616	1539	1251
Propeller	Hartzell 2 or 3-blade constant speed	Hartzell 2 or 3-blade constant speed	Hartzell 3-blade constant speed
Floats available			
PERFORMANCE			
Max speed	164 kts	195 kts	166 kts
Cruise speed	159 kts @ 75% 144 kts @ 55%	177 kts @ 75% 152 kts @ 55%	163 kts @ 75% 152 kts @ 55%
Efficiency (gph)	18 @ 75%	19.9 @ 75%	18.5 @ 75%
Stall speed - flaps / gear down	54 kts	56 kts	61 kts
Climb @ sea level (fpm)	1010	1120	1116
Range with reserves	784 nm @ 75% 869 nm @ 55%	730 nm @ 75% 843 nm @ 55%	740 nm @ 75% 800 nm @ 55%
Service ceiling (ft)	16,700	20,000	15,588
Take off (Ground run)(ft)	1183 / 1013	1110 / 960	1196
Take off (over 50ft obst)(ft)	1759 / 1573	1590 / 1420	1768
Landing (Ground roll)(ft)	732 / 650	752 / 650	645
Landing (over 50ft obst)(ft)	1612 / 1530	1725 / 1640	1520

Performance data included for both the 2 and 3-blade propeller versions. For example: The take off ground run of the Saratoga SP is 1183 feet with a 2-blade and 1013 feet with a 3-blade propeller.

The 1996 model PA-32R-301 Saratoga II HP s/n 3213098 registration N9296Z at Vero Beach. (R.W. Peperell)

PA-33

During 1966 and early 1967 Swearingen produced a pressurized cabin version of the PA-24 Comanche for Piper. It had a turbocharged 260 hp Lycoming TIO-540 engine, long Twin Comanche landing gear, a Comanche tail and wings and a new fuselage with gull-wing doors. The prototype PA-33 Pressurized Comanche s/n 33-1 registration N4600Y had its first flight on the 11th of March 1967. Unfortunately it crashed on take-off from Lock Haven on the 24th of May 1967 when a Lycoming test pilot had problems with the electrically controlled hydraulically operated nose gear steering. The project was about to be cancelled due to poor sales prospects when the prototype crashed. Mooney, one of the competition, cancelled their Mustang programme due to poor sales. The prototype was cancelled from the U.S. register in 1969.

PA-33 SPECIFICATION & PERFORMANCE

SPECIFICATION	33
Engine	260 hp Lycoming TIO-540
No of seats	6
Wing Span (ft/ins)	36/0
Length (ft/ins)	
Height (ft/ins)	
Useable fuel capacity (US gal)	
Gross weight (lbs)	
Empty weight (lbs)	
Useful load (lbs)	
Propeller	
Pressurization (psi)	
PERFORMANCE	
Max speed	
Cruise speed	
Stall speed - flaps / gear down	
Climb @ sea level (fpm)	
Range with reserves	
Service ceiling (ft)	

PA-33 Pressurized Comanche s/n 33-1 registration N4600Y at Vero Beach. (D.H. Smith)

PA-34 SENECA

As soon as initial tests were complete on the PA-32-260 Cherokee Six, two 115 hp Lycoming O-235 engines were added to the wings of the PA-32 prototype N9999W (which had the 250 hp Lycoming in the nose) and tests on the tri-motor configuration commenced. The PA-32-3M had its first flight in this configuration on the 13th of May 1965 at Vero Beach. With the centre engine shut down, tests showed that the 115 hp engines on the wings were not powerful enough, so these were replaced by the 150 hp Lycomings. The centre engine was also replaced by a 150 hp Lycoming engine. In this configuration it first flew in December 1965. Piper used Twin Comanche cowlings on the wing engines. The tri-motor configuration was abandoned because the drag of the unfeatherable propellers and fixed gear made the performance unacceptable and the extra cost and complication of three controllable pitch propellers was also unacceptable. This resulted in the a twin engined arrangement being developed named the Twin 6 with designation PA-34. Development work on this fixed gear twin started in January 1966.

The first prototype PA-34-180 Twin 6 s/n 34-E1 registration N3401K first flew on the 25th of April 1967. It had two 180 hp Lycoming O-360 engines with constant speed propellers, fixed landing gear and the wing span and vertical tail from the Cherokee Six. The second prototype s/n 34-E3 registration N3407K first flew on the 30th of August 1968. It also had the 180 hp Lycoming engines, but this aircraft had retractable landing gear. Later during development the wing span was increased by two feet and a larger vertical tail was fitted. Needing more power, a third prototype s/n 34-E4 registration N34PA had two 200 hp Lycoming IO-360-A1A engines (the starboard one was counter-rotating) and first flew on the 20th of October 1969. This also had an aileron / rudder interconnection system. Unfortunately the second prototype N3407K crashed at Vero Beach on the 3rd of June 1970 and was cancelled from the U.S. register. The first two production aircraft were s/n 34-7250001 registration N1021U completed on the 30th of April and s/n 34-7250002 registration N1022U completed on the 7th May 1971. FAA approval A7SO was granted on the 7th of May 1971. Piper announced the PA-34-200 with the name Seneca on the 23rd of September 1971 and deliveries from Vero Beach commenced with s/n 34-7250003 registration N1023U. The base price was $49,900.

For the 1973 model year the gross weight was increased by 200 pounds and de-icing and flight director options were available. For the 1974 model year the Seneca had the two extra fuselage windows (as per the Cherokee Six), the windows had a more rounded line, an improved nose wheel steering, improved ventilation, adjustable front seats, improved sound-proofing and full de-icing package was available as an option.

In October 1973 Piper received a NASA contract to fabricate a new wing and new propellers on the PA-34 Seneca. The initial design work was carried out by Kansas State University and Robertson under contract to NASA. This programme was called the ATLIT Study (Advanced Technology Light Twin). The Piper work was carried out at the Lakeland plant. The wing had the GA(W)-1 airfoil (General Aviation-Whitcomb) and had full span Fowler flaps and spoilers (and no ailerons) and was fitted to Seneca N1021U. This first flew on the 11th of October 1974. The new propellers were fitted to Seneca N1022U. Aircraft N1021U was delivered to NASA Langley Research Centre on the 26th of November 1974 for testing both the new wing and the propellers.

The original Seneca handled awkwardly and flew slowly (but still sold well - 933 in three years), so in 1973/74 Piper engineers revamped the Seneca and altered the handling and performance characteristics to create the PA-34-200T Seneca II. It had turbo-charged 200 hp Continental TSIO-360-E engines inside new streamlined nacelles. To improve in-flight handling characteristics Piper fitted aerodynamically balanced ailerons, an antiservo tab for increased rudder effectiveness and a redesigned stabilitor. To improve handling characteristics on the ground the aileron / rudder interconnect was removed and the nose gear steering linkage reworked. The empty and gross weights were increased. The experimental aircraft was N34PA which had the Continental engines fitted at the beginning of 1973. The pre-production aircraft, s/n 34-7570001 registration N41275 first flew in May 1974. This version was approved on the 18th of July 1974. Deliveries commenced with s/n 34-7570002 registration N44447 in late 1974. The base price was $63,995.

For the 1977 model year the Seneca had new brakes and tyres which reduced landing and take-off distances and increased service life, a new door latch, improved interior, new panel and optional conference style seating.

In March 1978 Piper carried out some preliminary design work on a pressurized Seneca IIP with 2.5 psi pressurization. It had 220 hp Continental engines, gross weight increased by 100 pounds, fuel capacity increased to 160 gallons. The predicted top speed was 200 knots. This never left the drawing board.

The experimental PA-32-3M s/n 32-01 registration N9999W at Vero Beach. (G.K. Gates)

Roll-out of the prototype PA-34 Twin 6 s/n 34-E1 registration N3401K at Vero Beach. (G.K. Gates)

The prototype PA-34-180 Twin 6 s/n 34-E1 registration N3401K on a test flight. (H.W. Barnhouse)

The second prototype PA-34-180 Twin 6 s/n 34-E3 registration N3407K with retractable gear. (G.K. Gates)

The second prototype PA-34-180 Twin 6 s/n 34-E3 registration N3407K with larger vertical tail. (via G.K. Gates)

The third prototype PA-34-200 Twin 6 s/n 34-E4 registration N34PA at Lakeland. (Piper Aircraft Corporation)

The first production PA-34-200 Seneca s/n 34-7250001 registration N1021U. (Piper Aircraft Corporation)

PA-34-200 s/n 34-7250001 registration N1021U with the ATLIT wing at Lakeland. (G.K. Gates)

1974 model PA-34-200 Seneca s/n 34-7450001 registration N15774. (Piper Aircraft Corporation)

PA-34 PRODUCTION DETAILS

Model Year	Serial Number Range From	To	Type	Total	Comments
Experimental	32-01		TriMotor	0	
Prototype	34-E1		Twin 6 180	1	Fixed gear
Prototype	34-E3		Twin 6 180	1	Retractable gear
Prototype	34-E4		Twin 6 200	1	to Seneca 200
1972	34-7250001	34-72500360	200	360	
1973	34-7350001	34-73500353	200	353	
1974	34-7450001	34-74500220	200	220	
Pre-production	34-7570001		200T 'II'	1	
1975	34-7570002	34-7570327	200T 'II'	326	
1976	34-7670001	34-7670371	200T 'II'	371	
1977	34-7770001	34-7770441	200T 'II'	441	
1978	34-7870001	34-7870474	200T 'II'	474	
1979	34-7970001	34-7970530 *	200T 'II'	516	
1980	34-8070001	34-8070367	200T 'II'	367	
1981	34-8170001	34-8170092	200T 'II'	92	
Prototype	34-8133001		220T 'III'	1	
1981	34-8133002	34-8133277	220T 'III'	276	
1982	34-8233001	34-8233205 *	220T 'III'	189	
1983	34-8333001	34-8333133 *	220T 'III'	113	
1984	34-8433001	34-8433088	220T 'III'	88	
1985	34-8533001	34-8533069	220T 'III'	69	
1986	34-8633001	34-8633031 *	220T 'III'	30	
1986	3433001	3433020	220T 'III'	20	
1986	3433022	3433025	220T 'III'	4	
1987	3433021		220T 'III'	1	
1987	3433026	3433080	220T 'III'	55	
1988	3433081	3433136	220T 'III'	56	
1989	3433137	3433168	220T 'III'	32	
1989	3433171	3433178	220T 'III'	8	
1989	3448001	3448004	220T 'III'	4	
1990	3433169	3433170	220T 'III'	2	
1990	3433179	3433216	220T 'III'	38	
1990	3448005	3448007	220T 'III'	3	
1990	3448009		220T 'III'	1	
1990	3448011	3448014	220T 'III'	4	
1991	3433217	3433238 *	220T 'III'	13	kits
1992	3448008 & 3448010		220T 'III'	2	
1992	3448015	3448022	220T 'III'	8	
1993	3448023	3448037 *	220T 'III'	13	
1994	3448038	3448061	220T 'IV'	24	
1995	3448062	3448085 *	220T 'IV'	18	
1995	3447001	3447012	220T 'IV'	12	
1996	3447013	3447029	220T 'IV'	17	
1997	3449001		220T 'V'	1	
1997	3449002		220T 'V'		

The experimental aircraft 32-01 has been included in the PA-32 manufactured total.
A total of 68 aircraft in the batches marked * were not delivered, instead they were updated to the next year's model and given new serial numbers or not built. See table below.
Total manufactured 4626 (All built at Vero Beach)

PA-34 SERIAL NUMBER CHANGES			
Model	Old Serial Number	New Serial Number	New Model (if different)
PA-34-200T	34-7970515-523	Not built	
PA-34-200T	34-7970525-529	Not built	
PA-34-220T	34-8233059	34-8333105	
PA-34-220T	34-8233100	34-8333085	
PA-34-220T	34-8233101	34-8333030	
PA-34-220T	34-8233114	34-8333057	
PA-34-220T	34-8233123	34-8333108	
PA-34-220T	34-8233133	34-8333058	
PA-34-220T	34-8233135	34-8333106	
PA-34-220T	34-8233139	34-8333029	
PA-34-220T	34-8233162	34-8333104	
PA-34-220T	34-8233163	34-8333068	
PA-34-220T	34-8233166	34-8333086	
PA-34-220T	34-8233169	34-8333027	
PA-34-220T	34-8233170	34-8333028	
PA-34-220T	34-8233177	34-8333099	
PA-34-220T	34-8233185	34-8333087	
PA-34-220T	34-8233186	34-8333107	
PA-34-220T	34-8333070	34-8433025	
PA-34-220T	34-8333074	34-8433024	
PA-34-220T	34-8333076	34-8433016	
PA-34-220T	34-8333089	34-8433014	
PA-34-220T	34-8333090	34-8433007	
PA-34-220T	34-8333091	34-8433017	
PA-34-220T	34-8333092	34-8433018	
PA-34-220T	34-8333093	34-8433020	
PA-34-220T	34-8333095	34-8433022	
PA-34-220T	34-8333096	34-8433006	
PA-34-220T	34-8333097	34-8433005	
PA-34-220T	34-8333110	34-8433023	
PA-34-220T	34-8333111	34-8433019	
PA-34-220T	34-8333112	34-8433026	
PA-34-220T	34-8333113	34-8433021	
PA-34-220T	34-8333116	34-8433015	
PA-34-220T	34-8333130-133	34-8433010-013	kits
PA-34-220T	34-8633022	3433001	
PA-34-220T	3433230-238	Kits not completed	
PA-34-220T 'III'	3448036	3448051	PA-34-220T 'IV'
PA-34-220T 'III'	3448037	3448060	PA-34-220T 'IV'
PA-34-220T	3448080	3447001	
PA-34-220T	3448081	3447002	
PA-34-220T	3448082	3447003	
PA-34-220T	3448083	3447004	
PA-34-220T	3448084	3447005	
PA-34-220T	3448085	3447006	

PA-34-200T Seneca II s/n 34-7570001 registration N41275. (Piper Aircraft Corporation)

The prototype PA-34-220T Seneca III s/n 34-813301 registration N8181C at Vero Beach. (R.W. Peperell)

PA-34 SPECIFICATION & PERFORMANCE

SPECIFICATION	34-200	34-200T 'II'	34-220T 'III'
Engine	200 hp Lycoming L/IO-360-A1A	200 hp Continental L/TSIO-360-E	220 hp Continental L/TSIO-360-KB2A
Engine TBO (hrs)	1400	1400	1800
No of seats	6/7	6/7	6/7
Wing Span (ft/ins)	38/11	38/11	38/11
Length (ft/ins)	28/6	28/6	28/7
Height (ft/ins)	9/11	9/11	9/11
Useable fuel capacity (US gal)	95	100, 123 (optional wing tanks)	93, 123 (optional wing tanks)
Gross weight (lbs)	4000 (72) 4200 (7250215 onwards, 73 & 74)	4570	4773
Empty weight (lbs)	2479-2623	2770-2848	2852-2875
Useful load (lbs)	1521-1601	1722-1800	1898-1921
Propellers	Hartzell 2-blade	Hartzell 2-blade	Hartzell 3-blade
Floats available			
PERFORMANCE			
Max speed	171 kts	198 kts	196 kts
Cruise speed	163 kts @ 75% 158 kts @ 55%	191 kts @ 75% 164 kts @ 55%	193 kts @ 75% 180 kts @ 55%
Efficiency (gph)	20.6 @ 75%	24 @ 75%	29 @ 75% 18.7 @ 55%
Stall speed - flaps / gear down	59 kts	60 kts	64 kts
Climb @ sea level (fpm)	1460 (72) 1360 (73 & 74)	1340	1400
Range with reserves	723-754 nm @ 75% 873-939 nm @55%	547 nm @ 75% 578 nm @ 55%	462 nm @ 75% 630 nm @ 55%
Optional fuel range with reserves		756 nm @ 75% 806 nm @ 55%	665 nm @ 75% 920 nm @ 55%
Service ceiling (ft)	20,000	25,000	25,000
Take off (Ground run)(ft)	750-800	900	920
Take off (over 50ft obst)(ft)	1140-1420	1240	1210
Landing (Ground roll)(ft)	700-705	1050-1380	1218
Landing (over 50ft obst)(ft)	1335	1760-2090	1978

In mid 1978 Piper started work on the Seneca III. Semi-tapered wings from the single-engine Cherokee series, but with same span as the Seneca II were fitted to aircraft N34PA in early 1979, designated the PA-34-201T but resulted in no increase in performance. A T-tail was also fitted in March 1979, but the aircraft didn't fly well in this configuration and was scrapped after three hours of flying. Piper re-designed the Seneca III by keeping the existing Seneca II wings and tail unit. They added 220 hp Continental L/TSIO-360-KB2A engines (220 hp available for take-off, 200 hp for continuous operation) with three bladed propellers, a new panel and interior, a one-piece windscreen and gave it an increase in useful load. The prototype PA-34-220T s/n 34-8133001 registration N8181C was completed in early 1980. This version was certified on the 27th of December. Deliveries commenced with s/n 34-8133002 registration N8282Y in January 1981. The list price was $138,250.

In 1989 Piper added 28 volt electrics to the Seneca III in support of advanced avionics (including Electronic Flight Instrumentation System) and started a new s/n series 3448xxx. The first aircraft was s/n 3448001 registration N9523N completed in September 1989 for Korean Airlines.

Piper put a new cowl, similar to the new Saratoga II HP cowl, onto the Seneca III in 1993 and renamed it the Seneca IV. Aircraft s/n 3448029 registration N9162Z was used as the experimental aircraft and first flew with the new cowl on the 3rd of September. The production prototype was s/n 3448038 registration N9219X completed on the 29th of November 1993. The Seneca IV has a modified window line, a new leather interior with window blinds and a new panel. The first production aircraft was s/n 3448039 registration N9208P completed on the 23rd of February 1994. The standard price was $424,900.

The first 28 volt Seneca III in final assembly at Vero Beach, s/n 3448001 registration N9523N. (R.W. Peperell)

The experimental PA-34-220T Seneca III s/n 3448029 registration N9162Z with the IV cowling after an icing test at Vero Beach. (via D. Schwartz)

PA-34-220T Seneca IV s/n 3448038 registration N9219X. (Piper Aircraft Corporation)

PA-34 SPECIFICATION & PERFORMANCE		
SPECIFICATION	34-220T 'IV'	34-220T 'V'
Engine	220 hp Continental L/TSIO-360-KB2A	220 hp Continental L/TSIO-360-RB
Engine TBO (hrs)	1800	
No of seats	6	6
Wing Span (ft/ins)	38/11	38/11
Length (ft/ins)	28/7	28/7
Height (ft/ins)	9/11	9/11
Useable fuel capacity (US gal)	123	
Gross weight (lbs)	4750	4750
Empty weight (lbs)	3314	
Useful load (lbs)	1436	
Propellers	McCauley 3-blade	
Floats available		
PERFORMANCE		
Max speed	196 kts	
Cruise speed	193 kts @ 75% 191 kts @ 65%	189 kts
Efficiency (gph)		
Stall speed - flaps / gear down	64 kts	
Climb @ sea level (fpm)	1400	
Range with reserves	990 nm @ 45%	
Service ceiling (ft)	25,000+	
Take off (Ground run)(ft)		
Take off (over 50ft obst)(ft)	1210	
Landing (Ground roll)(ft)		
Landing (over 50ft obst)(ft)	1978	

In 1995 Piper started to develop the Seneca V. It has improved cowling inlets, and at first had new 220 hp Lycoming TIO-360-X66 4 cylinder engines. The experimental aircraft was s/n 3448033 registration N9183N and this first flew on the 16th of June. This set up was not a total success, so the engines were replaced with improved 220 hp TCM L/TSIO-360-RB engines and this first flew on the 1st of December. These engines offer 220 hp continuous operation. The first production aircraft, s/n 3449001 registration N92987, first flew on the 23rd of April 1996. The Seneca V has a new air-conditioning unit, an updated panel with an overhead switch panel. The standard cabin interior will be configured for five, an entertainment console replacing the starboard aft-facing seat, but a six-seat interior is optional. It will be launched for 1997.

The Seneca is the best selling twin in its class, providing a combination of value, economy, performance and handling characteristics that are unmatched. It was in production at Vero Beach in December 1996.

In the field a conversion has been offered by Seguin of Texas to convert the Seneca (1) into the Princess. The modification includes new engine cowlings and wing fences. Sierra Industries (previously R/STOL & Robertson) offer the Super Seneca I and Super Seneca II with spoilers and full-span single slotted flaps. Examples of the Super Seneca are s/n 34-7250198 registration N2BL, s/n 34-7670167 registration N8703E and s/n 34-7670049 registration N4458X.

The experimental PA-34 Seneca V s/n 3448033 registration N9183N with Lycoming engines. (via D. Schwartz)

The first production PA-34-220T Seneca V s/n 3449001 registration N92897. (via D. Schwartz)

PA-34-200T Seneca II s/n 34-7670049 registration N4458X with Robertson STOL modifications. (J.M. Gradidge)

PA-35 POCONO

In 1965 Piper started to design a 16-18 place non-pressurized commuter airliner with two 400 hp engines at Vero Beach. The main part of the fuselage was to be a circular cylinder large enough that three people could be seated side by side, two on one side and with an aisle between the single seat on the other side. Piper announced its intentions on its commuter airliner in March 1967. Originally it was to be named the Cheyenne. Piper produced the 18 seat prototype PA-35 s/n 35-E1 registration N3535C, with 475 hp Lycoming TIO-720-BIA engines in 1968. It had its first flight on the 13th of May and was called the Pocono. During development the prototype's airframe was enlarged to improve flight characteristics. The fuselage was lengthened by over three feet and the tail area was also increased. First flight in the new configuration was on the 10th of December 1968.

The president of Piper, W.T. Piper Junior, announced early in 1969 that Piper would build a two million dollar factory at Lakeland Municipal Airport in Florida on 100 acres of land with an option on a further 100 acres. It was planned for the Pocono to be manufactured there from 1970.

Development was suspended during 1969, primarily to permit more rapid progress on other development programs at Vero Beach. There were other factors which also contributed to the decision to suspend the program, i.e. a serious question on the economic justification of the project and the fact that Piper were experiencing difficulty with the powerplant capability due to airframe growth (originally it was 400 hp, later needed 520 hp but only obtained 507 hp from the Lycoming engines). During 1969 and 1970 many U.S. third level commuter operators were experiencing difficulties and going out of business. The outlook for sales seemed very poor.

PA-35 SPECIFICATION & PERFORMANCE

SPECIFICATION	35 (1968)	35 (1969)
Engine	475 hp Lycoming TIO-720-B1A	520 hp Lycoming TIO-720-B1A
Engine TBO (hrs)		
No of seats	16	18
Wing Span (ft/ins)	51/0	51/0
Length (ft/ins)	39/3	42/4
Height (ft/ins)	17/5	
Useable fuel capacity (US gal)	200	200
Gross weight (lbs)	9500	9750
Empty weight (lbs)	4900	5572
Useful load (lbs)	4600	4178
Propellers		
Pressurization (psi)		
Floats available		
PERFORMANCE		
Max speed	242 mph	260 mph
Cruise speed	216 mph	235 mph @ 75%
Efficiency (gph)		
Stall speed - flaps / gear down		80 mph
Climb @ sea level (fpm)	1630	1680
Range with reserves	800 sm	700 sm @ 75%
Service ceiling (ft)	25,000	29,000
Take off (Ground run)(ft)		
Take off (over 50ft obst)(ft)		
Landing (Ground roll)(ft)		
Landing (over 50ft obst)(ft)		

PA-35 Pocono s/n 35-E1 registration N3535C. Note tufts. (Piper Aircraft Corporation)

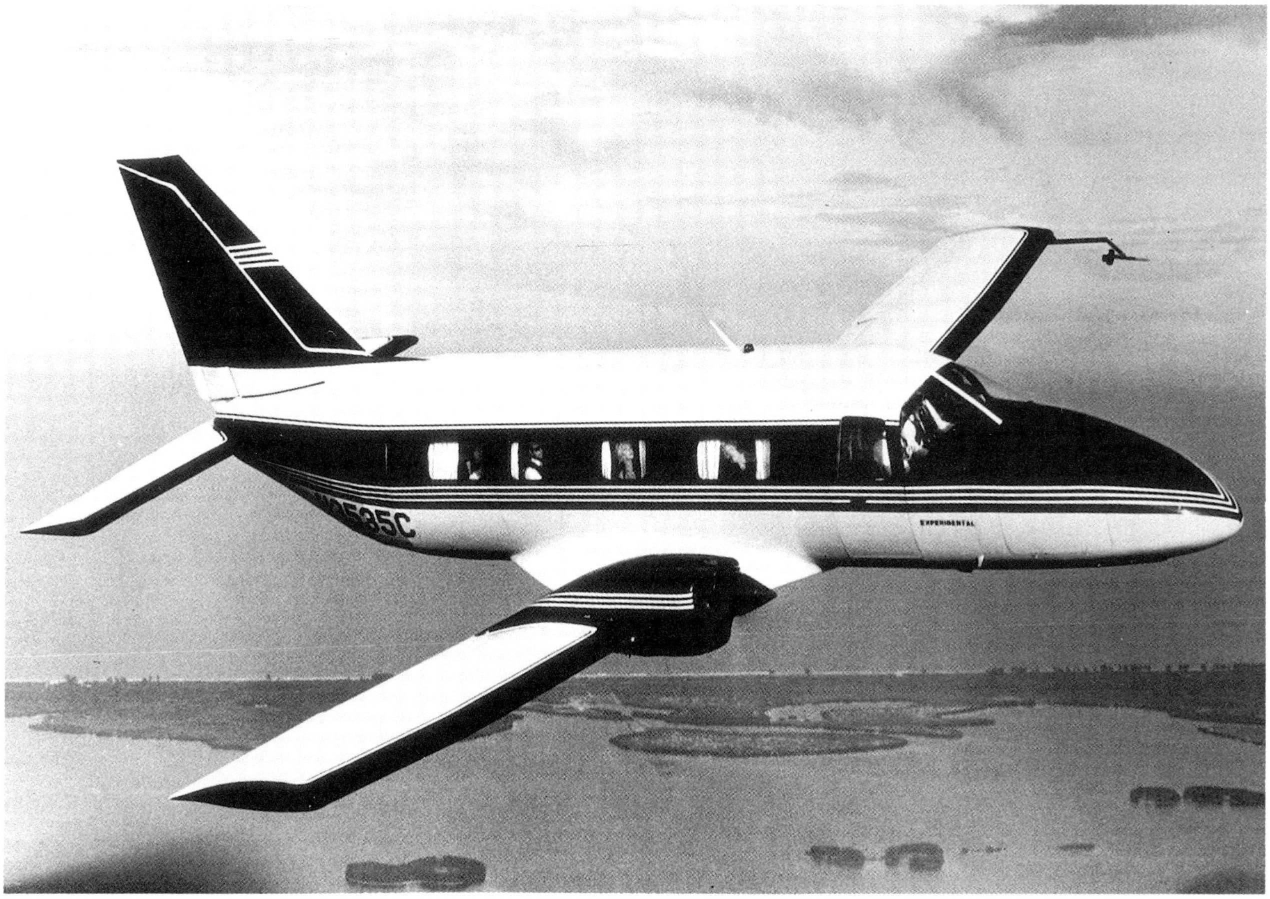

PA-35 Pocono s/n 35-E1 registration N3535C with extended fuselage and larger tail. (Piper Aircraft Corporation)

In May 1970 Piper proposed three new versions of the Pocono in addition to the original version. These were:-

A four engined version with 250 hp Lycoming TIO-540 engines,
A two engined version with 600 hp Pratt & Whitney R1340 engines, and
A turbo prop version with two 800 shp Pratt & Whitney PT-6A-30 engines with a stretched fuselage with 23 seats.

Garrett proposed a version with two TPE331 engines.

Pratt & Whitney proposed a version with two 680 shp P&W PT6A-27 engines

None of these derivatives was developed, and the prototype was flown from Vero Beach to Lakeland on the 23rd of October. It was seen engine-less at Lakeland in May 1976. At the end of 1976 the sole Pocono built was sold to Pezetel, Poland.

With the cancellation of the Pocono production, Lakeland didn't manufacture its first aircraft until June 1973 when the Chieftain line was built there.

Aerial view of the Piper factory at Lakeland. (Piper Aircraft Corporation)

Model of the Piper proposed four engined version of the PA-35 Pocono. (Piper Aircraft Corporation)

Drawing of the Pratt & Whitney proposed PT6 powered PA-35 Pocono. (Piper Aircraft Corporation)

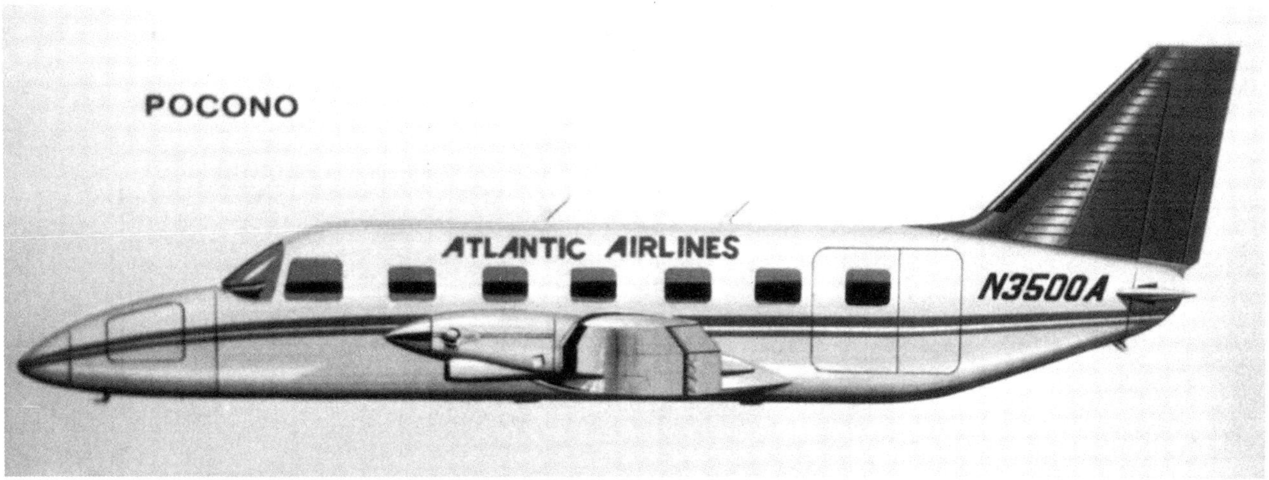

Drawing of the Piper proposed turbine powered stretched PA-35 Pocono. (via T. Heitzman)

PA-36 PAWNEE BRAVE

Piper designed a new agricultural aircraft, the PA-36 Pawnee II, in the late 1960's at Vero Beach. It was a bigger aircraft than the PA-25 Pawnee, with a bigger hopper capacity of 30 or 38 cu. ft., better pilot safety, the best dispersal equipment available, a strong design and it was easily maintainable. A fibreglass sprung landing gear was developed for the Pawnee II, and was fitted to Pawnee N6966Z in January 1967, but it was not proceeded with. The first prototype s/n 36-E1 registration N36PA first flew on the 17th of November 1969 and it had a 260 hp Lycoming O-540-E engine and a stabilator. Continental persuaded Piper to use the new Tiara engine in the Pawnee II. The engine had been flying in several Pipers during 1969 and 1970. It was proposed to produce the Pawnee II in two versions, one with a 285 hp Continental Tiara 6-285 engine and another with a 320 hp 6-320 engine. The Continental engine was put into the prototype during development as was a conventional stabilizer / elevator in place of the stabilator and a larger rudder and vertical tail. In support of the PA-36 programme Piper evaluated a Cessna 188 Agwagon registration N188TV during March 1971. The second prototype s/n 36-E3 registration N36TC was registered in 1971. FAA approval was granted on the 31st of May 1972 (A9SO - normal) and on the 31st of August 1972 (A10SO - restricted). The first pre-production aircraft now named the Pawnee Brave s/n 36-7360001 registration N55636 was built in early 1973. Production got under way with only the 285 hp version and deliveries from Vero Beach commenced with s/n 36-7360002 registration N55512 in May 1973.

The Continental engine was problematic, so in June 1974 Piper installed a 300 hp Lycoming IO-540-K1A5 engine in aircraft s/n 36-7460016 registration N43401 using the existing cowling. This was type certificated on the 22nd of November (normal) and on the 12th of December (restricted) of that year and would have used the serial number range 36-7561xxx had it gone into production at that time. From the 1975 model year onwards the Pawnee Brave was built at Lock Haven starting with s/n 36-7560001 completed on the 13th January 1975. Lock Haven wanted to keep the 285 hp Tiara and Continental appeared to solve the Tiara engine problems, so Piper stayed with the Tiara.

PA-36 PRODUCTION DETAILS

Model Year	Serial Number Range From	To	Type	Total	Comments
Prototype	36-E1		260	1	Built Vero Beach
Prototype	36-E3		285	1	Built Vero Beach
1973	36-7360001	36-7360073 *	285	63	Built Vero Beach
1974	36-7460001(1)	36-7460003(1) *	285	0	
1974	36-7460001(2)	36-7460003(2)	285	3	Built Vero Beach
1974	36-7460004	36-7460041	285	38	Built Vero Beach
1975	36-7560001	36-7560134	285	134	Built Lock Haven
1976	36-7660001	36-7660135	285	135	Built Lock Haven
1977	36-7760001	36-7760142	300	142	Built Lock Haven
1978	36-7860001	36-7860123 *	300	71	Built Lock Haven
1978	36-7802001	36-7802074	375	74	Built Lock Haven
1978	36T-7817001 *		Turbine	0	
1979	36-7960001	36-7960078 *	300	50	Built Lock Haven
1979	36-7902001	36-7902051	375	51	Built Lock Haven
1980	36-8060001	36-8060026	300	26	Built Lock Haven
1980	36-8002001	36-8002041 *	375	35	Built Lock Haven
1981	36-8160001	36-8160023	300	23	Built Lock Haven
1981	36-8102001	36-8102029	375	29	Built Lock Haven
1982	36-8202001	36-8202025	375	25	Built Lock Haven
1983	36-8302001	36-8302025	375	25	Built Lock Haven

A total of 100 aircraft in the batches marked * were not delivered, instead they were updated to the next year's model and given new serial numbers or not built. See table below.

Total manufactured 923

The prototype PA-36 Pawnee II s/n 36-E1 registration N36PA with stabilator and Lycoming engine at Vero Beach. (C. Diefendorf)

The prototype PA-36 Pawnee II s/n 36-E1 registration N36PA with elevator at Vero Beach. (Piper Aircraft Corporation)

The second prototype PA-36-285 Pawnee Brave s/n 36-E3 registration N36TC showing the access panels. (Piper Aircraft Corporation)

PA-36 SERIAL NUMBER CHANGES			
Model	Old Serial Number	New Serial Number	New Model (if different)
PA-36-285	36-7360050	36-7460001(2)	
PA-36-285	36-7360052	36-7460016	
PA-36-285	36-7360066	36-7460003(2)	
PA-36-285	36-7360067	36-7460004	
PA-36-285	36-7360068	36-7460005	
PA-36-285	36-7360069	36-7460006	
PA-36-285	36-7360070	36-7460007	
PA-36-285	36-7360071	36-7460011	
PA-36-285	36-7360072	36-7460012	
PA-36-285	36-7360073	36-7460002(2)	
PA-36-285	36-7460001(1)	36-7460008	
PA-36-285	36-7460002(1)	36-7460009	
PA-36-285	36-7460003(1)	36-7460010	
PA-36-300	36-7860002	36-7960040	
PA-36-300	36-7860004	36-7960041	
PA-36-300	36-7860005	36-7960042	
PA-36-300	36-7860006	36-7960043	
PA-36-300	36-7860008	36-7960044	
PA-36-300	36-7860009	36-7960045	
PA-36-300	36-7860016	36-7960046	
PA-36-300	36-7860025	36-7960071	
PA-36-300	36-7860027	36T-7817001	PA-36T
PA-36-300	36-7860032	36-7960047	
PA-36-300	36-7860033	36-7960048	
PA-36-300	36-7860035	36-7960049	
PA-36-300	36-7860038	36-7960072	
PA-36-300	36-7860039	36-7960073	
PA-36-300	36-7860040	36-7960050	
PA-36-300	36-7860042	36-7960074	
PA-36-300	36-7860046	36-7960075	
PA-36-300	36-7860048	36-7960051	
PA-36-300	36-7860052	36-7960052	
PA-36-300	36-7860053	36-7960053	
PA-36-300	36-7860054	36-7960054	
PA-36-300	36-7860055	36-7960055	
PA-36-300	36-7860056	36-7960056	
PA-36-300	36-7860057	36-7960057	
PA-36-300	36-7860058	36-7960058	
PA-36-300	36-7860059	36-7960059	
PA-36-300	36-7860060	36-7960076	
PA-36-300	36-7860064	36-7960060	
PA-36-300	36-7860065	36-7960061	
PA-36-300	36-7860066	36-7960062	
PA-36-300	36-7860067	36-7960063	
PA-36-300	36-7860068	36-7960064	
PA-36-300	36-7860070	36-7960065	
PA-36-300	36-7860072	36-7960066	
PA-36-300	36-7860080	36-7960077	
PA-36-300	36-7860084	36-7960078	
PA-36-300	36-7860099	36-7960001	
PA-36-300	36-7860100	36-7960002	

PA-36 SERIAL NUMBER CHANGES (continued)

Model	Old Serial Number	New Serial Number	New Model (if different)
PA-36-300	36-7860101	36-7960003	
PA-36-300	36-7860106	36-7960004	
PA-36-300	36-7860107	36-7960005	
PA-36-300	36-7860108	36-7960006	
PA-36-300	36-7860110	36-7960007	
PA-36-300	36-7860116	36-7960010	
PA-36-300	36-7860117	36-7960068	
PA-36-300	36-7860118	36-7960069	
PA-36-300	36-7860119	36-7960070	
PA-36-300	36-7860120	36-7960011	
PA-36-300	36-7860121	36-7960012	
PA-36T	36T-7817001	Not completed	
PA-36-300	36-7960002-006	Not completed	
PA-36-300	36-7960007	36-8060020	
PA-36-300	36-7960008	36-8060022	
PA-36-300	36-7960009	36-8060023	
PA-36-300	36-7960020-039	Not built	
PA-36-375	36-8002034-039	Not built	

During 1975 Piper looked at the more powerful 320 hp Tiara engine. Aircraft N55636 was converted at Mobile in May 1975 and s/n 36-7560067 registration N9956P first flew at Lock Haven on the 10th of October 1975. These two aircraft were put out on service test. Production of the PA-36-320 was planned for the 1976 model year in parallel with the 285 hp model. Continuing problems with the Tiara engine prevented the introduction of the 320 hp version.

In 1976 Piper put the 300 hp Lycoming engine in a modified the cowl on two aircraft; s/n 36-7560068 registration N9957P at Vero Beach which first flew on the 28th of July and s/n 36-7660078 registration N57770 at Lock Haven which first flew on the 19th of May. For the 1977 model year the 300 hp Lycoming IO-540-K1G5 engine replaced the 285 hp Tiara engine on the Pawnee Brave production line. Deliveries commenced with s/n 36-7760001 registration N57813. It was priced at $55,000. At the same time Piper produced a conversion kit for the field to convert the pre-1977 Pawnee Braves from the 285 hp Tiara engine to the 300 hp Lycoming engine. Eighteen kits have been supplied by Piper. TCM eventually solved the Tiara engine problems but it was too late. For the 1978 model year for the Pawnee Brave 300 was re-named the Brave 300.

STC Engineering of Oklahoma installed a Jacobs R-755A radial engine in aircraft s/n 36-7460003 registration N40915 in mid 1976. With the help of Page Industries, Piper were to launch this model, the PA-36-350 in February 1977 in parallel with the 300 hp Lycoming version. Due to concern at Piper about putting such an old engine in a modern airframe, this was not put into production.

Near the end of 1976 Piper discussed a 375 hp Brave. They tested a three bladed propeller on aircraft N9957P in March 1977 in preparation. This became the test aircraft with a 375 hp Lycoming IO-720-D1CD engine in a new style cowling and first flew at Vero Beach on the 8th of July 1977. FAA certification of the PA-36-375 was granted on the 4th of October 1977 for Normal and Restricted operations. Deliveries of the Brave 375 from Lock Haven commenced with s/n 36-7802001 registration N3778E which was completed on the 15th of February 1978.

The experimental PA-36-320 Pawnee Brave s/n 36-7360001 registration N55636 with 320 hp Tiara engine at Vero Beach. (Piper Aircraft Corporation)

PA-36-350 Pawnee Brave s/n 36-7460003 registration N40915 with 350 hp Jacobs engine and wing slats. (C. Diefendorf)

The experimental PA-36-300 Pawnee Brave s/n 36-7560068 registration N9957P at Vero Beach. (C. Diefendorf)

The experimental PA-36-375 Pawnee Brave s/n 36-7560068 registration N9957P. (Piper Aircraft Corporation)

The experimental PA-36T Turbine Pawnee Brave s/n 36-7660078 registration N57770. (via J. Maurielli)

PA-36 SPECIFICATION & PERFORMANCE

SPECIFICATION	36-285 (Normal)	36-285 (Restricted) 2 blade propeller	36-285 (Restricted) 2 blade propeller
Engine	285 hp Continental Tiara	285 hp Continental Tiara	285 hp Continental Tiara
Engine TBO (hrs)	1200	1200	1200
No of seats	1	1	1
Wing Span (ft/ins)	39/0	39/0	39/0
Length (ft/ins)	27/4	27/4	27/4
Height (ft/ins)	7/6	7/6	7/6
Useable fuel capacity (US gal)	90	90	90
Gross weight (lbs)	3900	4400	4400
Empty weight (lbs)	2185	2185	2203
Useful load (lbs)	1715	2215	2197
Propeller	Hartzell 2-blade	Hartzell 2-blade	Hartzell 3-blade
Hopper load (lbs)	1900	1900	1900
Hopper capacity (gals / cu.ft)	225/30	275/38	275/38
Floats available			
PERFORMANCE			
Max speed	131 mph (dust) 132 mph (spray)	124 mph (dust) 125 mph (spray)	121 mph
Cruise speed	107 mph (dust) 112 mph (spray)	101 mph (dust) 106 mph (spray)	96 mph
Efficiency (gph)	17.9 @ 75%	17.9	17.9
Stall speed - flaps / gear down	64 mph (dust) 63 mph (spray)	67 mph (dust) 66 mph (spray)	67 mph
Climb @ sea level (fpm)	493	355	355
Range with reserves	538 sm (dust) @ 75% 564 sm (spray) @ 75%	510 sm (dust) @ 75% 535 sm (spray) @ 75%	466 sm @ 75%
Service ceiling (ft)	8,800	5,900	5,900
Take off (Ground run)(ft)	1330	1829	1473
Take off (over 50ft obst)(ft)	2200	2600	2250
Landing (Ground roll)(ft)	625	715	715
Landing (over 50ft obst)(ft)	1390	1470	1470

In May 1977 Piper started to develop a turbo-prop powered PA-36T Pawnee Brave. A 585 shp Lycoming LTP-101 Series 600 engine was installed in a lengthened cowl (by 18 inches) in a strengthened Pawnee Brave 300 aircraft N57770 by a local fixed based operator at Stratford, Connecticut. This first flew on the 10th of September 1977. The prototype was s/n 36-7860027 which went to the experimental department in December to become s/n 36T-7817001, but the installation was not completed and was subsequently scrapped. The experimental aircraft didn't perform too well as the engine had to be torque limited to around 475 shp in support of airframe restrictions. During testing Piper used diesel fuel in this engine. Aircraft N57770 flew with a new wing on the 17th of July 1978 in order to support a higher gross weight. This programme was cancelled in August 1978. Piper also proposed developing a 475 shp Pratt & Whitney PT6A-11AG powered Brave at the end of 1977 designated the PA-36T2. This never left the drawing board being cancelled in April 1978. Later in 1978 Piper considered a further development of the Turbine Brave, the PA-36T4. This had a two feet eleven inches plug in the rear fuselage, but still had the PT6A-11AG engine. The turboprop derivative did not go into production.

In October 1982 the turbine programme was resurrected by Piper in response to a request by Placo Aircraft, the Piper South African dealer, who wished to sell it as a kit world-wide. This would have used the Brave 375 airframe with a 450 shp Lycoming LTP-101-600A engine and a gross weight of 4800 pounds, but was not proceeded with.

Piper looked at a Brave with wing leading edge slats, which was proposed by the University of Oklahoma. In July 1978 Brave 375 N9957P was delivered to Norman, Oklahoma on the 5th August for fitment. It was picked up by Piper on the 6th December and returned to Vero Beach for evaluation. Piper decided not to produce it and left it as an a Supplementary Type Certificate.

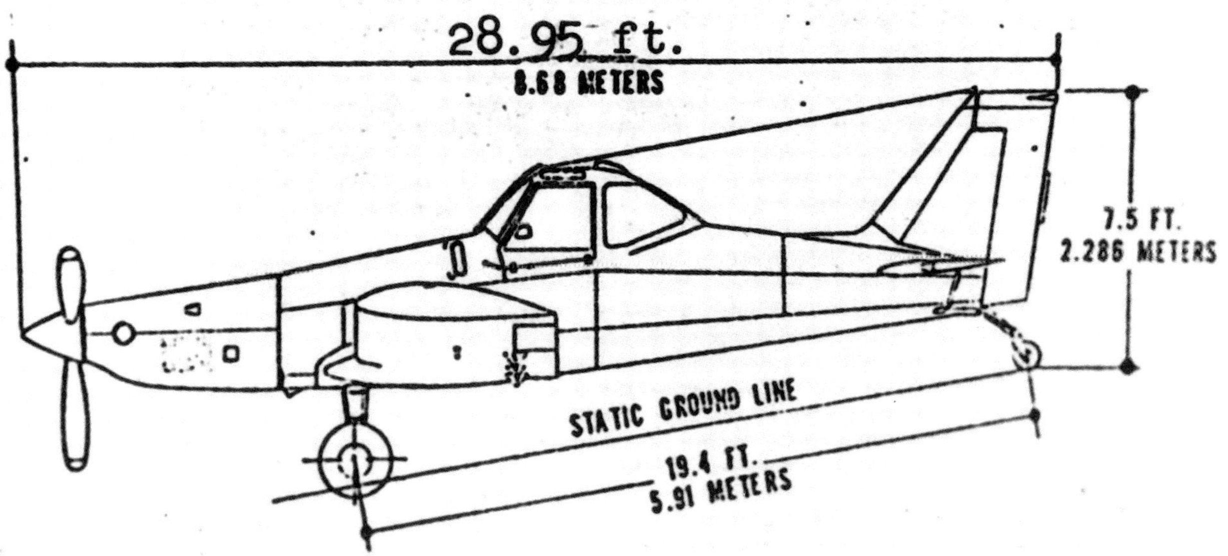

Drawing of the proposed Pratt & Whitney PT6 powered PA-36T2. (Piper Aircraft Corporation)

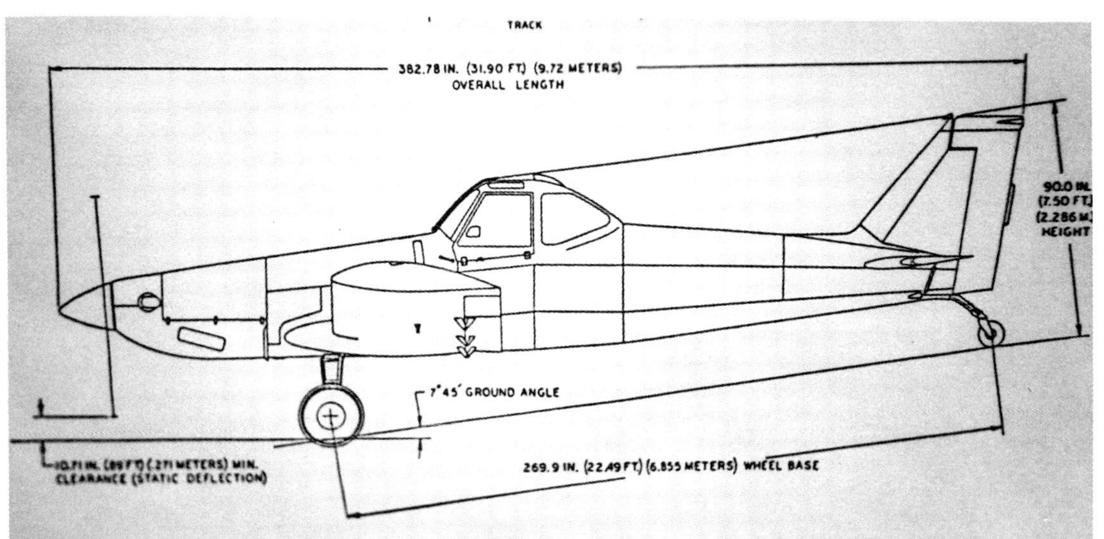

Drawing of the Pratt & Whitney PT6 powered PA-36T4 with lengthened fuselage. (Piper Aircraft Corporation)

PA-36-400 Pawnee Brave s/n 36-8202006 registration N2337X with 400 hp Lycoming engine. (N. Thelwell)

PA-36 SPECIFICATION & PERFORMANCE

SPECIFICATION	36-300	36-375	JAS 400
Engine	300 hp Lycoming IO-540-K1G5	375 hp Lycoming IO-720-D1CD	400 hp Lycoming IO-720-D1C
Engine TBO (hrs)	2000	1200	1200
No of seats	1	1	1
Wing Span (ft/ins)	38/9.5	38/9.5	38/9.5
Length (ft/ins)	26/10	27/6	27/6
Height (ft/ins)	7/6	7/6	7/6
Useable fuel capacity (US gal)	86	86	86
Gross weight (lbs)	3900 normal 4400 restricted	3900 normal 4400 restricted	3900 normal 4400 restricted
Empty weight (lbs)	2198-2200	2434-2465	
Useful load (lbs)	2200-2202	2335-2366	
Propeller	Hartzell 3-blade	Hartzell 3-blade	Hartzell 3-blade
Hopper load (lbs)	1900	1900	1900
Hopper capacity (gals / cu.ft)	225/30 or 275/38	275/38	275/38
Floats available			
PERFORMANCE			
Max speed	148 mph	160 mph	160 mph
Cruise speed	142 mph @ 75%	149 mph @ 75%	137 mph
Efficiency (gph)			
Stall speed - flaps / gear down	62 mph	66 mph	
Climb @ sea level (fpm)	770	1051	1051
Range with reserves	456 sm @ 75%	455 sm @ 75%	605 sm
Service ceiling (ft)	12,000	15,000	
Take off (Ground run)(ft)	960	715	
Take off (over 50ft obst)(ft)	1525	1208	
Landing (Ground roll)(ft)	700	740	
Landing (over 50ft obst)(ft)	1650	1850	

In 1978 Piper, Lockheed and NASA jointly worked on the design of an advanced safe agricultural aircraft. No aircraft was built as a result of this study.

In August 1981 Piper sold the marketing rights of the Brave 300 and 375 to WTA of Lubbock, Texas together with the 19 unsold 1981 model Brave 300 and 17 unsold 1981 model Brave 375 aircraft. Production of the 300 hp version ceased with s/n 36-8160023 registration N2397Y completed on the 4th of June 1981. WTA re-named the 375 hp model the New Brave 375. They also made the 400 hp Lycoming IO-720-D1C engine available in August 1982 as the New Brave 400. This engine was tested by Piper at Lock Haven in aircraft s/n 36-8202001 registration N2321X in July 1982. The last 375 / 400 hp version was s/n 36-8302025 registration N4365E completed on the 10th of January 1983.

In the field, Johnston Aircraft Service of Tulare, California offers several Brave 285 and 300 modifications including a 400 hp Super Brave conversion kit with Lycoming IO-720-D1C engine and a High Lift Wing leading edge kit. An example of the JAS Super Brave 400 is s/n 36-7360027 registration N56070. Avtek Aviation of Lubbock, Texas installed a 450 hp Pratt & Whitney R-985 radial engine in aircraft s/n 36-7560112 registration N57569 in 1977 and offered this PA-36-450 version for sale as a conversion. The conversion included a 30 gallon increase in hopper capacity and much improved field performance. Many of the Brave 300 aircraft in the field have had a turbo-charger installed on their engine.

At the end of 1974 Piper Lock Haven initiated design of a high wing bushplane called the Cargo Brave for the African and South American markets. It was based upon PA-36 components including the powerplant (320 hp Tiara), wings, tail and landing gear with a new cargo type fuselage, with either six seats or 170 cubic feet cargo volume, to make a low cost utility aircraft. It's length was to be 35 feet with a height of 10 feet 7 inches. Gross weight was planned at 4150 pounds. There were to be follow on versions to use the 375 hp Lycoming and turbine powerplants. This programme didn't get far as it was cancelled in early 1975.

PA-36-450 s/n 36-7560112 registration N57569 with Pratt & Whitney R-985 engine. (via C. Diefendorf)

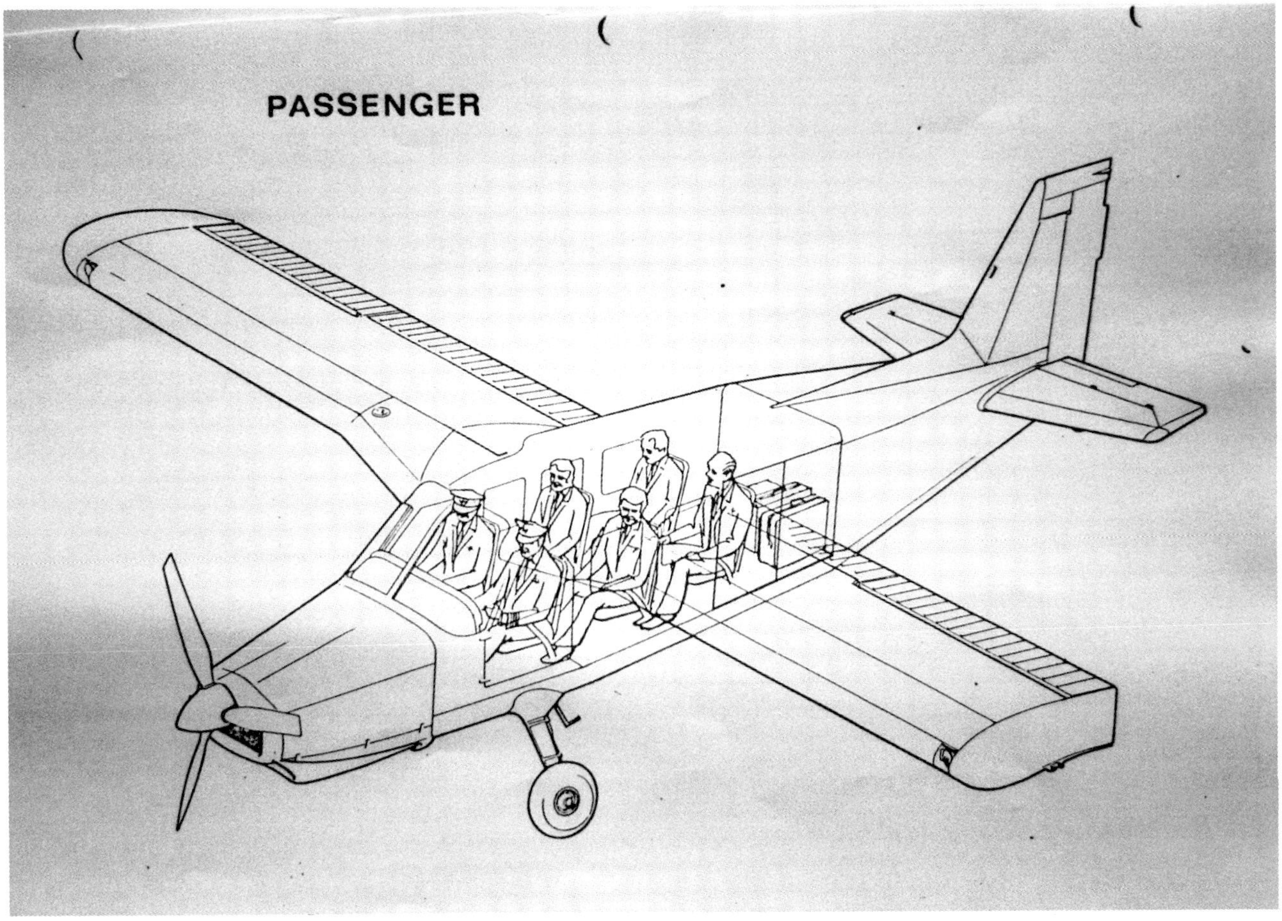

Drawing of the proposed Bushplane with passenger interior. (R. Edelstein)

PA-37

First discussed in May 1967, Piper started design work on a new pressurized twin in January 1969, designated PA-37. The first proposal was in January 1970 for a four to six place pressurized low wing twin engined retractable gear aircraft. The size was between the Twin Comanche and the Aztec D. Turbo-charged 280 to 300 hp hydra-torque engines were proposed. It was planned to certify this by March 1974. Several models and drawings were produced, one with a T-tail and another with pusher engines.

In order to design and produce the PA-37 concept aircraft in a shorter time, a modified pressurized Aztec was proposed in February 1970. This had a PA-31P front fuselage and a new rear fuselage, an Aztec tail, Aztec wings and Aztec F wing tips, Aztec gear and 300 hp Continental hydra-torque (Tiara) engines. The PA-37 programme was unaffordable and was cancelled in July 1970.

Piper started work on the PX-2 in late 1970, being a development of the PA-37 designation. In October 1971 a PX-2-9000 was proposed, based upon a cut down version of the Navajo with the ultimate goal of a pressurized aircraft. Three models were proposed:

1. Normally aspirated Continental 300 hp non-pressurized
2. Turbocharged Continental 300 hp non-pressurized
3. Turbocharged Continental 320 hp pressurized

This project was cancelled on the 26th August 1974.

PA-37 Proposed SPECIFICATION & PERFORMANCE

SPECIFICATION	PA-37	Aztec based	PX-2-9000
Engine	280-300 hp turbocharged hydra-torque	300 hp Continental hydra-torque	300 hp Continental Tiara 6-300 or 6-320
Engine TBO (hrs)			
No of seats	4-6		4-6
Wing Span (ft/ins)	37/6	36/3	36/0
Length (ft/ins)	31/4	32/11	31/4
Height (ft/ins)	12/7	10/5	11/9
Useable fuel capacity (US gal)		144	190
Gross weight (lbs)	5600	5450	5500-6000
Empty weight (lbs)	3500	3332	3100-3465
Useful load (lbs)	2100	2118	2400-2535
Propeller			
PERFORMANCE			
Max speed	264 mph	267 mph	240-283 mph
Cruise speed	249 mph @ 75%	197 mph @ 75%	213-261 mph @ 75%
Efficiency (gph)			
Stall speed - flaps / gear down	74 mph	70 mph	75-78 mph
Climb @ sea level (fpm)	1300	1775	1630-1700
Range with reserves			
Service ceiling (ft)	25,000	30,000	18,000-26,000
Take off (Ground run)(ft)			
Take off (over 50ft obst)(ft)	2080	1950	2360-2500
Landing (Ground roll)(ft)			
Landing (over 50ft obst)(ft)	2100	2060	1700-1980

Model of the proposed PA-37 with pusher engines. (J. Bryerton)

Drawing of the proposed PA-37. (D. Clark)

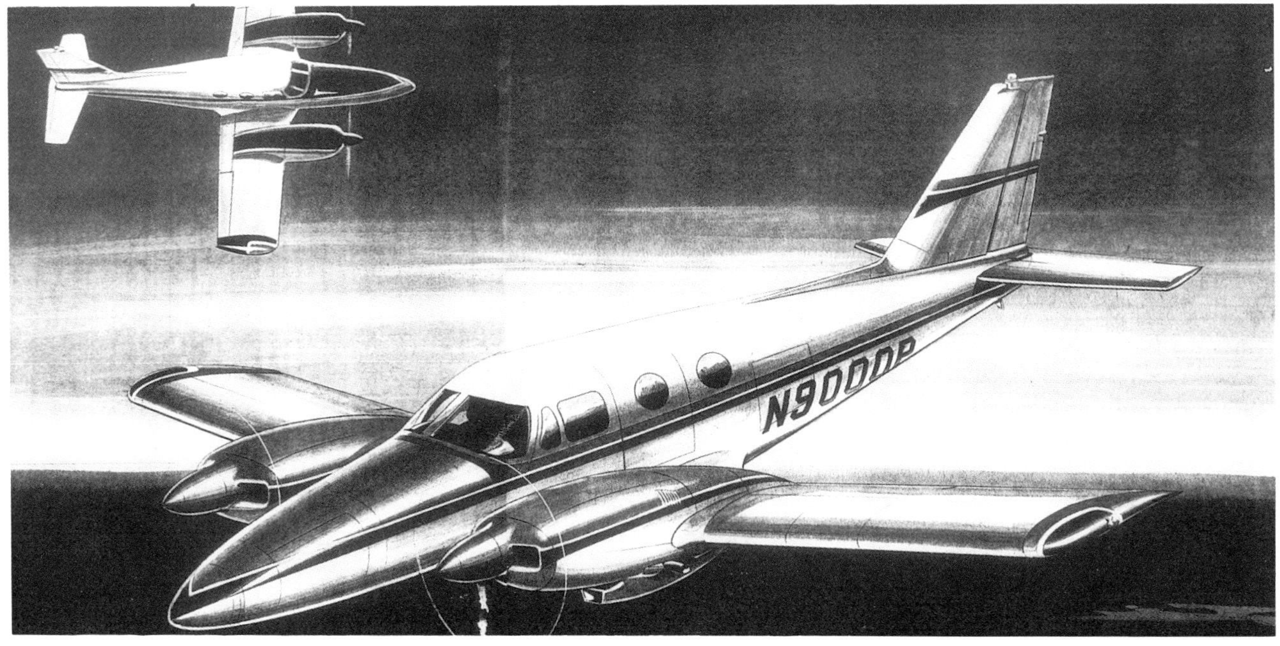

Drawing of the proposed PA-37 based upon a modified Aztec airframe. (Piper Aircraft Corporation)

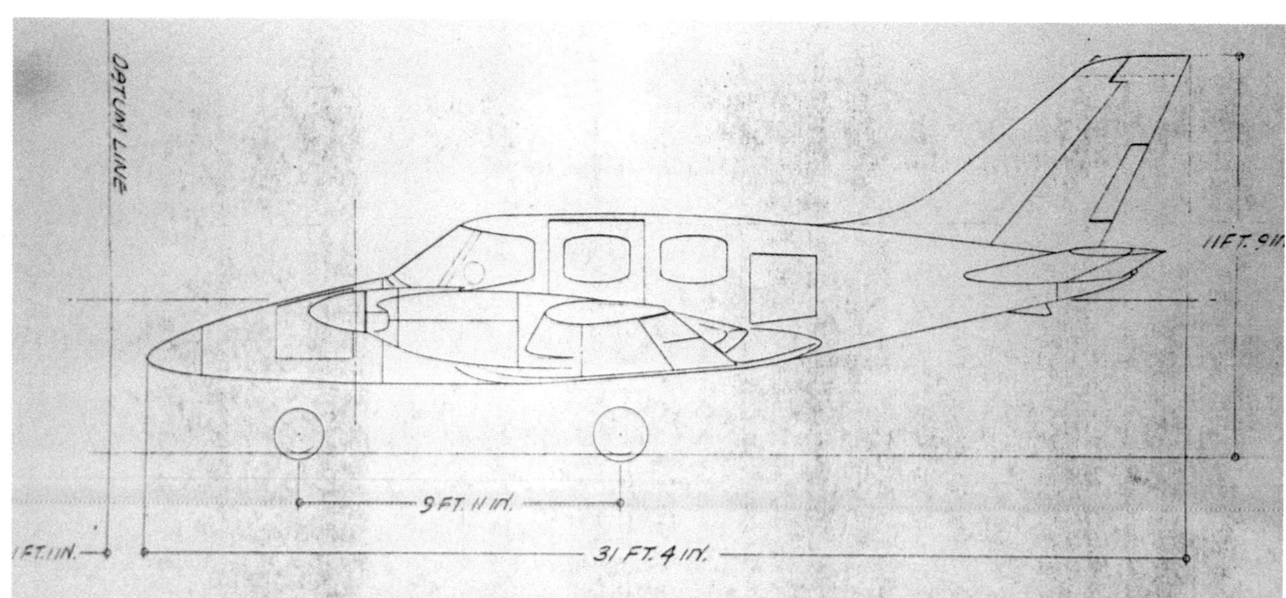

Drawing of the proposed PX-2-9000. (Piper Aircraft Corporation)

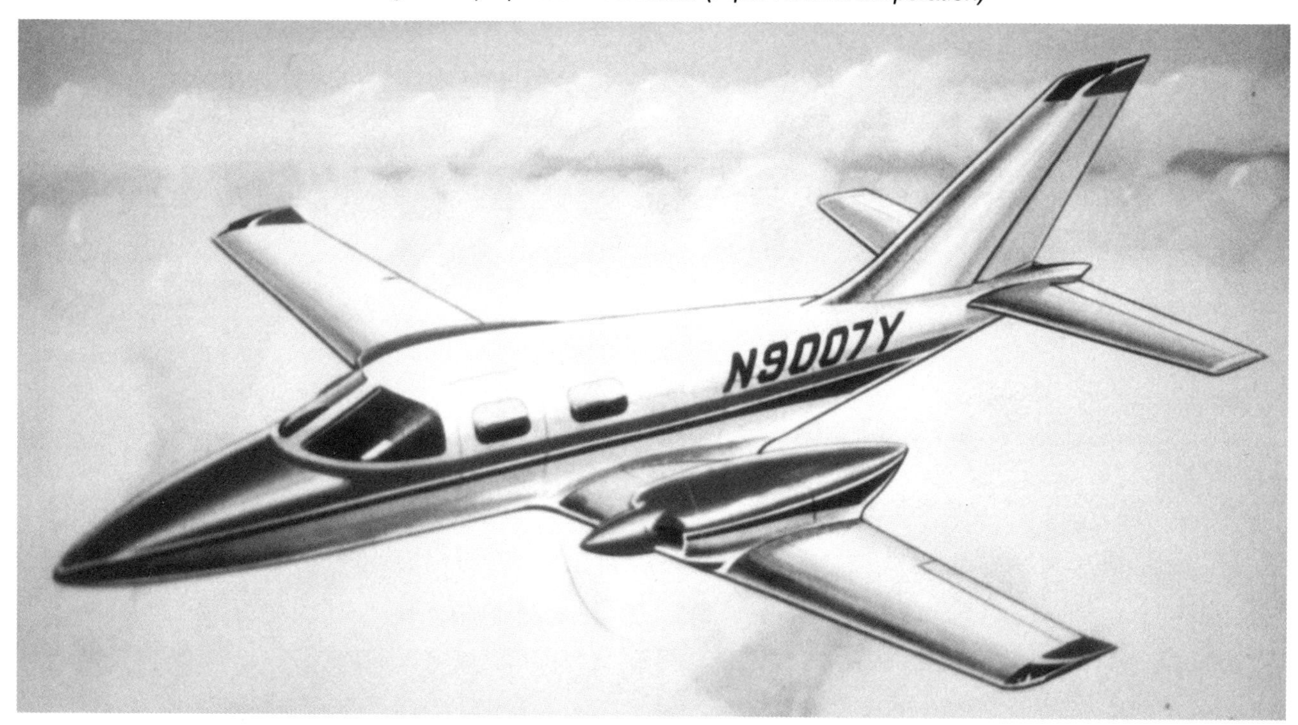

Drawing of the proposed PX-2-9000. (D. Clark)

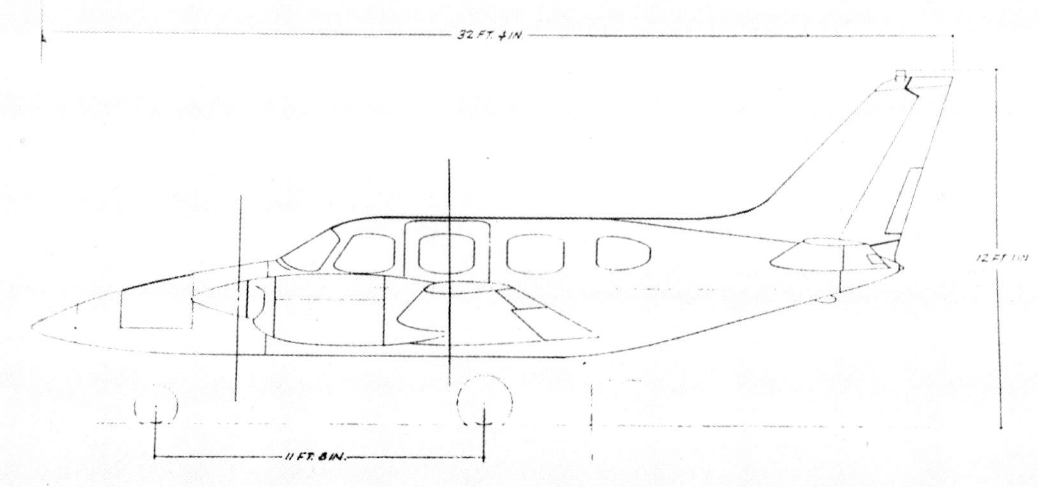

Another drawing of the PA-37 (PX-2) based upon the Navajo airframe. (via G.K. Gates)

PA-38 TOMAHAWK

Piper canvassed 10,000 flying instructors before fixing the specification of a new two-place basic trainer in late 1972. The experimental PA-38-100 aircraft s/n 38-7320001 registration N56346 first flew at Vero Beach on the 17th of July 1973. This aircraft was powered by a 100 hp engine and had a conventional low tail and trailing-beam main landing gear. The programme was stopped in mid December. In 1974 Piper tried to sell the design to Embraer whilst negotiations were underway on the kit build programme. Embraer didn't want it. Work restarted on the PA-38 at the end of 1974. Several T-tail designs were tested starting January 1975 through to March 1976 to improve spin control. Many other changes to the aircraft were tested in early 1975; tailcone size, horizontal stabilizer, main gear location and design, vertical tail size, rudder size, wing twist, canopy and wing cusp.

The prototype s/n 38-7738001 registration N38PA was built at Vero Beach and first flew on the 11th of June 1977. It was powered by a 112 hp Lycoming O-235-L2C engine. Piper announced the PA-38 Tomahawk, a new two-place basic trainer in October 1977. It had a T-tail, bubble canopy and a GA (W)-1 airfoil. The Piper dealers demonstrated their acceptance of the type by ordering 1,400. It was initially certified on the 20th of December 1977. The prototype (It's serial number was changed to 38-78A0001 in 1978) and the two pre-production aircraft s/n 38-78A0002 registration N381PT completed in September and s/n 38-78A0003 registration N382PT completed on the 3rd of October (both at Lock Haven) carried out the test flying. Final certification A18SO for the PA-38-112 was gained on 23rd of March 1978. The first production aircraft was s/n 38-78A0004 registration N383PT completed at Lock Haven on the 27th of January 1978. The Tomahawk has unlimited spinning clearance and good visibility from the bubble canopy as well as many other qualities any good basic trainer should have. Deliveries began in April 1978. It's price was $15,820. In the first two production years 2,000 aircraft were built at Lock Haven at a rate of 8 aircraft a day.

At the end of 1977, Piper looked at certifying a fully aerobatic version of the Tomahawk (+6g-3g). This was not proceeded with.

In late 1977 Piper introduced the Blue Sky scheme at its Flight Centers in the U.S.A. This scheme included fixed price solo and private-license courses and a video instruction program (VIP).

Wing stall strips were fitted to the Tomahawk in September 1978 and certified. Aircraft N382PT was used for testing these at Lock Haven.

In April 1979 Piper and Shorts of Belfast, Northern Ireland, announced that Shorts would produce the Tomahawk at Belfast. Shorts announced the formation of a new wholly-owned subsidiary company called Shorts Light Aircraft Company Ltd (SHORLAC). It was proposed that 200 aircraft per year were to be assembled from kits for the European market. Piper and Shorts had been discussing the deal since the end of 1977. Unfortunately later in 1979, due to unexpected difficulties of transferring U.S. certification and the downturn in Tomahawk demand, both parties agreed to abandon the plans. Piper looked at the Shorts 330 commuter airliner in 1979 for possible manufacture in the U.S., but no agreement was reached.

PA-38 PRODUCTION DETAILS

Model Year	Serial Number Range From	To	Type	Total	Comments
Experimental	38-7320001		100	1	Built Vero Beach
Prototype	38-7738001 *		112	0	
Prototype	38-78A0001		112	1	Built Vero Beach
Pre-production	38-78A0002	38-78A0003	112	2	Built Lock Haven
1978	38-78A0004	38-78A0844 *	112	820	Built Lock Haven
1979	38-79A0001	38-79A1179	112	1179	Built Lock Haven
1980	38-80A0001	38-80A0198	112	198	Built Lock Haven
1981	38-81A0001	38-81A0210 *	112 'II'	196	Built Lock Haven
1982	38-82A0001	38-82A0124 *	112 'II'	122	Built Lock Haven

A total of 38 aircraft in the batches marked * were not delivered, instead they were updated to the next year's model and given new serial numbers or not built. See table below.
Total manufactured 2519

PA-38 SERIAL NUMBER CHANGES

Model	Old Serial Number	New Serial Number	New Model (if different)
PA-38-112	38-7738001	38-78A0001	
PA-38-112	38-78A0822-828	Not built	
PA-38-112	38-78A0830-843	Not built	
PA-38-112	38-81A0177-190	Not built	
PA-38-112	38-82A0123-124	Not built	

The experimental PA-38-100 s/n 38-7320001 registration N56346 at Vero Beach. (G.K. Gates)

The experimental PA-38 s/n 38-7320001 registration N56346 with new T-tail and main gear at Vero Beach. (Piper Aircraft Corporation)

In September 1979 a Twin Tomahawk with two 100 hp Lycoming O-235-G2B engines and fixed gear was on the drawing board. Gross weight would be 2200 pounds and top speed was predicted to be 149 knots. The derivative never left the drawing board.

Piper tested Beech Skipper registration N6629X at Lock Haven in 1979 in order to compare it with the Tomahawk. Aircraft s/n 38-78A0688 registration N2383L was used.

During 1979 / 80 the Tomahawk II was developed with better equipment and sound proofing, a new colour scheme, bigger tyres and improved nose gear steering. Bigger tyres and a front fork change were tested on aircraft s/n 38-79A0416 registration N2400F on the 10th of April 1979. The bigger tyres were also on aircraft N38PA. The new sound proofing was on aircraft s/n 38-78A0017 registration N384PT. The first production aircraft s/n 38-81A0001 registration N25459 was registered in February 1981.

Piper carried out full spin testing at Lakeland for the British CAA in October 1980 using aircraft s/n 38-80A0098 registration N25424. This was completed satisfactorily.

Piper installed a 115 hp Pezetel PZL-F-4A engine in aircraft N38PA and this first flew on the 11th of January 1980 at Lock Haven. When compared to the standard Lycoming powered model performance was much the same, so the alternate engine was not proceeded with.

Production stopped with s/n 38-82A0122 registration N9255A at Lock Haven on the 26th of July 1982, as the demand for basic trainers disappeared in line with the general aviation slump of the early 1980's.

The experimental PA-38-112 s/n 38-7320001 registration N56346 with the definitive T-tail. (Piper Aircraft Corporation)

The prototype PA-38-112 Tomahawk s/n 38-7738001 registration N38PA. (Piper Aircraft Corporation)

PA-38-112 Tomahawk II s/n 38-81A0001 registration N25459. (Piper Aircraft Corporation)

PA-38 SPECIFICATION & PERFORMANCE		
SPECIFICATION	38-112	38-112 'II'
Engine	112 hp Lycoming O-235-L2C	112 hp Lycoming O-235-L2C
Engine TBO (hrs)	2000	2000
No of seats	2	2
Wing Span (ft/ins)	34/0	34/0
Length (ft/ins)	23/1	23/1
Height (ft/ins)	8/8	9/1
Useable fuel capacity (US gal)	30	30
Gross weight (lbs)	1670	1670
Empty weight (lbs)	1064-1088	1109-1128
Useful load (lbs)	582-606	542-561
Propeller		
Floats available		
PERFORMANCE		
Max speed	113 kts	109 kts
Cruise speed	109 kts @ 75%	108 kts @ 75%
Efficiency (gph)		4.9 @ 65%
Stall speed - flaps / gear down	46 kts	49 kts
Climb @ sea level (fpm)	700	718
Range with reserves	402 nm @ 75%	452 nm @ 75%
Service ceiling (ft)	12,850	13,000
Take off (Ground run)(ft)	945	820
Take off (over 50ft obst)(ft)	1400	1460
Landing (Ground roll)(ft)	642	707
Landing (over 50ft obst)(ft)	1374	1544

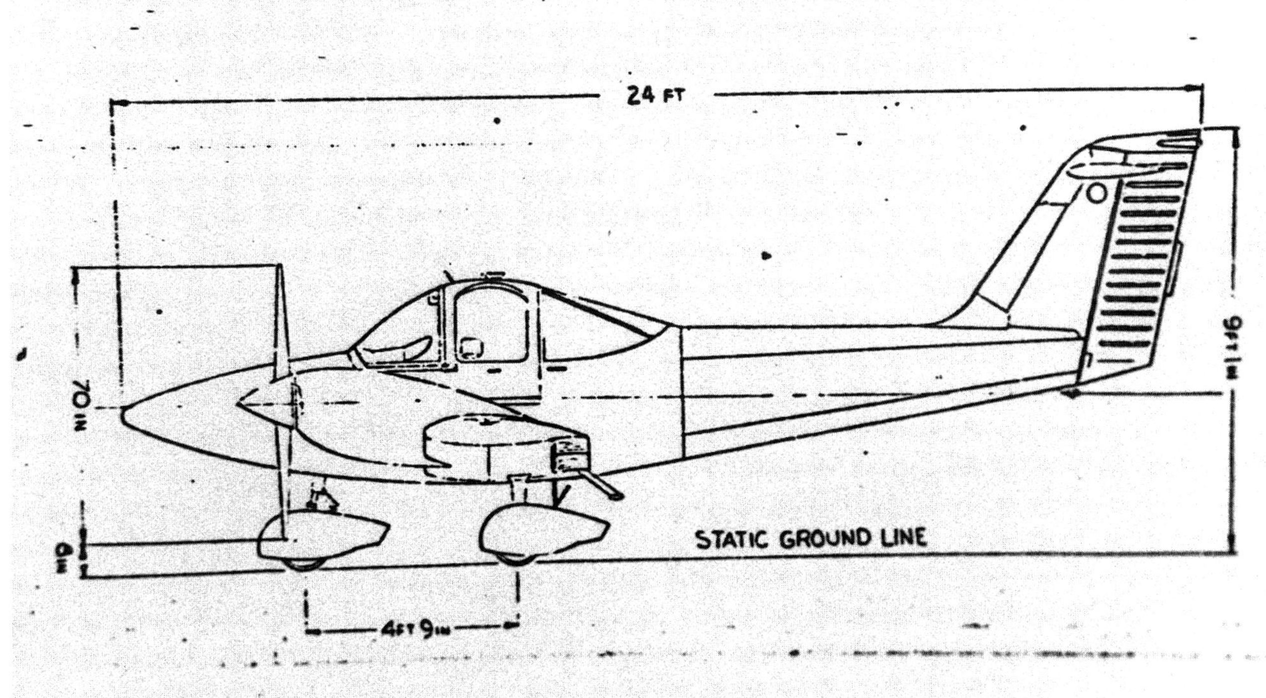

Drawing of the proposed Twin Tomahawk. (Piper Aircraft Corporation)

PA-39 TWIN COMANCHE C/R

Piper conducted many tests to improve the flight characteristics of the PA-30 using three aircraft N7003Y, N8568Y and s/n 30-1893 registration N8739Y between February and July 1969. Aircraft N8568Y flew with opposite rotating engine on the 27th March. Aircraft N7003Y flew with wing leading edge slots on the 10th of March. Aircraft N8739Y flew with flow fences and stall strips in May and with extended flaps and ailerons on the 8th of July. N7003Y flew with a 12 inch fuselage extension on the 11th of July. (This later flew with a 30 inch fuselage extension). N8739Y flew with wing tip extensions on the 11th of August. All the tests were reviewed by Piper and they decided that the combination of counter rotating L/IO-320-B1A engines and inconspicuous triangular-section flow strips on the leading edge of both wings outboard of the nacelles was the best combination for the new PA-39. This final configuration first flew on aircraft N8568Y on the 23rd of September 1969.

Two pre-production aircraft were converted, aircraft s/n 30-1979 registration N8821Y with normally aspirated 160 hp Lycoming L/IO-320-B1A engines and s/n 30-1981 registration N8823Y with turbo-charged 160 hp Lycoming L/TIO-320-C1A engines. The FAA type approval was received on the 3rd of December using the PA-30 certificate. The first production aircraft s/n 39-1 registration N8843Y was completed on the 23rd of December 1969. Piper announced the Twin Comanche C/R on the 15th of February 1970 and deliveries commenced in April. The first production aircraft with turbo-charged engines was s/n 39-3 registration N8844Y.

Aircraft N8843Y was modified with STOL modifications by Robertson in early 1971. Modifications included drooped wing leading edge, flap actuated drooped ailerons, dorsal fin, raked wing tips, gross weight up to 3800 pounds. Piper evaluated it between the 15th of April and the 31st of August 1971 when it was destroyed in an accident.

On the 28th of May 1970 Piper received approval for the PA-30 and PA-39 with flap and aileron interconnection, wing leading edge flow strips, rudder gap seal installation and stabilizer trim reductions. Aircraft s/n 30-1854 registration N8705Y, s/n 30-1948 registration N8790Y and s/n 30-1964 registration N8807Y were all converted and used for testing between March and May 1970.

Production ceased in June 1972 with the flood of the Lock Haven plant. The last built was 39-155 registration N8990Y completed on the 30th of May 1972.

In 1972 Piper proposed developing an improved version of the PA-39 Twin Comanche C/R. Many changes were proposed including a one-piece windshield. This project was cancelled in favour of the PA-40 new light twin

PA-39 PRODUCTION DETAILS

Model Year	Serial Number Range From	To	Type	Total	Comments
Experimental	30-1717			0	
Pre-production	30-1979, 30-1981			0	
1970	39-1	39-83		83	
1971	39-84	39-132		49	
1972	39-133	39-155		23	
-	39-156	39-162			Not built, see Appendix B
The experimental aircraft 30-1717 and the two pre-production aircraft 30-1979 & 1981 have been included in the PA-30 manufactured total. Total manufactured 155 (All built at Lock Haven)					

The experimental counter-rotating PA-30 Twin Comanche s/n 30-1717 registration N8568Y with Jack Wetzel at Lock Haven. (via J. Wetzel)

PA-39 Twin Comanche C/R s/n 30-1979 registration N8821Y. (Piper Aircraft Corporation)

PA-39 Twin Comanche C/R s/n 30-1981 registration N8823Y. (Piper Aircraft Corporation)

PA-39 SPECIFICATION & PERFORMANCE

SPECIFICATION	39	39 'Turbo'
Engine	160 hp Lycoming L/IO-320-B1A	160 hp Lycoming L/TIO-320-C1A
Engine TBO (hrs)	2000	1200
No of seats	6	6
Wing Span (ft/ins)	36/0, 36/9.5 with tip tanks	36/9.5
Length (ft/ins)	25/3	25/3
Height (ft/ins)	8/3	8/3
Useable fuel capacity (US gal)	90, 120 with tip tanks	120
Gross weight (lbs)	3600	3725
Empty weight (lbs)	2270	2416
Useful load (lbs)	1330	1309
Propellers	Hartzell 2 blade	Hartzell 2 blade
Floats available		
PERFORMANCE		
Max speed	205 mph	246 mph
Cruise speed	198 mph @ 75%	221 mph
Efficiency (gph)	19.6 @ 75%	22.6 @ 75%
Stall speed - flaps / gear down	70 mph	70 mph
Climb @ sea level (fpm)	1460	1290
Range with reserves	830 sm @ 75% 1200 sm @ 75% with tip tanks	1270 sm @ 75%
Service ceiling (ft)	20,000	25,000
Take off (Ground run)(ft)	940	990
Take off (over 50ft obst)(ft)	1530	1590
Landing (Ground roll)(ft)	700	725
Landing (over 50ft obst)(ft)	1870	1900

The first production PA-39 s/n 39-1 registration N8843Y at Lock Haven. (Piper Aircraft Corporation)

PA-40 ARAPAHO

Between 1972 and 1974 Piper developed a new light twin to replace the PA-39 Twin Comanche C/R. The experimental aircraft was Twin Comanche s/n 30-4000 registration N8300Y. In March 1972 zero timed C/R engines from N8843Y (which had crashed in 1971) were installed. This first flew at Lock Haven on the 20th. In April many tests were carried out including: with flow strips, wing fillets, extended ailerons and flaps, wing fillets outboard of the engines. It was damaged in the June 1972 flood at Lock Haven. (It was disassembled in August 1973 and scrapped in 1974). The prototype s/n 40-1 registration N9999P was damaged in production in the same flood. It was repaired and its serial number changed to 40-7300001. It's first flight was on the 16th of January 1973. The PA-40 Arapaho which was similar in size to the Twin Comanche with six seats but with longer landing gear legs (5.5 inches longer), undercambered cuff at wing leading edge, larger cabin windows, hydraulic landing gear, simplified fuel management, additional cabin sound reduction, increase in useful load, one-piece windshield and the panel was lowered by one half of one inch. It had counter-rotating 160 hp Lycoming IO-320 engines with propellers that had rounded tip blades. Unfortunately it crashed near Lock Haven on the 21st of September 1973 during spin trails and was cancelled from the U.S. Register. Piper then built a stall / spin evaluation radio-controlled model and took it to NASA Langley for a series of tests. The aircraft was re-designed with strakes and dorsal fin. Two pre-production models were s/n 40-7400002 registration N9998P which first flew on the 5th of April 1974 and was turbocharged and s/n 40-7400003 registration N9997P which first flew on the 2nd of April 1974 and was normally aspirated. The normally aspirated model was FAA certified on the 18th of July 1974 using the same type certificate A1EA as the PA-30. Aircraft N9997P was delivered from Engineering to the Sales Department in November 1974.

In July 1974 a growth version was proposed with 180 hp Lycoming L/IO-320 engines. Also a T-tail version was proposed in November. The aircraft was to be launched for the 1975 model year but there was not a big enough market for it and Piper management wished to use the Cherokee as a basis for its new models, so the project was cancelled in February 1975. The turbocharged version had not been certified when the project was cancelled. The first five production fuselages were built and they were scrapped at Lock Haven in June 1975. Later the two pre-production models were given to Purdue University.

PA-40 PRODUCTION DETAILS

Model Year	Serial Number Range From	To	Type	Total	Comments
Experimental	30-4000			0	
Prototype	40-1*			0	
Prototype	40-7300001			1	
Pre-production	40-7400002	40-7400003		2	
The experimental aircraft 30-4000 has been included in the PA-30 manufactured total. Total manufactured 3 (All built at Lock Haven)					

PA-40 SERIAL NUMBER CHANGES

Model	Old Serial Number	New Serial Number	New Model (if different)
PA-40	40-1	40-7300001	

The prototype PA-40 Arapaho s/n 40-7300001 registration N9999P at Lock Haven. (Piper Aviation Museum)

Cal Wilson and the stall / spin PA-40 model. (via C. Wilson)

PA-40 Turbo Arapaho s/n 40-7400002 registration N9998P at Lakeland. (K. Donald)

PA-40 SPECIFICATION & PERFORMANCE	
SPECIFICATION	40
Engine	160 hp Lycoming L/IO-320-B1A
Engine TBO (hrs)	
No of seats	6
Wing Span (ft/ins)	36/5
Length (ft/ins)	25/2
Height (ft/ins)	9/5
Useable fuel capacity (US gal)	120
Gross weight (lbs)	3800
Empty weight (lbs)	2336
Useful load (lbs)	1464
Propellers	
Floats available	
PERFORMANCE	
Max speed	201 mph
Cruise speed	181 mph @ 75%
Efficiency (gph)	
Stall speed - flaps / gear down	69 mph
Climb @ sea level (fpm)	1330
Range with reserves	1115 sm
Service ceiling (ft)	17,700
Take off (Ground run)(ft)	910
Take off (over 50ft obst)(ft)	1435
Landing (Ground roll)(ft)	920
Landing (over 50ft obst)(ft)	1500

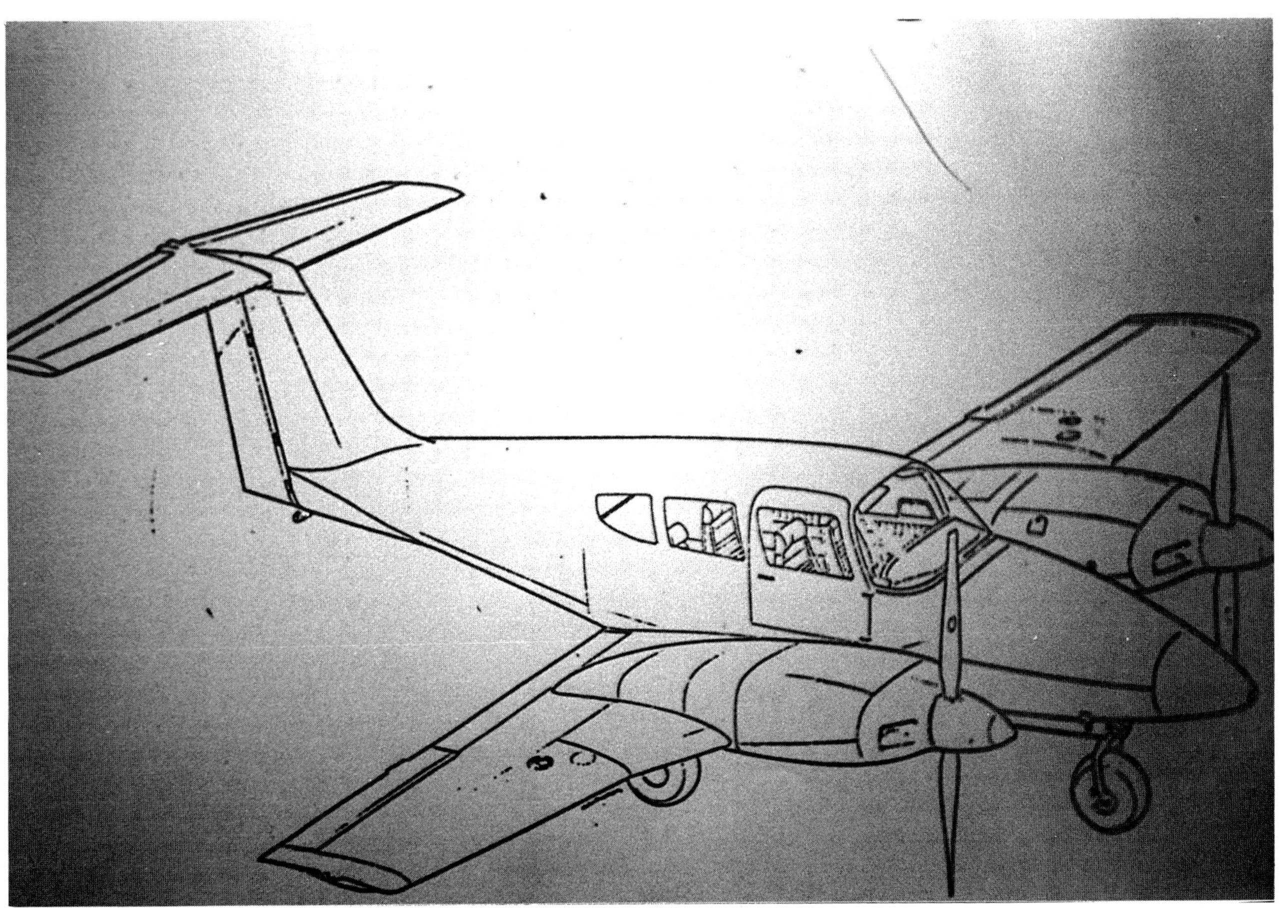

Drawing of the proposed PA-40 with T-tail. (Piper Aircraft Corporation)

PA-41P

During 1972 and 1973 Piper designed a pressurized cabin version of its PA-23-250 Aztec. The experimental aircraft was Aztec s/n 27-4426 registration N13775. It was fitted with experimental 270 hp counter-rotating Lycoming L/TIO-540-L1AD engines and first flew on the 26th of March 1973 and after considerable testing they were removed in September. Piper did consider fitting TCM Tiara engines instead of 285 hp Lycoming engines in March 1973. The prototype PA-41P Pressurized Aztec was s/n 41P-1 registration N9941P and first flew on the 21st of February 1974. The pressurized Aztec was an attempt at making a low cost pressurized aircraft out of a totally unsuitable airframe which had flat sides and was more than 20 years old. It was not a success. The project was cancelled in June 1974 and the prototype given to the Raspet Flight Research Laboratory at the Mississippi State University on the 15th December. There, it was used for cooling drag tests funded by NASA which resulted in the round 'bug-eye' cowlings. These were first used on the Arrow III in 1976.

PA-41P SPECIFICATION & PERFORMANCE

SPECIFICATION	41P
Engine	270 hp Lycoming L/TIO-540-L1AD
Engine TBO (hrs)	
No of seats	6
Wing Span (ft/ins)	37/2
Length (ft/ins)	31/2
Height (ft/ins)	10/3
Useable fuel capacity (US gal)	144
Gross weight (lbs)	5200
Empty weight (lbs)	3280
Useful load (lbs)	1920
Propellers	
Pressurization (psi)	5.5
Floats available	
PERFORMANCE	
Max speed	248 mph
Cruise speed	215 mph
Efficiency (gph)	
Stall speed - flaps / gear down	68 mph
Climb @ sea level (fpm)	1480
Range with reserves	975 sm
Service ceiling (ft)	30,000
Take off (Ground run)(ft)	1110
Take off (over 50ft obst)(ft)	1580
Landing (Ground roll)(ft)	1620
Landing (over 50ft obst)(ft)	2220

PA-41P Pressurized Aztec s/n 41P-1 registration N9941P. (J. Hensen, Mississippi State University)

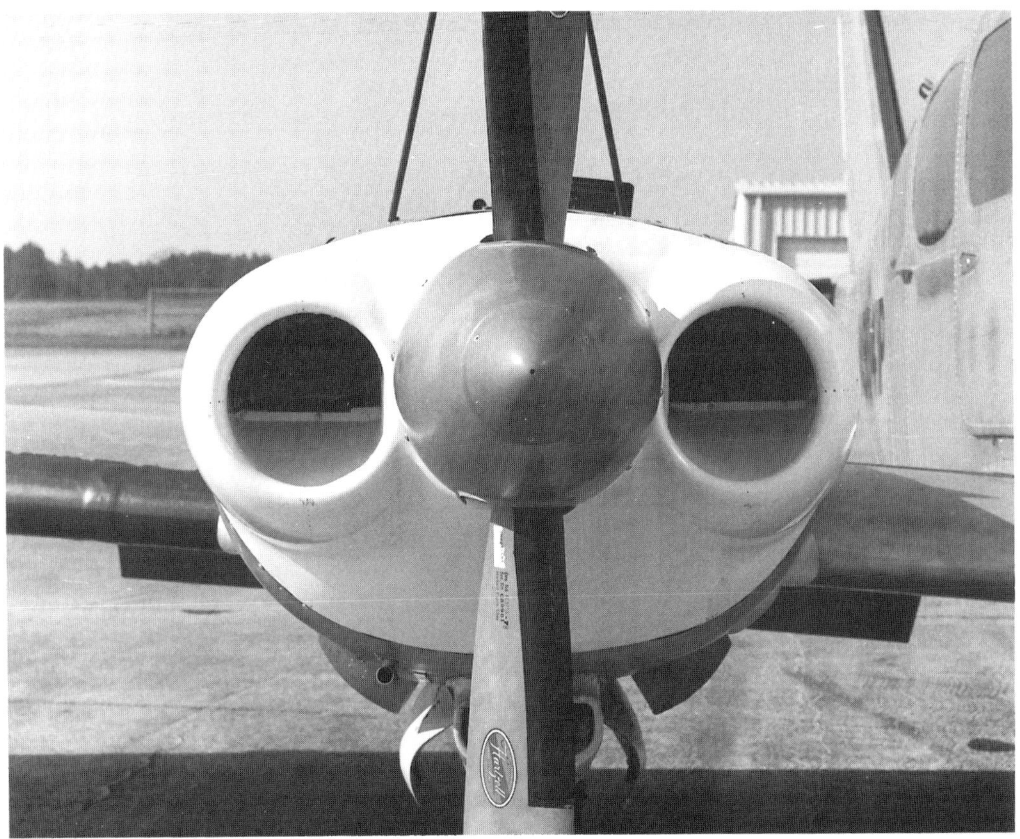

The round 'bug-eye' cowlings of the PA-41P Pressurized Aztec s/n 41P-1 registration N9941P. (J. Hensen, Mississippi State University)

PA-42 CHEYENNE III / IV / 400

Design at Lock Haven had started in 1972 with the PA-31-350P Pressurized Chieftain. This was developed further including a T-tail and given a new designation, the PA-42 and transferred to Lakeland on the 1st of July 1975. The design was changed to turbo-prop engines and the original design became the PA-43 in August 1975. The PA-42 design was firmed up by December 1975. A Chieftain, s/n 31-5003 registration N7676L was used as the experimental aircraft. The conversion was carried out by Hayes International at Birmingham, Alabama. They retained the Chieftain fuselage without pressurization, added Cheyenne wings and a T-tail. The 680 shp Pratt & Whitney PT6A-41 turbo-prop engines were added to the airframe. This first flew on the 20th of August 1976. Extensive testing was carried out for the next twelve months. Piper announced the PA-42 Cheyenne III on the 26th of September 1977. The first two prototypes (with a pressurized fuselage) were s/n 42-7800001 registration N420PA which first flew on the 15th of March 1978 and s/n 42-7800002 registration N420PT registered on the 5th of April 1978. The Cheyenne III fuselage was 8 feet 8 inches longer than the Cheyenne II and the wing span increased by 4 feet.

In September 1978 Piper decided to delay the launch of the Cheyenne III by over a year for two reasons; to stretch the fuselage by three feet in order to increase cabin size and to increase the size of the tail in order to improve stall characteristics. In addition 720 shp Pratt & Whitney PT6A-41 engines were used and moved forward by 14 inches. It could seat 2 crew and 9 passengers. The two prototypes were reworked in early 1979, N420PT having its first flight after conversion on the 16th July. The first of the stretched PA-42 pre-production aircraft, s/n 42-7801003 registration N142PC, first flew on the 13th of September 1979, the second s/n 42-7801004 registration N242PC first flew on the 11th of December 1979. FAA certification (A23SO) was received for the PA-42 on the 18th December. The experimental aircraft N7676L was cancelled from the U.S. register in 1980. Deliveries from Lakeland commenced with s/n 42-8001001 registration N442PC at the end of 1980. It was priced at $1,100,000.

In late 1982 and early 1983, Piper developed an updated model, the PA-42-720 Cheyenne IIIA with a new interior, a higher service ceiling and 720 shp Pratt and Whitney PT6A-61 turbo-prop engines. The prototype N420PA first flew in August 1982 with new engines. FAA certification was granted on the 24th March 1983. Deliveries commenced with s/n 42-8301002 registration N420PC in late summer of 1983. The first production IIIA s/n 42-8301001 registration N842PC was retained by the company as a demonstrator. At the same time a new delivery centre was opened at Lakeland bringing the total Piper operation at the airport to 710,200 sq. ft.

In August 1983 the serial number series was changed on the Cheyenne IIIA to remove the model year from the series and replace it with the Lakeland plant code (5) repeated. Thus 42-<u>83</u>01xxx became 42-<u>55</u>01xxx.

In January 1985 Piper announced the closure of it's Lakeland plant, and its move to consolidate all operations at Vero Beach. New production facilities were built at Vero Beach to manufacture the Cheyenne models, adding to the existing 1,000,000 sq. ft. Production of the Cheyenne IIIA at Lakeland stopped at s/n 42-5501031 in October 1985. Production re-started at Vero Beach with s/n 42-5501032 in 1986.

Piper developed the Cheyenne IV between 1981 and 1984. They wanted more power than the existing P&W PT6 engines on the III and counter rotating operation. Pratt & Whitney didn't have an engine, so Piper went to Garrett. In early 1983 Piper announced the PA-42-1000 Cheyenne IV. It was basically a redesigned Cheyenne III airframe with structural changes and counter-rotating 1,000 shp Garrett TPE331-14 turbo prop engines. The prototype s/n 42-8427001 registration N400PT first flew at Lakeland on the 23rd of February 1983. The production prototypes were s/n 42-8427002 registration N400PS which first flew on the 26th of June 1983 and s/n 42-8427003 registration N400PJ which was registered later in 1983. In August 1983 the serial number series was changed on the Cheyenne IV from 42-8427001, 2 and 3 to 42-5527001, 2 and 3. FAA certification of the Cheyenne IV was granted on the 13th of July 1984. In September 1984 it was renamed the Cheyenne 400LS, the '400' to show that the aircraft can go to 400 mph and the 'LS' to indicate Lear Siegler its new parent company. The FAA re-certified it and deliveries from Lakeland commenced with s/n 42-5527004 registration N290T in December 1984. The price with IFR equipment was $1,774,500.

The experimental PA-42 Cheyenne III s/n 31-5003 registration N7676L. (W. Bubb)

The experimental PA-42 Cheyenne III s/n 31-5003 registration N7676L painted. (Piper Aircraft Corporation)

The prototype PA-42 Cheyenne III s/n 42-7800001 registration N420PA at Lakeland (prior to fuselage stretch). (W. Bubb)

The definitive PA-42 Cheyenne III s/n 42-7801003 registration N142PC. (Piper Aircraft Corporation)

PA-42-720 Cheyenne IIIA s/n 42-8301001 registration N842PC. (Piper Aircraft Corporation)

PA-42 PRODUCTION DETAILS

Model Year	Serial Number Range From	To	Type	Total	Comments
Experimental	31-5003			0	
Prototypes	42-7800001	42-7800002		2	Built Lakeland, to 'III'
Pre-production	42-7801003	42-7801004	'III'	2	Built Lakeland
1980	42-8001001	42-8001004	'III'	4	Built Lakeland
1981	42-8001005	42-8001060	'III'	56	Built Lakeland
1982	42-8001061	42-8001096 *	'III'	19	Built Lakeland
1983	42-8001101	42-8001106	'III'	6	Built Lakeland
1983	42-8301001	42-8301002	720 'IIIA'	2	Built Lakeland
1983	42-5501003	42-5501010	720 'IIIA'	8	Built Lakeland
1984	42-5501011	42-5501023	720 'IIIA'	13	Built Lakeland
1985	42-5501024	42-5501031	720 'IIIA' & 720R	8	Built Lakeland
Prototypes	42-8427001	42-8427003 *	1000 'IV'	0	Built Lakeland
Prototypes	42-5527001	42-5527003	1000 '400LS'	3	Built Lakeland
1985	42-5527004	42-5527029	1000 '400LS'	26	Built Lakeland
1986	42-5501032	42-5501039	720 'IIIA' & 720R	8	Built Vero Beach
1986	42-5527030	42-5527035	1000 '400LS'	6	Built Vero Beach
1987	42-5501041	42-5501047	720 'IIIA'	7	Built Vero Beach
1987	42-5527036	42-5527037	1000 '400'	2	Built Vero Beach
1988	42-5527038		1000 '400'	1	Built Vero Beach
1989	42-5501040		720 'IIIA'	1	Built Vero Beach
1989	42-5527039 & 42-5527041		1000 '400'	2	Built Vero Beach
1990	42-5501048	42-5501056	720 'IIIA'	9	Built Vero Beach
1990	42-5527040		1000 '400'	1	Built Vero Beach
1990	42-5527042	42-5527043 *	1000 '400'	1	Built Vero Beach
1991	42-5501057	42-5501058	720 'IIIA'	2	Built Vero Beach
1991	42-5527044		1000 '400'	1	Built Vero Beach
1992	42-5501059		720 'IIIA'	1	Built Vero Beach
1993	42-5501060		720 'IIIA'	1	Built Vero Beach

The experimental aircraft has been included in the PA-31-350 manufactured total and 18 aircraft in the batches marked * were not delivered, instead they were updated to the next year's model and given new serial numbers or not built. See table below.
Total manufactured 'III / IIIA' 149 '400' 43

Between 1982 and 1986 Piper promoted both the Cheyenne IIIA and 400LS with specialist equipment for a variety of new roles, including maritime surveillance, search and rescue, airways calibration, high altitude photogrammetry, counter-insurgency and target towing.

As with other Piper models, in November 1982 Piper looked at installing the TCM TP-500 turboprop engines on the PA-42. This was not done.

In September 1983 Piper submitted a paper proposal for a special Operational Support Cheyenne version known as the IIIAF for the Sabreliner replacement program for the U.S.A.F. who required 40 aircraft. It had a quick change interior and special avionics including Tacan, VLF / Omega, UHF and HF. The contract was awarded to Beechcraft with their King Air 200 (C-12).

The Cheyenne 400LS holds many speed and time-to-climb records. Chuck Yeager set a speed record of 568.86 km / hr between New York and Gander on the 1st of October 1984. In April 1985 time-to-climb records were set in Oregon for 3000, 6000, 9000, and 12,000 metres.

In May 1985 Piper proposed the Cheyenne IIIA for the FAA Flight Inspection aircraft for checking airways. Piper didn't get the contract.

The prototype PA-42-1000 Cheyenne IV s/n 42-8427001 registration N400PT. (Piper Aircraft Corporation)

The experimental PA-42-720R Customs Cheyenne III s/n 42-7800001 with flight test crew at Vero Beach. (via D. Schwartz)

PA-42 SERIAL NUMBER CHANGES

Model	Old Serial Number	New Serial Number	New Model (if different)
PA-42	42-8001076	42-8001101	
PA-42	42-8001077	42-8001102	
PA-42	42-8001082	42-8001103	
PA-42	42-8001083	42-8001104	
PA-42	42-8001084	42-8001105	
PA-42	42-8001085	42-8301001	PA-42-720
PA-42	42-8001086	42-8001106	
PA-42	42-8001087	42-5501005	PA-42-720
PA-42	42-8001088	42-8301002	PA-42-720
PA-42	42-8001089	42-5501003	PA-42-720
PA-42	42-8001090	42-5501004	PA-42-720
PA-42	42-8001091	42-5501006	PA-42-720
PA-42	42-8001092	42-5501007	PA-42-720
PA-42	42-8001093	42-5501008	PA-42-720
PA-42	42-8001094	42-5501009	PA-42-720
PA-42	42-8001095	42-5501010	PA-42-720
PA-42	42-8001096	42-5501011	PA-42-720
PA-42-1000	42-8427001	42-5527001	
PA-42-1000	42-8427002	42-5527002	
PA-42-1000	42-8427003	42-5527003	
PA-42-1000	42-5527042	Not built	

Production of the Cheyenne 400LS at Lakeland stopped at s/n 42-5527029 in October 1985. Production re-started at Vero Beach with s/n 42-5527030 in 1986.

A modified PA-42 was used by the US Customs Agency during 1984. This resulted in the PA-42-720R being developed with Electrospace Systems, Westinghouse Electric and Texas Instruments for the U.S. Customs Agency in 1985. These C.H.E.T. (Customs High Endurance Tracker) aircraft have infrared sensors, long range radar in the nose and a fuselage down-looking camera. Aircraft N420PA was used as the development PA-42-720R and s/n 42-5501024 registration N41182 was the first production aircraft. FAA approval (A32SO - restricted) was granted on the 31st of March 1986. All the production 720R aircraft were licensed at Vero Beach during 1986.

In February 1986 Piper proposed the Cheyenne 400LS with a large cargo door as the UX-X for the U.S. Army. No contract was awarded.

Once Lear Siegler had sold Piper, the Cheyenne 400LS was renamed the Cheyenne 400.

In November 1987 Piper discussed license manufacture of the Cheyenne 400 by Hindustan Aeronautics in India. A number of operators including carrier Vayudoot were considering operating the aircraft. No deal was forthcoming.

Piper were successful in selling to the Airline Training market during the late 1980s with both the IIIA and the 400. Airlines which operated them were Lufthansa, Alitalia, All Nippon, Austrian and Korean Airlines.

Production of the Cheyenne 400 and Cheyenne IIIA ended at Vero Beach in September 1991 with s/n 42-5527044 registration N91940 for Korean Airlines. The Cheyenne IIIA ended in February 1993 with s/n 42-5501060 registration N9115X for China.

PA-42 SPECIFICATION & PERFORMANCE

SPECIFICATION	42	42 'III'	42-720 'IIIA'
Engine	680 shp Pratt & Whitney PT6A-41	720 shp Pratt & Whitney PT6A-41	720 shp Pratt & Whitney PT6A-61
Engine TBO (hrs)		2,500	
No of seats	6-11	6-11	6-11
Wing Span (ft/ins)	47/6	47/8	47/8
Length (ft/ins)	39/3	43/4	43/4
Height (ft/ins)	12/4	14/9	14/9
Useable fuel capacity (US gal)	392	578	560
Gross weight (lbs)	10500	11080 (80) 11285 (81/82)	11285
Empty weight (lbs)	5750	6389-6630	6837
Useful load (lbs)	4750	4450-4896	4448
Propellers	Hartzell 3-blade Q-tip	Hartzell 3-blade Q-tip	Hartzell 3-blade Q-tip
Pressurization (psi)	6.3	6.3	6.3
Floats available			
PERFORMANCE			
Max speed		299 kts	
Cruise speed	301 kts	265-290 kts	282-305 kts
Efficiency (gph)			
Stall speed - flaps / gear down		87 kts	89 kts
Climb @ sea level (fpm)	2450	2236	2380
Range with reserves	1145 nm	1400-2240 nm	1372-2270 nm
Service ceiling (ft)	33,000	32,000	35,840
Take off (Ground run)(ft)		2560 (82)	1465
Take off (over 50ft obst)(ft)	2320	2369-3230	2280
Landing (Ground roll)(ft)		1337	1457
Landing (over 50ft obst)(ft)		2135	2586

PA-42-720R Customs Cheyenne IIIA s/n 42-5501024 registration N41182. (C. Diefendorf)

PA-42 SPECIFICATION & PERFORMANCE

SPECIFICATION	42-1000
Engine	1000 shp Garrett TPE331-14A/14B
Engine TBO (hrs)	No TBO Hot section 2,000
No of seats	7-9
Wing Span (ft/ins)	47/8
Length (ft/ins)	43/5
Height (ft/ins)	17/0
Useable fuel capacity (US gal)	570
Gross weight (lbs)	12135
Empty weight (lbs)	7565
Useful load (lbs)	4570
Propellers	Dowty-Rotol 4-blade composite
Pressurization (psi)	7.6
Floats available	
PERFORMANCE	
Max speed	351 kts
Cruise speed	294-351 kts
Efficiency (gph)	
Stall speed - flaps / gear down	84 kts
Climb @ sea level (fpm)	3242
Range with reserves	1234-2176 nm
Service ceiling (ft)	41,000
Take off (Ground run)(ft)	1425
Take off (over 50ft obst)(ft)	2325
Landing (Ground roll)(ft)	820
Landing (over 50ft obst)(ft)	2038

PA-42-720 Cheyenne IIIA s/n 42-5501041 registration D-IOSA for Lufthansa at Vero Beach. (R.W. Peperell)

PA-43

When the PA-42 design changed to turbo-prop engines in July 1975 the original piston engined PA-42 design received the PA-43 designation. The engines were to be 375 hp counter-rotating Lycoming L/TIGO-480. There were two versions, the PA-43 without pressurization and the pressurized PA-43P with 5.5 psi. They were to use the PA-31-350 fuselage, the original PA-42 T-tail, PA-31T main gear, PA-31P nose gear and PA-42 seats. The PA-43P was dropped in 1976 in favour of the PA-43.

During June 1977 aircraft PA-31-350 N7463L test flew with a 375 hp Lycoming TIGO-480-E engine in a PA-43 cowl. By July it was flying with both 375 hp engines installed.

The prototype PA-43 s/n 43-7800001 was under construction on the assembly line in 1978 when the project was cancelled. This was due to a shortage of staff to develop both the PA-42 and PA-43. Piper chose to concentrate their resources on the PA-42.

PA-43 Proposed SPECIFICATION & PERFORMANCE

SPECIFICATION	43	43P
Engine	375 hp Lycoming L/TIGO-480-E1AD	375 hp Lycoming L/TIGO-480-D1AD
No of seats		
Wing Span (ft/ins)	47/8	47/8
Length (ft/ins)	35/10	35/10
Height (ft/ins)	12/11	12/11
Useable fuel capacity (US gal)		
Gross weight (lbs)	8300	
Empty weight (lbs)	4728	
Useful load (lbs)	2572	
Propellers		
Pressurization (psi)		5.5
PERFORMANCE		
Max speed	269 mph	
Cruise speed		
Stall speed - flaps / gear down		
Climb @ sea level (fpm)		
Range with reserves		
Service ceiling (ft)		

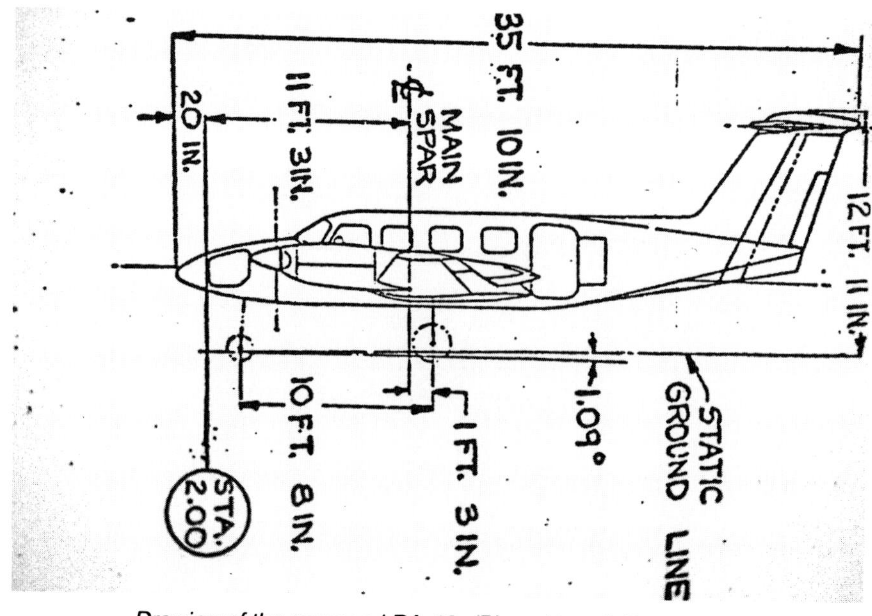

Drawing of the proposed PA-43. (Piper Aircraft Corporation)

PA-44 SEMINOLE

Piper started development work on a Twin Arrow at the end of 1974 as a replacement to the PA-39 Twin Comanche C/R and the PA-40 Arapaho. The experimental aircraft s/n 44-7812001 registration N998P with two counter-rotating 180 hp Lycoming O-360-E1A6D engines and T-tail first flew in May 1976. The registration was chosen to be very similar to the Arapaho N9998P plus it was painted in the same paint scheme. This was to mislead the casual observer into thinking that Piper had put a T-tail on the company Arapaho which was based at Vero Beach. In March 1978 the rear of this aircraft was re-engineered with a smaller T-tail. After further development this aircraft was scrapped and the prototype PA-44-180 Seminole, with s/n 44-7995001 using the same registration N998P was completed at the end of 1977. FAA certification A19SO for this four seater was received on the 10th of March 1978. Deliveries from Vero Beach commenced with s/n 44-7995002 registration N9666C in July 1978. The basic list price was $73,900.

In 1979 Piper developed the PA-44-180T Turbo Seminole with weather radar, propeller de-icing, optional oxygen systems and 180 hp turbo charged Lycoming L/TO-360-EIA6D engines. The prototype N998P was converted in the late summer of 1979. This version was approved on the 29th November. Deliveries from Vero Beach began with s/n 44-8107001 registration N8154H in April 1980.

Production on the normally aspirated Seminole stopped in November 1981 with s/n 44-8195026 registration N9587N and the Turbo Seminole ended in October 1982 with s/n 44-8207020 registration N8236B.

The Seminole was revived in 1988 to fulfill a requirement by Training Schools for a light twin. A customer aircraft s/n 44-7995215 registration N2083N was leased by Piper and new 180 hp Lycoming L/O-360-A1H6 engines were installed. It first flew on the 16th of March 1989. Production re-commenced with s/n 4495001 registration N9178Z completed in August 1989.

The Seminole was in production at Vero Beach in December 1996.

PA-44 PRODUCTION DETAILS

Model Year	Serial Number Range From	To	Type	Total	Comments
Experimental	44-7812001		180	1	
Prototype	44-7995001		180	1	
1979	44-7995002	44-7995329	180	328	
1980	44-8095001	44-8095027	180	27	
1981	44-8195001	44-8195026	180	26	
1981	44-8107001	44-8107066	180T	66	
1982	44-8207001	44-8207020	180T	20	
1989	4495001	4495009	180	9	
1990	4495010	4495012	180	3	
1993	4495013		180	1	
1995	4495014 *		180	0	
1995	4496001	4496005	180	5	
1996	4496006	4496013	180	8	
1997	4496014		180		

One aircraft in the batch marked * was not delivered, instead it was given a new serial number. See table below.
Total manufactured 494 (All built at Vero Beach)

PA-44 SERIAL NUMBER CHANGES

Model	Old Serial number	New Serial Number	New Model (if different)
PA-44-180	4495014	4496001	

The experimental PA-44 s/n 44-7812001 registration N998P at Vero Beach. (W. Moreu)

The experimental PA-44 s/n 44-7812001 registration N998P with modified fuselage & tail at Vero Beach. (H.W. Barnhouse)

The prototype PA-44-180 Seminole s/n 44-7995001 registration N998P. (Piper Aircraft Corporation)

PA-44-180T Turbo Seminole s/n 44-8107001 registration N8154H. (Piper Aircraft Corporation)

PA-44 SPECIFICATION & PERFORMANCE			
SPECIFICATION	**44-180**	**44-180T**	**44-180 (1988-1996)**
Engine	180 hp Lycoming L/O-360-E1A6D	180 hp Lycoming L/TO-360-E1A6D	180 hp Lycoming L/O-360-A1H6
Engine TBO (hrs)	2000	1800	2000
No of seats	4	4	4
Wing Span (ft/ins)	38/7	38/7	38/7
Length (ft/ins)	27/7	27/7	27/7
Height (ft/ins)	8/6	8/6	8/6
Useable fuel capacity (US gal)	108	108	108
Gross weight (lbs)	3816	3943	3800
Empty weight (lbs)	2316-2422	2430-2461	2536-2593
Useful load (lbs)	1394-1500	1482-1513	1280-1207
Propellers	Hartzell 2 or 3 blade	Hartzell 2 or 3 blade	Hartzell 2 or 3 blade
Floats available			
PERFORMANCE			
Max speed	168 kts	195 kts	169 kts
Cruise speed	166 kts @ 75%	183 kts @ 75%	162 kts @ 75% 157 kts @ 65%
Efficiency (gph)	19.3 @ 75%	20.8 @ 75%	14.0-23.3
Stall speed - flaps / gear down	55 kts	56 kts	59 kts
Climb @ sea level (fpm)	1340	1290	1340
Range with reserves	690-915 nm	710-820 nm	612-942 nm
Service ceiling (ft)	17,100	20,000	15,000
Take off (Ground run)(ft)	880	900	1175
Take off (over 50ft obst)(ft)	1400	1500	1520
Landing (Ground roll)(ft)	590	590	770
Landing (over 50ft obst)(ft)	1400	1400	1230

The experimental PA-44-180 Seminole s/n 44-7995215 registration N2183N at Vero Beach. This was used by Piper to test and certify the new Lycoming engines in 1989. (R.W. Peperell)

The first new production PA-44-180 Seminole s/n 4495001 registration N9178Z at Vero Beach. (G.K. Gates)

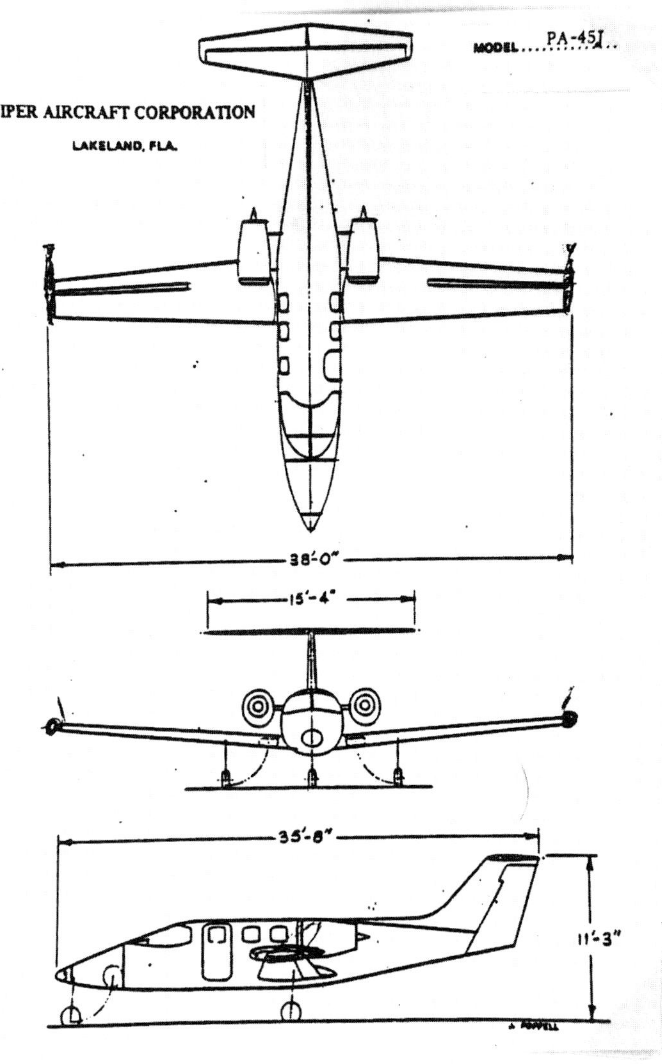

Drawing of the proposed PA-45J. (Piper Aircraft Corporation)

9
NEW DESIGNS

PA-45

Piper wanted to buy the Aerostar line in early 1977, but Ted Smith wanted too much money. In November 1977 Piper proposed an in-house designed series of aircraft at Lakeland using the designation PA-45 as a replacement for the Aztec which would be expanded into a series of aircraft. It was a six seater, T-tail aircraft with full span wing flaps and spoilers for roll control. Five derivatives were proposed.

PA-45	-	Non -pressurized with two turbocharged engines
PA-45P	-	Pressurized with two turbocharged engines
PA-45T	-	Pressurized with two turboprop engines
PA-45ST	-	Pressurized with a single turboprop engine
PA-45J	-	Pressurized with two jet engines

This proposal was not proceeded with as Piper decided to buy the Aerostar line in April 1978 when Ted Smith returned to Piper to sell it.

PA-45 Proposed SPECIFICATION & PERFORMANCE

SPECIFICATION	45	45P	45T, 45ST, 45J
Engine	285 hp Continental TSIO-520R	285 hp Continental TSIO-520R	
Engine TBO (hrs)			
No of seats	6	6	6
Wing Span (ft/ins)	38/0	38/0	38/0
Length (ft/ins)	30/4	30/4	30/4, 31/1, 35/8
Height (ft/ins)	11/3	11/3	11/3
Useable fuel capacity (US gal)	184	184	
Gross weight (lbs)	5800	5800	
Empty weight (lbs)	3744	3447	
Useful load (lbs)	1756	2353	
Propellers			
Pressurization (psi)			
Floats available			
PERFORMANCE			
Max speed	248 kts	228 kts	
Cruise speed	233 kts @ 75%	204 kts @ 75%	
Efficiency (gph)			
Stall speed - flaps / gear down	64 kts	64 kts	
Climb @ sea level (fpm)			
Range with reserves			
Service ceiling (ft)			
Take off (Ground run)(ft)			
Take off (over 50ft obst)(ft)	1570	1572	
Landing (Ground roll)(ft)			
Landing (over 50ft obst)(ft)	2040	2036	

In 1979 Piper revived the Aerostar 800 programme. The prototype N72TS was flying with Lycoming IO-720 engines at the Santa Maria plant. It was to have 375 hp Continental GTSIO-520 engines and was designated by Piper, the PA-45. The fuselage was delivered to Vero Beach, but the programme was cancelled due to cost and the fuselage scrapped. Had it gone into production, it would have used the serial number range 60-yy64xxx.

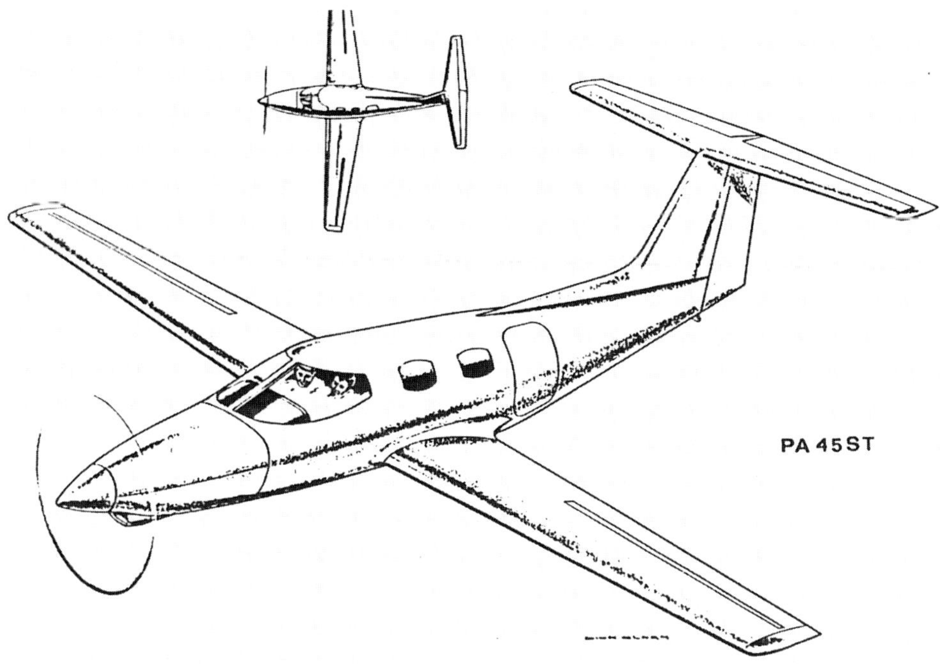

Drawing of the proposed PA-45ST. (Piper Aircraft Corporation)

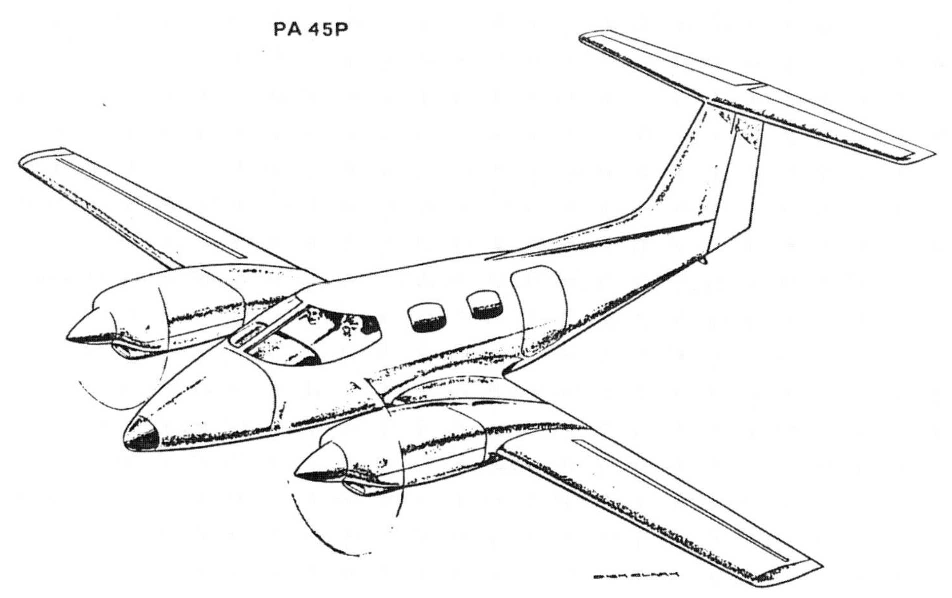

Drawing of the proposed PA-45P. (Piper Aircraft Corporation)

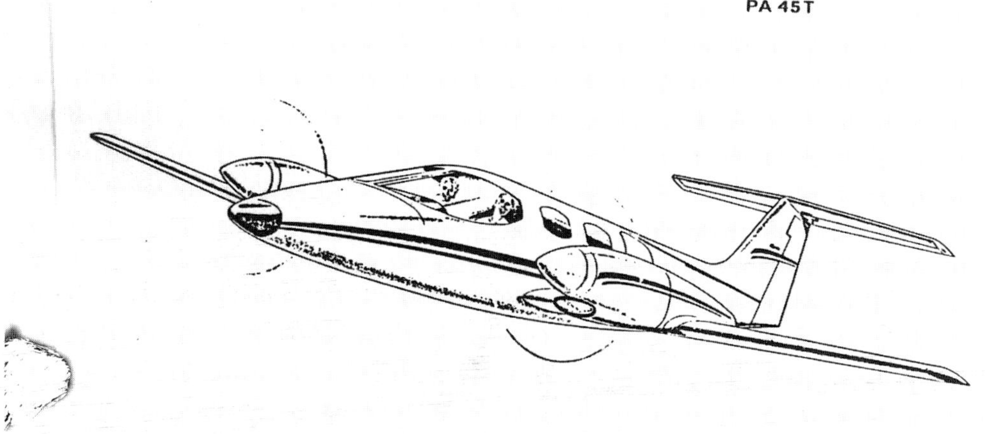

Drawing of the proposed PA-45T. (Piper Aircraft Corporation)

PA-46 MALIBU

Piper experimented with a new 6 seater single engined aircraft in 1979. The PA-46-300T experimental aircraft s/n 46-E1 registration N35646 was registered on the 12th of October and first flew on the 30th of November 1979. The fuselage was not pressurized and was made of poplar wood and metal and had a 300 hp Lycoming IO-540 engine with an STC'd turbocharger installed. This had a narrow chord vertical tail. This was later modified in May 1980 with the 'King Kong' dorsal fillet during initial spin testing. The engine was changed to the 310 hp Continental TSIO-520-BE and the fuselage / empennage transition was smoothed out and a large chord vertical tail was installed. After further testing this aircraft was scrapped in July 1982 and the prototype PA-46-310P pressurized Malibu s/n 46-8408001 using the same registration N35646 first flew on the 21st of August 1982. It has a long wing span (43 feet) with flaps along two thirds of the span, and a conventional tailplane and elevator (not the usual Piper stabilitor). The pre-production aircraft s/n 46-8408002 registration N43000 first flew on the 27th of July 1983. FAA certification (A25SO) for the PA-46-310P was received on the 27th of September 1983 and customer deliveries from Vero Beach commenced in December 1983 with s/n 46-8408004 registration N84PM. The basic IFR equipped price was $275,000.

In December 1979 Piper had proposed a new range of models with the PA-46 design:

- Single engined (310P Continental) 6 place pressurized
- Twin engined (2 X 230 hp 4 cylinder Lycoming TIO-370-X47 engines) 8-9 place, large cargo door with or without luggage nacelles
- fixed gear 4 place
- retractable gear 4 place
- 2 place
- 400 hp Malibu III

Once the initial development of the 310P was well underway, Piper looked at the other proposals. All these proposals except for the 310P died due to Lear Siegler having only so much money, and the PA-42 project got it.

In 1983 Piper considered putting the Malibu wing on the PA-28/32/44 series of aircraft. This was not done.

In March 1985 Malibu s/n 46-8508013 registration N43783 claimed two world speed records on two flights over the Pacific. Flying from Oakland, California to Honolulu and then on to Sydney, Australia, Stewart Reid averaged 200 mph on the first leg of 2409 miles and 204 mph on the second leg of 3082 miles. The Malibu had extra fuel tanks fitted by Globe Aero which added 171 gallons.

In April 1986 Piper considered putting the TCM TP-500 engine (derated to 350 shp) in a PA-46-310P Malibu. This was not proceeded with.

In late 1986 Piper started development of a 350 hp Lycoming powered version of the Malibu. In November construction of a prototype s/n 4619001 was started (with completion expected in March 1987), but the project was cancelled. This was to have had a 350 hp Lycoming TIO-540-X83 engine.

In December 1987 Piper asked operators to stop flying their Malibu aircraft after a higher-than-expected number of engine failures. As Teledyne Continental attempted to find the cause of the failures, Piper offered to buy first-class air tickets for people who would otherwise use their Malibu on essential company business. Teledyne and the FAA worked on a mandatory aircraft directive (AD) for the engine.

In late 1987 Piper initiated two Malibu programmes in parallel, the PA-46-311P with a 310 hp Lycoming TIO-540-X90 engine and the PA-46-350P with a 350 hp Lycoming TIO-540-AE2A engine. The 310 hp was dropped in favour of the 350 hp engine. There were two prototypes: s/n 4622001 registration N9134F first flew on the 21st of December 1987 and was converted from s/n 4608067 registration N9124X and s/n 4622002 registration N9135D first flew on the 30th of January 1988 and was converted from s/n 4608098 registration N9122R. In addition to the 350 hp Lycoming engine, additional redundancy was installed such as dual intercoolers, both alternators belt driven, dual vacuum pumps continuously engine driven. There was a new leather interior, new panel, new paint and a new fuel management system. The Malibu Mirage was certified on the 30th of August 1988. Deliveries commenced in January 1989 with s/n 4622005 registration N9148V. The basic list price was $349,000.

The experimental PA-46 s/n 46-E1 registration N35646 at Sebring, Florida. (W. Moreu)

The experimental PA-46 s/n 46-E1 registration N35646 with the big tail at Sebring, Florida. (W. Moreu)

The prototype PA-46-310P Malibu s/n 46-8408001 registration N35646 at Vero Beach. (R.W. Peperell)

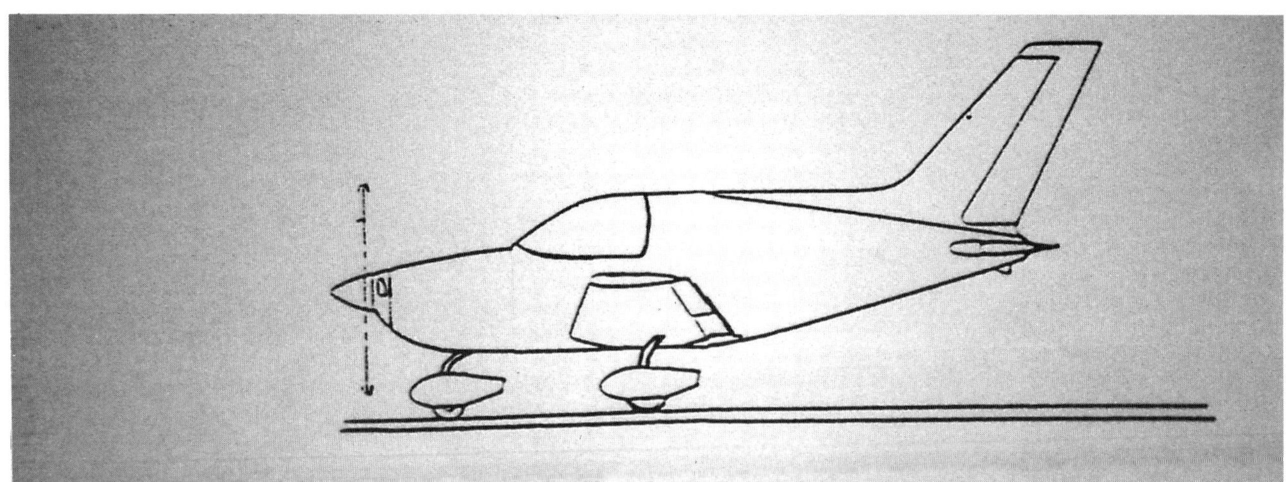

Drawing of the proposed two-place Malibu. (R.W. Peperell)

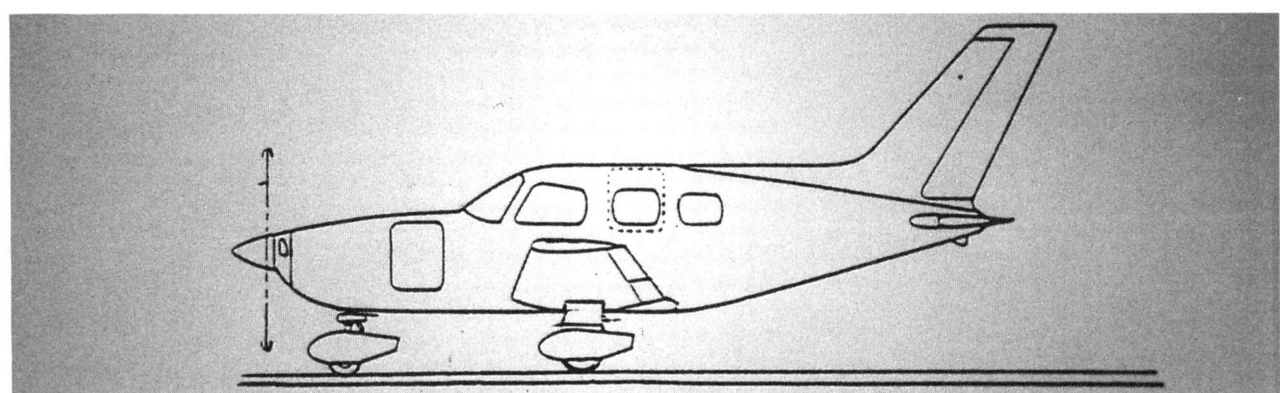

Drawing of the proposed four-place fixed gear Malibu. (R.W. Peperell)

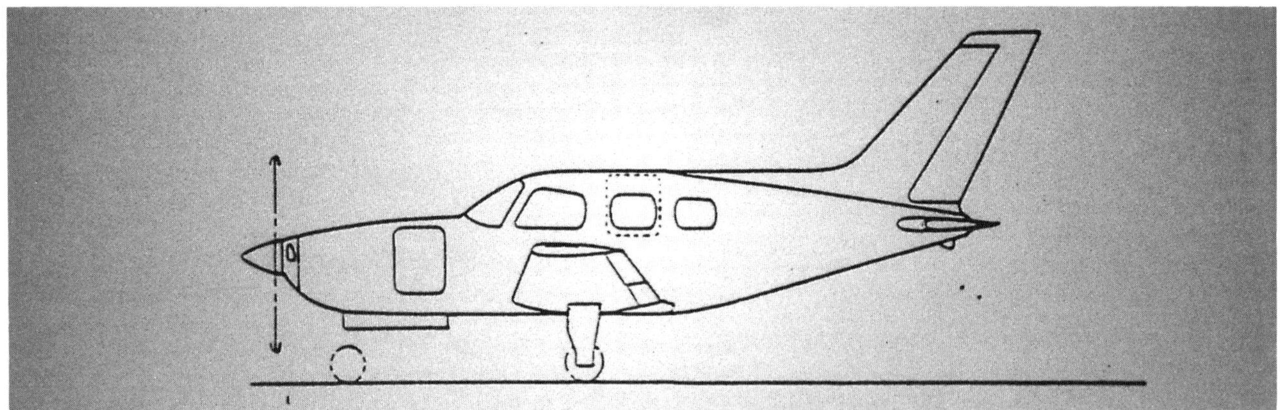

Drawing of the proposed four-place retractable gear Malibu. (R.W. Peperell)

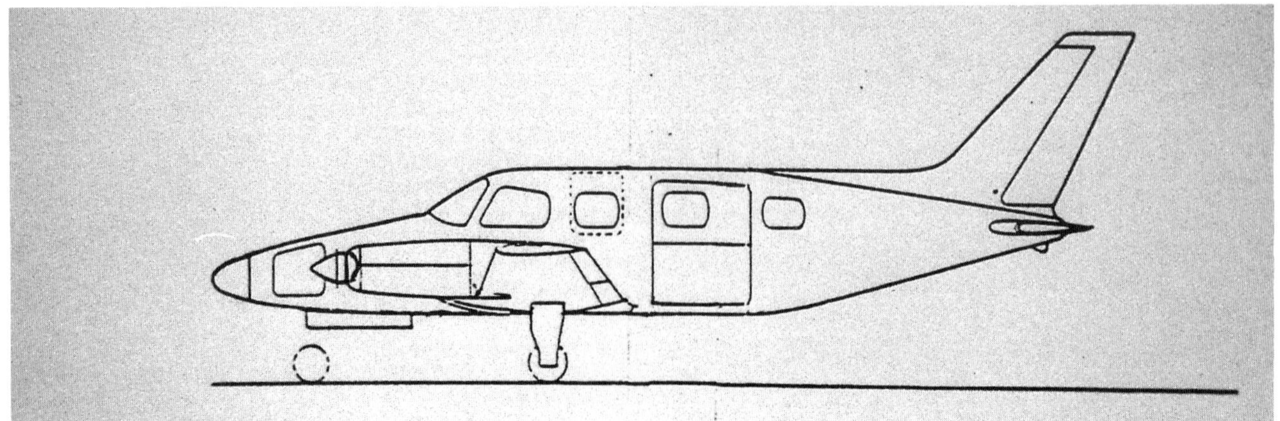

Drawing of the proposed Twin Malibu. (R.W. Peperell)

PA-46-310P Malibu s/n 4608064 registration N221FP awaiting delivery at Vero Beach. (R.W. Peperell)

The prototype PA-46-350P Malibu Mirage s/n 4622001 registration N9134F. (Piper Aircraft Corporation)

The second prototype PA-46-350P Malibu Mirage s/n 4622002 at Vero Beach. (G.K. Gates)

PA-46 PRODUCTION DETAILS

Model Year	Serial Number Range From	To	Type	Total	Comments
Experimental	46-E1		300	1	
Prototype	46-8408001		310P	1	
Pre-production	46-8408002		310P	1	
1984	46-8408003	46-8408087	310P	85	
1985	46-8508001	46-8508109	310P	109	
1986	46-8608001	46-8608088 *	310P	67	
1986	4608001	4608029	310P	29	
1986	4608031	4608047	310P	18	
1986	4608049		310P	1	
1987	4608030 & 4608048		310P	2	
1987	4608050	4608102 *	310P	46	
1988	4608103	4608140	310P	38	
Prototypes	4622001	4622002	350P	2	4622001 re-manufactured as 1990 model
1989	4622003	4622084	350P	82	
1989	4622086	4622093	350P	8	
1990	4622085		350P	1	
1990	4622094	4622117	350P	24	
1991	4622118		350P	1	
1992	4522119	4622126	350P	8	
1993	4622127	4622141	350P	15	
1993	4622143	4622145	350P	3	
1994	4622142		350P	1	
1994	4622146	4622171	350P	26	
1995	4622172	4622210 *	350P	29	
1995	4636001	4636020	350P	20	
1996	4622220 *		350P	0	
1996	4636021	4636076	350P	56	
1997	4636077		350P		

A total of 34 aircraft in the batches marked * were not delivered, instead they were updated to the next year's model and given new serial numbers. See table below.

Total manufactured 674 (All built at Vero Beach)

PA-46 SERIAL NUMBER CHANGES

Model	Old Serial Number	New Serial Number	New Model (if different)
PA-46-310P	46-8608068	4608001	
PA-46-310P	46-8608069	4608002	
PA-46-310P	46-8608070	4608003	
PA-46-310P	46-8608071	4608004	
PA-46-310P	46-8608072	4608005	
PA-46-310P	46-8608073	4608006	
PA-46-310P	46-8608074	4608007	
PA-46-310P	46-8608075	4608008	
PA-46-310P	46-8608076	4608009	
PA-46-310P	46-8608077	4608010	
PA-46-310P	46-8608078	4608011	
PA-46-310P	46-8608079	4608012	
PA-46-310P	46-8608080	4608013	
PA-46-310P	46-8608081	4608014	
PA-46-310P	46-8608082	4608015	
PA-46-310P	46-8608083	4608016	
PA-46-310P	46-8608084	4608017	
PA-46-310P	46-8608085	4608018	
PA-46-310P	46-8608086	4608019	
PA-46-310P	46-8608087	4608020	
PA-46-310P	46-8608088	4608021	
PA-46-310P	4608067	4622001	PA-46-350P
PA-46-310P	4608098	4822002	PA-46-350P
PA-46-350P	4622201	4636001	
PA-46-350P	4622202	4636002	
PA-46-350P	4622203	4636003	
PA-46-350P	4622204	4636004	
PA-46-350P	4622205	4636005	
PA-46-350P	4622206	4636006	
PA-46-350P	4622207	4636007	
PA-46-350P	4622208	4636008	
PA-46-350P	4622209	4636009	
PA-46-350P	4622210	4636010	
PA-46-350P	4622220	4636021	

At the beginning of 1988 Piper started to work on their own turbine Malibu programme, the TP-600. Piper made a one fifth scale model of the Turbine Malibu and had it tested at the University of Washington in August and September 1988. A single exhaust 400 shp Pratt & Whitney PT6A-11 engine was installed in a redesigned nose on aircraft N35646. A 4 inch plug was put in the cockpit and a 3 foot 6 inch plug with an additional window was put in the fuselage aft of the wing. The rudder area and the horizontal tail span were increased. The aircraft first flew on the 26th of September 1988. Production aircraft would have had the 600 shp PT6A-61 engine and an increase in gross weight to 5,300 pounds. A cruising speed of 300 knots at 31,000 feet was predicted. Piper cancelled the project due to the small market size and the new Phoenix programme. The engine was removed and the airframe was parked outside the experimental building. Next Piper wanted to put a 450 hp Lycoming TIO-720 engine into a Malibu. Aircraft N35646 was towed across the airport to LoPresti Piper for fitment of the engine. A market research survey indicted little interest in the PA-46-450P, so the project was quietly dropped and the airframe (without engine) was towed back to Piper experimental, where it sat for over a year. The airframe (without serial number and registration) was sold to Van Kesteren Leasing Inc. of St. Petersburg, Florida in July 1992 (see Chapter 16).

The Piper experimental PA-46T s/n 46-8408001 registration N35646 on its first flight on the 26th of September 1988. (Piper Aircraft Corporation)

PA-46 s/n 4608059 registration N9127Z with Allison turbine engine. (D. Schwartz)

The experimental PA-46 s/n 4608059 registration N9127Z with TCM TIOL-550 engine at Vero Beach. (G.K. Gates)

PA-46-350P s/n 4622002 registration N9135D at Vero Beach. This was used by Piper to re-test the design in 1990. (Piper Aircraft Corporation)

PA-46 SPECIFICATION & PERFORMANCE

SPECIFICATION	46-310P	46-350P	46-400
Engine	310 hp Continental TSIO-520-BE	350 hp Lycoming TIO-540-AE2A	400 shp P&W PT6A-11
Engine TBO (hrs)	2000	2000	
No of seats	6	6	8
Wing Span (ft/ins)	43/0	43/0	43/0
Length (ft/ins)	28/5	28/7	34/1
Height (ft/ins)	11/4	11/6	11/7
Useable fuel capacity (US gal)	120	120	120
Gross weight (lbs)	4118	4300	4400
Empty weight (lbs)	2460-2466	2626-3048	
Useful load (lbs)	1652-1658	1270-1692	
Propeller	Hartzell 2-blade	Hartzell 2-blade	
Pressurization (psi)	5.5	5.5	5.5
Floats available			
PERFORMANCE			
Max speed	234 kts	232 kts	240 kts
Cruise speed	215 kts @ 75% 196 kts @ 55%	168-225 kts	
Efficiency (gph)	16 @ 65% 13.8 @ 55%		
Stall speed - flaps / gear down	58 kts	60 kts	
Climb @ sea level (fpm)	1143	1218	1500
Range with reserves	1330 nm @ 75% 1555 nm @ 55%	990-1450 nm	
Service ceiling (ft)	25,000	25,000+	25,000
Take off (Ground run)(ft)	1440	1450-1530	
Take off (over 50ft obst)(ft)	2025	2375-2550	
Landing (Ground roll)(ft)	1070	932-1018	
Landing (over 50ft obst)(ft)	1800	1952-1964	

Bobby Allison, the racing driver, had his Piper-sponsored Malibu s/n 4608059 registration N9127Z converted in Alabama by replacing the engine with a turbine powered Allison 250-B17F engine. This first flew on the 6th of May 1988. It was brought to Vero Beach for review in August. Unfortunately performance was not up to expectations (the top speed at altitude was less than the standard aircraft), so the engine was removed. Later in 1988 Piper experimented with a liquid-cooled TCM TIOL-550 engine in this same aircraft at Vero Beach. This first flew on the 3rd of October. Piper did not proceed with this either, both the programme and the aircraft were sold to TCM at Mobile, Alabama in the middle of 1989.

In 1989 Piper started on a new programme named the Phoenix, which was largely based upon the Malibu airframe. Six models were proposed, ‘A’ through ‘F’, with two different fuselage cross sections, one with T-tail, two different fuselage lengths and five different engines including Allison and Pratt & Whitney. Piper favoured the Phoenix C with two flat-rated 700 shp Pratt & Whitney PT6B-35F engines driving a single propeller via a Soloy DualPac gearbox (equates to 1100 shp) with a larger and longer fuselage and T-tail. Piper announced the programme at the October 1990 NBAA in order to try to find a partner for joint development. The programme died due to Piper’s cash problems.

At the end of March 1991 the FAA virtually grounded all Malibu aircraft. Seven in-flight break-ups over the previous few years prompted the FAA to ban flights into known weather, until they could find out what was wrong. Piper had been re-testing the Malibu since June 1990 using aircraft N9135D as a result of an accident in California. In early July 1991 the FAA and the NTSB allowed the Malibu to fly again into weather, but not thunderstorms. The Malibu AD was finally rescinded by the FAA / NTSB in February 1992 and they gave the Malibu a clean bill of health.

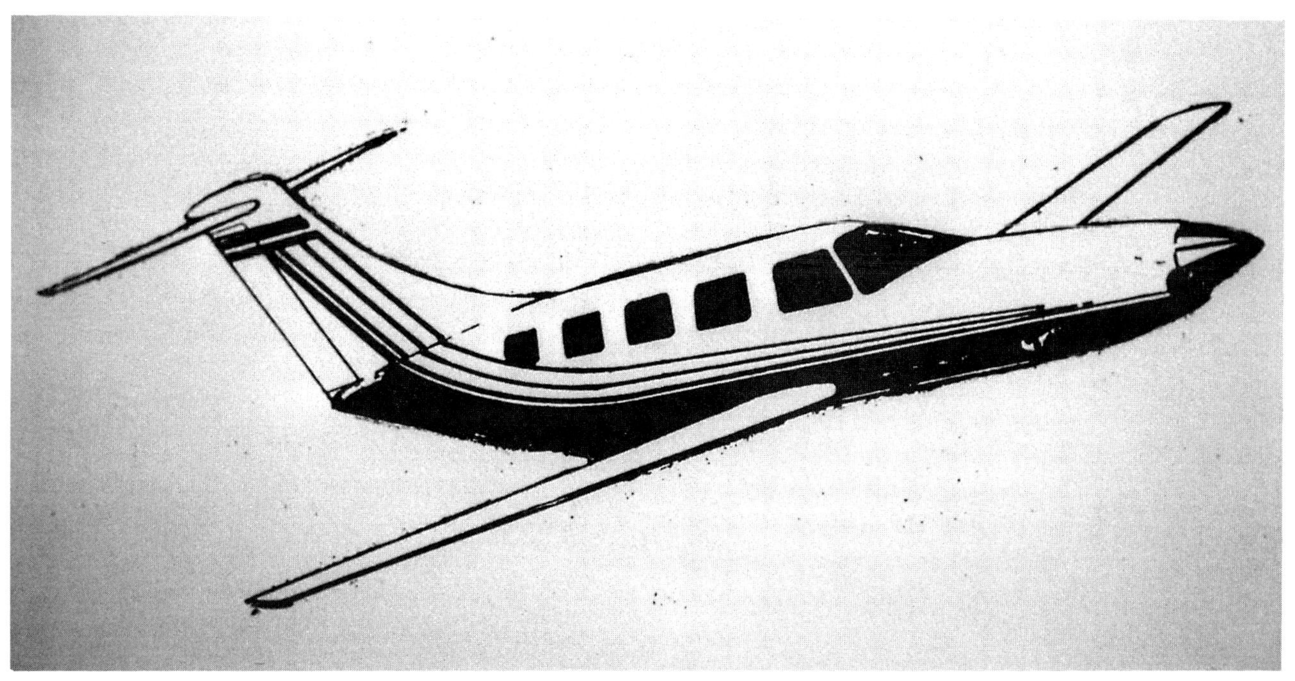

Drawing of the proposed Piper Phoenix. (Piper Aircraft Corporation)

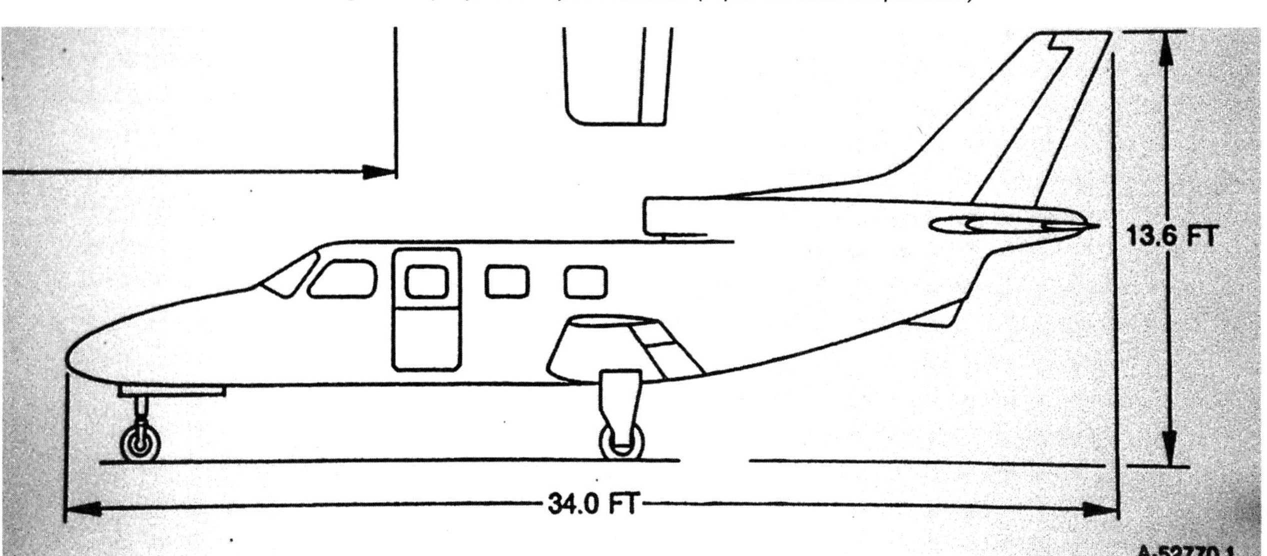

Drawing of the proposed PA-46J Jet Malibu. (Piper Aircraft Corporation)

The first PA-46-350P Malibu Mirage with EFIS, s/n 4622085 registration N9188D at Vero Beach. (R.W. Peperell)

PA-46 Proposed SPECIFICATION & PERFORMANCE

SPECIFICATION	PA-46-JW / JP	Phoenix 'C'
Engine	Williams FJ-44 or Pratt & Whitney JT15D-1	700 shp Pratt & Whitney PT6B-35F Dual Pac
Engine TBO (hrs)		
No of seats		
Wing Span (ft/ins)		
Length (ft/ins)	43/0	45/0
Height (ft/ins)	34/0	36/0
Useable fuel capacity (US gal)	13/7	13/6
Gross weight (lbs)	5340, 5440	8500
Empty weight (lbs)	2800, 2875	6155
Useful load (lbs)	2540, 2565	2345
Propeller		5 blade
Pressurization (psi)		7.5
Floats available		
PERFORMANCE		
Max speed	369, 382 kts	250 kts
Cruise speed	310, 321 kts	
Efficiency (gph)		
Stall speed - flaps / gear down	60 kts	
Climb @ sea level (fpm)	3250, 3500	
Range with reserves	1050-1385	
Service ceiling (ft)	45,000, 46,000	35,000
Take off (Ground run)(ft)		
Take off (over 50ft obst)(ft)	1880, 1780	
Landing (Ground roll)(ft)		
Landing (over 50ft obst)(ft)	1950, 1975	

In 1988 and 1989, Piper revived plans for a new family of aircraft using the Malibu knowledge and experiences as a base. The Twin Malibu was looked at and dropped. Some work was carried out on the PA-46J Jet Malibu, but this never left the drawing board. Two versions were proposed the PA-46-JW with a Williams FJ-44 engine and the PA-46-JP with a Pratt & Whitney JT15D-1 engine. This design had the Malibu wing and fuselage, the engine installation was in the rear fuselage with a single intake above, the Malibu tail with a small dorsal extension. Some design work was carried out on the four place Malibu for a possible order of trainers for Lufthansa, the German airline. There were three versions looked at:

- standard size Malibu with the smaller Lycoming IO-540 engine and four seats,
- smaller fuselage with four seats and the Lycoming IO-540 engine,
- four seat with the water-cooled Continental TIOL-550 engine

Unfortunately Piper couldn't meet the tough noise requirements requested by Lufthansa, so no order was forthcoming. The Twin, Jet and the Four-place were all dropped due to Piper's cash problems.

In mid 1990 Piper introduced an option of EFIS avionics on the Mirage, the Allied Signal Aerospace and Bendix-King electronic flight instrument system. The EHI 40 was integrated with the Bendix-King RDS-81 / 82VP weather radar systems that were mounted in a pod under the aircraft's right wing. This was first tested on the Piper retained Malibu Mirage prototype N9135D.

For the 1996 model year Piper updated the Malibu Mirage with overhead switches, new control yoke mechanism, new air-conditioner. Aircraft N9135D was the experimental aircraft. The first production aircraft s/n 4636021 registration N92696 (which had its serial number changed from 4622220 on the production line) was completed in November 1995. The Malibu Mirage was in production at Vero Beach in December 1996.

In the field, V.K. Leasing Inc. offer a conversion for the TCM powered Malibu. A 350 hp Continental TSIO-550-C engine derated to 310 hp replaces the standard engine. The first aircraft converted at St. Petersburg, Florida was s/n 46-8508105 registration N26025 in late 1993. It was re-registered N550VK on the 18th of November.

1996 model PA-46-350P Malibu Mirage s/n 4636021 registration N92696 in the paint shop at Vero Beach. (R.W. Peperell)

PA-46-310P s/n 46-8508105 registration N550VK with TCM TSIO-550-C engine at St. Petersburg, Fl. (H. Van Kesteren)

PA-47

This model number has not yet been assigned. Over the years several of the Malibu derivatives have proposed using the PA-47 designation.

10
MUSTANG

ENFORCER

The original Piper Enforcer programme was a Cavalier programme, based on the North American P-51 Mustang with a Lycoming T55 turboprop engine, taken over by Piper in the early 1970s. There were two prototypes, the first was the PE1 s/n PE1-1001 registration N201PE which first flew on the 28th of April 1971. This aircraft was cancelled in 1973 but was restored to the U.S. Register in 1975. The second was the PE2 s/n PE2-1001 registration N202PE was registered in 1971. Unfortunately it was written off in a crash at Vero Beach on the 12th of July 1971. Both aircraft used original Mustang airframes as a basis, the U.S. register showed that the PE1 airframe was built in 1941. Piper submitted the Enforcer to the U.S.A.F. in response to the AX tank killer requirement, as did Fairchild (with the A-10 Thunderbolt II), which Fairchild won. As a result the U.S.A.F. had no official requirement for the Enforcer, but areas for improvement were pointed out to Piper.

Piper's intensive lobbying of the U.S.A.F. throughout the mid 1970's led to an allocation of 12 million dollars to produce 2 Enforcers for evaluation - in the Close Support Role - in the early 1980's

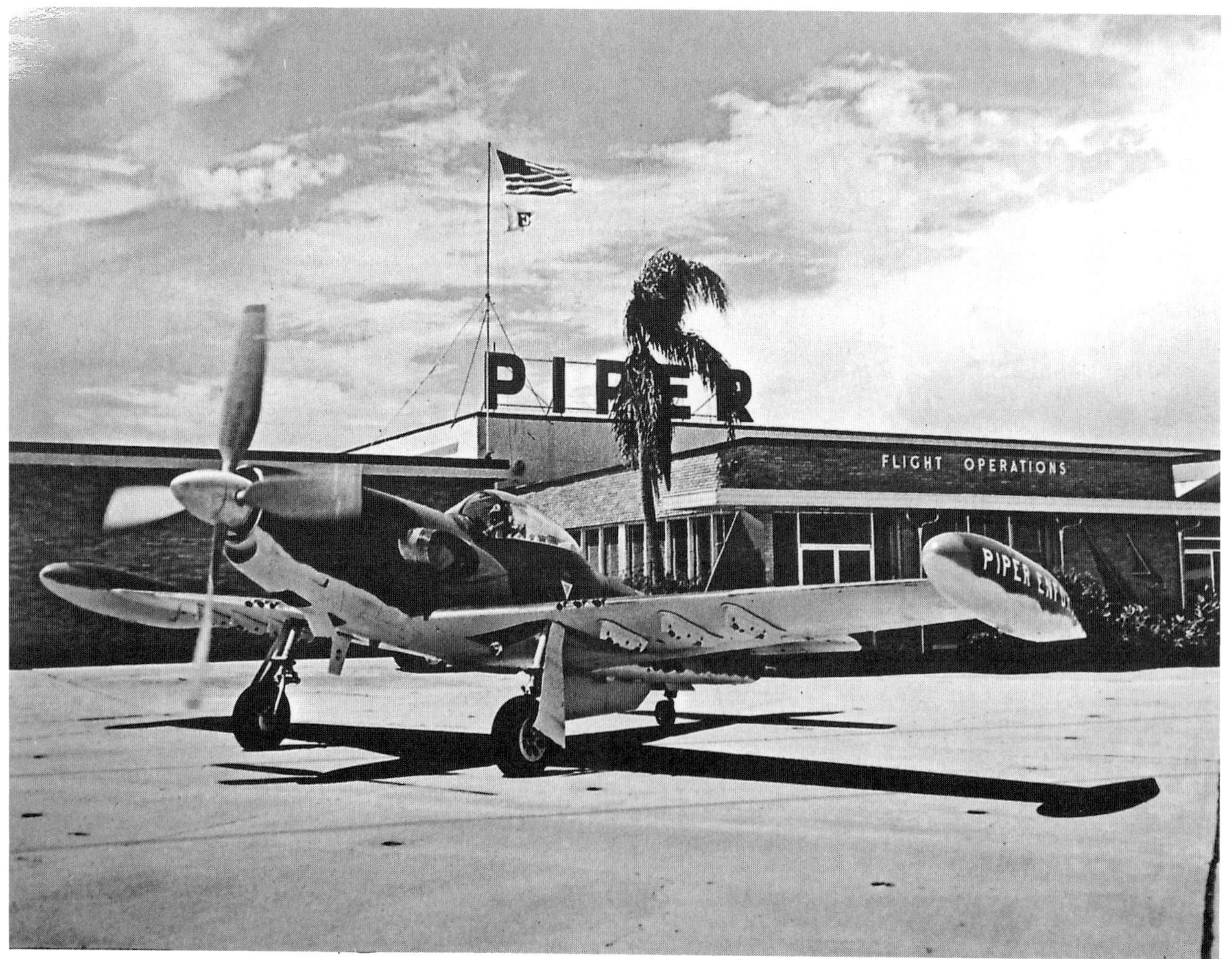

Piper Enforcer PE1 s/n PE1-1001 registration N201PE at Vero Beach. (via W.T. Piper Jr.)

Piper Enforcer PE2 s/n PE2-1001 registration N202PE. (Piper Aircraft Corporation)

PA-48 Enforcer s/n 48-8301001 registration N481PE on take off at Lakeland. (Piper Aircraft Corporation)

PA-48 Enforcer s/n 48-8301002 registration N482PE in open storage. (D. Lawrence)

PA-48 ENFORCER

On the 4th of September 1981 Piper announced the receipt of a contract from the U.S.A.F. for the PA-48 programme. The PA-48 Enforcer was developed at Lakeland between 1981 and 1984. The next logical PA number was PA-47, but this was not used for the Enforcer so as not to confuse it with the P-47 Thunderbolt. So PA-48 was assigned. The original prototype Enforcer N201PE, loaned to Piper by Mr. David Lindsay, was used as a pattern aircraft. Major design changes were made to the original Enforcer to create the PA-48. The aft fuselage was extended by 19 inches. New longerons were added and the rear fuselage cross section was refined. The rudder and fin area was increased by 9% and the tailplane area increased by 35.8%, a Yaw stability augmentation system (Y-SAS) was fitted as was a Yankee rocket escape system for the pilot. It had a Lycoming 2445 shp T55-L-9 engine with a A-1E Skyraider Aeroproducts four bladed propeller (cut-down) in a long nose. The prototypes were s/n 48-8301001 registration N481PE which first flew on the 9th of April 1983 and s/n 48-8301002 registration N482PE which first flew on the 8th of July 1983. The Enforcer had six underwing pylons. The main weapons would be G.E. Gepod 30 mm 4 barrel rotary cannons. Other mission loads were to include the Canadian CRV-7 2.75 inch unguided rocket, 7.62 mm minigun pods and CBU-55 or Rockeye Mk. 20 cluster bombs. Piper handed over the two aircraft to the U.S.A.F. in late 1984 for trials to be carried out. It is doubtful that these trials took place and later they were flown to the Aerospace Maintenance and Regeneration Centre (AMARC) at Davis Mothan Air Force Base in Arizona. They were displayed at Dayton Air Force Museum and Edwards Air Force Museum in mid 1990. Had it gone into production, it would have used the serial number range 48-yy73xxx, and had a 3000 shp engine with a Dowty Rotol or Hamilton-Standard propeller.

PE / PA-48 SPECIFICATION & PERFORMANCE

SPECIFICATION	PE	48
Engine	Lycoming T55	2455 shp Lycoming T55-L-9
Engine TBO (hrs)		
No of seats	1	1
Wing Span (ft/ins)	39/10	41/4
Length (ft/ins)	32/7	34/2
Height (ft/ins)		13/1
Useable fuel capacity (US gal)		1472 lbs + 1920 lbs tip tanks
Gross weight (lbs)		14,000
Empty weight (lbs)		
Useful load (lbs)		5680
Propeller		Skyraider Aeroproducts 4 blade
Floats available		
PERFORMANCE		
Max speed		350 kts
Cruise speed		315 kts
Efficiency (gph)		
Stall speed - flaps / gear down		100 kts
Climb @ sea level (fpm)		4790
Range with reserves		400 nm
Service ceiling (ft)		37,600
Take off (Ground run)(ft)		
Take off (over 50ft obst)(ft)		1680
Landing (Ground roll)(ft)		
Landing (over 50ft obst)(ft)		1720

11 AEROSTAR

The Aerostar was designed by Ted Smith and he began production of the Aerostar 600 and 601 at Santa Maria, California in 1968. The original prototype was the Aerostar 360 s/n 36-0001 registration N540TS which first flew in November 1966. This was FAA type approved with number A11WE. The Aerostar 600 prototype (with 290 hp Lycoming engines) was s/n 60-0001 registration N588TS which first flew in October 1967. FAA type approval A17WE was granted on the 27th of March 1968. In 1968 the Aerostar 601 with turbo-charged engines was also produced. The prototype was s/n 61-0001 registration N587TS which first flew in July 1968. FAA type approval was granted in November 1968. A single Aerostar 620 was built in 1969 with a pressurized fuselage and 310 hp turbocharged engines. This was s/n 62-001 registration N620TS. (The New Piper Aircraft Inc. owned this aircraft in 1996). On the 16th of February 1970 the Aerostar assets were acquired by Butler Aviation International. Butler did not complete any aircraft but they did finish some wings. Ted Smith re-acquired the Aerostar line in 1972 and re-started production in 1973. The serial number format was switched at this time from 'type-airframe number within type-airframe number of all Aerostars' to 'type-airframe number of all Aerostars-airframe number within type'. In 1974 the pressurized Aerostar 601P was developed and put into production. The prototype was s/n 61P-0157-001 registration N601P. In 1976 an improved 601 was produced, the 601A and an improved 600 was produced, the 600A. In 1977 the 601 was improved again into the 601B. Ted Smith also produced a 601P with lengthened fuselage and two 350 hp Lycoming engines. The fuselage was increased by 32 inches with a plug behind the pilot's seat with a door in it. Both the vertical and horizontal tail surfaces were increased in area. Aircraft s/n 60-0026-044 registration N72TS was the prototype 700 Super Star. This developed into the Aerostar 800 with 400 hp Lycoming IO-720 engines. They had also proposed the 1000 with 450 hp Lycoming or 435 hp Continental engines. None of these derivatives went into production. In 1979 Piper revived the Aerostar 800 programme. (see chapter 9, PA-45)

In early 1977 Piper wanted to purchase the Aerostar line but Ted Smith wanted too much money. Ted Smith returned to Piper later and on the 28th of April 1978 Piper acquired the Aerostar line. Production aircraft could seat one pilot and five passengers. The 600A had two 290 hp Lycoming IO-540-K1J5 engines, the 601B had an increased wing span and gross weight as compared to the 600A and turbo charged 290 hp Lycoming TIO-540-S1A5 engines, and the 601P was a 601B with a pressurized cabin. The only changes Piper made to these aircraft was new 'Piper' paint schemes and an improved fuel gauge system. The aircraft continued to be produced at Santa Maria, California.

In February 1981 Piper announced the Sequoya. This was an Aerostar 601P with new low compression 290 hp Lycoming TIO-540-AA1A5 engines. The prototype s/n 62P-0750-8165001 registration N6081P was converted from s/n 61P-0750-8063370. The first production aircraft was s/n 62P-0861-8165002 registration N602PC registered in March 1981. It's basic price was $333,500. The Sequoya name was dropped shortly after launch because of a conflict with the name of a kitplane manufacturer, the Sequoia Aircraft Company, and the name Aerostar 602P was adopted.

In the summer of 1981 Piper stopped production of the 600A and 601B at Santa Maria, California and moved production of the 602P to Vero Beach. A new 3.7 million dollar assembly building was built at Vero Beach for Aerostar and Malibu production. Production restarted at the end of 1981 with the 602P now designated the PA-60-602P. The first off the production line was s/n 60-8265001 registration N6897Q. Production of the 602P stopped with s/n 60-8365021 registration N9538N in May 1983 when it was replaced by the PA-60-700P Aerostar.

The Aerostar 700P had 350 hp counter rotating Lycoming TIO-540-U2A engines (similar to those used on the Chieftain but counter rotating away from the fuselage instead of towards the fuselage) and a new optional 40 gallon fuel tank. The prototype s/n 60-8223001 registration N68907 was converted from s/n 62P-0874-8165011 and first flew at Vero Beach in September 1981. The first production aircraft s/n 60-8423001 registration N6905A was registered in January 1984. FAA approval was received in May 1984 and IFR equipped price was $499,300. Production ended with s/n 60-8423025 registration N9516N in October 1984.

Mooney Aircraft had changed hands in early 1984 to the owners of Lake Aircraft and Euralair. When Piper terminated production of the Aerostar 700P, they tried to get the new owners of Mooney to take over the entire stock of unsold Aerostars. Terms could not be agreed. The last few unsold examples were sold off in March and April 1985 at a big discount.

The Aerostar factory at Santa Maria, California. (Piper Aircraft Corporation)

Aerostar 800 s/n 60-0026-44 registration N72TS at Santa Maria. (G.K. Gates)

1980 model Piper Aerostar 600A s/n 60-0620-7961198 registration N8219J. (Piper Aircraft Corporation)

1981 model Piper Aerostar 601B s/n 60-0788-8062150 registration N3637E. (Piper Aircraft Corporation)

1980 model Piper Aerostar 601P s/n 61P-0619-7963280 registration N8218J. (Piper Aircraft Corporation)

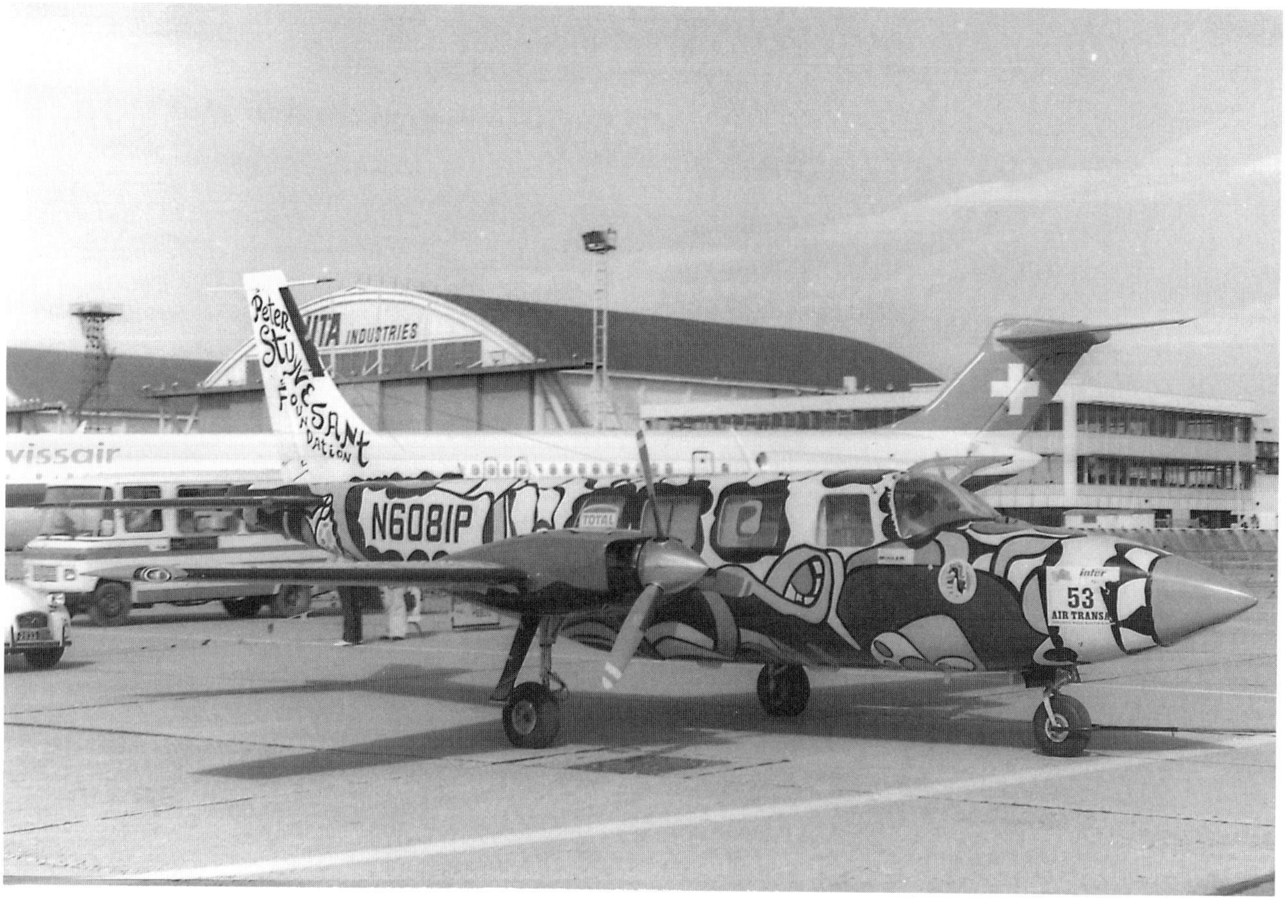

The prototype Piper Aerostar 602P s/n 62P-0750-8165001 registration N6081P in a special paint scheme at the Paris Air Show. This was originally named the Sequoya. (J.M. Gradidge)

Piper Aerostar 601P s/n 61P-0843-8163444 registration N36444. This was the Piper Sequoya show aircraft and has the name 'Sequoia' on the nose. (Piper Aircraft Corporation)

Ted Smith Aerostar PRODUCTION DETAILS

Model Year	Serial Number Range From	To	Type	Total	Comments
Prototype	36-0001-001		360	1	
1968-1970	60-0001-003	60-0056-128	600	56	
1973-1978	60-0130-057	60-0496-161 *	600 / 600A	103	
1968-1970	61-0001-004	61-0070-129	601	70	
1973-1978	61-0132-071	61-0480-127	601 / 601A / 601B	57	
1969	62-001		602	1	
1974-1978	61P-0157-001	61P-0495-203	601P	203	

* s/n -131-00 and -133-00 were fuselages only, 002-00 was static test
Total manufactured 491 (All built at Santa Maria)

Piper Aerostar PRODUCTION DETAILS

Model Year	Serial Number Range From	To	Type	Total	Comments (built)
1978	60-500-162	60-0560-182	600A	21	Santa Maria
1978	61-0497-128	61-0537-132	601B	5	Santa Maria
1978	61P-0498-204	61P-0559-241	601P	38	Santa Maria
1979	60-0563-7961183	60-0713-7961221	600A	39	Santa Maria
1979	61-0573-7962133	61-0698-7962143	601B	11	Santa Maria
1979	61P-0561-242	61P-0562-243	601P	2	Santa Maria
1979	61P-0564-7963244	61P-0714-7963345	601P	102	Santa Maria
1980	60-0715-8061222	60-0824-8061236	600A	15	Santa Maria
1980	61-0717-8062144	61-0838-8062152	601B	9	Santa Maria
1980	61P-0716-8063346	61P-0825-8063433 *	601P	87	Santa Maria
1981	60-0833-8161237	60-0933-8161262	600A	26	Santa Maria
1981	61-0844-8162153	61-0880-8162157	601B	5	Santa Maria
1981	61P-0826-8163434	61P-0860-8163455	601P	22	Santa Maria
Prototype	62P-0750-8165001		Sequoya	1	Santa Maria
1981	62P-0861-8165002	62P-0932-8165055 *	602P	53	Santa Maria
1982	60-8265001	60-8265057 *	60-602P	36	Vero Beach
1983	60-8365001	60-8365021	60-602P	21	Vero Beach
Prototype	60-8223001		60-700P	1	Vero Beach
1984	60-8423001	60-8423025	60-700P	25	Vero Beach

A total of 24 aircraft in the batches marked * were not delivered, instead they were updated to the next year's model and given new serial numbers. See table below.
Total manufactured 519

Piper Aerostar SERIAL NUMBER CHANGES			
Model	Old Serial Number	New Serial Number	New Model (if different)
Aerostar 601P	61P-0750-8063370	62P-0750-8165001	Aerostar 602P
Aerostar 602P	62P-0874-8165011	60-8223001	PA-60-700P
PA-60-602P	60-8265016	60-8365011	
PA-60-602P	60-8265022	60-8365008	
PA-60-602P	60-8265025	60-8365005	
PA-60-602P	60-8265029	60-8365010	
PA-60-602P	60-8265030	60-8365007	
PA-60-602P	60-8265032	60-8365009	
PA-60-602P	60-8265035	60-8365002	
PA-60-602P	60-8265037	60-8365003	
PA-60-602P	60-8265038	60-8365012	
PA-60-602P	60-8265041	60-8365004	
PA-60-602P	60-8265042	60-8365006	
PA-60-602P	60-8265047	60-8365001	
PA-60-602P	60-8265048	60-8265047 (2)	
PA-60-602P	60-8265049	60-8365013	
PA-60-602P	60-8265050	60-8365014	
PA-60-602P	60-8265051	60-8365015	
PA-60-602P	60-8265052	60-8365016	
PA-60-602P	60-8265053	60-8365017	
PA-60-602P	60-8265054	60-8365018	
PA-60-602P	60-8265055	60-8365019	
PA-60-602P	60-8265056	60-8365021	
PA-60-602P	60-8265057	60-8365020	

Prior to Piper purchasing the Aerostar line, there were many proposals for jet versions. Ted Smith had proposed developing two jet Aerostars, the 3000 and 4000 in the mid 1970s. Neither of these left the drawing board. In October 1981, Williams proposed a short fuselage Aerostar powered by Williams WR44-2 jet engines. The William WR44-2 engine was of approximately 1200 pound thrust. After Piper discounted the Aerospatiale Corvette in 1981, they looked at a jet powered Aerostar, the PA-60-700XP, one with Williams engines (1500 pound thrust) and another with Garrett TFE76-4A (F109-GA-100) engines but using the extended 800 fuselage. None of these derivatives went into production due to lack of funds. Had it done, it would have used serial number range 60-yy17xxx. In October 1985 Piper revived the Jet Aerostar project as the new technology light jet with the Williams FJ44 engines, but again it was dropped. Piper did briefly review the applicability of the Williams FJ44 engine to the Cherokee line of aircraft in October 1985.

The three pressurized Aerostars, the 601P, 602P and 700P were recognised as the best twins in their class, flying higher, faster, further and more economically than any other type.

In the field, Machen at Seattle, Washington offer a conversion called the Superstar 700. It is an Aerostar 601P with 350 hp Lycoming engines and was first shown at the NBAA show in October 1982. An example is s/n 61P-0755-8063374 registration N6081X. Another conversion available is an Aerostar 680 with 340 hp Lycoming IO-540-AA1A5 engines. An example is an Aerostar 602P s/n 60-8265012 registration N68980. Also the Superstar 650 was offered which put 325 hp Lycoming engines on the 601P. By 1986, 65 conversions had been completed. Other examples have been s/n 61P-0658-7963306 registration N222L and s/n 61P-0743-8063365 registration N4PC.

In 1991 Aerostar 601P s/n 61P-0860-8163455 registration N312BA was modified by installing two 420 shp Allison 250B-17D propjet engines. This was brought to Vero Beach on the 9th of July 1991 but was not reviewed by Piper.

Piper sold the Aerostar type certificate to AAC (Machen) in May 1991. AAC immediately announced that they were to develop the Jet Star 1, an Aerostar with two Williams 44 jet engines. Nothing more is known about this project.

Piper Aerostar SPECIFICATION & PERFORMANCE			
SPECIFICATION	600A	601B	601P
Engine	290 hp Lycoming IO-540-K1JS	290 hp Lycoming TIO-540-S1AS	290 hp Lycoming TIO-540-S1AS
Engine TBO (hrs)	2000	1800	1800
No of seats	6	6	6
Wing Span (ft/ins)	34/2	34/2	34/2
Length (ft/ins)	34/10	34/10	34/10
Height (ft/ins)	12/2	12/2	12/2
Useable fuel capacity (US gal)	165.5	165.5	165.5
Gross weight (lbs)	5500-5525	6000	6000
Empty weight (lbs)	3740-3780	3958-3985	4095
Useful load (lbs)	1720-1788	2015-2042	1905
Propellers	Hartzell 3-blade	Hartzell 3-blade	Hartzell 3-blade
Pressurization (psi)	n/a	n/a	4.25
Floats available			
PERFORMANCE			
Max speed	226 kts	257 kts	257 kts
Cruise speed	197-220 kts	218-257 kts	235 kts
Efficiency (gph)			
Stall speed - flaps / gear down	74 kts	77 kts	77 kts
Climb @ sea level (fpm)	1800	1460	
Range with reserves	983-1201 nm	1024-1173 nm	1024-1173 nm
Service ceiling (ft)	21,200	30,000	30,000
Take off (Ground run)(ft)	1550	1900	1900
Take off (over 50ft obst)(ft)	1950	2490	2490
Landing (Ground roll)(ft)	1040	1230	1230
Landing (over 50ft obst)(ft)	1840	2030	2030

The prototype Piper Aerostar 700P s/n 60-8223001 registration N68907. (Piper Aircraft Corporation)

Piper Aerostar 601P s/n 61P-0860-8163455 registration N312BA with Allison propjet engines. (via H. Van Kesteren)

Machen Superstar III showing four bladed propellers. This is a 1980 model Piper Aerostar. (via J. Taylor)

Piper Aerostar SPECIFICATION & PERFORMANCE			
SPECIFICATION	60-602P	60-700P	Machen 650 / 680
Engine	290 hp Lycoming TIO-540-AA1A5	350 hp Lycoming L/TIO-540-U2A	325 hp or 340 hp Lycoming TIO-540
Engine TBO (hrs)	1800	1800	1800
No of seats	6	6	6
Wing Span (ft/ins)	36/8	36/8	36/8
Length (ft/ins)	34/10	34/10	34/10
Height (ft/ins)	12/2	12/2	12/2
Useable fuel capacity (US gal)	165.5	205.5	
Gross weight (lbs)	6029	6356	6200
Empty weight (lbs)	4075-4125	4275	4106
Useful load (lbs)	1904-1954	2081	2094
Propellers	Hartzell 3-blade	Hartzell 3-blade	3-blade
Pressurization (psi)	4.25	4.25	4.25
Floats available			
PERFORMANCE			
Max speed	262 kts	266 kts	265 kts
Cruise speed	247 kts @ 75% 228 kts @ 65%	261 kts @ 75% 230 kts @ 65%	240-250 kts
Efficiency (gph)	32.4 @ 65%		
Stall speed - flaps / gear down	77 kts	80 kts	77 kts
Climb @ sea level (fpm)	1755	1840	1955
Range with reserves	1094-1143 nm	868 nm @ 75%	1137 nm
Service ceiling (ft)	28,000	25,000	25,000
Take off (Ground run)(ft)	1800	1950	
Take off (over 50ft obst)(ft)	2250	3080	1980
Landing (Ground roll)(ft)	1217	1440	
Landing (over 50ft obst)(ft)	2076	2140	

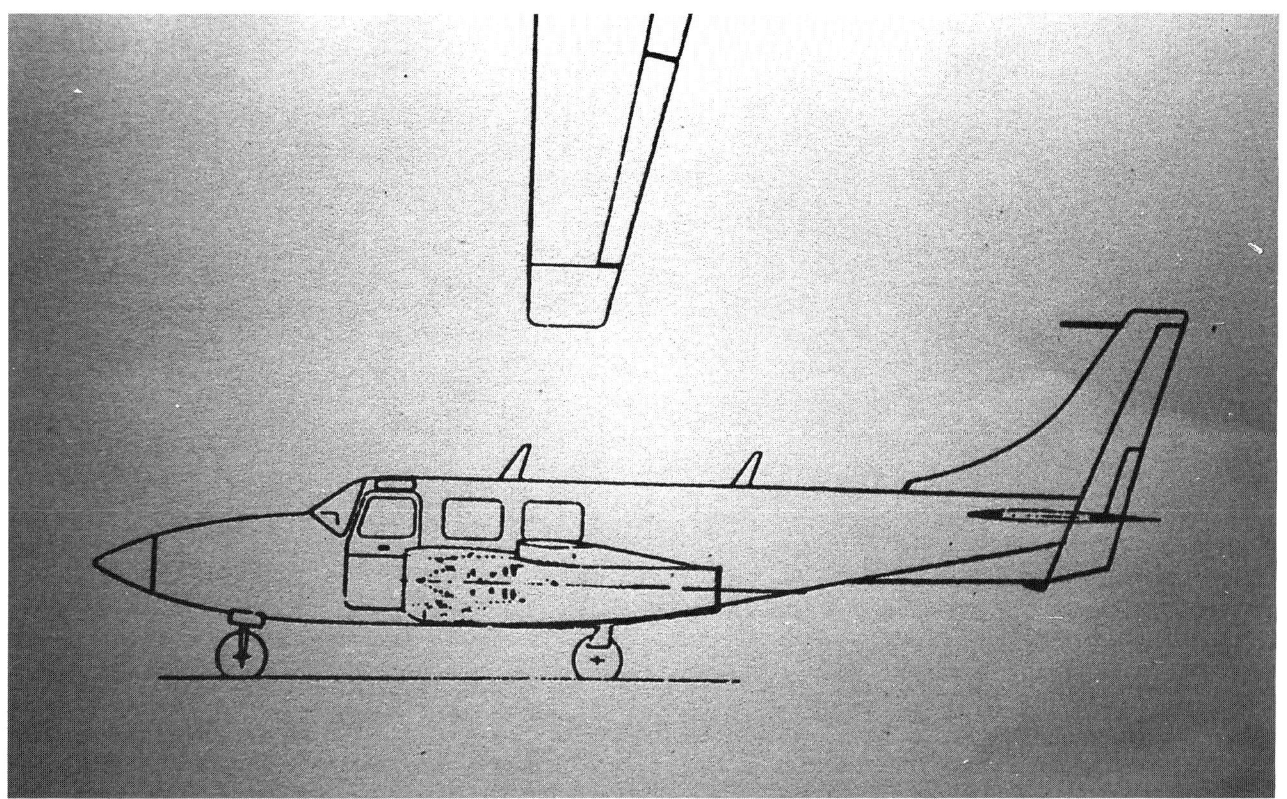

Drawing of the Piper proposed Jet Aerostar. (via G.K. Gates)

12
LOPRESTI-PIPER

Romeo Charlie Inc. established LoPresti-Piper advanced engineering group at Vero Beach in December 1987. Piper acquired the rights to the Globe Swift in early 1988. The Globe GC-1 Swift was initially awarded its type certificate in the spring of 1942 with the 145 hp Continental C-145 engine with production starting after World War II. LoPresti-Piper's first Swift project was the Swiftfire. They purchased a 1946 Swift s/n 246 registration N80843 and replaced the 235 hp Franklin engine with a 420 shp Allison 250B-17C engine, fitted a new McCauley propeller and cleaned up the airframe. This first flew on the 19th of September 1988 as registration N345LP. Later in August 1989, the engine was removed and the airframe sold. Next was the LP-1 Swiftfury. They had purchased another two 1946 Swifts; s/n 310 registration N80907 and registration N15HN, this latter one as their photo / chase aircraft. Firstly s/n 310 had an aerodynamic clean-up including wing fences and stall strips and a 180 hp Lycoming O-320 engine fitted. This first flew on the 27th of February 1989 as registration N207LP. This was launched at Sun N' Fun at Lakeland, Florida in April 1989 where the order book was opened and 200 were taken. They had planned to amend the Swift type certificate, but the amendment would have necessitated 99% re-testing, so they went for a new certification. By December 1989 a 200 hp Lycoming IO-360 engine was installed in a longer cowl. It was repainted in Yippee! yellow, the registration was changed to N217LP and the orders poured in. The Swiftfury was to be manufactured by Piper North, with Piper making some of the parts. Swiftfury orders stood at 550 when LoPresti-Piper was closed down in December 1990, a casualty of Piper's financial problems. LoPresti-Piper and the Swiftfury project was sold by Romeo Charlie Inc. to LoPresti Speed Merchants, Vero Beach who planned to certify it and manufacture the Swiftfury. Pipers involvement in the project ceased. LoPresti Speed Merchants didn't have the resources or money to certify it so the project was dropped. The aircraft resided in the back of the LoPresti hangar at Vero Beach in 1995.

In 1989 LoPresti-Piper proposed an improved Comanche with a modified fuselage with an upward hinging door and a turbocharged 350 hp Lycoming TIO-540 engine. A new panel would be designed including a holographic Head Up Display (HUD). The projected cruise speed was 226 knots at 25,000 feet. Comanche s/n 24-4965 registration N9457P was purchased. The first new door was designed and built as well some of the new fuselage components, but the project was shelved in order to concentrate resources on the Swiftfury project.

LoPresti Speed Merchants went on to produce a series of 'go-faster' kits for Piper aircraft. An example is the Comanche 'Holey Cowl', s/n 24-4112 registration N8665P converted during early 1995.

LoPresti Piper Swiftfire s/n 246 registration N345LP. (C. LoPresti)

LoPresti Piper LP-1 Swiftfury s/n 310 registration N207LP. (C. LoPresti)

LoPresti Piper LP-1 Swiftfury s/n 310 registration N207LP with 200 hp Lycoming engine. (C. LoPresti)

Drawing of the proposed LoPresti Piper Comanche. (C. LoPresti)

LoPresti Piper SPECIFICATION & PERFORMANCE		
SPECIFICATION	Swiftfire	LP-1 Swiftfury
Engine	420 shp Allison 250B17C	200 hp Lycoming IO-360
Engine TBO (hrs)		
No of seats	2	2
Wing Span (ft/ins)		29/3.5
Length (ft/ins)		
Height (ft/ins)		
Useable fuel capacity (US gal)		50
Gross weight (lbs)		2300
Empty weight (lbs)		1736 (1450 target)
Useful load (lbs)		564 (850 target)
Propeller	McCauley 3AFR-34-C80Q	constant speed
Pressurization (psi)		
Floats available		
PERFORMANCE		
Max speed	345 mph	217 mph
Cruise speed		200 mph
Efficiency (gph)		10
Stall speed - flaps / gear down		57 kts
Climb @ sea level (fpm)	4000	1100
Range with reserves		1000 sm
Service ceiling (ft)		
Take off (Ground run)(ft)		
Take off (over 50ft obst)(ft)		
Landing (Ground roll)(ft)		
Landing (over 50ft obst)(ft)		

PA-24-260 Comanche with LoPresti speed modifications (including propeller & cowl) at Vero Beach. (R.W. Peperell)

13
OTHER AIRCRAFT

Piper have proposed aircraft designs over the years which were not based on existing designs and were not assigned a PA- designation. Some of these are listed below:

Piper single engine proposals

In October 1970 Piper Lock Haven Engineering proposed a four place single engined turboprop aircraft. There were two versions proposed, both with a 425 shp Pratt & Whitney PT6A-28 engine, gross weight of 3900 pounds with a predicted maximum speed of above 300 mph. They were not produced.

Piper Ducted Fan

In June / July 1973 Piper Lock Haven did a feasibility study of a series of six-place, twin 450 hp engines, ducted-fan, T-tailed aircraft called Alpha, Beta and Gamma. The design had a gross weight of 7400 pounds, span of 40 feet, length of 36 feet and a height of 9 feet. They never left the drawing board.

Piper HOPI Airliners

Piper looked at developing a series of commuter aircraft in July 1980 called the Hopi airliners. The Hopi I was a renamed commuter version of the PA-31-350 Chieftain which was under development and there were two new designs called the Hopi II and III. The Hopi II and III were similar in size (resembling a Douglas DC-9 / Boeing 737) but with 19 and 30 seats capacity respectively and turbine engines. It was proposed that this line of commuters would establish Piper as the manufacturer of choice of the U.S. commuter operators. The Hopi II and III were not developed, but Piper did look at a 17 seat commuter stretched PA-31T.

Piper 2 + 2

In 1987 Piper designed a new all metal 2 + 2 seat aircraft with a 240 hp Lycoming TIO-360 engine with three-bladed propeller. It was to be similar in size to the LoPresti-Piper Swiftfury and would have a gross weight of 2525 pounds and a maximum speed of 200 knots. It was cancelled as Piper thought that the Swiftfury would cost less to bring to production status.

In some cases Piper carried out sub-contract work for other companies or were involved in bidding for contracts which involved modifying existing designs. Some of these are listed below, several were through Lear Siegler, Piper's parent company in the 1980s:

X-27A Target

Piper designed the modified landing gear and nose tow arms on the Aero 27A winged tow target and submitted a bid to the U.S. Navy in January 1950. Flight tests took place at Patuxent. They didn't get the contract.

Piper sub-contracts in the early 1950s

In an effort to fully employ its skilled workforce, Piper did some sub-contract work in the early 1950s. It made the gas tank, ventral fin and tail boom for helicopters for Bell during late 1951. It manufactured dollies for Lycoming in late 1952. Grumman windshields were manufactured between 1951 and 1955 at 50 per month.

Drawing of the tractor engined version of the Piper single engine proposal of 1970. (Piper Aircraft Corporation)

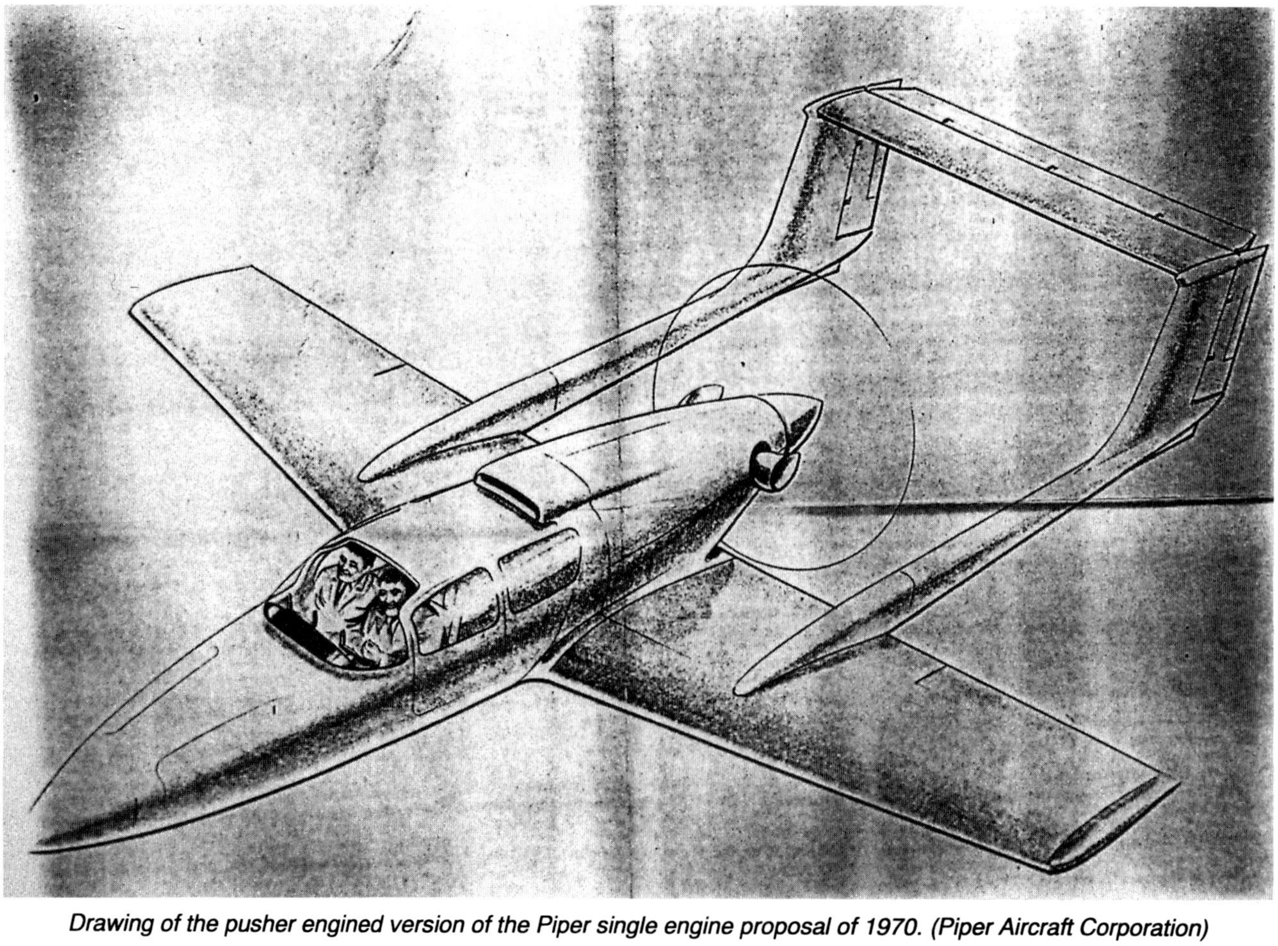

Drawing of the pusher engined version of the Piper single engine proposal of 1970. (Piper Aircraft Corporation)

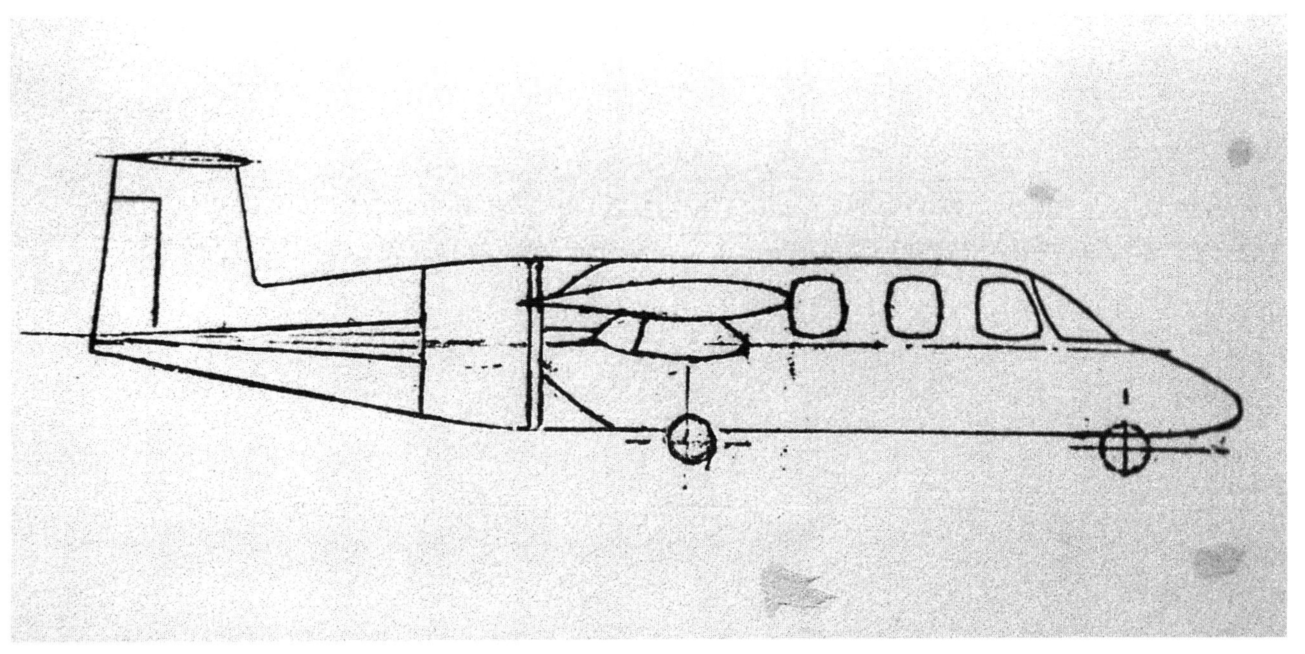

Drawing of the proposed Alpha version of the Piper ducted fan twin. (Piper Aircraft Corporation)

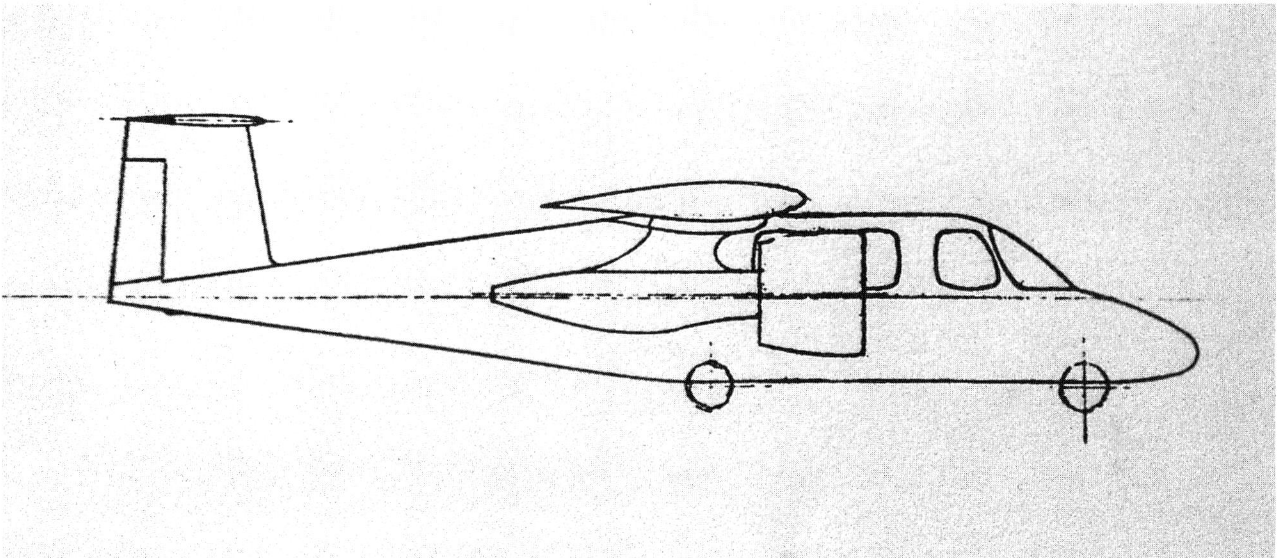

Drawing of the proposed Beta version of the Piper ducted fan twin. (Piper Aircraft Corporation)

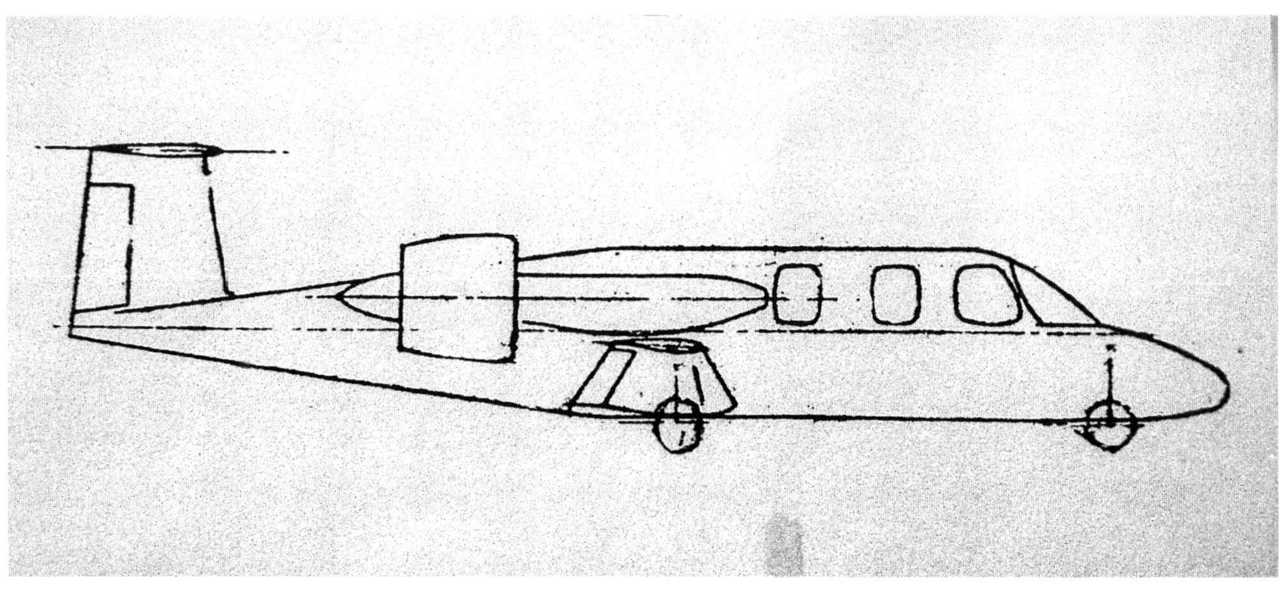

Drawing of the proposed Gamma version of the Piper ducted fan twin. (Piper Aircraft Corporation)

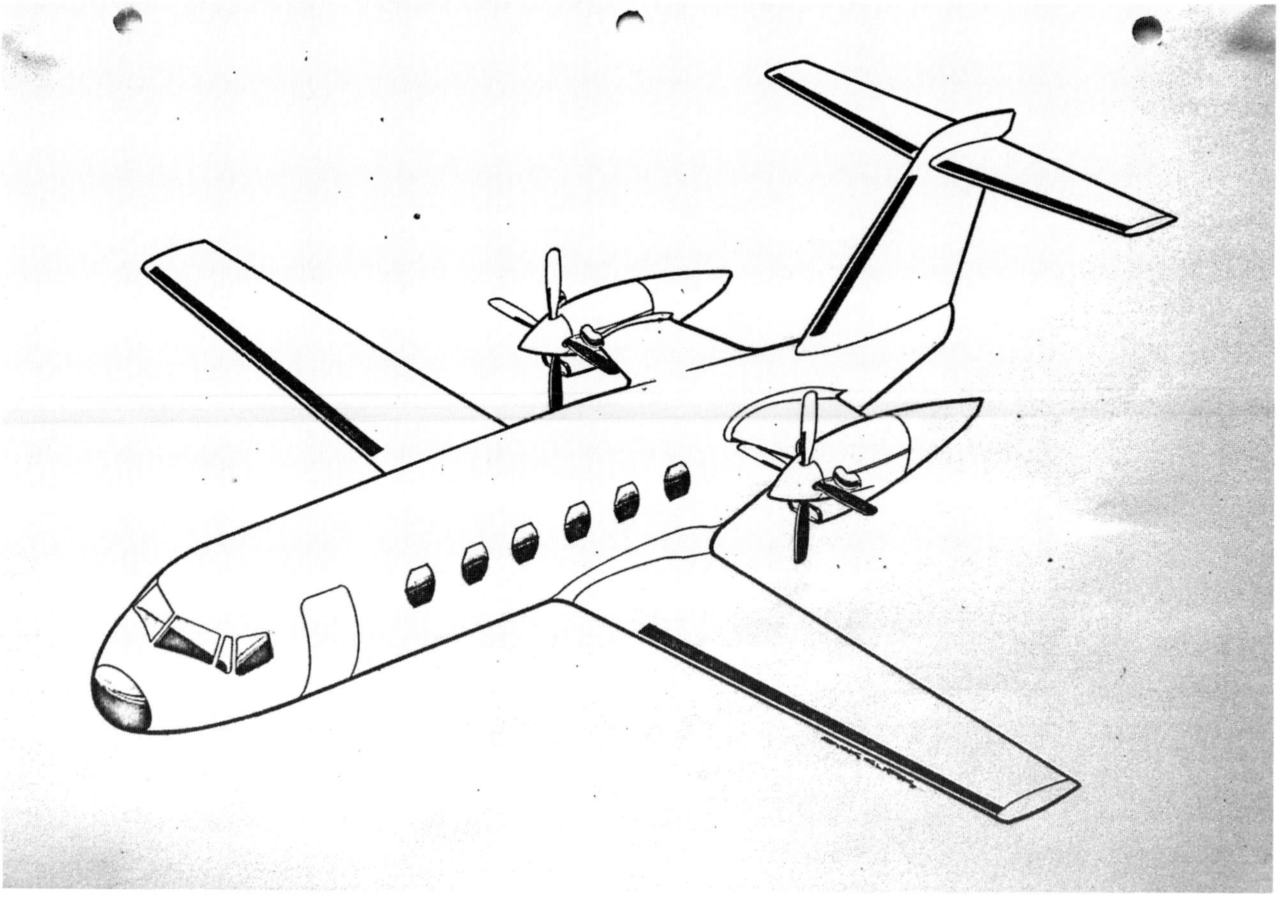

Drawing of the proposed Piper Hopi II / III airliner. (D. Marshall)

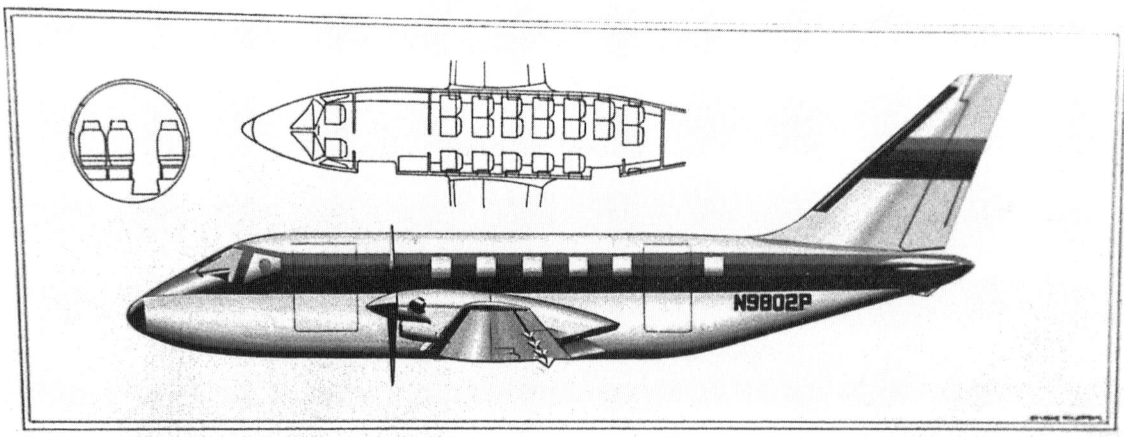

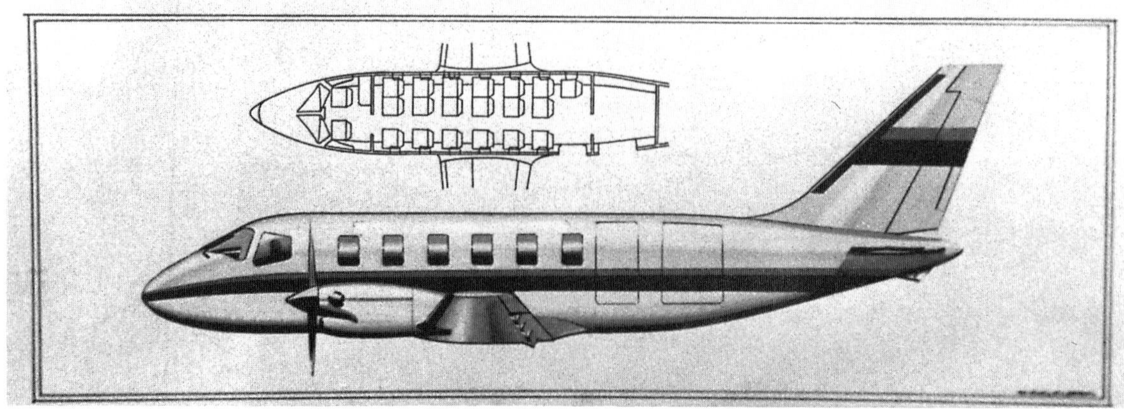

Two more drawings of the proposed Piper airliner. (Piper Aircraft Corporation)

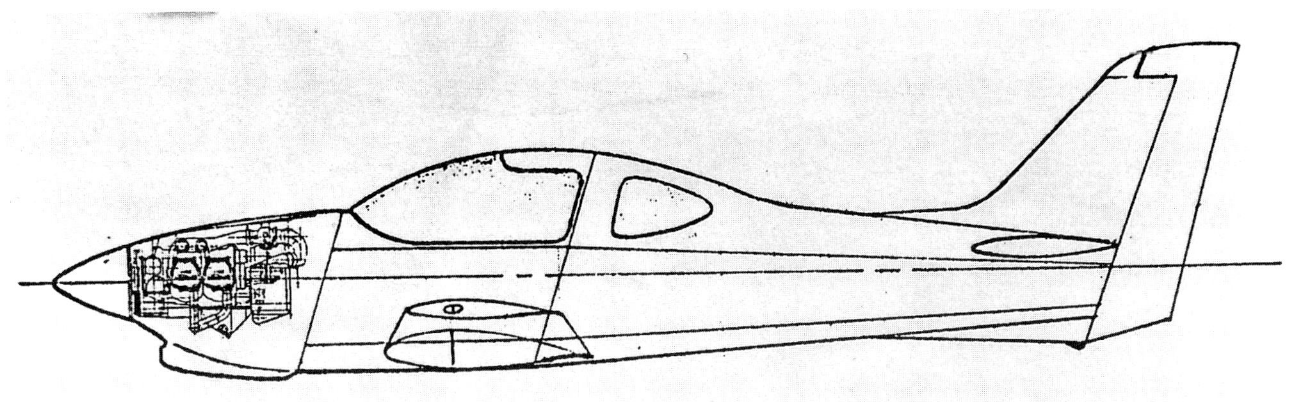

Drawing of the proposed Piper 2+2 Sport. (via G.K. Gates)

X-27A Target at Lock Haven. (Piper Aircraft Corporation)

The manufacture of components for Bell Helicopters by Piper at Lock Haven. (Piper Aircraft Corporation)

The manufacture of windshields for Grumman by Piper at Lock Haven. (Piper Aircraft Corporation)

CASA 212

Piper bid for the U.S.A.F. contract for a small transport aircraft with a Piper built CASA 212 in early 1984. The contract was won by Shorts with the Sherpa.

Later in March 1985 Piper proposed certifying the CASA 212 Series 200 Aviocar with Pratt & Whitney PT6A-45R engines under Regulation (FAR) 25 and obtain an Supplementary Type Certificate under Regulation (FAR) 21. This included new engine mounts and nacelles and cowls. This never went ahead and CASA then developed the Series 300 with 900 shp Garrett TPE-331-10R engines.

T-33 Skyfox

In early 1984 Lear Siegler looked at the Fox programme which was the re-manufacture of the T-33 with a Garrett TFE-731-3 turbofan engine. In January 1985 Piper was asked to manufacture the airframe and some components. No contract was awarded.

QF-106

In January 1986 Lear Siegler Industries, bid for a contract to convert the Convair F-106 Delta Dart into a pilot-less radio controlled full-scale QF-106 aerial target. Piper would have been involved in this work had Lear Siegler got the contract, but in the event they did not.

Grumman S-2 Tracker update

The Instrument and Avionics Systems Division of Lear Siegler proposed an updated Grumman S-2 Tracker with Garrett TPE-331 turbine engines for the Brazilian Air Force in early 1987. Piper declined to participate with Lear Siegler by June.

Piper have been involved with aircraft designs from other companies over the years, either where Piper approached them or the other company approached Piper. Some of these are listed below:

Schweizer 1-30

In December 1960, Schweizer tried to get Piper Lock Haven to manufacture the single seat 1-30 aircraft. Aircraft s/n 1 registration N3840A was brought to Lock Haven for trials.

Victa Airtourer

Between November 1965 and March 1966 Piper evaluated the Victa Airtourer 100 as a possible trainer for mass production in the USA. One aircraft was imported for evaluation at Vero Beach s/n 74 registration N6300V. It was owned for five months and then sold. The Victa had a 100 hp engine versus the 150 hp engine of the Cherokee 140. Training schools were looking for something with 100 hp, but it would have been expensive for Piper as the Victa would be unique in Piper's line-up. There is a possibility that another Victa Airtourer aircraft s/n 49 registration N4350Y was tested by Piper at Lock Haven in 1963, but this is unconfirmed.

Beagle

Piper Vero Beach looked at the Beagle B.121 Pup s/n B121-013 registration N556MA on the 21st/22nd of April 1969. It was on loan from U.S. Pup dealer Miami Air Service at Opa Locka, Florida who wanted Piper to build it for the U.S. market. Pug Piper didn't think it was a good idea, so it was returned to Opa Locka.

Beagle brought their twin-engined B.206 Series 2 s/n 057 registration N966B to Vero Beach on the 12th of May 1967 for Piper to review. Piper was not interested.

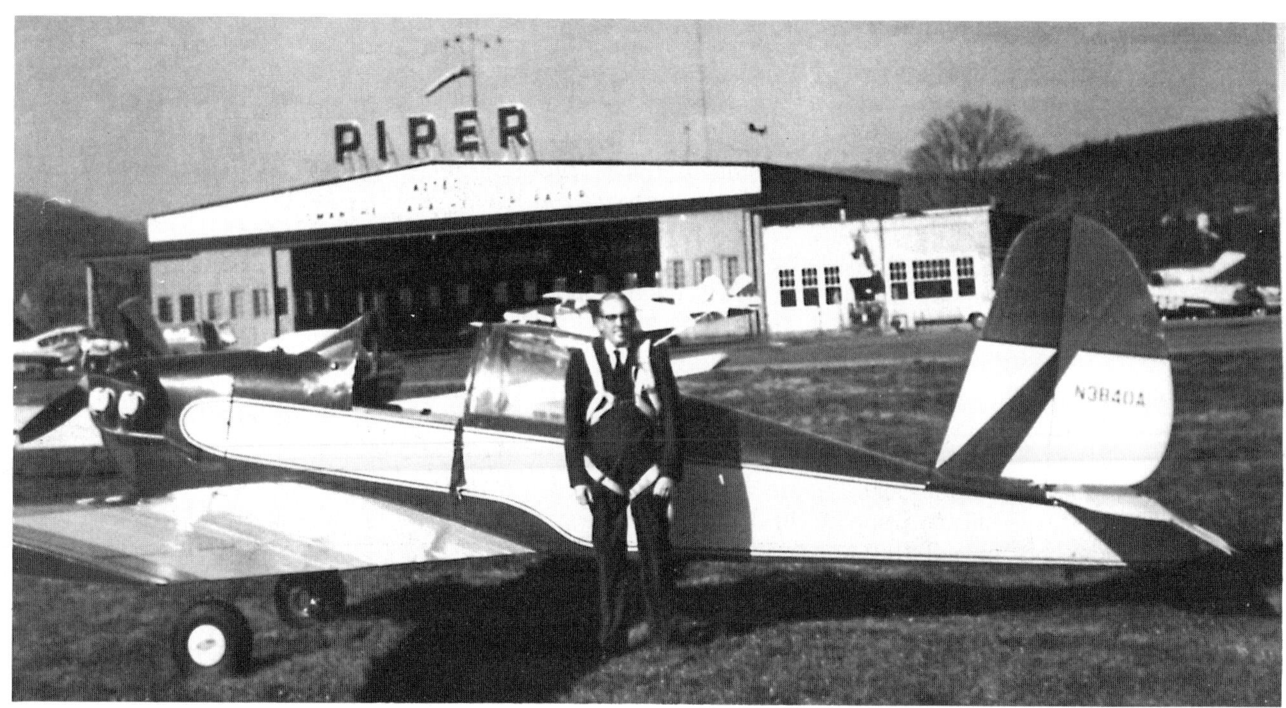

Schweizer 1-30 s/n 1 registration N3840A with Fred Strickland at Lock Haven. (via D. Strickland)

Victa Airtourer s/n 74 registration N6300V at Vero Beach. (P. Peck)

Beagle Pup s/n B121-013 registration N556MA at Opa Locka. (via I. McConnell)

Bolkow Bo.209

In 1970 Piper tested the market with the Bolkow Bo.209 Monsun 160FV s/n V-0 registration D-EMHK in the U.S.A. to see if there was any demand for it. There was not.

Swearingen Merlin / Metro

On the 26th of August 1971 Piper announced a proposal to acquire the assets of Swearingen Aircraft for a price in excess of $16m. Piper was to form a new fully-owned subsidiary to assume the present aircraft manufacturing, sales and service operation of Swearingen. Piper would complement the present Garrett AiResearch domestic distribution network and would assume responsibility for all sales of the new Metro airliner and International sales of the Merlin II, III and IV series of turboprop aircraft. Unfortunately final approval was not reached between Piper and Swearingen and the acquisition fell through. Subsequently Fairchild purchased Swearingen on the 2nd November 1971.

Nord 262

Nord of France invited Piper to take over the Nord 262 programme in the 1970s. Piper declined.

Gulfstream I

After the PA-35 Pocono programme had died, Piper did a review in May 1979 of the Grumman Gulfstream I to see if by re-engineering it with Lycoming T-55 engines they could turn it into a commuter airliner. Piper did not proceed with this.

BAe Jetstream 3101

In 1979 British Aerospace offered Piper the Jetstream 31 design. BAe were developing the Jetstream 31, with 940 shp Garrett TPE-331 engines. Piper thought they might stretch the fuselage, but decided not to purchase the programme. BAe went on the develop the project with the prototype aircraft s/n 227 registration G-JSSD first flying in March 1980.

Aerospatiale Corvette

In January 1981 Piper reviewed taking over the complete SN.601 Corvette programme from Aerospatiale, but decided against it. Aerospatiale had stopped building the Corvette in 1978 as lack of demand curtailed production. Aerospatiale had planned a family of jets.

Piaggio

Between February and May 1983 Piper were invited to become a joint partner in the Piaggio P-180 Avanti project. Piper would manufacture the fuselage and under-carriage in the U.S. A mock-up aircraft was completed by Dave Ellies Industrial Design at Dallas, Texas. The programme was quite advanced with prototype E-01 to be completed by Piaggio and E-03 to be completed by Piper in November 1985, when unfortunately Piper and Piaggio couldn't agree terms. Subsequently Piaggio went to Gates and the design became the GP-180.

During work on the Avanti, Piper proposed a project to convert the LTP101-700 engined P-166 to PT6A-135 engines. This was stopped in June 1983 due to lack of market demand mainly because the P-166 fuselage was not pressurized.

Also in May 1983 a combination of a new fuselage (similar styling to the Avanti) and Cheyenne IV wings and tail was looked at, named the Cheyenne V. This was stopped when Piaggio went to Gates.

In June 1987 discussions were held between Piper and Piaggio on the possibility of Piper manufacturing the Avanti in the U.S.A. Piaggio had been looking for a U.S. partner since Gates dropped out of the program. The venture required too much money.

Bolkow Bo.209 Monsun s/n V-0 registration D-EMHK. (Piper Aircraft Corporation)

Swearingen Merlin III s/n T-201 registration N5292M. (Aerospace Publishing)

The mock-up of the Piaggio P-180 Avanti. (C. Diefendorf)

Trago Mills SAH-1

Trago Mills approached Piper in 1988 with a view to getting Piper to manufacture the SAH-1 for the U.S. market. It did not fit Pipers needs.

Sukhoi

Piper had talks with Sukhoi in the second half of 1989 with a view to:

- collaborating on a new aircraft,
- for Sukhoi to build Piper aircraft from kits,
- FAA certification training and skills

Sukhoi were talking to Grumman at the same time and nothing came of the Piper discussions mainly due to Piper's cash flow problems in 1990.

Pilatus PC-12

In 1990 Piper offered to help Pilatus obtain Regulation (FAR) 23 certification for the PC-12 by running the full scale fatigue test. Pilatus declined. Later in April 1993, as part of the take-over talks with Pilatus, Piper were to manufacture the PC-12 at Vero Beach, but the Courts rejected the Pilatus bid.

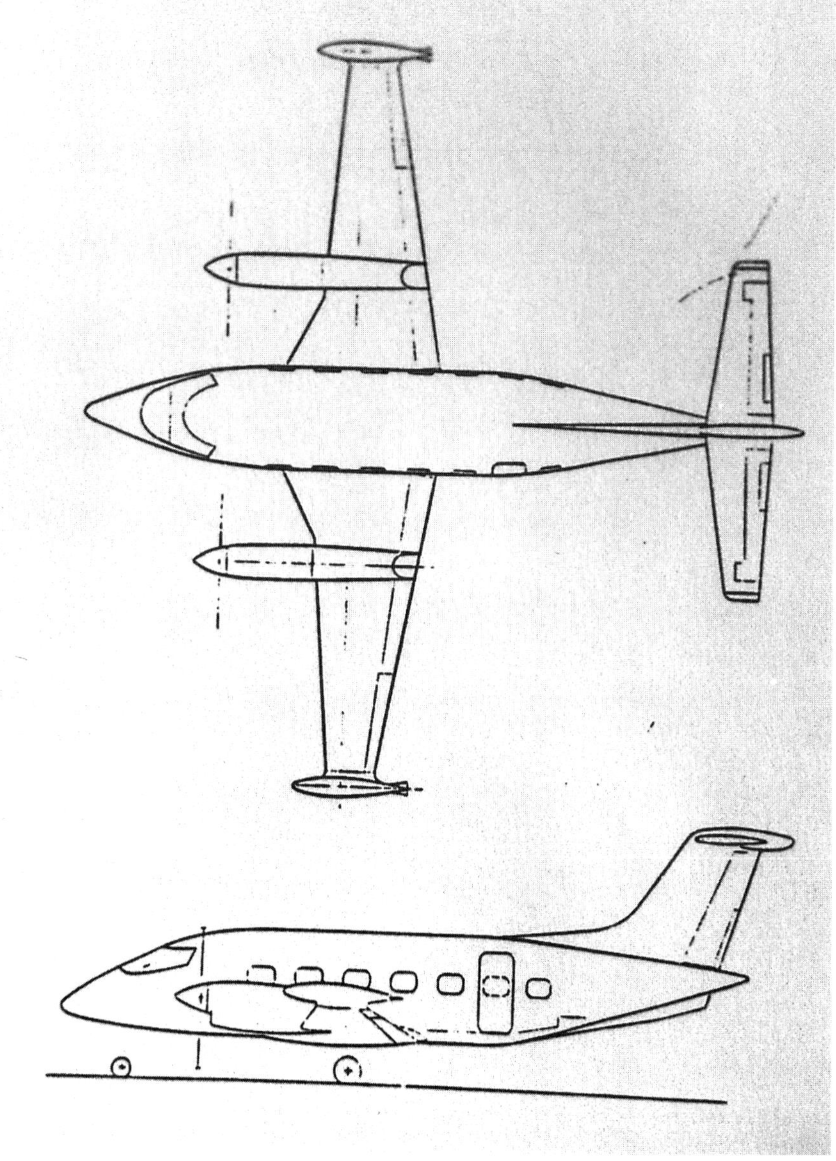

Drawing of the proposed Piper Cheyenne V. (Piper Aircraft Corporation)

Aerial view of the Piper factory at Vero Beach in 1989. (Piper Aircraft Corporation)

PA-28 production line at a standstill at Vero Beach in 1990. At the front is PA-28-161 Cadet s/n 2841324 registration N92156 painted but awaiting engine, propeller and avionics. (Piper Aircraft Corporation)

14
PIPER TODAY

The Piper Aircraft Corporation no longer exists as a result of the Chapter 11 reorganisation. The New Piper Aircraft Inc. was born on the 17th of July 1995, buying most of the assets of the old organisation. The new owners are Dimeling, Schreiber & Park, Teledyne Industries and a trust of Piper's creditors and shareholders. The old company and now New Piper has been revamping its model line over the past year, e.g. Warrior III, Archer III, Seneca IV / V, Saratoga II HP and there are more to come. Its is currently looking at developing a new line of aircraft to be produced in a few years time. Production is slowly increasing and they plan to produce 188 aircraft in 1996 and 210 in 1997. They have recently introduced updated 1996 models of the Saratoga II HP and the Malibu Mirage and will introduce the Saratoga II TC and the Seneca V for the 1997 model year.

The following models were in production in December 1996:-

Warrior III, Archer III, Arrow, Saratoga II HP, Seneca IV / V, Seminole, Malibu Mirage.

The New Piper vision is based on technology-driven innovations in current products and providing the foundation for development of the new platforms. To achieve the vision they feel it is imperative to maintain a responsible, growth oriented, but bottom-line approach to the marketplace.

During 1996 Piper has been evaluating several new designs including a turbine Malibu. The company's goal is to bring to market the next generation of private and business aircraft. After significant research has been completed and considered, Piper will embark on development of the new designs.

Two Warrior III aircraft awaiting delivery at Vero Beach to Heights of Georgia Tech, PA-28-161 s/n 2842006 registration N281HG and s/n 2842007 registration N282HG. (The New Piper Aircraft Inc.)

View of the Piper Aircraft International facility at Geneva in 1966 with various Pipers awaiting delivery to Europe and Africa. (Aerospace Publishing)

15
FOREIGN ASSEMBLY PROGRAM

Many of the exported Pipers are put into a wooden crate (the fuselage and wings separated) and delivered by road / sea / road to the foreign distributors where they are re-assembled for delivery to customers. For many years from 1962 through to the 1970s Piper Aircraft International had a large facility at Geneva, Switzerland which was responsible for most of the European and African markets. The U.K. and Scandinavia were served by C.S.E. Aviation and Nyge-Aero respectively.

Over the years Piper has offered to deliver aircraft to countries as kits rather than completed aircraft. This reduces the price of the aircraft as Piper saves some of the labour cost. It also helps to develop the local aviation industry.

Kits were delivered to Denmark in 1937 and 1939 for delivery throughout Europe.

Denmark KITS		
Model	Total	Serial Numbers
J-2	16	987, 993, 1155-1164, 1316--1319
J-3	24	1995-1998, 2475,2479-2482, 2485, 2486, 2491, 2492, 2503-2505, 2532-2535, 3157-3160
J-4	8	4-565, 4-566, 4-567, 4-568, 4-597, 4-598, 4-599, 4-600

From June 1936 until November 1941, kits were assembled by Cub Aircraft in Hamilton, Ontario, Canada. The factory was in the east part of the city, not at the airport. Part completed aircraft were trucked to the airport. The first eleven kits were shipped to Cub Aircraft without Taylor serial numbers and Cub aircraft put a C in front of the fuselage number to produce the s/n. After World War II the company became a division of Transvision Television (Canada) Ltd. Between November 1945 and 1947 (plus one more in 1952) Cub Aircraft built 150 J-3C-65 Cub Prospector aircraft from kits supplied by the Lock Haven factory. Cub Aircraft assigned their own serial numbers. The Cub Prospector had an enlarged baggage compartment; an auxiliary fuel tank may be installed increasing range.

Cub Aircraft KITS		
Model	Total	Serial Numbers
J-2	34	C838, C906, C909, C1005, C1006, C1080, C1082, C1083, C1089, C1091, C1092, C1100, C1103-C1124,
J-3	37	C1125-C1130, C2250, C2370, C2416, C2422, C2437, C2438, C2476, C2477, C2681, C2727, C2739, C3059, C3060, C3085, C3152, C3154, C3155, C3383-C3392, C7015-C7018
J-3C-65	150	101C-249C, C250

Kits were shipped to Argentina in 1941.

Argentina (1940s) KITS		
Model	Total	Serial Numbers
J-3	16	6862-6865, 7300-7303, 7728-7735

The completeness of the kit aircraft at Piper is referred to as one of eight phases, e.g. a kit completely assembled but unpainted and not test flown or certified is called 'Phase I' and a kit supplied in sub-assemblies and detail parts for the customer to assemble is called 'Phase VIII'.

View of the workforce at Cub Aircraft at Hamilton, Ontario in 1946 with Cub Prospector s/n 219C registration CF-EES in the background. (A. Casper)

Aerial view of the Cub facility in Denmark in the late 1930s. (The Cub Flier)

(CHINCUL) S.A.C.A.I.F.I. (ARGENTINA)

Chincul S.A.C.A.I.F.I. of Buenos Aires is a wholly owned subsidiary of La Marcarerra SA. It was formed in 1972 as the Piper Argentine distributor. The factory at San Juan is now shut down but they assembled 706 aircraft of 28 different types from kits produced by Piper there. (See below). In addition Chincul has built 11 Super Cub and 27 Pawnee aircraft without it being a kit sourced from Piper. Chincul assembled aircraft have an additional A (for Argentina) in the type, additional Chincul serial numbers (two ranges, one for Vero Beach models and another for Lock Haven / Lakeland models) and modified Piper serial numbers with an AR added (for Argentina), e.g. PA-A-28 registration LV-LJA s/n AR-0449 s/n AR28-7405167 and PA-A-38 registration LV-OOA s/n AR-0374 s/n AR38-80A0196. In a few minor cases the actual serial number has been changed by Chincul, e.g. Piper s/n 1809089 to 099 became AR1809001 to 011.

Chincul have also developed what was known as the Chincul Cherokee Arrow which was built for the Argentine armed forces training division in 1978. It was the PA-A-28R-260T Cherokee Arrow III with a 260 Lycoming AEIO-540 engine, side by side seating for two under a sliding canopy and a 7.62 mm gun. The prototype was s/n AR28-7703285 registration LV-X67 and was previously LV-MCS. The Air Force didn't want it, so was converted back to a Turbo Arrow III and registered LV-WCT and sold.

Chincul SPECIFICATION & PERFORMANCE	
SPECIFICATION	PA-A-28R-260T
Engine	260 hp Lycoming AEIO-540
Engine TBO (hrs)	
No of seats	2
Wing Span (ft/ins)	35/0
Length (ft/ins)	23/9.5
Height (ft/ins)	7/3.5
Useable fuel capacity (US gal)	
Gross weight (lbs)	2900
Empty weight (lbs)	1730
Useful load (lbs)	1170
Propeller	
Pressurization (psi)	
Floats available	
PERFORMANCE	
Max speed	195 mph
Cruise speed	180 mph @ 75%
Efficiency (gph)	
Stall speed - flaps / gear down	
Climb @ sea level (fpm)	780
Range with reserves	840 sm @ 75%
Service ceiling (ft)	13,000
Take off (Ground run)(ft)	744
Take off (over 50ft obst)(ft)	
Landing (Ground roll)(ft)	990
Landing (over 50ft obst)(ft)	

In early 1982 Aero Boero offered a modified PA-A-38-112 with dorsal fillet and speed pants. An example was s/n AR38-80A0131 registration LV-OHJ.

Chincul developed a two-seat Pawnee in 1985 with the second seat in the hopper area. The prototype was s/n AR25-8556002 registration LV-OHT. Two production examples were built for the Argentine Armed Forces s/n AR25-8056011 registration PG-433 and s/n AR25-8456012 registration PG-434.

Chincul also modified a PA-A-34 Seneca for an off-shore observer role and a PA-A-23-250 Aztec with wing pylons for rockets and bombs for the Argentine Army.

View of the Chincul factory at San Juan, Argentina. (via J. Taylor)

Cherokees being assembled by Chincul at San Juan. (Aerospace Publishing)

PA-A-28R-200 s/n AR28R-7535149 registration LV-LXU at San Juan. (Chincul)

PA-A-28R-260T s/n AR28R-7703285 registration LV-X67. (via J. Taylor)

PA-A-31-350 s/n AR31-7405490 registration LV-LSC at San Juan. (via J. Taylor)

Chincul and Embraer agreed on the 17th of May 1989 to jointly produce and market Piper aircraft in Argentina and Brazil. According to the agreement, Embraer would produce at Neiva the EMB-720D and the EMB-810D. Chincul would produce the PA-A-18-115 and -150, PA-A-28-161, PA-A-28-181, PA-A-28-236, PA-A-28RT-201 and -201T, PA-A-25-235 and -260, PA-A-36-375, PA-A-31-350, PA-A-31T and PA-A-42.

Chincul KITS

Model	Total	Serial Numbers
PA-A-23-250	17	AR27-7305220, 221 AR27-7405371, 377, 388, 398, 438, 447, 451, 455 AR27-7554104 AR27-7654022, 031, 153 AR27-7754163 AR27-7854057, 102
PA-A-25-235 / 260	135	AR25-7305528, 530, 532 AR25-7405591, 596, 613, 620, 631, 642, 652, 658, 662, 672, 679, 686, 694, 698, 708, 714, 716 AR25-7556030, 035, 040, 045, 065, 067, 069, 071, 090, 095, 100, 105, 110, 115, 120, 125, 135, 140, 145, 150, 226-230 AR25-7656078, 091 AR25-7756072-095 AR25-7856001-004, 006, 008, 010, 012, 016, 018, 020, 022, 032, 034, 036, 038, 043, 045, 047, 049, 055, 057, 063, 065-067, 069, 071 AR25-7956004, 006, 009-012, 014, 016, 019, 020, 022, 025, 027, 029, 031, 033, 036, 038, 041, 042 AR25-8056004, 005, 008, 009, 011, 013, 016, 018, 021, 022, 026, 028, 041, 043, 046, 048
PA-A-28-180	22	AR28-7305315, 316, 480, 499 AR28-7405136-139, 158, 160, 161, 167, 184-187 AR28-7505138, 148, 168, 169, 189, 260
PA-A-28-181	50	AR28-7790571, 605 AR28-7890185, 351, 352, 406, 407, 463, 464, 480, 481, 507, 508, 534 AR28-8090203, 243, 274, 349 AR28-8190032, 098, 099, 174, 175, 200, 201, 261, 262, 317, 318 AR28-8290020-022, 122-125, 146-149 AR28-8390057-060 AR28-8690061-062 AR2890035, 036, 168, 169
PA-A-28-140	64	AR28-7225490-499 AR28-7325238, 371-379, 508, 516, 525, 526, 555-558, 580, 581, 599, 600 AR28-7425217, 222, 224, 271-279, 304-307 AR28-7525142, 144, 177, 197, 201, 215-218, 230, 243, 244, 246, 247 AR28-7625272, 273
PA-A-28-161	12	AR2816006, 007, 020-022, 034-036, 047, 048, 095, 096
PA-A-28-235	8	AR28-7310152, 153 AR28-7410074, 078 AR28-7510072, 073 AR28-7710068, 089
PA-A-28-236	15	AR28-7911027 AR28-8011062, 095, 107 AR28-8111030, 038, 070 AR28-8411021-024, 026-029
PA-A-28R-200	17	AR28R-7335201, 202, 326, 328, 395, 397 AR28R-7435214, 229, 252, 253 AR28R-7535146, 149, 167, 168, 214, 217 AR28R-7635377
PA-A-28R-201	19	AR28R-7737119 AR28R-7837076, 148, 149, 188, 189, 225, 226, 248, 249, 273, 274, 294, 316, 317 AR2837046-049

PA-A-28R-201T	18	AR28R-7703285 AR28R-7803064, 207, 208, 251, 291-293, 299, 300, 317, 318, 344, 370, 371 AR2803013-015
PA-A-28RT-201	5	AR28R-8118029, 054, 078 AR28R-8218015, 016
PA-28RT-201T	3	AR28R-8131029, 083, 183
PA-A-31 / PA-A-31-325	11	AR31-856 AR31-7400991 AR31-7512002, 026 AR31-7812011, 053, 070, 080, 101, 122 AR31-8012067
PA-A-31-350	13	AR31-7405218, 238, 485, 490 AR31-7552043, 076 AR31-7652144 AR31-7852014, 042, 110, 133 AR31-8052009, 083
PA-A-31P	5	AR31P-7400211, 213, 219, 230 AR31P-7530016
PA-A-31T	11	AR31T-7920017, 031, 033, 050, 080, 085 AR31T-8020013, 028, 054, 079, 092
PA-A-31T1	1	AR31T-7904045
PA-A-32-300	15	AR32-7240120, 123, 126, 129, 132 AR32-7340133, 155, 159, 160, 172 AR32-7540114, 136 AR32-7640127 AR32-7740100 AR32-7840028
PA-A-32R-300	6	AR32R-7680409, 410 AR32R-7780520 AR32R-7880058, 067, 068
PA-A-32RT-300	16	AR32R-7885027, 099, 100, 176, 177, 213-215, 234-237, 259, 260, 285 AR32R-7985027
PA-A-32RT-300T	2	AR32R-7887222 AR32R-7987050
PA-A-34-200	5	AR34-7350283, 299, 300 AR34-7450162, 187
PA-A-34-200T	23	AR34-7570074, 136 AR34-7670071, 072, 312 AR34-7770357 AR34-7870069, 133, 174, 212, 213, 252, 313, 314, 367, 410, 411, 443, 473, 474 AR34-7970021, 051 AR34-8070132
PA-A-34-220T	10	AR34-8133039, 083, 129, 169, 208, 244 AR34-8433084, 088 AR3433188, 189
PA-A-36-300	33	AR36-7860095-098, 102-105, 109, 111, 112, 122, 123 AR36-7960001, 010-019 AR36-8060002, 003, 007, 010, 015, 020-023
PA-A-36-375	13	AR36-7802050, 074 AR36-7902048-051 AR36-7802005, 006, 011, 013, 016, 018, 025
PA-A-38-112	157	AR38-78A0344, 358, 424, 439, 624, 639, 734, 749, 829, 844 AR38-79A0058, 088, 114, 156, 221, 236, 271, 301 AR38-79A1042, 1051, 1056, 1061, 1115, 1117, 1122, 1126, 1158, 1162, 1165, 1168 AR38-80A0015, 019, 022, 025, 035, 038-051, 054, 056, 057, 060, 063, 077, 080, 083, 086, 104, 113, 120, 123-165, 169-198 AR38-81A0136-138, 191-210
Total	706	

Chincul build		
Model	Total	Serial Numbers
PA-A-18	11	AR18-8009001-011
PA-A-25	6	AR25-8556001-006
PA-A-25	5	AR25-8656001-005
PA-A-25	16	AR2556006-021
Total	38	

Two seat PA-A-25 s/n AR25-8556002 registration LV-OHT at San Juan. (via J. Taylor)

PA-A-38-112 s/n AR38-80A0131 registration LV-OHJ with Aero Boero modifications. (via J. Taylor)

EMBRAER (BRAZIL)

On the 19th of August 1974 Piper made an agreement with Embraer to assemble Piper aircraft in Brazil. Initially Embraer built aircraft from knocked down kits but after a year all aircraft were built from either sub-assemblies or piece parts manufactured by Piper. All the Embraer aircraft carry new Embraer serial numbers and Piper also assign a Piper serial number to all the aircraft sets sent to Embraer. Initially 6 types were built, a seventh was added in 1979.

The first aircraft of each of the 7 types were as follows:

Embraer type	Embraer s/n	Piper type	Piper s/n	Registration	Date Registered
710 Carioca	710001	Cherokee 235	28-7510051	PT-NAB	Sept ember 1975
711 Corisco	711001	Cherokee Arrow	28R-7535143	PT-NAA	August 1975
712 Tupi (also Carioquinha)	712001	Archer II	28-7890061	PT-NRG	November 1979
720 Minuano	720001	Cherokee Six 300	32-7540112	PT-EAC	September 1975
721 Sertanejo	721001	Cherokee Lance	32R-7680011	PT-EBK	June 1976
810 Seneca	810001	Seneca II	34-7570099	PT-EAA	July 1975
820 Navajo	820001	Navajo Chieftain	31-7552080	PT-EBN	July 1976

Embraer wanted Piper to market their EMB-110 Bandeirante turboprop commuter airliner in 1974. Piper declined.

All construction of Piper aircraft in Brazil was transferred from Sao Jose dos Campos to Neiva, a subsidiary of Embraer at Botucatu in mid 1983.

In 1984 Neiva agreed with Schafer for Neiva to convert 50 Embraer 820 Navajos into the NE 821 Caraja (the Schafer Comanchero 500B conversion) with Pratt and Whitney 578 shp PT6A-27 engines. First flight of the first conversion was on the 9th of March 1984 and was registered PT-ZNA (previously PT-RGV) with s/n 820136.

By May 1992, 2370 kits had been supplied to Embraer. Unfortunately due to both Piper's and Embraer's cash flow problems, delivery of kits and assembly stopped. In the last two years only the Saratoga and Seneca III were built. Data is correct according to Piper, but it appears that either Piper shipped more kits in 1991 than they recorded or Neiva assembled some from other sources. Piper shows that the last Saratoga delivered was s/n 3206088 (= Embraer s/n 720289) and the last Seneca III was s/n 3433229 (= Embraer s/n 810799). Neiva certifications ended with s/n 720291 registration PT-VPO and s/n 810846 registration PT-VSC.

PA-28RT-201T phase III kits s/n 2831009, 2831010 and 2831011 for Embraer at Vero Beach. (R.W. Peperell)

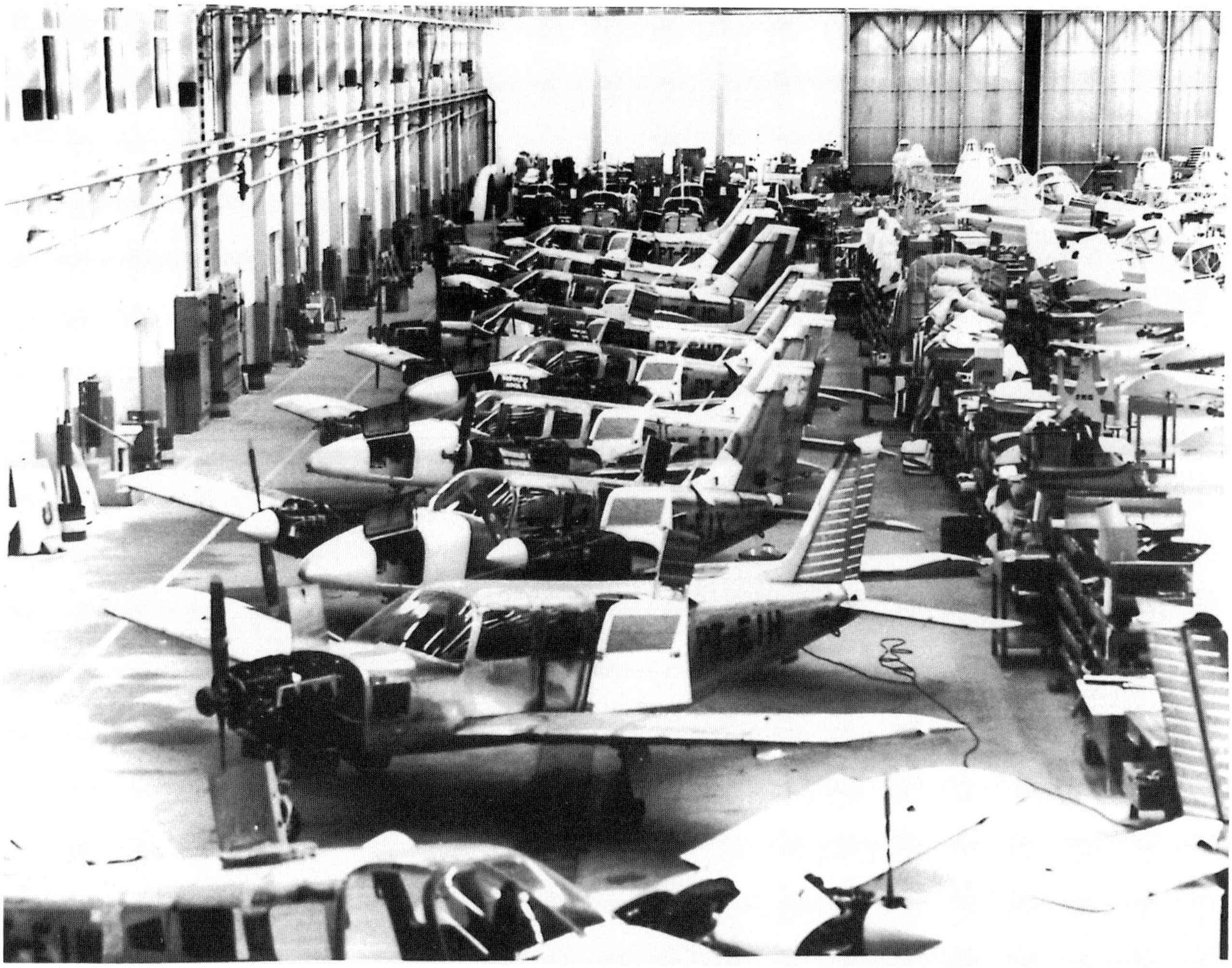

Embraer EMB-720 / 721 / 810 production line at Sao Jose dos Campos, Brazil. Sertanejo s/n 721048 registration PT-EIH is near the front followed by Seneca s/n 810083 registration PT-EIX. (Aerospace Publishing)

Embraer EMB-710C Carioca s/n 710003 registration PT-NAE. (Aerospace Publishing)

Embraer EMB-711C Corisco s/n 711016 registration PT-NBK. (Aerospace Publishing)

Embraer EMB-712 Tupi s/n 712109 registration PT-RXB. (Embraer)

Embraer EMB-720C Minuano s/n 720019 registration PT-EBX. (Aerospace Publishing)

PRODUCTION DETAILS				
Embraer type	Piper type	Built by	Embraer Serial numbers From	To
EMB-710C Carioca	PA-28-235	Neiva	710001	710264
EMB-710D Carioca	PA-28-236	Neiva	710265	710288
EMB-711C Corisco	PA-28R-200 II	Neiva	711001	711219
EMB-711B Corisco	PA-28R-201 III *	Neiva	711220	711251
EMB-711S Corisco II	PA-28RT-201 IV	Neiva	711252	711443
EMB-711ST Corisco II	PA-28RT-201T IV	Neiva	711252	711477
EMB-712 Tupi	PA-28-181	Neiva	712001	712145
EMB-720C Minuano	PA-32-300	Embraer	720001	720126
EMB-720D Minuano	PA-32-301	Embraer	720127	720291 **
EMB-721C Sertanejo	PA-32R-300 *	Embraer	721001	721150
EMB-721D Sertanejo	PA-32R-301	Embraer	721151	721205
EMB-810C Seneca	PA-34-200T II	Embraer	810001	810452
EMB-810D Seneca III	PA-34-220T III	Embraer	810453	810846 **
EMB-820 Navajo	PA-31-350	Embraer	820001	820168

* Embraer s/n 711250 and 711251 are Piper type PA-28-235
Embraer s/n 721149 and 721150 are Piper type PA-32RT-300

** Piper shipped to the equivalent of 720289 and 810799

Embraer EMB-721C Sertanejo s/n 721004 registration PT-ECX. (Aerospace Publishing)

Embraer KITS

Model	Total	Serial Numbers
PA-28-181	145	28-7890061, 062, 182-184, 239-241, 287-289, 353-355, 404, 405 28-7990249, 250, 307, 308, 358, 359, 413, 414, 464, 465, 522, 523, 571, 572 28-8090018, 019, 088, 089, 138, 139, 170, 171, 201, 202, 208, 209, 239-242, 270-273, 303-310, 335-348, 350-352, 356-358 28-8190007-012, 028-031, 067-070, 094-097, 118-121, 144-147, 176-178, 197-199, 230-232 28-8590033, 034, 071, 072, 084, 085 28-8690007, 008, 027, 028, 040, 041 2890018, 019, 023-025, 037-048, 057-059
PA-28-235	266	28-7510051-056, 059, 060, 062, 064, 066, 067, 069, 071, 076-084, 096-107, 112-135 28-7610003-014, 021-032, 038-044, 049-061, 067-072, 080-083, 090-094, 099-103, 111-117, 123-135, 141-150, 153-167, 169-202 28-7710003-009, 011-017, 024-030, 034-040, 047-054, 057-064, 069-088
PA-28-236	24	28-8011120, 121, 128, 129, 134, 135, 138, 139 28-8111008, 017, 028, 029, 036, 037, 057, 059, 066, 067, 078, 079, 085, 086, 093, 094
PA-28R-200	219	28R-7535143, 144, 175-178, 185, 193, 196, 203, 240, 242, 245, 246, 250, 252, 292-296, 332-337, 372-377 28R-7635023-028, 058-063, 082-084, 104-109, 135-137, 139-143, 167-169, 171-175, 199-206, 237-242, 274-281, 305-314, 343-352, 378-389, 419-430, 463-545
PA-28R-201	30	28R-7737120-122, 143-148, 174-178 28R-7837009-011, 030-037, 146, 147, 185-187
PA-28RT-201	44	28R-7918148-151, 189-191, 224-226, 243-245, 255-257 28R-8018010-012, 051-054, 071-074, 082-084, 096, 097, 105, 106 28R-8118015, 070, 071, 075-077, 079-082
PA-28RT-201T	182	28R-8031026-028, 037-039, 043-045, 058-061, 078-081, 097-100, 118-122, 134-137, 139-144, 157-162, 174-176 28R-8131011-014, 030-034, 046-050, 065-069, 084-094, 101-111, 124-134, 148-158, 173-182, 196-206 28R-8231070-080 28R-8331003-006, 008, 009, 020, 021 2831002-035
PA-31-350	167	31-7552080, 085, 090, 093, 100, 104, 112, 117, 120, 122, 125, 127, 129 31-7652005, 008, 011, 013, 015, 018, 021, 024-027, 029, 031, 034, 036, 038, 040, 042, 045, 047, 050, 052, 054, 060, 063, 066, 069, 085, 089, 092, 096, 103, 106, 108, 111, 113, 116, 118, 121, 123, 126, 128, 131, 136, 138, 140, 143, 146, 149, 152, 155, 158, 160, 161, 177 31-7752003, 007, 010, 014, 017-026, 037, 039, 041, 043, 051, 053, 055, 057, 067, 069, 071, 073, 082, 084, 086, 088, 098, 100, 102, 104, 115, 116, 132, 133, 155-158, 177-179, 191, 192 31-7952093, 116, 130, 144, 163, 164, 176-178, 211, 212, 236-238 31-8052015, 016, 041-043, 080-082, 099-101, 132, 133, 150, 151, 156-158, 187, 188, 190-192, 201, 209-211, 213-216, 220, 221 31-8152021-023, 052, 064
PA-32-300	126	32-7540112, 113, 125, 127, 128, 137-139, 156-159, 174-177, 185-188 32-7640013-015, 027-029, 036-038, 046-048, 054-056, 067-069, 077, 083, 091, 092, 096, 097, 102, 103, 110, 111, 119, 120, 128-130 32-7740009-011, 018-021, 028-030, 040-042, 051-053, 057-059, 067-069, 078-080, 089-091, 101-103 32-7840005, 006, 016, 017, 041, 042 32-7940048-050, 075-077, 107-109, 138-140, 173-175, 208-210, 237-239, 255-257, 260-262, 265-267, 281-283, 288-290
PA-32-301	163	32-8006007-009, 019-021, 033-036, 054-057, 067-070, 082-089, 100-106 32-8106012, 013, 023, 024, 032-034, 044, 045, 052, 053, 059-061, 071, 072, 081, 082, 091, 092

		32-8306011, 012, 014, 015 32-8506002, 003, 005, 006, 008, 009, 011, 012, 014, 015, 018-021 32-8506002-017, 020-023 3206001, 002, 006-010, 012, 013, 015-041, 045, 046, 048, 049, 056-059, 061-088
PA-32R-300	148	32R-7680011, 012, 049-053, 085-089, 125-130, 163-167, 212-218, 265-270, 312-317, 364-369, 411-416, 463-468, 513-519, 32R-7780041-047, 089-094, 130-136, 180-186, 227-232, 282-291, 337-343, 394-401, 452-458, 498-505, 540-543 32R-7880034-036, 056
PA-32RT-300	2	32R-7885257, 258
PA-32R-301	55	32R-8013057, 058, 076, 077, 096-099, 110-119, 124-127, 129-131, 137-139 32R-8113009-011, 021-023, 031-033, 041-043, 053, 054, 062, 063, 073-076, 089-091, 106 109
PA-34-200T	452	34-7570099-101, 137-139, 177, 180, 185, 203, 205, 209, 211, 256-259, 293-296, 324-327 34-7670031-034, 056-059, 091-094, 115-118, 143-146, 171-175, 200-203, 227-232, 252-260, 284-292, 313-321, 344-352, 363-371 34-7770038-046, 071-079, 103-111, 138-146, 170-177, 207-216, 243-251, 279-287, 317-325, 358-366, 407-411, 436-441 34-7870030-033, 067, 068, 134-138, 175, 176, 253-256, 309-312, 363-366, 406-409, 439-442, 469-472 34-7970018-020, 049, 050, 080-086, 123-130, 164, 165, 202-204, 248-253, 303-313, 363-373, 408-419, 459-471, 505-508, 510, 511 34-8070039-044, 066-071, 090-095, 124-131, 158-165, 193-201, 236-249, 270-275, 291-297, 310-313, 317-327, 343-350 34-8170004-011, 035-040, 060-065, 077-082, 086-088, 090-092
PA-34-220T	347	34-8133080-082, 121-124, 163-168, 202-207 34-8233102-105, 125-128, 154-157, 181-184, 188-195, 200-203 34-8333010-013, 022-025, 038-041, 044-047, 049-052, 064-067, 077-080, 100-103, 117-120, 125-129 34-8433003, 004, 008, 009, 027, 028, 052-054, 064-066, 070-074, 076-082, 085-087 34-8533004-006, 010-012, 021-023, 026-028, 031-033, 037-040, 042-054, 058-060, 064-069 34-8633002-013, 015-017, 019-021, 023-031 3433002-012, 016-019, 022-025, 029-036, 045-052, 057-088, 092-101, 103-110, 116-119, 124-127, 134, 135, 141-144, 147-150, 162-167, 173-187, 190-229
Total	2370	

Embraer EMB-810C Seneca s/n 810004 registration PT-EAE. (Aerospace Publishing)

Embraer EMB-820C Navajo s/n 820004 registration PT-EBT. (Aerospace Publishing)

Neiva NE 821 Caraja s/n 820136 registration PT-ZNA. (Embraer)

PEZETEL (POLAND)

At the end of 1976 Piper made an agreement with Pezetel of Mielex, Poland for them to produce 400 Seneca aircraft from kits with 220 hp PZL engines (Franklin) to be sold in the Eastern European countries. A PZL M.20.00 Mewa (Gull), registration SP-GKA (registered the 5th of August 1976) was shown at the 1977 Paris Air Show with its original s/n 34-7670279 and 200 hp PZL (Franklin) engines. Others known to be air delivered to PZL were s/n 34-7670121 which was registered SP-NBA on the 10th of February 1976 and s/n 34-7870199 registered SP-DKC on the 17th of April 1978. Four kits were delivered to PZL in 1978 and 1979. The first PZL built aircraft s/n 1AHP01-01 registration SP-PKA first flew on the 25th of July 1979. Five more kits were delivered in 1980. The first M.20.01 Mewa built by PZL was s/n 1AH002-02 registration SP-PKE first flew on the 22nd of September 1982. The Polish type certificate was granted on the 22nd of September 1983. In 1985 PZL developed the M.20.02 Mewa with 220 hp PZL-F6A-350C engines and Polish equipment. The prototype s/n 1AHP01-01 re-registered SP-DMA first flew on the 10th of October 1985. Unfortunately production versions of the PZL-F engine were not available so PZL reverted to the 220 hp TCM engines. The M.20.02 was dropped. This then became the M.20.03 with 220 hp TCM engines, increased gross weight and 28 volt electrics. The prototype was the same SP-DMA and first flew on the 13th of October 1988. Production was underway in 1995 and was marketed as the Gemini in Germany, Austria and South Africa. In 1995 PZL were developing the M.20.04 with a strengthened spar and wing allowing a gross weight increase to 4753 pounds. All PZL built M.20 Mewa aircraft carry new serial numbers.

PZL have also produced a Seneca derived two seat Military trainer with a single 205 hp PZL 6A-350CI engine named the PZL M.26 Iskierka (Little Spark). The prototype was s/n 1APP01-01 registration SP-PIA and first flew on the 18th of July 1986. The M.26 was later re-engined with a 260 hp Lycoming and was being promoted to the civilian market in the U.S.A.

After the Pocono prototype was sold to Pezetel at the end of 1976, Piper and Pezetel worked on a turbine powered commuter aircraft in early 1979 under the name 333P. This was a 30 seater aircraft to be built by Pezetel with components to be supplied by Piper. It was to be powered by Pratt & Whitney PT6 engines. The wing span was to be 64 feet, the length 56 feet and the height 19 feet. It never left the drawing board.

In February 1991, Piper signed an agreement with PZL for them to build any Piper model from kits similar to Piper's agreements with Chincul and Embraer.

Pezetel KITS

Model	Total	Serial Numbers
PA-34-200T	9	34-7870157, 217 34-7970087, 088 34-8070276-280
Total	9	

Pezetel serial numbers

Model	Total	Serial Numbers
M.20.00	4	1AHP01-01 to -04
M.20.01	5	1AH002-02 to - 06
M.20.03	11	1AH002-07 to -17
Total	20	

Pezetel M-20 Mewa s/n IAHP01-01 registration SP-DMA at the Farnborough Air Show. (C. Chatfield)

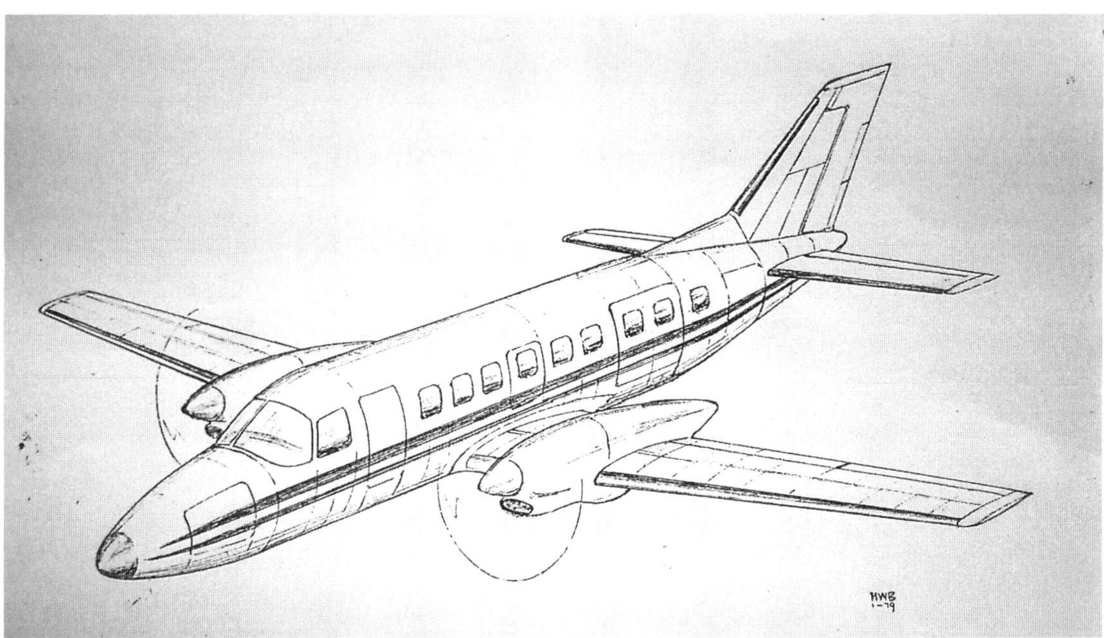

Drawing of the proposed Pezetel 333P commuter. (H.W. Barnhouse)

AERO SALFA (CHILE)

Aero Salfa were the distributors for Piper aircraft in Chile. In 1981 Piper supplied 3 kit aircraft of 3 different types for them to assemble.

Aero Salfa KITS		
Model	Total	Serial Numbers
PA-18-150	1	18-8109023
PA-28-181	1	28-8190122
PA-28-161	1	28-8116108
Total	3	

ENAER (CHILE)

Empressa Nacional de Aeronautica (ENAER) of El Bosque, Santiago, Chile assemble aircraft from kits produced by Piper. In 1980 they started assembling Dakota aircraft for the Chile Air Force training division. A pattern aircraft was delivered in 1979, s/n 28-7911177 registration N29365 and it became FaCh215. Twenty four aircraft were assembled with Chile Air Force markings FaCh216 to FaCh239.

ENAER assemble the PA-28R-300 kits which, after assembly, became the T-35 Pillan with new ENAER serial numbers consisting of the unit number built starting at 100 followed by the year assembled. Known examples are s/n 10081 through to 18688.

In late 1985 ENAER developed a turboprop version of the Pillan named the T-35TX Aucan. Pillan CC-EFS was converted by Soloy, Olympia, Washington in early 1986 and it was re-registered CC-PZC. It first flew on the 14th February. It had a 420 shp Allison 250B-17D engine giving it much improved maximum and cruise speed, climb and service ceiling over the Pillan. In 1989 Piper marketed the Pillan in the USA, but no sales resulted from this. Aircraft s/n 18688 registration CC-PZG was based at Vero Beach for this. Later this aircraft was also converted with a 420 shp Allison 250B-17D engine and a new canopy and first flew in March 1991. This was designated the T-35DT and was evaluated by ENAER until 1994.

ENAER developed a single seat version of the Pillan. The T-35S prototype was s/n 10182 converted from CC-EFP and re-registered CC-PZB. This first flew with a 300 hp Lycoming IO-540-K1K5 engine on the 5th of March 1988. They were planning two production versions, one with the 300 hp Lycoming and the other with the 420 shp Allison 250B-17 engine.

ENAER KITS

Model	Total	Serial Numbers
PA-28-236	24	28-8011063, 077, 132, 133, 146, 147-151 28-81111039, 040, 089-092 28-8211037-040, 046-049
PA-28R-300	120	28R-8319001-035, 28R-2219036-120
Total	144	

ENAER T-35 production line at Santiago, Chile. (G.K. Gates)

ENAER T-35TX s/n 10484 registration CC-PZC. (ENAER)

ENAER T-35DT s/n 18688 registration CC-PZG at the Farnborough Air Show. (J.M. Gradidge)

ENAER T-35S s/n 10182 registration CC-PZB. (via G.K. Gates)

View of the Aero Mercantile assembly line at Guaymaral, Columbia. The PA-34-220T Seneca III is s/n 34-8133262 registration HK-2780-X. (Piper Aircraft Corporation)

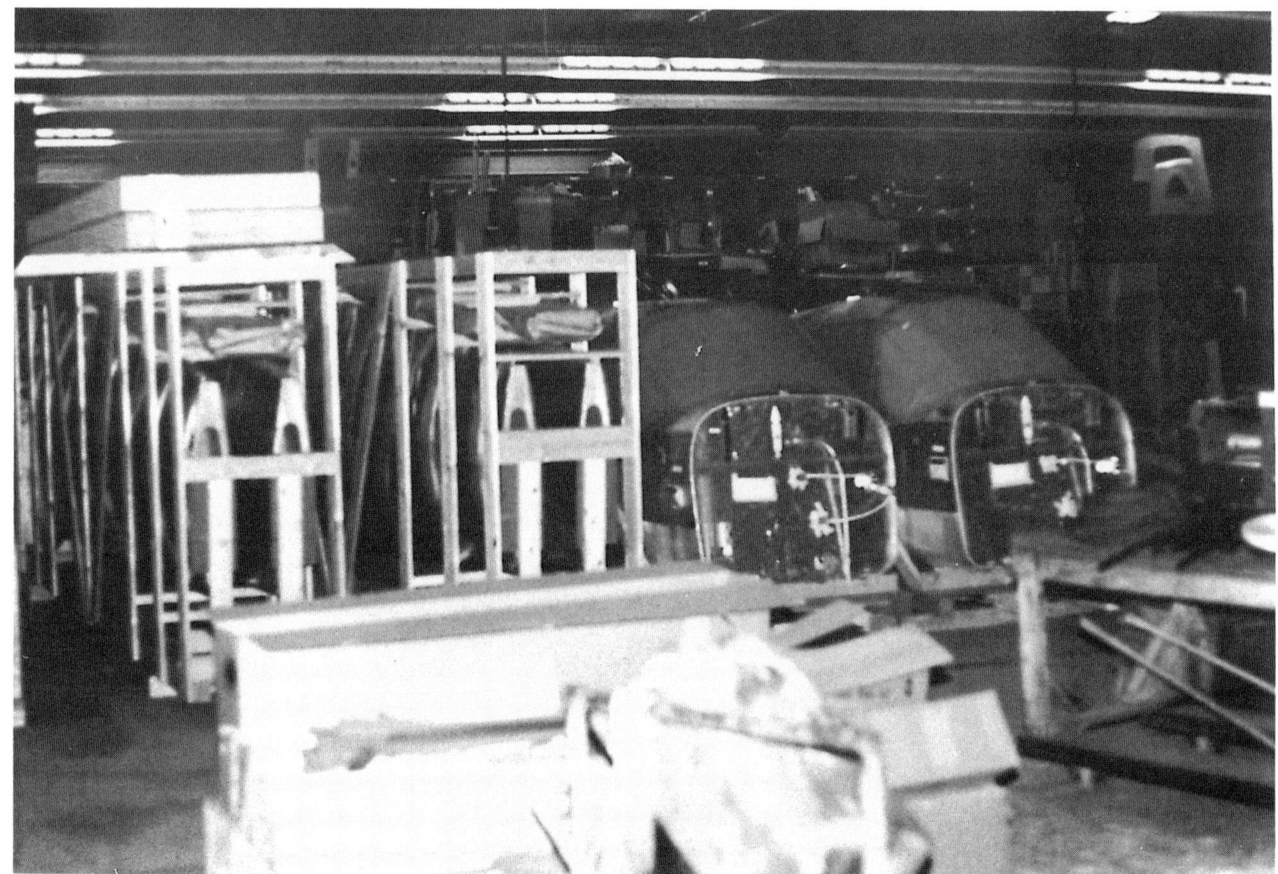

PA-28-161 kits s/n 2816091 and 2816092 for Aero Mercantile at Vero Beach. (R.W. Peperell)

AERO MERCANTILE (COLUMBIA)

In 1968 Aero Industrial Columbiana SA (AICSA) of Guaymaral, Bogata, Columbia was established to assemble Piper aircraft from kits. The Columbian Air Force owned 51% and the Industrial Development Agency of Columbia owned 49%. Aero Mercantile were the distributors for Piper aircraft in Colombia and as far as Piper were concerned they are the customers for the kits. By May 1992 Piper had supplied 491 kit aircraft of 36 different types. Unfortunately due to Pipers cash problems delivery of kits and assembly had to stop. Unlike Chincul, the Aero Mercantile assembled aircraft keep their Piper type and serial number.

Aero Mercantile KITS

Model	Total	Serial Numbers
PA-23-250	1	27-7405396
PA-25-235 / 260	57	25-4894, 25-5027, 5030, 5033, 5057, 5066, 5069, 5072, 5075, 5097, 5100, 5102, 5106, 5269, 5271, 5273, 5275, 5284-5293, 5315, 5316, 5318, 5320, 5454, 5455, 5456, 5457 25-7405690, 5692, 5696, 5701, 5704-5706 25-7556050, 052,057,062,073, 075, 077, 080, 153, 159, 162, 166, 231-233
PA-28-180	8	28-5047,5178, 5262, 5397, 5435 28-7405223 28-7505159,179
PA-28-181	21	28-7690044,361,362 28-7790056, 111, 343, 344, 388, 533 28-7890060, 290, 465, 466, 509, 510, 550, 551 28-7990158, 251 28-8390031, 032
PA-28-140	16	28-24660, 24701 28-7425383, 384 28-7525180, 181, 182, 238 28-7625060, 061, 130, 144, 274, 275 28-7725053, 188
PA-28-161	9	28-7816330 28-7916235 28-8016266 28-8116157, 158 28-8316031, 032 2816091, 092
PA-28-235	20	28-11077, 11101, 11140, 11180, 11200, 11212, 11227, 11254, 11255, 11370-373 28-7310074, 172 28-7410089, 090 28-7610087, 168 28-7710033
PA-28-236	16	28-7911028-030, 136, 219-221, 252 28-8011020, 021, 092-094 28-8111058, 068, 069
PA-28-201T	1	28-7921085
PA-28R-180	5	28R-30861, 30952, 30972, 31043, 31091
PA-28R-200	2	28R-7335377, 387
PA-28R-201T	14	28R-7703069, 132, 184, 185, 382 28R-7803156, 294, 295, 319, 320, 360, 361, 372, 373
PA-28RT-201T	7	28R-7931122, 205, 206, 262, 296, 297 28R-8031062
PA-30	1	30-1728
PA-31/ PA-31-325	23	31-7812116 31-8012045, 056, 071, 083, 089, 101, 102 31-8112037, 044, 052, 061, 072, 073, 077 31-8212023, 024, 028, 029, 034, 036 31-8312002, 007

PA-31-350	33	31-7552073 31-7652099 31-7852081, 123, 169 31-7952067, 140, 184, 231 31-8052145, 217-219 31-8152067, 068, 122, 123, 144, 145, 201-203 31-8252024, 037, 046, 058, 070, 071, 084, 085 31-8352002, 003, 036
PA-31T	11	31T-7920076 31T-8020040, 047, 077 31T-8120015, 032, 037, 047, 051, 062, 064
PA-31T2	4	31T-8166019, 035, 053, 073
PA-32-300	19	32-40491, 40503, 40518, 40532, 40544, 40545, 40746, 40965, 40966, 40968-974 32-7440144 32-7940141, 240
PA-32-301	3	32-8006090 32-8106043 3206005
PA-32-301T	11	32-8024031, 032 32-8124011, 017, 018, 035, 036 32-8224011, 013, 014 32-8324006
PA-32R-300	1	32R-7880057
PA-32RT-300T	4	32R-7887036, 081 32R-7987085, 122
PA-32R-301T	4	32R-8029121 32R-8129041 32R-8229065 32R-8329017
PA-34-200	1	34-7450211
PA-34-200T	65	34-7570193, 292 34-7670045, 168, 261 34-7770037, 137, 206, 288, 316, 367, 368, 406 34-7870098, 171-173, 214-216, 257, 258, 368, 369, 444-446 34-7970052-054, 131-133, 205-207, 374-376, 472-475, 512-514 34-8070045, 096-099, 202-205, 298-301 34-8170012-015
PA-34-220T	71	34-8133125-128, 209-212, 240-243, 261-264 34-8233129-132, 158-161, 196-199 34-8333014-017, 034-037, 081-084, 121-124 34-8433010-013, 042-045 34-8533014-017 34-8633018 3433013-015, 026-028, 039, 040, 053-056, 145, 146
PA-36-285	11	36-7360050 36-7460011-015 36-7560088 36-7660085, 088, 091, 094
PA-36-300	29	36-7760018, 034, 047, 051, 055, 120, 121, 123, 125, 129, 132 36-7860010-012, 043, 045, 047, 049-051, 069, 071, 073, 089-094
PA-36-375	13	36-7802034, 061-063 36-7902001-003, 020, 022, 024, 033, 035, 037
PA-38-112	5	38-78A0464 38-79A0699, 713, 1131, 1134
PA-42	1	42-8001059
PA-42-1000	1	42-5527037
PA-44-180	2	44-7995235, 298
Aerostar 602P	1	62P-0916-8165041
Total	491	

AEROSPATIALE

On the 1st of June 1971 Piper announced an agreement with Societe Nationale Industrielle Aerospatiale of France to include Cherokee production at Tarbes. Two PA-28-140 kits were assembled there in December 1972 and were subsequently sold through Piper International at Geneva. Piper with the help of Fairchild looked at the ST60 Rallye 7-300 for possible manufacture in the U.S. Piper test flew aircraft F-ZWRR at Tarbes, France on the 22nd September 1971. In the 1970s Aerospatiale promoted the MS.884 Rallye Minerva with a 235 hp Franklin 4A-235 engine for manufacture in the U.S. for the American market. Piper tested aircraft s/n 888 registration N991WA in 1973. The complete agreement eventually fell through.

Aerospatiale KITS

Model	Total	Serial Numbers
PA-28-140	2	28-7225118, 130
Total	2	

VENEZUELA

In June 1975 Piper proposed to Venezuelan officials that they locally assemble certain Piper aircraft from kits and develop the aviation industry in Venezuela. Production of PA-31T, PA-31-350, PA-28R-200 and PA-36 aircraft was proposed, up to 150 a year in total starting in late 1975. To support this Piper would help Venezuela establish the factory, production organisation and provide training for personnel to assemble the aircraft from kits. In addition Piper proposed allowing Venezuela to manufacture the UX-1 utility aircraft (the Cargo Brave) for the South American market. The UX-1 programme schedule indicated prototype first flight at Lakeland (even though the design was initiated at Lock Haven) in September 1976 and production starting in 1978. The Venezuelan government, the local Piper dealer and Piper were unable to agree terms nor afford the start up costs, so Piper continued to build and deliver aircraft from the U.S. for Venezuela.

Aerospatiale ST60 Rallye 7-300 s/n 2 registration F-ZWRR. (Aerospace Publishing)

Aerospatiale MS.884 Rallye Minerva s/n 888 registration N991WA. (R.W. Simpson)

16
KIT, HOME BUILT AND CONVERSIONS

Wag-Aero of Lyons, Wisconsin

Drawings and kits are supplied by Wag-Aero to the home builder to enable reproduction early Piper aircraft to be built. By 1986 more than 2000 plans / kits had been sold. The first design was the Wag-Aero Sport Trainer (J3) and the first one flew in March 1975. Four versions of the J3 replica are available; Sport Trainer, Aero Trainer (clipped wing), Observer (L-4) and Super Sport (structural modifications). The Wag-a-bond (PA-15) is available as the Classic or Traveller (updated with two doors, skylight window)). The first one was produced in May 1978. The 2+2 Sportsman (PA-14) is also available.

Some examples of each type are:

Type	Registration	Serial number
Wag-Aero Cuby	N818W	513
Cuby Sport Trainer	N3WA	1
Cuby PA-11	N99615	HCB-2
PA-14-R	C-GCSZ	001
Super Cuby	N82DH	1101
Cuby L-21B-135	N90293	690
Wagabond	C-GGDG	093
Cuby J-3	C-GDCY	997
Wag Chubby Cuby	N65WA	1
Wagabond Traveller	N36GM	GM-2
Wagaero 2+2 Sportsman	N200DM	73
Wagaero Super Canadian	C-GDPR	008

McHolland XPA-11

The McHolland XPA-11 is based on the 1947 PA-11 drawings, usually with all new components made to the Piper drawings and some composite materials also used. The engine is a Continental C-85-12F. The wing span was increased to 35 feet 6 inches and the gross weight increased to 1300 lbs and empty weight to 846 lbs. The prototype was s/n 1 registration N11XP.

Wagaero Sport Trainer (L-4) s/n PFA108-12647 U.S. Army serial 39624 (G-BVMH) at Cranfield, England. (R.W. Peperell)

McHolland XPA-11 s/n 1 registration N11XP at Oshkosh. (J.M. Gradidge)

Bagimer II (converted L-4) s/n 01 registration F-PFAR. (via J. Taylor)

Poullin PJ.5A (converted J-3) s/n 1 registration F-PDVD. (J.M. Gradidge)

Rhone et Sudest (converted L-4) s/n 1 registration F-PERB. (J.M. Gradidge)

MDC Trailer (converted Cub) s/n MDC-1038 registration HB-RAL. (J.M. Gradidge)

P.A.T. 1 s/n 1 registration N15PT at Oshkosh. (J.M. Gradidge)

VK100TP (with the extended fuselage) s/n 1 registration N100VK. (H. Van Kesteren)

VK100TP (with fuselage plug removed) s/n 1 registration N100VK at St. Petersburg, Florida. (R.W. Peperell)

Other conversions

Examples of other Piper types registered in the Home-built / Experimental category:

Type	Registration	Serial number
Super Cruiser	N84MS	621B
Super Cub	N2769D	1
J-3 Trainer	N1391P	1
Clipped-wing Cub	N23CK	DM3
Weaver Skycoupe Cub	CF-RGP	DW1
Clipped Special	CF-RCJ	1
J-2 Cub Trainer	CF-RBX	WP-1
Bushmaster Super 22	C-FBAN	B.004
J-3C Marabout	D-EGWH	EN1
J-3 Marabout	F-PGKH	EN2
Rippert A.1-65 Cub	F-PHOQ	1
Comandre 1	F-PHUF	01
Bagimer II	F-PFAR	01
Rhone et Sudest	F-PERB	1
Poullin PJ.5A	F-PDVD	1
Poullin PJ.5B	F-BAQC	6
MDC Trailer	HB-RAL	MDC-1038

Piper Advanced Technology Inc.

Pug Piper left Piper and approached Burt Rutan about putting the twin engined Defiant into production. The project eventually foundered. Pug then joined with George Mead, an RAF alumnus and set up the Piper Advanced Technology company in Wichita, Kansas in 1980. They produced a single experimental four seater aircraft in late 1980, the P.A.T.1 It had a 160 hp Lycoming O-320 engine and was registered N15PT. Unfortunately it crashed in late 1981 and was destroyed, killing Mead.

V.K. Leasing Inc.

Van Kesteren at St. Petersburg, Florida purchased the Piper turbine Malibu airframe without engine in July 1992. A twin exhaust 550 shp Pratt & Whitney PT6A-20 engine was installed by April 1993. In June 1994 they shortened the fuselage by removing the extra centre section that Piper had installed. This is registered as a VK100TP, s/n 1 registration N100VK.

APPENDICES

Appendix A

The relationship of U.S.A.A.F. and U.S.N. serial numbers and Piper serial numbers are shown:

Military Serial / Piper Serial Number cross reference

Type	Military Serial Number (Piper Serial Number)
YO-59	42-460 (7513) and 42-461 (7528) to 42-463 (7530)
O-59	42-7813 (7842) and 42-7814 (7845) to 42-7852 (7883)
O-59A	42-15159 (8278) to 42-15329 (8448), 42-36325 (8449) to 42-36745 (8869)
L-4A	42-36746 (8870) to 42-36824 (8948), 42-38380 (8949) to 42-38457 (9026), 43-29048 (10339) to 43-29246 (10537)
L-4B	43-491 (9352) to 43-1470 (10331) (originally ordered as 42-59301 to 42-60280)
C-83	42-79551 (5-513), 42-79552 (5-515), 42-79553 (5-514), 42-79554 (5-211)
C-83A	42-79557 (6170), 42-79558 (6167)
C-83B	42-79555 (4-1323)
L-4C	43-2923 (7555), 43-2925 (9067),43-2927 (7577), 43-2932 (9070), 43-2959 (7318), 43-2960 (7346), 43-2961 (7546), 43-2962 (7634), 43-2967 (9068)
L-4D	43-2914 (9059), 43-2924 (7521), 43-2995 (9058), 43-2996 (9057)
L-4E	43-2954 (4-1612), 43-2955 (4-1623), 43-2956 (4-1599), 43-2957 (4-1642), 43-2973 (4-1307), 43-2974 (4-1378), 43-2958 (4-1643), 43-2989 (4-1632), 43-2990 (4-1640), 43-3003 (4-1644), 43-3004 (4-1608), 43-3005 (4-1637), 43-3006 (4-1633), 43-3007 (4-1638), 43-3008 (4-1627)
L-4F	42-57507 (5-1080), 42-107425 (5-928), 43-2909 (5-1205), 43-2910 (5-1203), 43-2911 (5-1201), 43-2912 (5-1206), 43-2915 (5-1224), 43-2916 (5-1238), 43-2917 (5-1237), 43-2918 (5-1236), 43-2919 (5-1153), 43-2920 (5-1208), 43-2922 (5-1144), 43-2926 (5-1141), 43-2930 (5-1308), 43-2931 (5-929), 43-2933 (5-1272), 43-2934 (5-1240), 43-2935 (5-1328), 43-2937 (5-407), 43-2938 (5-866), 43-2939 (5-871), 43-2941 (5-1337), 43-2947 (5-1299), 43-2949 (5-1301), 43-2952 (5-1284), 43-2953 (5-1362), 43-2964 (5-1225), 43-2965 (5-946), 43-2966 (5-1068), 43-2968 (5-1122), 43-2969 (5-1226), 43-2970 (5-1060), 43-2978 (5-1282), 43-2980 (5-1346), 43-2984 (5-1380), 43-2991 (5-1317), 43-2993 (5-1311), 43-2999 (5-1377), 43-3000 (5-1371), 43-3001 (5-1384), 43-3002 (5-1383), 44-52988 (5-1120)
L-4G	43-2913 (5-1125), 43-2921 (5-1096), 43-2928 (5-1161), 43-2929 (5-1135), 43-2936 (5-1331), 43-2940 (5-1095), 43-2942 (5-1151), 43-2943 (5-1218), 43-2944 (5-1214), 43-2945 (5-1220), 43-2946 (5-1296), 43-2948 (5-106), 43-2950 (5-1274), 43-2951 (5-1285), 43-2963 (5-1103), 43-2971 (5-1298), 43-2972 (5-1322), 43-2975 (5-1273), 43-2976 (5-1281), 43-2977 (5-1289), 43-2979 (5-1336), 43-2981 (5-1343), 43-2982 (5-1292), 43-2983 (5-1334), 43-2985 (5-1090), 43-2986 (5-1361), 43-2987 (5-1279), 43-2988 (5-1360), 43-2992 (5-1324), 43-2994 (5-1344), 43-2997 (5-1359), 43-2998 (5-1376)
L-4H	43-29049, 29073, 29144, 29150, 29172, 29173, 29175 ex L-4A above, 43-29247 (10538) to 43-30547 (11838), 44-79545 (11841) to 44-80044 (12340)
L-4J	44-80045 (12341) to 44-80844 (13140) 45-4401 (13141) to 45-5200 (13940), 45-55175 (13941) to 45-55215 (13981), 45-55224 (13990) to 45-55257 (14023), 45-55259 (14025) to 45-55260 (14026), 45-55263 (14029) to 45-55264 (14030) and 45-55267 (14033) 45-55216 (13982) to 45-55223 (13989)) 45-55258 (14024)) These were cancelled and 45-53261 (14027) to 45-55262 (14028)) completed post war as 45-55265 (14031) to 45-55266 (14032)) J-3C-65 Cubs 45-55268 (14034) to 45-55325 (14091)) 45-55326 (14092) to 45-55524 (14290) - cancelled, not built
L-4K	42-36519 ex L-4A 43-518, 522, 537, 545, 546, 1004, 1027, 1037, 1297, 1336, 1388, 1391, 1440 ex L-4B 43-29150 ex L-4H

L-4	51-16086 (?) to 51-16091 (?) supplied to Iran
YL-14	45-55525 (5-3001) to 45-55529 (5-3005)
L-14	45-55530 (5-3006) to 45-55538 (5-3014) cancelled, to civil market, 45-55539 (5-3015) to 45-56374 (5-3850), cancelled, not built
TG-8	43-3009 (G-1) to 43-3258 (G-250), 43-12499 (G-251) to 43-12501 (G-253)
XLNP-1	36425 (ex 43-3065), 36426 (ex 43-3070), 36427 (ex 43-3075)
HE-1	30197 (5-1400) to 30296 (5-1499)
NE-1	26196 (8015), 26197 (8037), 26198 (8039), 26199 (8020), 26200 (8018), 26201 (8088), 26202 (8021), 26203 (8046), 26204 (8082), 26205 (8114), 26206 (8128), 26207 (8162), 26208 (8167), 26209 (8090), 26210 (8152), 26211 (8166), 26212 (8108), 26213 (8164), 26214 (8158), 26215 (8163), 26216 (8068), 26217 (8110), 26218 (8098), 26219 (8091), 26220 (8159), 26221 (8126), 26222 (8115), 26223 (8033), 26224 (8041), 26225 (8094), 26226 (8134), 26227 (8130), 26228 (8245), 26229 (8101), 26230 (8102), 26231 (8112), 26232 (8103), 26233 (8109), 26234 (8151), 26235 (8153), 26236 (8146), 26237 (8148), 26238 (8147), 26239 (8155), 26240 (8141), 26241 (8165), 26242 (8168), 26243 (8181), 26244 (8193), 26245 (8192), 26246 (8054), 26247 (8197), 26248 (8060), 26249 (8085), 26250 (7924), 26251 (7928), 26252 (7929), 26253 (7923), 26254 (7927), 26255 (7953), 26256 (8180), 26257 (8205), 26258 (8007), 26259 (8019), 26260 (8206), 26261 (8022), 26262 (8160), 26263 (8172), 26264 (8171), 26265 (8016), 26266 (8097), 26267 (7787), 26268 (8099), 26269 (8119), 26270 (7805), 26271 (7808), 26272 (8169), 26273 (8181), 26274 (8184), 26275 (8106), 26276 (8187), 26277 (8188), 26278 (8186), 26279 (8183), 26280 (8182), 26281 (8174), 26282 (8170), 26283 (8067), 26284 (8173), 26285 (8178), 26286 (8023), 26287 (8038), 26288 (8053), 26289 (8084), 26290 (8059), 26291 (8053), 26292 (8111), 26293 (8118), 26294 (8105), 26295 (8107), 26296 (8113), 26297 (8121), 26298 (8211), 26299 (8185), 26300 (8221), 26301 (8220), 26302 (8212), 26303 (8219), 26304 (8239), 26305 (8240), 26306 (8241), 26307 (8243), 26308 (8244), 26309 (8246), 26310 (8247), 26311 (8248), 26312 (8249), 26313 (8242), 26314 (8250), 26315 (8238), 26316 (8207), 26317 (8208), 26318 (8223), 26319 (8202), 26320 (8179), 26321 (8210), 26322 (8213), 26323 (8225), 26324 (8222), 26325 (8203), 26326 (8204), 26327 (8224), 26328 (8251), 26329 (8252), 26330 (8253), 26331 (8254), 26332 (8255), 26333 (8256), 26334 (8257), 26335 (8258), 26336 (8259), 26337 (8260), 26338 (8261), 26339 (8262), 26340 (8209), 26341 (8199), 26342 (8191), 26343 (8234), 26344 (8231), 26345 (8236), 26346 (8263), 26347 (8264), 26348 (8265), 26349 (8266), 26350 (8267), 26351 (8268), 26352 (8269), 26353 (8270), 26354 (8271), 26355 (8272), 26356 (8273), 26357 (8274), 26358 (8277-11), 26359 (8277-12), 26360 (8277-13), 26361 (8277-14), 26362 (8277-15), 26263 (8277-16), 26364 (8275), 26365 (8276), 26366 (8277-1), 26367 (8277-2), 26368 (8277-40), 26369 (8277-4), 26370 (8277-5), 26371 (8277-6), 26372 (8277-7), 26373 (8277-8), 26374 (8277-9), 26375 (8277-10), 26376 (8233), 26377 (8190), 26378 (8218), 26379 (8040), 26380 (8069), 26381 (8086), 26382 (8087), 26383 (8122), 26384 (8120), 26385 (8214), 26386 (8237), 26387 (8226), 26388 (8216), 26389 (8232), 26390 (8093), 26391 (8277-20), 26392 (8277-17), 26393 (8014), 26394 (8228), 26395 (8215), 26396 (8230), 26397 (8189), 26398 (8200), 26399 (8235), 26400 (8229), 26401 (8201), 26402 (8195), 26403 (8196), 26404 (8194), 26405 (8198), 26406 (8227), 26407 (8277-23), 26408 (8277-24), 26409 (8104), 26410 (8277-26), 26411 (8277-27), 26412 (8277-28), 26413 (8277-29), 26414 (8277-30), 26415 (8277-31), 26416 (8277-32), 26417 (8277-33), 26418 (8277-34), 26419 (8277-35), 26420 (8277-36), 26421 (8277-37), 26422 (8277-38), 26423 (8277-39), 26424 (8277-25), 26425 (8217) Note: 26243 and 26273 are both quoted as Piper s/n 8181, one is 8161 and the other is 8181
NE-2	29669 (ex 45-5191) to 29678 (ex 45-5200), 29679 (ex 45-55199) to 29688 (ex 45-55208), (29689 to 29698 not delivered)
LBP-1	85165 (1) to 85167 (3), (85168(4) to 85264 (100) not built)
L-18B	49-2774 (11-1249) to 49-2878 (11-1353)
L-18C	50-1745 (18-401) to 50-1812 (18-468), 51-15272 (18-969) to 51-15329 (18-1026), 51-15330 (18-1330) to 51-15653 (18-1653), 52-2376 (18-1976) to 52-2539 (18-2139), 53-4665 (18-3065) to 53-4848 (18-3248), 54-719 (18-3419) to 54-758 (18-3458)
YL-21	51-6495 (18-749) and 51-6496 (18-750)
L-21A	51-15654 (18-571) to 51-15662 (18-579), 51-15663 (18-570), 51-15664 (18-550) to 51-15683 (18-569), 51-15684 (18-849) to 51-15803 (18-968)
L-21B	52-6220 (18-2538) to 52-6294 (18-2612), 53-3738 (18-2738) to 53-3784 (18-2784), 53-4849 (18-2949) to 53-4877 (18-2977), 53-7718 (18-3318) to 53-7779 (18-3379), 54-2309 (18-3509) to 54-2408 (18-3608), 54-2409 (18-3809) to 54-2663 (18-4063),

	54-2826 (18-4226) to 54-2835 (18-4235), 55-4578 (18-5478) to 55-4581 (18-5481), 55-4749 (18-4470), 61-2928 (18-7724) and 61-2929 (18-7723)
UO-1	149050 (27-259), 149051 (27-264), 149052 (27-268), 149053 (27-275), 149054 (27-280), 149055 (27-286), 149056 (27-291), 149057 (27-298), 149058 (27-304), 149059 (27-311), 149060 (27-316), 149061 (27-328), 149062 (27-333), 149063 (27-337), 149064 (27-342), 149065 (27-347), 149066 (27-352), 149067 (27-357), 149068 (27-362), 149069 (27-364)

Piper L-4H s/n 10663 U.S. Army serial 43-29372 at Lock Haven. (Piper Aircraft Corporation)

U.S. Army Piper L-4F. (Piper Aviation Museum)

Appendix B

There have been several floods and flood scares at Lock Haven due to the proximity of the factory and airport to the West branch of the Susquehanna River. The major ones are listed below:

Lock Haven Flood 28th of May 1946

This flood affected the following 13 aircraft:

Lock Haven May 1946 - FLOOD			
Type	Serial Number	Registration	Disposition
J-3C-65	17695	NC70675	Re-inspected
J-3C-65	17696	NC70676	Repaired
J-3C-65	17697	NC70679	Re-inspected
J-3C-65	17701	NC70681	Re-inspected
J-3C-65	17702	NC70682	Repaired
J-3C-65	17703	NC70683	Re-manufactured
J-3C-65	17704	NC70684	Re-inspected
J-3C-65	17705	NC70685	Re-inspected
J-3C-65	17706	NC70686	Re-inspected
J-3C-65	17707	NC70687	Rebuilt-to s/n 17793 registration NC70689
J-3C-65	17708	NC70691	Re-inspected
J-3C-65	17709 (1) ?	unknown	Rebuilt-to s/n 17792 registration NC70688
PA-12	12-68	None - for export	Rebuilt-to s/n 12-219

Aerial view of the 1946 flood of the Piper factory at Lock Haven. (Piper Pilot)

Lock Haven Flood 23rd November 1950

This flood affected the following 108 aircraft:

Lock Haven November 1950 - FLOOD		
Type	Serial Number	Disposition
PA-18	18-266	Repaired with new fuselage
PA-18	18-520 to 18-527	Scrapped - replaced by new aircraft
PA-18	18-528	Repaired with new wing
PA-18	18-529 to 18-538	Reconditioned
PA-18	18-539 to 18-548	Repaired with new or reconditioned fuselage, wings or engine
PA-18	18-549	Scrapped - replaced by new aircraft
PA-18	18-583	Scrapped - replaced by new aircraft
PA-18	18-585 to 18-588	Scrapped - replaced by new aircraft
PA-18	18-590 to 18-591	Scrapped - replaced by new aircraft
PA-18	18-593	Scrapped - replaced by new aircraft
PA-18	18-594	Repaired with reconditioned fuselage and wings
PA-18	18-595 to 18-599	Scrapped - replaced by new aircraft
PA-18	18-602 to 18-606	Scrapped - replaced by new aircraft
PA-18	18-607 to 18-614	Repaired with new or reconditioned fuselage, wings or engine
PA-18	18-615 to 18-618	Repaired with reconditioned fuselage and wings and new engine
PA-18	18-619 to 18-630	Repaired with reconditioned fuselage, wings or engine
PA-18	18-632 to 18-648	Repaired with new or reconditioned fuselage, wings or engine
PA-18	18-650	Repaired with new fuselage and wings
PA-18	18-653	Repaired with new fuselage, wings and engine
PA-20	20-552	Reconditioned
PA-20	20-553	Repaired with new fuselage
PA-20	20-559 to 20-561	Repaired with new fuselage
PA-20	20-564	Repaired with new fuselage
PA-20	20-566 to 20-569	Repaired with new fuselage
PA-20	20-570	Scrapped - replaced by new aircraft
PA-20	20-571	Repaired with new fuselage and engine
PA-20	20-573	Scrapped - replaced by new aircraft

Lock Haven Flood scare 26th February 1961

No aircraft were damaged.

Lock Haven Flood 10th of March 1964

Aircraft were moved to the high ground points on the airport, none were damaged.

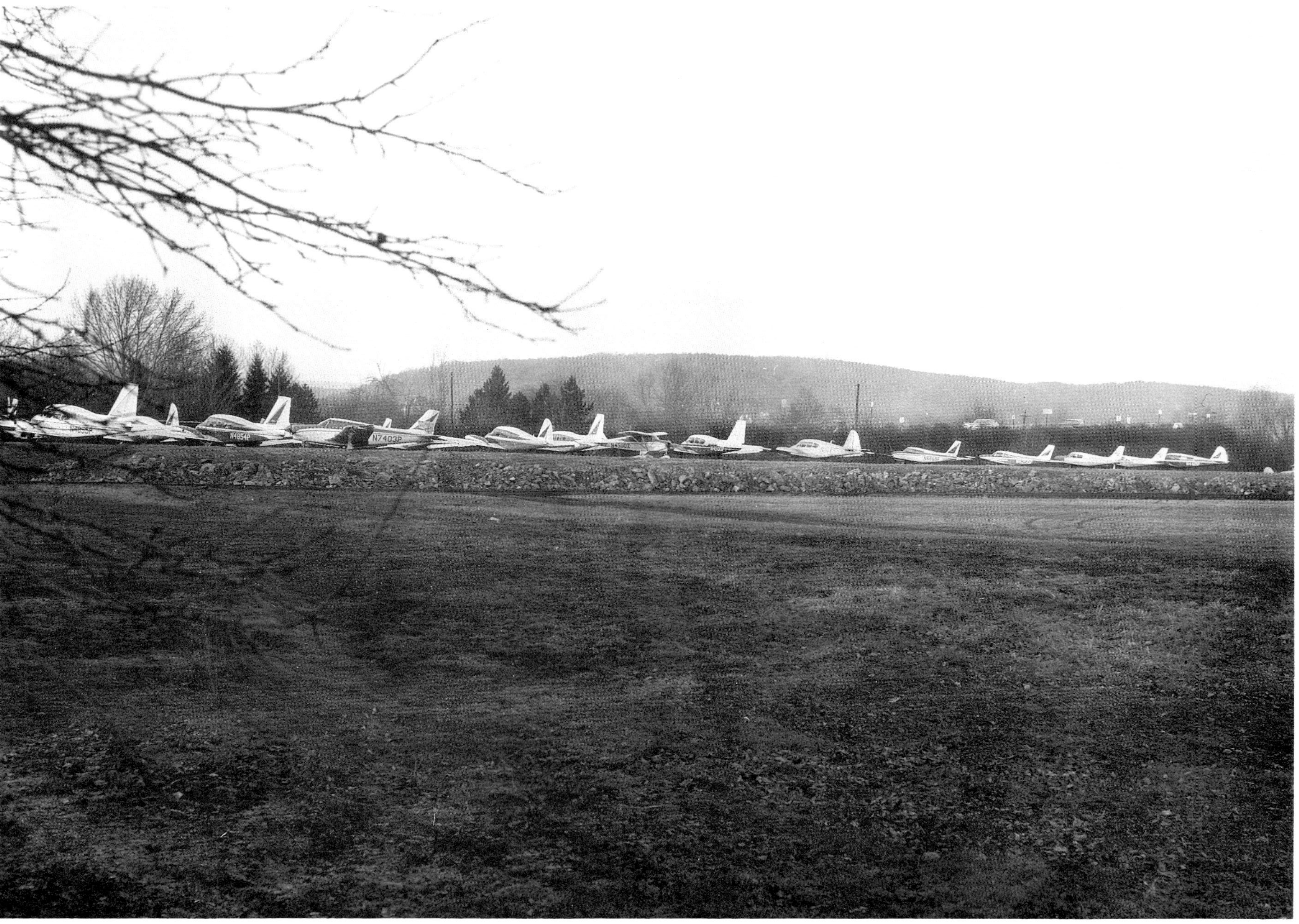

Aircraft moved to 'high ground' next to the highway 150 road during the flood scare at Lock Haven in February 1961. There are many interesting aircraft in this picture, from the right: PA-23 N4418P, PA-24 N5165P, experimental PA-24-380 N5316P, PA-24-250 N8250P, PA-24 N6868P, PA-23 N10F, PA-23-250 N4500P, prototype PA-22-108 N4500Z.

Aerial view of aircraft on the high ground near the paint shop during the flood of Lock Haven in June 1972. This photograph was taken after the flood waters had receded. In the picture at the bottom centre are the prototype Turbine Navajo N7500L and the experimental PA-30 N8300Y used for the PA-40 programme. (Piper Aircraft Corporation).

Aerial view of the 'high ground' next to highway 150 during the flood of Lock Haven in June 1972. (Piper Aircraft Corporation)

PA-31P Pressurized Navajo s/n 31P-74 with temporary registration N9697N wrecked by the flood at Lock Haven in June 1972. This aircraft went to NASA and was used by them for crash testing. (via W.T. Piper Jr.)

Lock Haven Flood 23rd of June 1972

Many finished aircraft were destroyed when tropical storm 'Agnes' caused the Susquehanna river to rise 31.3 feet above normal and flood the Lock Haven plant on the 23rd June 1972. Also many unfinished aircraft (component parts) were destroyed.

In 1972 there were two high spots on the airport, one in front of the paint shop and the other (slightly lower) by the highway 150 road bridge over the river. Both areas were under water, the latter area is shown as 'high ground' in the table below.

Some of the finished aircraft and most of the unfinished aircraft were scrapped. Many of the aircraft were sold to Brazil and the Sudan and some went to NASA for crash testing.

Listed below are the flood victims (serial number and registration) and their fate:

Lock Haven 23rd of June 1972 - FLOOD				
Type	Serial Number	Registration	Production status (where on airport)	Disposition
PA-18-150	18-8991	N9728N	high ground	repaired - to Air Leasing
PA-18-150	18-8998	N9406P	high ground	repaired
PA-18-150	18-9002	N9416P	high ground	repaired - to Martins PT-IJN
PA-18-150	18-9003	N9418P	high ground	repaired - to Martins
PA-18-150	18-9004	N9421P	paint shop	repaired - to experimental
PA-18-150	18-9005	N9422P	fuselage & wings mated	destroyed - scrapped
PA-18-150	18-9006	N9432P	fuselage & wings mated	destroyed
PA-18-150	18-9007	N9442P	fuselage & wings mated	destroyed
PA-18-150	18-9008	N9448P	fuselage	destroyed
PA-18-150	18-9009	N9461P	fuselage	destroyed
PA-18-150	18-9010 to 18-9015	-	component parts	destroyed
PA-23-250	27-2000	N5000Y *	Service hangar	demolished
PA-23-250	27-2321	CF-GAS *	Mod centre	repaired - to USA
PA-23-250	27-3782	N6485Y *	high ground	repaired
PA-23-250	27-4053	N6722Y	high ground	demolished
PA-23-250	27-4568	G-AYTO *	high ground	repaired - to USA
PA-23-250	27-4588	N13972	paint shop	demolished
PA-23-250	27-4721	N14157	high ground	repaired
PA-23-250	27-4772	N14214 *	high ground	demolished
PA-23-250	27-4773	LV-PRT	high ground	repaired - to Air Leasing
PA-23-250	27-4788	N14230	paint shop ramp	repaired - to experimental
PA-23-250	27-4808	ZP-PGD	paint shop ramp	repaired - to Martins PT-IFG
PA-23-250	27-4817	LV-PSA	high ground	repaired - to Air Leasing
PA-23-250	27-4826	N14267	paint shop ramp	repaired - to Aero Mercantile
PA-23-250	27-4834	N14321	outside shop	demolished
PA-23-250	27-4836	N14292	Moodys	repaired - to Africa
PA-23-250	27-4839	N14276	high ground	repaired - to Martins PT-IOW
PA-23-250	27-4842	N14280	high ground	repaired - to Martins PT-IIZ
PA-23-250	27-4843	N14281	high ground	repaired - to experimental
PA-23-250	27-4844	N9740N	paint shop	repaired - to Martins PT-IPU
PA-23-250	27-4854	N14293	paint shop	repaired - to Martins PT-IIJ
PA-23-250	27-4858	N14297	paint shop	repaired - to Martins ntu, to USA
PA-23-250	27-4860	N14298	outside shop	to NASA
PA-23-250	27-4862	(N14299)	paint shop	to NASA
PA-23-250	27-4863	N14300	paint shop	repaired - to Venezuela
PA-23-250	27-4864	N14301	paint shop	repaired - to experimental
PA-23-250	27-4865	N9663N	paint shop	repaired - to Martins PT-IOG
PA-23-250	27-4866	N14302	outside shop	repaired - to Martins PT-IIH

PA-23-250	27-4867	TG-WIH	paint shop	demolished
PA-23-250	27-4868	N14303	paint shop	demolished
PA-23-250	27-4869	(N14304)	paint shop	demolished
PA-23-250	27-4870	(N909PS)	paint shop	to NASA
PA-23-250	27-4871	N14305	paint shop	demolished
PA-23-250	27-4872	CF-SAR	paint shop ramp	demolished
PA-23-250	27-4873	N14306	paint shop	demolished
PA-23-250	27-4874	N14307	paint shop ramp	to CAMI
PA-23-250	27-4875	N14308	east side paint shop	to NASA
PA-23-250	27-4876	N14309	outside shop	demolished
PA-23-250	27-4877	N14310	outside shop	to Chincul
PA-23-250	27-4878	N14311	outside shop	demolished
PA-23-250	27-4879	N14312	outside shop	demolished
PA-23-250	27-4880	N14314	fuselage & wings mated	destroyed
PA-23-250	27-4881	N14315	fuselage & wings mated	destroyed
PA-23-250	27-4882	N14316	fuselage & wings mated	destroyed
PA-23-250	27-4883	N14318	fuselage & wings mated	destroyed
PA-23-250	27-4884	N14323	fuselage & wings mated	destroyed
PA-23-250	27-4885	N9702N	fuselage & wings mated	destroyed
PA-23-250	27-4886	N9703N	fuselage & wings mated	destroyed
PA-23-250	27-4887	N14324	fuselage	destroyed
PA-23-250	27-4888	N14325	fuselage	destroyed
PA-23-250	27-4889	N14326	fuselage	destroyed
PA-23-250	27-4890	N14327	fuselage	destroyed
PA-23-250	27-4891	N14328	fuselage	destroyed
PA-23-250	27-4892	N14329	fuselage	destroyed
PA-23-250	27-4893	N14331	fuselage	destroyed
PA-23-250	27-4894	N14332	fuselage	destroyed
PA-23-250	27-4895	N14333	fuselage	destroyed
PA-23-250	27-4896	-	fuselage	destroyed
PA-23-250	27-4897	-	fuselage	destroyed
PA-23-250	27-4898	-	fuselage	destroyed
PA-23-250	27-4899 to 27-4916	-	component parts	destroyed
PA-24-180	24-1463	N6353P *	high ground	repaired
PA-24-250	24-3056	N7836P *	high ground	repaired
PA-24-180	24-3440	N8184P *	high ground	repaired
PA-24-260	24-4919	N9414P	high ground	repaired - to C-GVBM
PA-24-260	24-4963	N9455P	paint shop ramp	demolished
PA-24-260	24-5027	N9509P	paint shop	repaired - to Martins PT-IKU
PA-24-260	24-5028	N9510P	high ground	repaired - to Martins PT-IGM
PA-24-260	24-5029	N9511P	high ground	to CAMI
PA-24-260	24-5030	(N9512P)	outside shop	to CAMI
PA-24-260	24-5031	N9513P	fuselage & wings mated	to NAFEC
PA-24-260	24-5032	N9514P	fuselage & wings mated	to NAFEC
PA-24-260	24-5033	N9515P	fuselage & wings mated	to NAFEC
PA-24-260	24-5034	N9516P	fuselage & wings mated	to NAFEC
PA-24-260	24-5035	N9517P	fuselage/no tail	to NAFEC
PA-24-260	24-5036	N9518P	fuselage/no tail	destroyed
PA-24-260	24-5037	N9519P	fuselage/no tail	to NAFEC
PA-24-260	24-5038	N9520P	fuselage/no tail	to NAFEC
PA-24-260	24-5039	-	fuselage/no tail	to experimental
PA-24-260	24-5040	-	fuselage/no tail	to NAFEC
PA-24-260	24-5041	-	fuselage/no tail	to experimental model static test
PA-24-300	24-6000	N9300P	high ground	demolished
PA-25-260	25-5445	LV-PSB	high ground	repaired - to Sudan
PA-25-260	25-5453	N9654N	paint shop	repaired - to Sudan
PA-25-260	25-5472	TG-KAX-F	high ground	repaired - to Sudan
PA-25-260	25-5474	TG-KAY-F	high ground	repaired - to Sudan

PA-25-260	25-5476	N9687N	paint shop	repaired - to Sudan
PA-25-260	25-5481	N8793L	high ground	repaired - to Sudan
PA-25-235	25-5484	N6474L	high ground	repaired
PA-25-260	25-5487	- *	in crate	repaired - to Kenya ++
PA-25-235	25-5489	-	high ground	destroyed
PA-25-235	25-5491	N6574L	high ground	demolished
PA-25-235	25-5492	N6590L	high ground	repaired - to Sudan
PA-25-235	25-5493	N6592L	high ground	repaired - to Sudan
PA-25-235	25-5494	N6609L	paint shop	demolished
PA-25-235	25-5495	AN-BFF	paint shop	demolished
PA-25-235	25-5496	N6612L	paint shop	demolished
PA-25-235	25-5497	N6712L	paint shop	to Chincul for parts
PA-25-235	25-5498	N6714L	paint shop	demolished
PA-25	25-5499	N6721L	paint shop	demolished
PA-25	25-5500	(N6724L)	paint shop	demolished
PA-25	25-5501	N6734L	fuselage & wings mated	demolished
PA-25	25-5502	N6740L	fuselage & wings mated	destroyed
PA-25	25-5503	N6741L	fuselage	destroyed
PA-25	25-5504	-	fuselage	destroyed
PA-25	25-5505	-	fuselage	destroyed
PA-25	25-5506	-	fuselage	destroyed
PA-25	25-5507	-	fuselage	destroyed
PA-25	25-5508	-	fuselage	destroyed
PA-25	25-5509 to 25-5521	-	component parts	destroyed
PA-28-180	28-3979	N9780J *	high ground	repaired
PA-28-180	28-5495	N2343R *	high ground	repaired
PA-28-180	28-7205239	N5012T	high ground	to NASA
PA-28-180	28-7205240	N5026T	high ground	to NASA
PA-28-140	28-24891	N5552F *	high ground	repaired
PA-28-140	28-7225029	N1877T	high ground	repaired - to Chincul
PA-28-140	28-7225279	N4912T	high ground	repaired - to Martins PT-IQR
PA-28-140	28-7225424	N5310T	high ground	repaired
PA-28-235	28-7210019	N5019T	high ground	repaired - to Martins PT-ILT
PA-28R-200	28R-7135133	N1916T	high ground	to NASA
PA-28R-200	28R-7135136	N1917T	service hangar	demolished
PA-28R-200	28R-7235112	N4803T	service hangar	repaired - to Martins PT-ITI
PA-28R-200	28R-7235183	N5048T	high ground	repaired - to Chincul
PA-28R-200	28R-7235209	N5261T *	Globe Aero	repaired
PA-28R-200	28R-7235225	N5348T *	Globe Aero	repaired
PA-30	30-1010	N7920Y *	high ground	repaired
PA-30-200	30-4000	N8300Y	paint shop	demolished - scrapped
PA-31	31-346	PT-BMK *	paint shop	repaired
PA-31	31-660	N6758L	paint shop	repaired - to experimental
PA-31	31-778	N7422L	paint shop	repaired - to Martins PP-EFF
PA-31	31-800	N9715N	paint shop	repaired - to Martins PT-IHH
PA-31	31-801	N7416L	paint shop	repaired - to Martins PT-IIC
PA-31	31-802	YV-O-TFA-1	paint shop ramp	repaired - to Martins PT-IJV
PA-31	31-805	N7420L	ramp	repaired - to UK
PA-31	31-809	PT-IDO	paint shop	repaired - to Martins PT-IFP
PA-31	31-814	N7427L	paint shop ramp	repaired - to Martins PT-DXB
PA-31	31-827	PT-IBF	paint shop	repaired - to Martins PT-IBF
PA-31	31-831	PT-IDQ	paint shop	repaired - to Martins PT-IDQ
PA-31	31-833	F-BTMT *	Moody's	repaired - to N7510L
PA-31	31-835	N9711N	paint shop	repaired - to Martins PT-IGS
PA-31	31-837	F-BTMV *	Moodys	repaired - to N7511L
PA-31	31-842	N100TA	outside shop back door	repaired - to Martins PT-IMF
PA-31	31-844	N7441L	paint shop	repaired
PA-31	31-845	SE-GAC	Globe Aero hangar	repaired - to Air Leasing

PA-31	31-846	N7450L	paint shop	repaired - to Africair
PA-31	31-848	PT-IFT	paint shop	repaired - to Martins PT-IFT
PA-31	31-850	N7453L	paint shop ramp	repaired
PA-31	31-851	N7454L	paint shop	to CIP mock-up
PA-31	31-852	N7455L	paint shop ramp	repaired - to Martins PT-IIU
PA-31	31-853	N7456L	paint shop	repaired - to Martins PT-IIK
PA-31	31-854	N100DA	paint shop ramp	repaired - to Martins PP-EFD
PA-31	31-855	N7458L	paint shop	to NASA
PA-31	31-856	N9682N	outside shop back door	to Chincul
PA-31	31-857	N7459L	paint shop	to NASA
PA-31	31-858	(N7460L)	inside paint shop	to NAFEC
PA-31	31-859	N7461L	paint shop	to NAFEC
PA-31	31-860	N7462L	paint shop ramp	to NASA
PA-31	31-861	N7463L	paint shop ramp	repaired - to experimental
PA-31	31-862	N7464L	paint shop ramp	demolished
PA-31	31-863	(N7466L)	paint shop	demolished - scrapped
PA-31	31-864	(N7467L)	complete aircraft	demolished
PA-31	31-865	N7468L	fuselage & wings mated	to NAFEC
PA-31	31-866	N7469L	fuselage & wings mated	to Lakeland
PA-31	31-867	N7470L	fuselage & wings mated	to NAFEC
PA-31	31-868	N7471L	fuselage & wings mated	destroyed
PA-31	31-869	N7472L	fuselage & wings mated	to NAFEC
PA-31	31-870	N7473L	fuselage & wings mated	destroyed
PA-31	31-871	N7474L	fuselage & wings mated	to NAFEC
PA-31	31-872	N7476L	fuselage & wings mated	to NAFEC
PA-31	31-873	N7478L	fuselage	destroyed
PA-31	31-874	N7479L	fuselage	destroyed
PA-31	31-875	-	fuselage	destroyed
PA-31	31-876	-	fuselage	destroyed
PA-31	31-877	-	fuselage	destroyed
PA-31	31-878	-	fuselage	destroyed
PA-31	31-879	-	fuselage	destroyed
PA-31	31-880	-	fuselage	destroyed
PA-31	31-881	-	fuselage	destroyed
PA-31	31-882	-	fuselage	destroyed
PA-31	31-883	-	fuselage	destroyed
PA-31	31-884	-	fuselage	destroyed
PA-31	31-885	-	fuselage	to NAFEC
PA-31	31-886	-	fuselage	to NAFEC
PA-31	31-887 to 31-900	-	component parts	destroyed
PA-31-350	31-0000	-	fuselage	to Chincul
PA-31-350	31-5002	-	static test model	to experimental
PA-31-350	31-5003	N7676L	Engineering	repaired
PA-31-350	31-5004	N7677L	fuselage	to NAFEC
PA-31P	31P-36	XB-CAN	ramp	repaired
PA-31P	31P-61	LV-PRZ	paint shop	repaired - to Air Leasing
PA-31P	31P-62	LV-PRY	paint shop (east)	repaired - to Martins PT-DTK
PA-31P	31P-63	N7310L	ramp	demolished
PA-31P	31P-72	N7319L	paint shop	repaired - to Martins PT-IID
PA-31P	31P-73	(N7320L)	paint shop spray booth	repaired - to experimental N10F
PA-31P	31P-74	N9697N	paint shop	to NASA
PA-31P	31P-75	N7322L	inside paint shop	repaired - to experimental
PA-31P	31P-77	N7324L	paint shop ramp	to NASA
PA-31P	31P-78	N7325L	paint shop	repaired - to Chincul
PA-31P	31P-79	N7326L	paint shop ramp	repaired - to Martins PT-IIS
PA-31P	31P-81	N7328L	paint shop	to NASA
PA-31P	31P-82	N7329L	paint shop	to NASA
PA-31P	31P-83	N7330L	paint shop	to NASA

PA-31P	31P-84	N7331L	paint shop ramp	to NASA
PA-31P	31P-85	N7332L	paint shop	to NASA
PA-31P	31P-86	N7333L	outside shop back door	to NASA
PA-31P	31P-87	N7334L	paint shop	to NASA
PA-31P	31P-88	N7335L	fuselage & wings mated	destroyed
PA-31P	31P-89	N7336L	fuselage & wings mated	destroyed
PA-31P	31P-90	N7337L	fuselage & wings mated	destroyed
PA-31P	31P-91	N7338L	fuselage & wings mated	destroyed
PA-31P	31P-92	N7339L	fuselage	destroyed
PA-31P	31P-93	N7340L	fuselage	destroyed
PA-31P	31P-94	N7341L	fuselage	destroyed
PA-31P	31P-95	N7342L	fuselage	destroyed
PA-31P	31P-96	N7343L	fuselage	destroyed
PA-31P	31P-97	N7344L	fuselage	destroyed
PA-31P	31P-98	-	fuselage	destroyed
PA-31P	31P-99 to 31P-109	-	component parts	destroyed
PA-31T	31T-1	N7500L	paint shop ramp	repaired
PA-32-300	32-7240001	N8651N	high ground	repaired - to Martins PT-IJW
PA-34-200	34-7250207	N5273T	high ground	repaired - to Martins PT-IIK
PA-34-200	34-7250212	N5030T *	Moody's	repaired
PA-34-200	34-7250227	N5245T	Moody's	repaired - to Martins PT-ISF
PA-39	39-103	N8942Y	service hangar	demolished
PA-39	39-107	N8946Y	high ground	demolished
PA-39	39-110	N8950Y	high ground	demolished
PA-39	39-120	N8960Y	paint shop	demolished
PA-39	39-135	N9705N	high ground	demolished
PA-39	39-153	N8988Y	high ground	repaired - to Martins PT-IUN
PA-39	39-154	N8989Y	outside shop back door	demolished
PA-39	39-155	N8990Y	paint shop	repaired - to Martins PT-IIV
PA-39	39-156	N8991Y	paint shop	to NAFEC
PA-39	39-157	(N8992Y)	paint shop	to NAFEC
PA-39	39-158	N8993Y	outside shop back door	demolished
PA-39	39-159	N8994Y	outside shop back door	demolished
PA-39	39-160	N8995Y	fuselage & wings mated	to NAFEC
PA-39	39-161	N8996Y	fuselage & wings mated	to NAFEC
PA-39	39-162	N8997Y	fuselage & wings mated	to NAFEC
PA-39	39-163	N8998Y		demolished
PA-39	39-164	N9710N	fuselage/no tail	to NAFEC
PA-39	39-165	N8999Y	fuselage/no tail	to NAFEC
PA-39	39-166	N9801P	fuselage/no tail	to NAFEC
PA-39	39-167	-	fuselage/no tail	to NAFEC
PA-39	39-168	-	fuselage/no tail	to NAFEC
PA-39	39-169	-	fuselage/no tail	to NAFEC
PA-39	39-170	-	fuselage/no tail	to tooling dept for PA-40 dev
PA-40	40-1	-	component parts	repaired

* = not owned by Piper, either privately owned, FBO or delivery company.
++ = possibly not a flood victim, but delivered in a crate prior to the flood.

Production resumed in 1972 after the flood as follows:

Type	s/n	Date completed
PA-18-150	18-7309016	28th of June 1973
PA-23-250	27-7304917	24th of August 1972
PA-25	25-7305522	25th of April 1973
PA-31 '310'	31-7300901	25th of August 1972
PA-31-350	31-7305005	7th of November 1972
PA-31P	31P-7300110	7th of October 1972

The 'boneyard' at Lock Haven (after the June 1972 flood) where all the flood damaged aircraft components were stored prior to being broken up. (Lock Haven Express)

The first production aircraft after the June 1972 flood, PA-23-250 s/n 27-7304917 registration N14334, nearly ready for roll-out in August 1972. (Lock Haven Express)

Lock Haven Flood 24th of February 1975

No aircraft were damaged.

Lock Haven Flood scare 24th of February 1977

Many aircraft were flown to the nearby (not yet opened) Highway 220 to escape the flood scare at the airport. No aircraft were damaged.

Line up of Navajos and Pressurized Navajos on the not yet opened Highway 220 next to Lock Haven, flown there to escape the rising waters of the Susquehanna River in February 1977. (Lock Haven Express)

Appendix C

Piper sales by calendar year

Year	Commercial	Military	Year	Commercial	Military
1930	1		1964	3196	
1931	23		1965	3775	
1932	22		1966	4437	
1933	17		1967	4490	
1934	72		1968	4228	
1935	212		1969	3952	
1936	522		1970	1678	
1937	683		1971	2055	
1938	701		1972	2465	
1939	1750		1973	3233	
1940	3005		1974	3414	
1941	2881		1975	3043	
1942	462	1731	1976	4043	
1943		1282	1977	4499	
1944		2154	1978	5264	
1945	938	864	1979	5253	
1946	7773	9	1980	2958	
1947	3492		1981	2495	
1948	1479		1982	1043	
1949	1278	105	1983	660	
1950	1108	68	1984	664	
1951	1081	328	1985	540	
1952	1161	412	1986	326	
1953	1639	525	1987	282	
1954	1191	348	1988	282	
1955	1870	56	1989	621	
1956	2329	67	1990	178	
1957	2300	11	1991	41	
1958	2162	1	1992	85	
1959	2530		1993	99	
1960	2313	20	1994	132	
1961	2646		1995	165	
1962	2139	2	1996	188 (planned)	
1963	2321		1997	210 (planned)	

Note: These figures may not agree with production (Appendix D) because re-sales and 'ex-company' aircraft are included in the sales figures.

Appendix D

Piper aircraft production summary by type

Type	Built	Comment
Early	12	Built by Taylor, etc. *
E / F / G / H-2	348	Built by Taylor *
J-2	1,169	(1,119 built by Taylor, Aircraft Associates & Cub Aircraft) *
J-3	20,056	(150 by Cub Aircraft) *
TG-8	253	
J-4	1,251	
J-5	1,506	
P-1	1	
P-2	1	
P-4	1	
PT-1	1	
LBP-1	3	(1 built by D. Barber) *
PWA-1	1	
PA-6	2	
PA-8	2	
PA-11	1,541	
PA-12	3,759	
PA-14	238	
PA-15	387	
PA-16	736	
PA-17	214	
Stinson 108-3	125	Sold 325 (built 125) +
PA-18	10,326	
PA-19	3	
PA-20	1,120	
PA-21	0	Not completed
PA-22	9,490	
PA-23	2,047	
PA-23 (27-)	4,930	
PA-24	4,717	
PA-24 (26-)	148	
PA-25	5,167	
PA-28	7,455	
PA-28-181	3,710	Current - last counted 2843066
PA-28-140	10,089	
PA-28-151 / 161	5,303	Current - last counted 2842018
PA-28-235 / 236	2,856	
PA-28-201T	91	
PA-28R	6,791	Current - last counted 2844011
PA-28R-300	122	
PA-29	1	
PA-30	2,001	
PA-31	1,785	
PA-31-350	1,827	
PA-31-350 T-1020	21	
PA-31-353	2	
PA-31P	259	
PA-31P-350	50	
PA-31T	526	
PA-31T1	215	

PA-31T2	82	
PA-31T3 T-1040	24	
PA-32	3,876	
PA-32-301	544	
PA-32R	2,881	Current - last counted 3246059
PA-33	1	
PA-34	4,626	Current - last counted 3447029 3449001
PA-35	1	
PA-36	923	
PA-38	2,519	
PA-39	155	
PA-40	3	
PA-41P	1	
PA-42 / PA-42-720	149	
PA-42-1000	43	
PA-44	494	Current - last counted 4496013
PA-46	674	Current - last counted 4636076
Enforcer	2	
PA-48	2	
Aerostar	1010	491 built by Ted Smith *
LoPresti Piper	2	
Total	130,671	
	2,132	* Not built by Piper
Total built by Piper	128,539	
	200	+ Sold, not built
Total built & sold by Piper	128,739	

PA-34-220T Seneca IV s/n 3447012 registration N9262B on the Vero Beach production line in 1995. This aircraft was delivered to Italy. (R.W. Peperell)

Appendix E

Aircraft Serial Number / Model Number Identification

Serial number block	Model Number	Manufacturing plant	Serial number block	Model Number	Manufacturing plant
--00--	PA-32-260	VRB	--40--	PA-32-300	VRB
--01--	PA-42	LAL / VRB	--41--	PA-28-161	VRB
--02--	PA-36-375	LHV	--42--	PA-28-161	VRB
--03--	PA-28R-201T	VRB	--43--	PA-28-181	VRB
--04--	PA-31T1	LHV	--44--	PA-28R-201	VRB
--05--	PA-28-180	VRB	--45--	PA-32-300L	LAL
--06--	PA-32-301	VRB	--46--	PA-32R-301	VRB
--07--	PA-44-180T	VRB	--47--	PA-34-220T	VRB
--08--	PA-46-310P	VRB	--48--	PA-34-220T	VRB
--09--	PA-18-150	LHV	--49--	PA-34-220T	VRB
--10--	PA-28-235	VRB	--50--	PA-34-200	VRB
--11--	PA-28-236	VRB	--51--		
--12--	PA-31 / PA-31-325	LAL	--52--	PA-31-350	LAL
--13--	PA-32R-301	VRB	--53--	PA-31-350 T-1020	LAL
--14--	PA-31P-350	LHV	--54--	PA-23-250	LHV
--15--	PA-28-151	VRB	--55--		
--16--	PA-28-161	VRB	--56--	PA-25-235 / 260	LHV
--17--	PA-36T PA-60-700XP	LHV VRB	--57--	PA-31-353 PA-32R-301T	LAL VRB
--18--	PA-28RT-201	VRB	--58--	PA-31-353 T-1020	LAL
--19--	PA-28R-300	VRB	--59--		
--20--	PA-31T	LHV	--60--	PA-36-285 / 300	VRB / LHV
--21--	PA-28-201T	VRB	--61--	PA-36-300 Aerostar 600	VRB SM
--22--	PA-31T2a PA-46-350P	LHV VRB	--62--	Aerostar 601	SM
--23--	PA-60-700P	VRB	--63--	Aerostar 601P	SM
--24--	PA-32-301T	VRB	--64--	PA-45 Aerostar 800	VRB
--25--	PA-28-140	VRB	--65--	Aerostar 602P / PA-60 602P	SM / VRB
--26--	PA-28R-221T	VRB	--66--	PA-31T2	LHV
--27--	PA-42-1000	LAL / VRB	--67--		
--28--			--68--		
--29--	PA-32R-301T	VRB	--69--		
--30--	PA-31P PA-28R-180	LHV VRB	--70--	PA-34-200T	VRB
--31--	PA-28RT-201T	VRB	--71--		
--32--			--72--		
--33--	PA-34-220T	VRB	--73--	PA-48	LAL
--34--			--74--		
--35--	PA-28R-200	VRB	--75--	PA-31T3	LHV
--36--	PA-46-350P	VRB	--76--		
--37--	PA-28R-201	VRB	--77--		
--38--	PA-38	Reserved	--78--		
--39--	PA-38	Reserved	--79--		

--80--	PA-32R-300	VRB	--90--	PA-28-181	VRB
--81--			--91--		
--82--			--92--		
--83--			--93--		
--84--			--94--		
--85--	PA-32RT-300	VRB	--95--	PA-44-180	VRB
--86--			--96--	PA-44-180	VRB
--87--	PA-32RT-300T	VRB	--97--		
--88--			--98--		
--89--			--99--	Reserved for spare parts return	
			--A---	PA-38-112	LHV

LHV	Lock Haven
LAL	Lakeland
SM	Santa Maria
VRB	Vero Beach

PA-28-181 Archer III s/n 2843018 registration N9262R in quality control at Vero Beach in 1995. This aircraft was delivered to the United Kingdom. (R.W. Peperell)

Index